Desktop and Mo
Programming wi
.NET MAUI and C#

KAMIL PAKULA

To my beloved wife Barbara and sons Chris and Adam

CONTENTS

Preface

This book covers all the basics that you need to start programming desktop and mobile applications with C# and .NET MAUI. I assume you have no prior knowledge of the .NET MAUI, but you should have at least some basic knowledge of the C# programming language and the object-oriented programming paradigm.

After a short introduction to .NET MAUI, we'll start by setting up our working environment. Then we'll be talking about some basic stuff like views, layouts, content pages, content views and XAML. Next, we'll discuss properties, styles, themes, visual states, control templates, markup extensions, platform differences, namespaces, data binding, the MVVM pattern, navigation, animation, sound and popups, to mention just the most important topics. In parallel, we'll be creating the Slugrace project - a racing game that we will be developing throughout the whole book. You will find the code and assets that you need for the project (images and sound files) on Github. There is a separate branch for each chapter. You will find the links at the beginning of each chapter. Finally we'll deploy the app to Windows and Android.

There's one convention I'm using in the book - the parts of code that were modified or added are highlighted in a shade of yellow so that you can immediately see the changes. Portions of code that did not change but I'd like to draw your attention to are highlighted in gray.

I hope you'll have at least as much fun reading the book as I had writing it.

Chapter 1 - Introduction to .NET MAUI and the Slugrace Project

In this book we will learn the basics of .NET MAUI, which is a cross-platform framework used for GUI applications of any kind. As learning by doing is a concept I'm a big fan of, throughout the book we'll be creating an app, which actually is a betting/racing game. We'll be creating two versions of the game, for desktop and mobile. Before we have a closer look at the app we're about to start creating, though, let's talk about the .NET MAUI framework.

What Is .NET MAUI?

Let's start with the name: .NET MAUI stands for .NET Multi-platform App UI, so, as you can see, it's a cross-platform framework for creating native mobile and desktop applications. It's open-source and relatively new, as of the time of writing this book. It's the evolution of Xamarin.Forms, if you know that framework.

In .NET MAUI we use C# to write the code. Although we can use just C# for most of our project, there's also the XAML markup language that, although optional, is practically always used because it makes it so much easier to create the presentation part of the app. In our project we'll be using C# and XAML.

You can use .NET MAUI to create apps for Windows, macOS, Android and iOS from a single shared code base.

How Does .NET MAUI Work?

The idea behind .NET MAUI is to put as much code as possible in a single code base. But still, you can tweak the code for particular platforms if need arises. The code you write interacts with the .NET MAUI API, which, in turn, directly consumes the native platform APIs: WinUI 3, .NET Android, .NET iOS and .NET macOS. Building apps for macOS and iOS requires a Mac computer. In this book we'll be building our app for Windows and Android.

The Slugrace Project

Before we start working on the Slugrace project, let's have a look at what it's all about. Slugrace is a game that combines a typical GUI application with animated graphics. This is a game for one to four players who put their bets on four slugs. Let's have a look at the final version of the app now.

The app is going to contain three pages that need access to data (Settings Page, Race Page and Game Over Page and one that doesn't (Instructions Page).

Settings Page

When you start the game, you first see the Settings Page. Here's the desktop version:

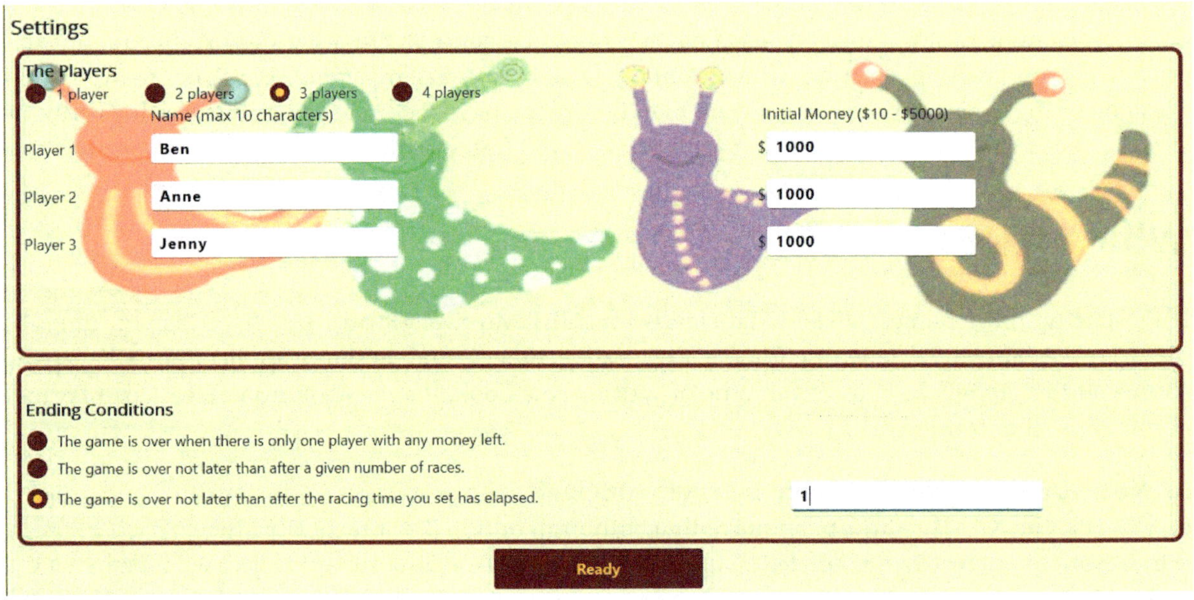

There's a background image of the four slugs in the upper part of the page. The slugs even have names. From left to right these are:

- Iffy - a slug that is not extremely reliable,
- Trusty - a slug that is pretty reliable,
- Speedster - a fast slug that often wins, hence his low odds,
- Slowpoke - a slug that is usually pretty slow, but sometimes can surprise you - if he wins and you bet on him, you can make a lot of money.

In this page you can set the following:

- the number of players (1-4),
- the names of the players (if you don't, the generic names Player 1, Player 2, etc. will be used),
- the initial money each player has when the game begins (there's $1000 by default),

- the ending conditions (when the game should end – there are three options to choose from).

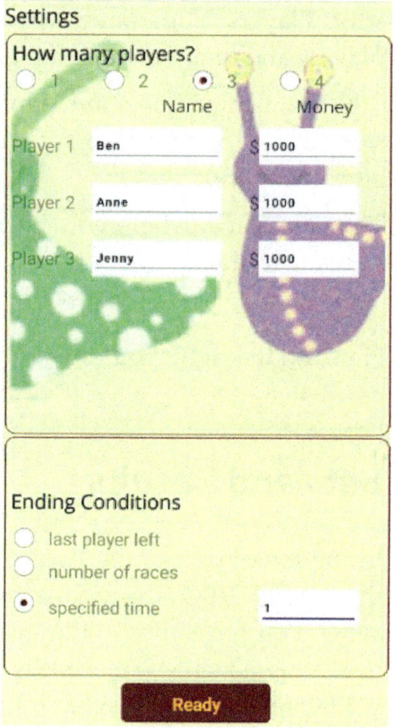

The mobile version looks a bit different, but it has the same functionality. Here you can see only a small portion of the background image.

Race Page

When you're done setting the players' names and initial money, and the ending condition, you just press the Ready button. When you do, you navigate to the Race Page, which is the main page of the app. You will spend most of your time on this page unless you lose right away.

Again, there are some differences between the two platforms. The desktop version looks like this:

This screen is divided into several panels:

- the Game Info panel where you can see the number of the race, the time of the game, etc.,

- the Slugs' Stats panel where you can see the names of the slugs and their wins (as both absolute values and percentages),

- the Players' Stats panel where you can see the names of the players and their current amount of money,

- the main game panel in the middle with the racetrack where the slugs run (you can also see the odds here, which are updated after each race),

- the Bets panel where you can place your bets by typing them in or using a slider.

Here, on the right, you can see the mobile version of this page.

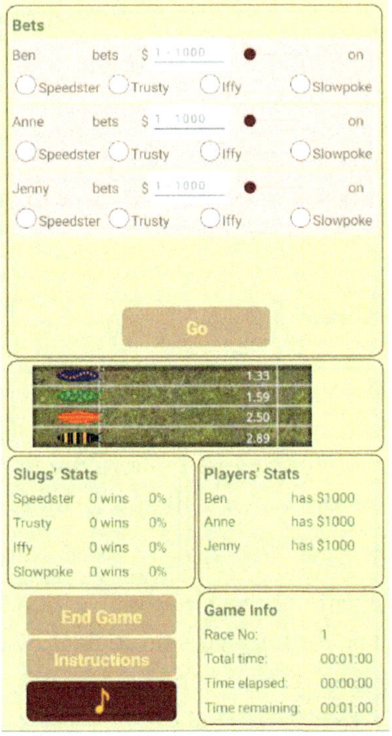

Bets and Results

In the lower part of the Race Page (in the desktop version) or in the upper part (in the mobile version), you can see the Bets panel. When you press the Go button, the race begins. When the race is over, this panel is replaced by the Results panel, where you can see the results. Here's what it looks like on a desktop:

You can see how much money each player had before the last race, how much they bet and on which slug and whether they won or lost and how much.

When you press the Next Race button in the Results panel, it'll change back to the Bets panel.

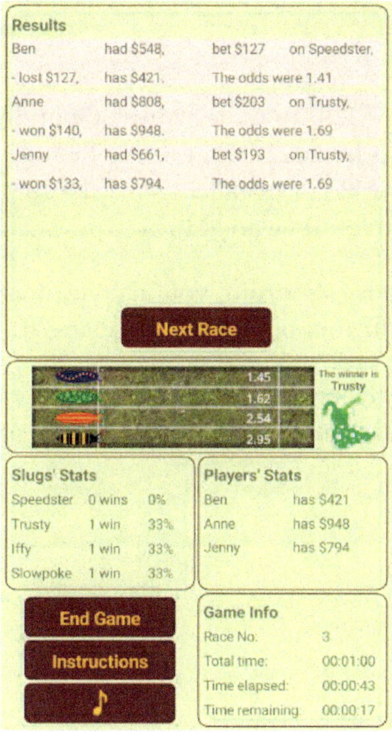

On a mobile device the Results panel is near the top of the screen.

What else do we have in the Race Page? In the upper right (desktop) or lower left (mobile) corner there are three buttons:

- End Game – this button lets you end the game at any time and takes you to the Game Over Page,

- Instructions – this button takes you to the Instructions Page,

- Sound – this button toggles the sound on or off.

Game Over Page

When the game is over, which happens after the ending condition you set is met or after you end it manually, you'll be taken to the Game Over Page.

The desktop version of this page looks like so:

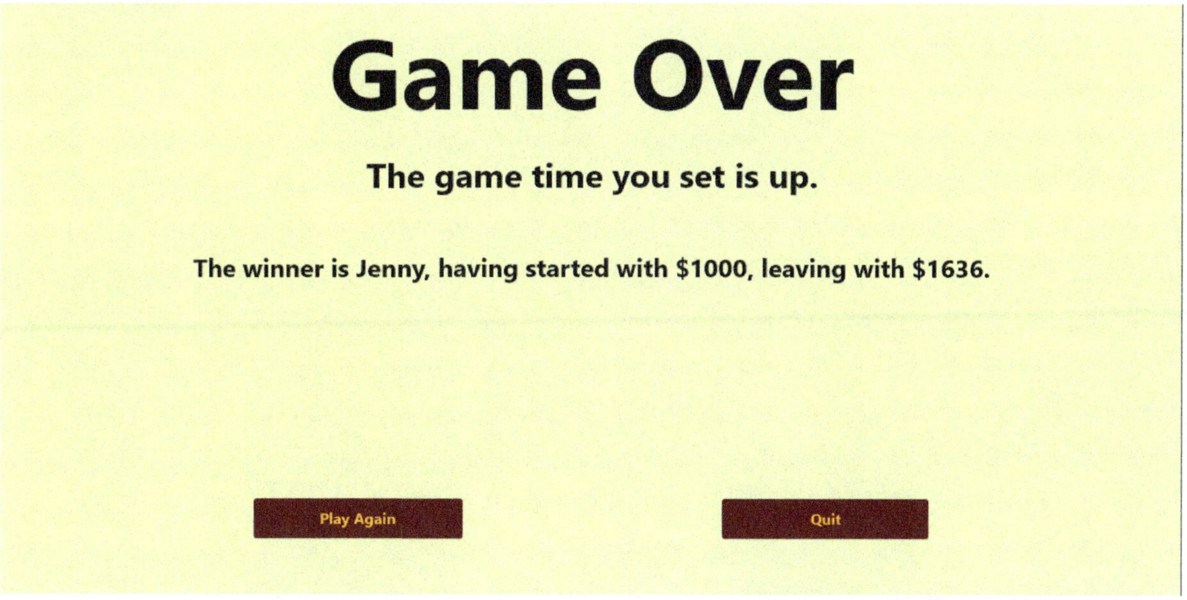

The mobile version looks pretty much the same, as you can see below.

So, this is the application we're going to create using the .NET MAUI framework and C#. But what do we need to get started?

What You Need

You definitely need a text editor or IDE to write your code in. In this book we'll be using Visual Studio 2022 with the .NET Multi-platform App UI development workload installed, so make sure you have it on your computer and you'll be good to go.

As we want to build our app also for Android, you also need an Android device or an emulator. In this book we'll be using the latter.

In the next chapter we'll create the project and we'll create an Android emulator.

Chapter 2 – Creating the Project

code: https://github.com/prospero-apps/Slugrace/tree/chapter2

In chapter 1 we talked about the project we're going to create. Now it's time to actually create the project in Visual Studio. So, without further ado, let's jump right in.

Open Visual Studio and click on Create a new project.

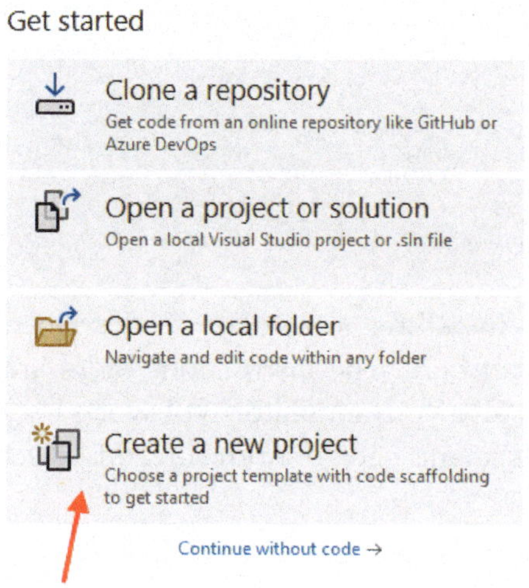

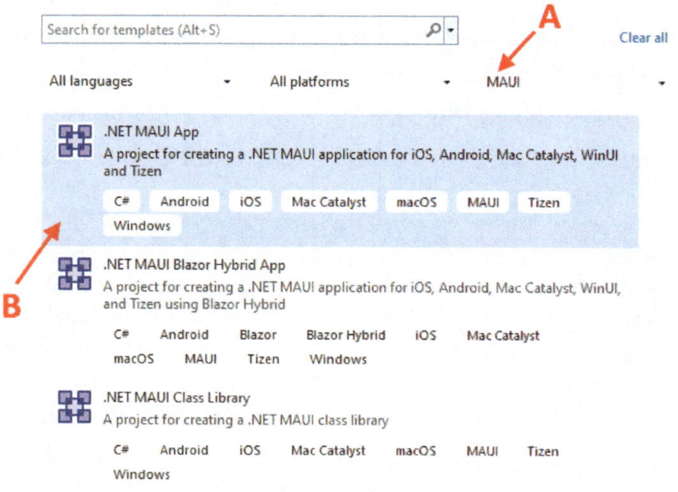

Then find MAUI in the dropdown list (A), select the .NET MAUI App project template (B) and hit the Next button.

Set the project name to Slugrace (A), select a location for your project (B) and hit Next.

We're going to target .NET 8.0, so make sure it's selected in the dropdown list. Then hit Create.

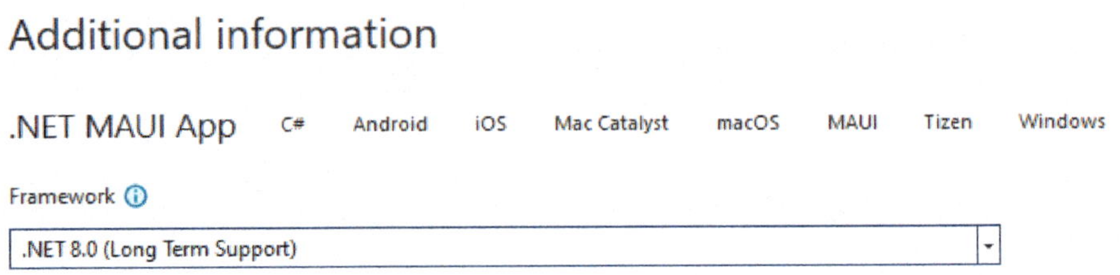

This will create the project for you.

Android Emulator

For the Android version of the app we'll be using an emulator. Installing an emulator is described in the .NET MAUI documentation, so I'm not going to repeat it here. The instructions there are pretty clear. Just make sure to enable hardware acceleration or else your emulator will work very slowly. To create an emulator, in Visual Studio, in the Tools menu, go to Android and select Android Device Manager:

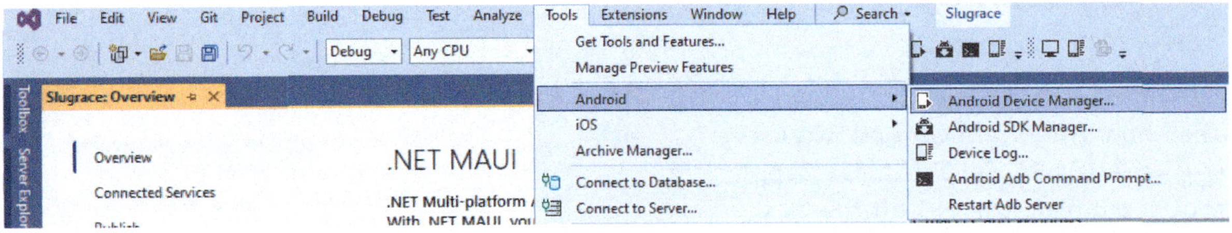

In the manager you'll see the list of all installed devices:

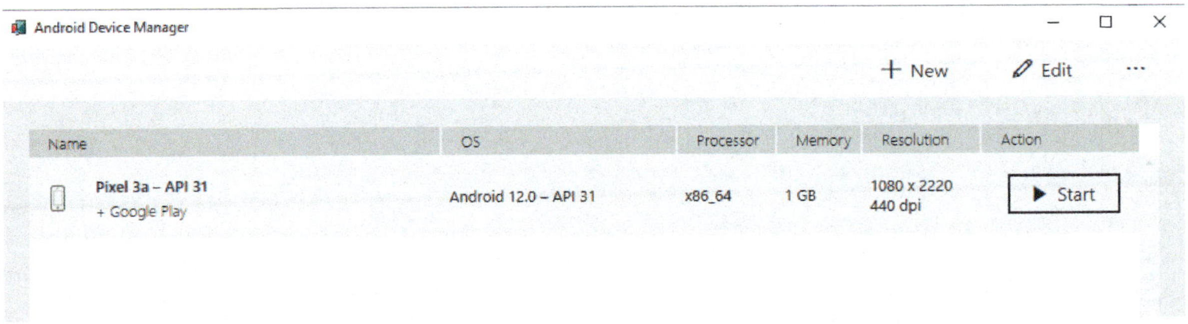

There's just one on my machine right now. Your list will most probably be empty when you open this window for the first time. Just click the +New button and select the device you want to use to emulate a real Android device. The installation may take some time. You can pick a model and set some properties of the device:

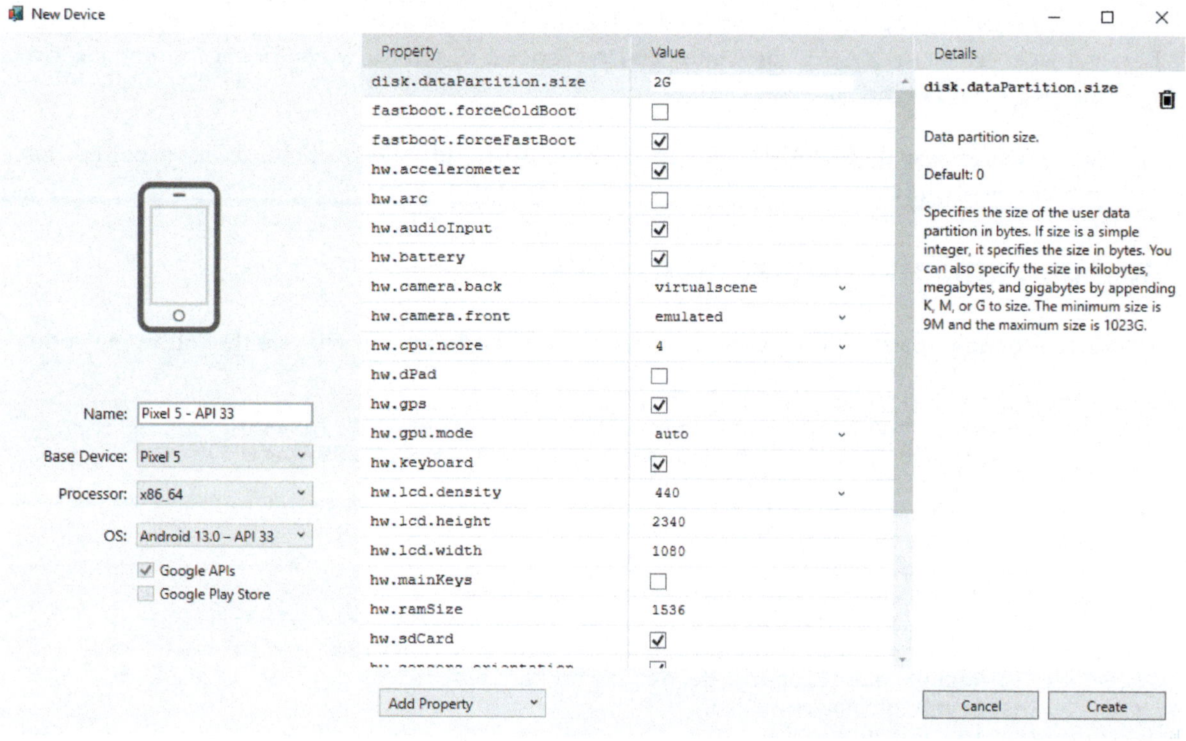

Hit the Create button when you're done. Consult the documentation for more details. Anyway, I assume you have Visual Studio 2022 installed (the free Community version is just fine) and also an Android emulator. If so, we're good to go.

Anatomy of a .NET MAUI Project

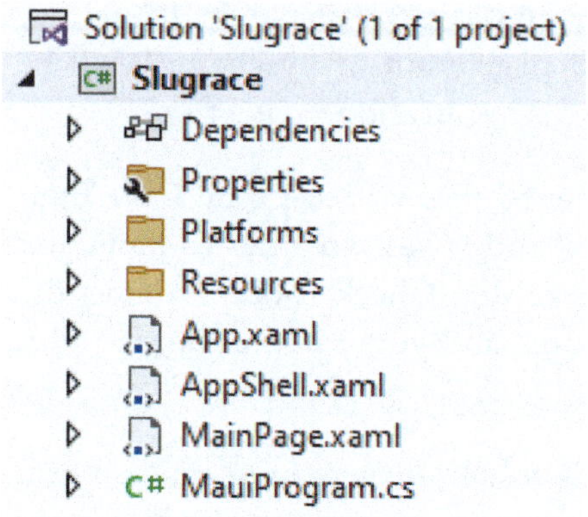

If you look at the Solution Explorer, you'll see there is just one project in the solution. We don't have separate projects for the particular platforms, the whole code sits in just one project.

There are three files with a **.xaml** extension. These files contain XAML code. Hit the little triangles to the left of their names to expand them and you will see the three C# files that accompany them.

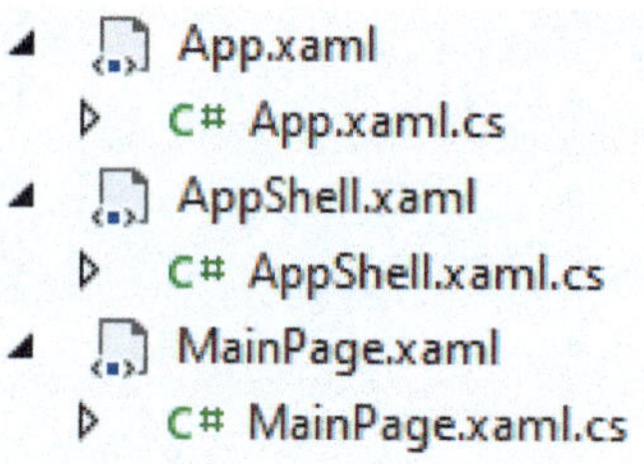

These are the code-behind files that are used to handle the logic of their corresponding XAML files. Whenever we create a XAML file later in the book, it will always be accompanied by a corresponding code-behind file.

Anyway, what are these three XAML files and their corresponding code-behind files for? Let's have a look at them one by one.

The App.xaml and App.xaml.cs Files

Let's start with the **App.xaml** file. If you open the file in the editor, you will see the following code:

```
<?xml version = "1.0" encoding = "UTF-8" ?>
<Application xmlns="http://schemas.microsoft.com/dotnet/2021/maui"
             xmlns:x="http://schemas.microsoft.com/winfx/2009/xaml"
             xmlns:local="clr-namespace:Slugrace"
             x:Class="Slugrace.App">
    <Application.Resources>
        <ResourceDictionary>
            <ResourceDictionary.MergedDictionaries>
                <ResourceDictionary Source="Resources/Styles/Colors.xaml" />
                <ResourceDictionary Source="Resources/Styles/Styles.xaml" />
            </ResourceDictionary.MergedDictionaries>
        </ResourceDictionary>
    </Application.Resources>
</Application>
```

We're going to talk about XAML syntax in detail later in the book, but if you know XML, you will notice lots of similarities here. So, here we have the root element, **`Application`**, and in it is nested the **`Application.Resources`** element. The nesting is clearly visible due to indentation. Inside the **`Application.Resources`** element, you can see the **`ResourceDictionary`** element, the latter nested in the former. If we move deeper and deeper in the hierarchy, we have the **`ResourceDictionary.MergedDictionaries`** element and in it two **`ResourceDictionary`** elements. The **App.xaml** file defines the application resources that are available in the entire application. Not just in a single page, not in a couple selected pages, but everywhere. We'll be talking about **`ResourceDictionary`** elements and their scope in the application in due time.

Now, if you look at the innermost **`ResourceDictionary`** elements, you will see they have their **`Source`** attributes set to the **Colors.xaml** and **Styles.xaml** files contained in the **Styles** folder inside the **Resources** folder. Check it out. Expand the **Resources** folder in the Solution Explorer and you will see the two files there.

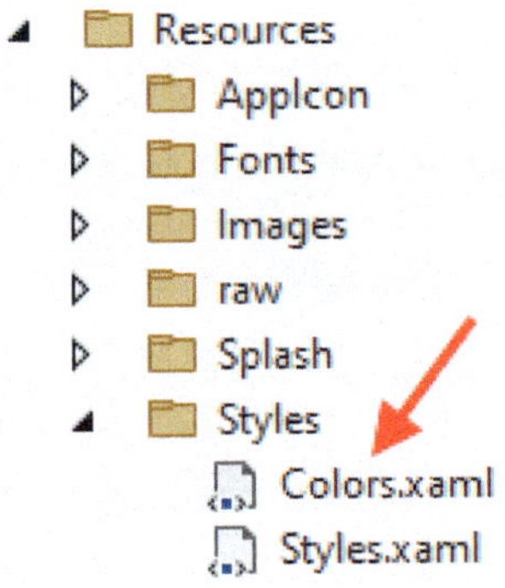

We'll be talking about the **Resources** folder in a minute, but as you probably suspect, this is the place where you can put style files, among other things. The **Colors.xaml** and **Styles.xaml** files define the styles used in the app. In the **App.xaml** file the two resource dictionaries are merged together in a **ResourceDictionary.MergedDictionaries** element.

Fine, and now let's open the code-behind file:

```
namespace Slugrace;

public partial class App : Application
{
    public App()
    {
        InitializeComponent();

         MainPage = new AppShell();
    }
}
```

Here we have the **App** class that inherits from **Application**. This class represents the application at runtime. As you can see, the class is defined as partial, which means the code you see in the file is not the full code the class consists of. The rest of the code is somewhere else, and to be precise, it's in the XAML file. So, the code in the **App.xaml** file is combined with the code in the code-behind file to produce the complete **App** class.

In the constructor, you can see the **InitializeComponent** method. This method is called right to create the class instance by merging with the code in the XAML file. You will see this method in every constructor in the code-behind files that have an accompanying XAML file. On the other hand, you won't see it if you write all your code in C#, without the XAML file, which is also possible (we'll see how to do it soon), although not recommended.

Finally, the code in the constructor creates the initial app window and assigns it to the **MainPage** property. This way the application knows what to display when you run it. As you can see, the initial window is created by instantiating the **AppShell** class. Speaking of which…

The AppShell.xaml and AppShell.xaml.cs Files

Let's have a look at the **AppShell.xaml** file:

```
<?xml version="1.0" encoding="UTF-8" ?>
<Shell
    x:Class="Slugrace.AppShell"
    xmlns="http://schemas.microsoft.com/dotnet/2021/maui"
    xmlns:x="http://schemas.microsoft.com/winfx/2009/xaml"
    xmlns:local="clr-namespace:Slugrace"
    Shell.FlyoutBehavior="Disabled"
    Title="Slugrace">


    <ShellContent
        Title="Home"
        ContentTemplate="{DataTemplate local:MainPage}"
        Route="MainPage" />
</Shell>
```

Here we have **Shell** as the root element. The purpose of this element is to give your app some structure.

Your app may be structured in a couple ways. There may be a flyout, there may be tabs or just a single page, which is the case here.

The single page that we get out of the box is represented by the **ShellContent** element. The attributes that are set on this element include the title of the page, the template of the page and the URI-based route to **MainPage**, which is to be displayed when the app starts running.

The **AppShell.xaml.cs** file is very simple:

```
namespace Slugrace;

public partial class AppShell : Shell
{
    public AppShell()
    {
        InitializeComponent();
    }
}
```

We just have the **InitializeComponent** method in the constructor that instantiates the **AppShell** class.

As you can see in the XAML file above, the first page that is going to be displayed is **MainPage**. Let's have a look at it next.

The MainPage.xaml and MainPage.xaml.cs Files

In the XAML file we have some sample code:

```
<?xml version="1.0" encoding="utf-8" ?>
<ContentPage xmlns="http://schemas.microsoft.com/dotnet/2021/maui"
             xmlns:x="http://schemas.microsoft.com/winfx/2009/xaml"
             x:Class="Slugrace.MainPage">

    <ScrollView>
        <VerticalStackLayout
            Padding="30,0"
            Spacing="25">
            <Image
                Source="dotnet_bot.png"
                HeightRequest="185"
                Aspect="AspectFit"
                SemanticProperties.Description="dot net bot in a race car number eight" />

            <Label
                Text="Hello, World!"
                Style="{StaticResource Headline}"
                SemanticProperties.HeadingLevel="Level1" />
```

```
            <Label
                Text="Welcome to &#10;.NET Multi-platform App UI"
                Style="{StaticResource SubHeadline}"
                SemanticProperties.HeadingLevel="Level2"
                SemanticProperties.Description="Welcome to dot net Multi platform App U I" />

            <Button
                x:Name="CounterBtn"
                Text="Click me"
                SemanticProperties.Hint="Counts the number of times you click"
                Clicked="OnCounterClicked"
                HorizontalOptions="Fill" />
        </VerticalStackLayout>
    </ScrollView>

</ContentPage>
```

This is the page that will be displayed when you run the app. The root element is **ContentPage** and inside it is a **ScrollView** element. This element contains a **VerticalStackLayout**, which in turn contains an image, two labels and a button.

These elements are added here so that you can see something on your screen when you run the app, but eventually we will cut out all the code between the opening and closing tags of the **ContentPage** and replace it with our own code. But let's leave it for now. What can you expect to see? Well, you'll see an image, two labels and a button arranged vertically (this is what the **VerticalStackLayout** is for). Besides, if the view is too large to fit in your screen, a scrollbar will be provided (this is what the **ScrollView** is for).

Before we run the app and see what it all looks like, let's have a look at the code-behind file. If you open the **MainPage.xaml.cs** file, you'll see this:

```
namespace Slugrace;

public partial class MainPage : ContentPage
{
    int count = 0;

    public MainPage()
    {
        InitializeComponent();
    }

    private void OnCounterClicked(object sender, EventArgs e)
    {
        count++;

        if (count == 1)
            CounterBtn.Text = $"Clicked {count} time";

        else
            CounterBtn.Text = $"Clicked {count} times";

        SemanticScreenReader.Announce(CounterBtn.Text);
    }
}
```

Here we have more code than in the other two code-behind files. In the constructor we have the **InitializeComponent** method again. Below the constructor we have another method, **OnCounterClicked**. This method takes care of the button click event and just displays the number of clicks on the button. This method is needed for the button to work. So, let's now run the app and see what the **MainPage** looks like. Let's run it twice, actually, first on Windows, then on Android.

Under the top menu you can see the Play button with a filled green triangle on it. It's used to run the app with debugging. Make sure Windows Machine is selected in the dropdown next to it.

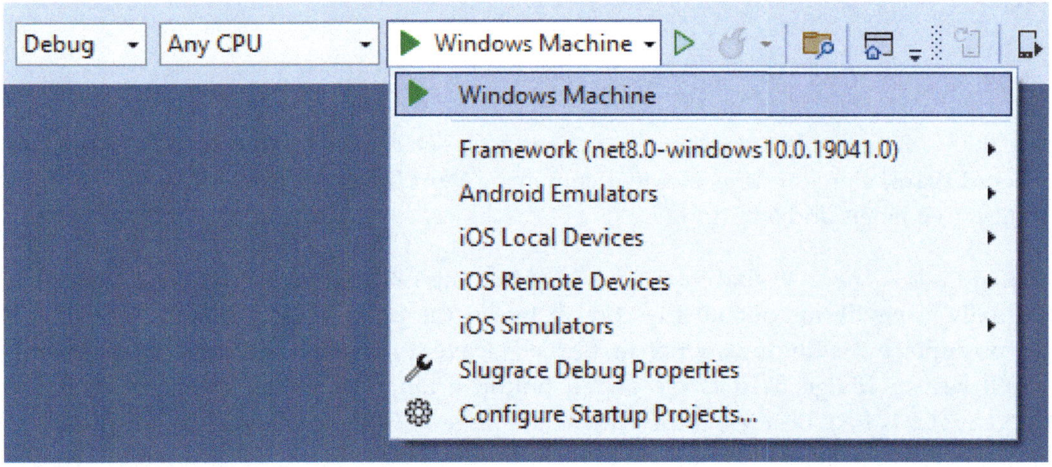

Press the Play button. Visual Studio may prompt you to enable Developer Mode if you haven't done it before. Just click the settings for developers link and switch on Developer Mode. Close the Enable Developer Mode for Windows dialog and now you can proceed. The app builds and runs. You can now see the image, the two labels and the button stacked vertically:

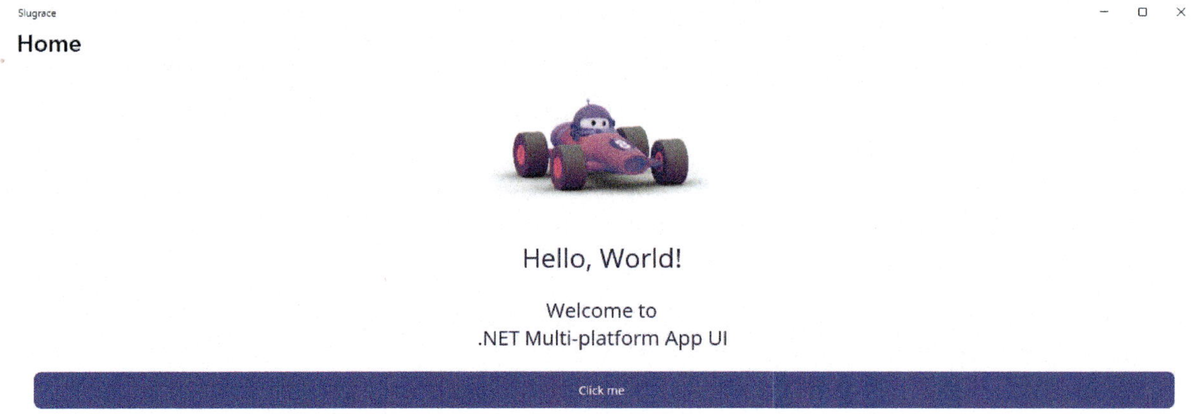

You can also see some other elements, like the page title in the upper left corner, which we didn't define in the **MainPage** file, but they are defined somewhere else, in the layout, which we're going to see later on. Anyway, let's try the app out. Click the button several times and watch the text on it. Here's what I could see after clicking the button 8 times.

Let's close the app. You can close the app window directly (A) or hit the Stop button in Visual Studio (B).

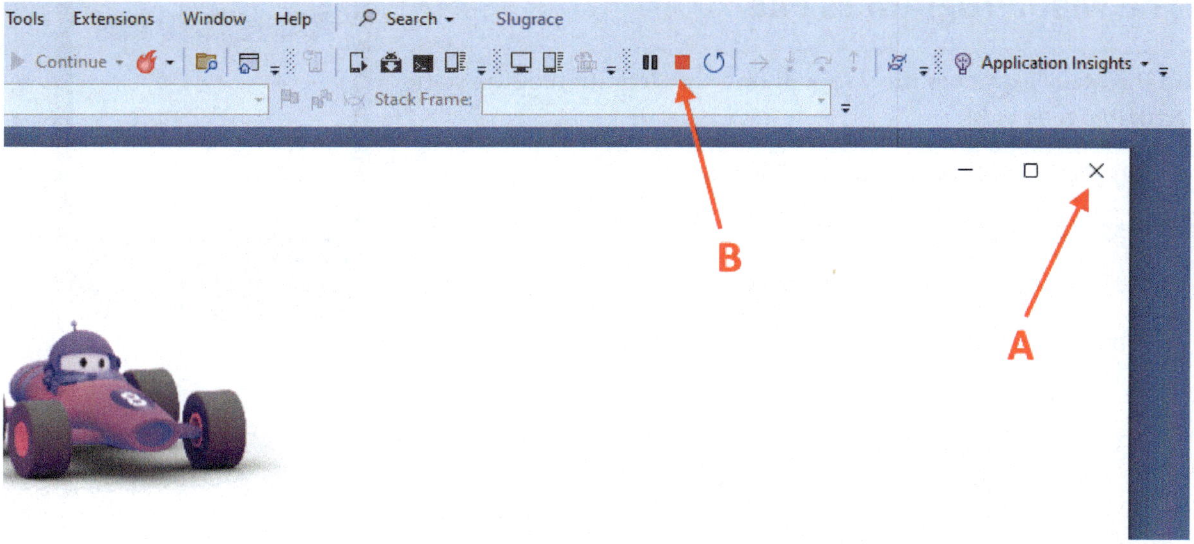

And now let's run the app on Android. First of all, we have to select the device that we created in before:

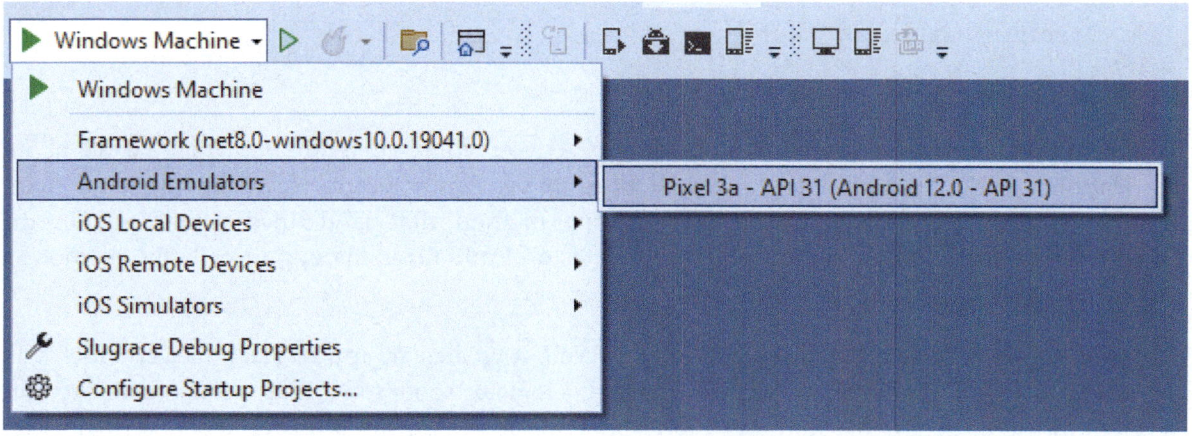

Now we can hit the Play button. It can take some time to start the first time, but the next time it'll be much faster. Anyway, here's what we can see after clicking the button several times.

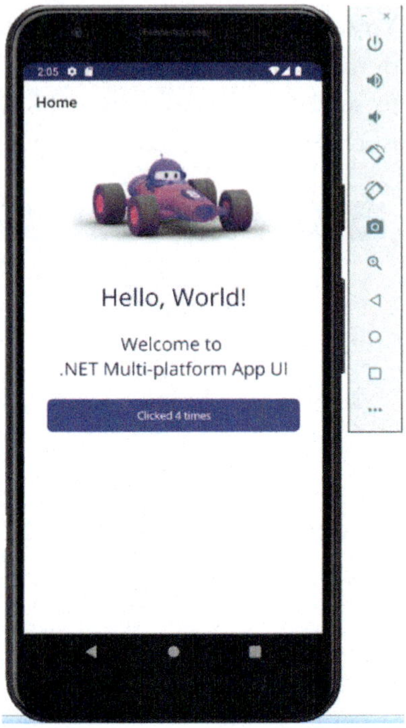

Fine, stop the app now and let's continue with our overview of the project.

The next file I'd like to draw your attention to is the **MauiProgram.cs** file.

The MauiProgram.cs File

In the **MauiProgram.cs** file you will find the definition of the static `MauiProgram` class:

```
using Microsoft.Extensions.Logging;

namespace Slugrace;

public static class MauiProgram
{
    public static MauiApp CreateMauiApp()
    {
        var builder = MauiApp.CreateBuilder();
        builder
            .UseMauiApp<App>()
            .ConfigureFonts(fonts =>
            {
                fonts.AddFont("OpenSans-Regular.ttf", "OpenSansRegular");
                fonts.AddFont("OpenSans-Semibold.ttf", "OpenSansSemibold");
            });

#if DEBUG
        builder.Logging.AddDebug();
#endif

        return builder.Build();
    }
}
```

This class is the common entry point for your app. As you will see in a minute, when we talk about the **Platforms** folder, each native platform defines its own entry point. However, the entry point code of each platform calls the **`CreateMauiApp`** method that is defined right here, in the **`MauiProgram`** class. So, when each platform creates and initializes the app, it calls the method in this common class.

But what does the **`CreateMauiApp`** method do? Well, it creates an app **`builder`** object which you can use to configure your app. Here you can see it register some fonts, but we also use it to add services for dependency injection and more. There is one thing the **`builder`** object always takes care of. It associates the application with the application class. To do that, it calls the generic **`UseMauiApp`** method and passes the application class as the type parameter, **App**. From now on, the application is identified with the **App** class that we discussed before.

Now, as I mentioned, each platform has its own entry point. To see how it works, let's move on to the **Platforms** folder.

The Platforms Folder

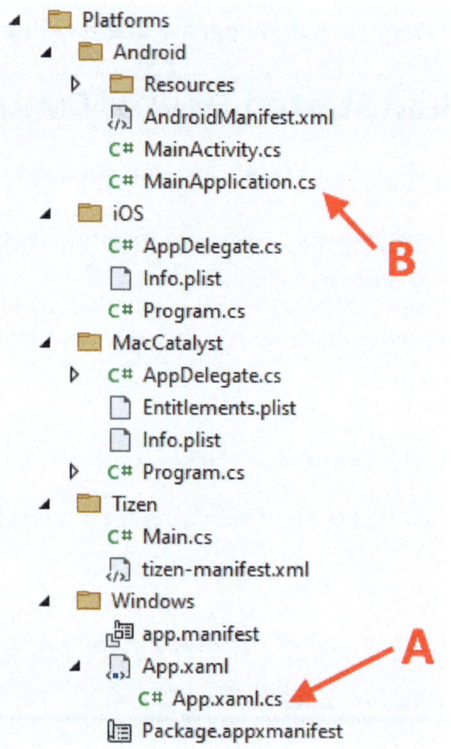

Expand the **Platforms** folder to view its hierarchy. Each platform has its own set of files and each platform contains a file with app initialization.

In case of Windows it's **App.xaml.cs** (A), in case of Android it's **MainApplication.cs** (B), and there are naturally initialization files in the other platforms as well.

If you open the initialization file of any platform, you'll see that the **`MauiProgram.CreateMauiApp`** method is called.

Let's have a look at the **App.xaml.cs** file in the Windows folder first:

```
using Microsoft.UI.Xaml;

namespace Slugrace.WinUI;

public partial class App : MauiWinUIApplication
{
    public App()
    {
        this.InitializeComponent();
    }

    protected override MauiApp CreateMauiApp() => MauiProgram.CreateMauiApp();
}
```

For clarity, I removed the comments. The method is called in the last line of the code.

And now let's have a look at the **MainApplication.cs** file in the Android folder:

```
using Android.App;
using Android.Runtime;

namespace Slugrace;
```

```
[Application]
public class MainApplication : MauiApplication
{
    public MainApplication(IntPtr handle, JniHandleOwnership ownership)
        : base(handle, ownership)
    {
    }

    protected override MauiApp CreateMauiApp() => MauiProgram.CreateMauiApp();
}
```

Again, the **MauiProgram.CreateMauiApp** method is called in the last line of the code.

App Startup Flow of Control

So, let's recap. What is going on when the app starts? Here are the steps:

1. Platform-specific initialization code is executed and calls the **CreateMauiApp** method in the **MauiProgram** class.

```
protected override MauiApp CreateMauiApp() => MauiProgram.CreateMauiApp();
```

2. The **CreateMauiApp** method creates the app **builder** object.

```
var builder = MauiApp.CreateBuilder();
```

3. The **builder** object associates the application with the **App** class.

```
builder.UseMauiApp<App>()
```

4. In the **App** object constructor the main app window is instantiated.

```
MainPage = new AppShell();
```

And only now the **MainPage** is displayed to you. Fine, and now let's have a look at the remaining folders in the project hierarchy.

The Project File

The project file, with the extension **.csproj**, contains some important information about your app. To open it, double-click on the name of the Project in the Solution Explorer, which in our case is **Slugrace**. Here's the code with the comments removed:

```
<Project Sdk="Microsoft.NET.Sdk">

	<PropertyGroup>
		<TargetFrameworks>net8.0-android;net8.0-ios;net8.0-maccatalyst</TargetFrameworks>
		<TargetFrameworks
Condition="$([MSBuild]::IsOSPlatform('windows'))">$(TargetFrameworks);net8.0-
windows10.0.19041.0</TargetFrameworks>

		<OutputType>Exe</OutputType>
		<RootNamespace>Slugrace</RootNamespace>
		<UseMaui>true</UseMaui>
		<SingleProject>true</SingleProject>
		<ImplicitUsings>enable</ImplicitUsings>
		<Nullable>enable</Nullable>

		<!-- Display name -->
		<ApplicationTitle>Slugrace</ApplicationTitle>

		<!-- App Identifier -->
		<ApplicationId>com.companyname.slugrace</ApplicationId>

		<!-- Versions -->
		<ApplicationDisplayVersion>1.0</ApplicationDisplayVersion>
		<ApplicationVersion>1</ApplicationVersion>

		<SupportedOSPlatformVersion
Condition="$([MSBuild]::GetTargetPlatformIdentifier('$(TargetFramework)')) ==
'ios'">11.0</SupportedOSPlatformVersion>
		<SupportedOSPlatformVersion
Condition="$([MSBuild]::GetTargetPlatformIdentifier('$(TargetFramework)')) ==
'maccatalyst'">13.1</SupportedOSPlatformVersion>
		<SupportedOSPlatformVersion
Condition="$([MSBuild]::GetTargetPlatformIdentifier('$(TargetFramework)')) ==
'android'">21.0</SupportedOSPlatformVersion>
		<SupportedOSPlatformVersion
Condition="$([MSBuild]::GetTargetPlatformIdentifier('$(TargetFramework)')) ==
'windows'">10.0.17763.0</SupportedOSPlatformVersion>
		<TargetPlatformMinVersion
Condition="$([MSBuild]::GetTargetPlatformIdentifier('$(TargetFramework)')) ==
'windows'">10.0.17763.0</TargetPlatformMinVersion>
		<SupportedOSPlatformVersion
Condition="$([MSBuild]::GetTargetPlatformIdentifier('$(TargetFramework)')) ==
'tizen'">6.5</SupportedOSPlatformVersion>
	</PropertyGroup>

	<ItemGroup>
		<!-- App Icon -->
		<MauiIcon Include="Resources\AppIcon\appicon.svg"
ForegroundFile="Resources\AppIcon\appiconfg.svg" Color="#512BD4" />

		<!-- Splash Screen -->
		<MauiSplashScreen Include="Resources\Splash\splash.svg" Color="#512BD4"
BaseSize="128,128" />

		<!-- Images -->
		<MauiImage Include="Resources\Images\*" />
```

```
                <MauiImage Update="Resources\Images\dotnet_bot.png" Resize="True"
BaseSize="300,185" />

                <!-- Custom Fonts -->
                <MauiFont Include="Resources\Fonts\*" />

                <!-- Raw Assets (also remove the "Resources\Raw" prefix) -->
                <MauiAsset Include="Resources\Raw\**"
LogicalName="%(RecursiveDir)%(Filename)%(Extension)" />
        </ItemGroup>

        <ItemGroup>
                <PackageReference Include="Microsoft.Maui.Controls" Version="$(MauiVersion)" />
                <PackageReference Include="Microsoft.Maui.Controls.Compatibility"
Version="$(MauiVersion)" />
                <PackageReference Include="Microsoft.Extensions.Logging.Debug" Version="8.0.0" />
        </ItemGroup>

</Project>
```

Here you can see a **PropertyGroup** section and two **ItemGroup** sections. The **PropertyGroup** contains information about the frameworks your app targets, app title, app version, and so on. You can modify this code if you need to.

In the **ItemGroup** below you can see information about resources. The section specifies an app icon, the splash screen and the default locations for images, fonts and other assets used by the app.

So, the project file contains information about the resources used in the app. But where actually are the resources?

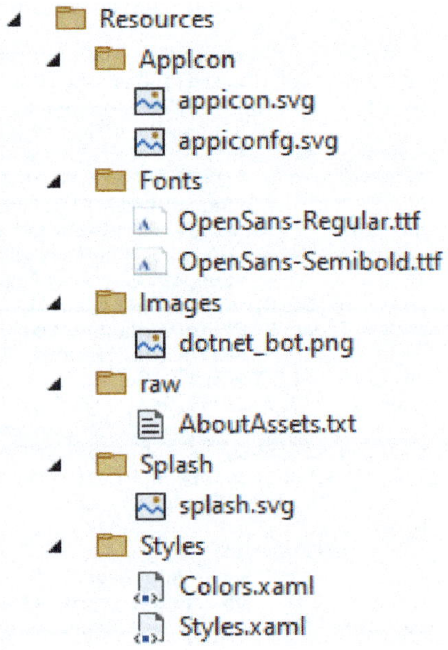

The Resources Folder

The answer is here, in the **Resources** folder. Expand it and you will see all the resources described in the project file. This is where we'll be adding all the resources that our app needs to make use of.

The Other Folders

The two remaining folders in our project hierarchy are **Dependencies** and **Properties**. The former contains .NET dependencies for the specific platforms. The latter contains a JSON file with launch settings.

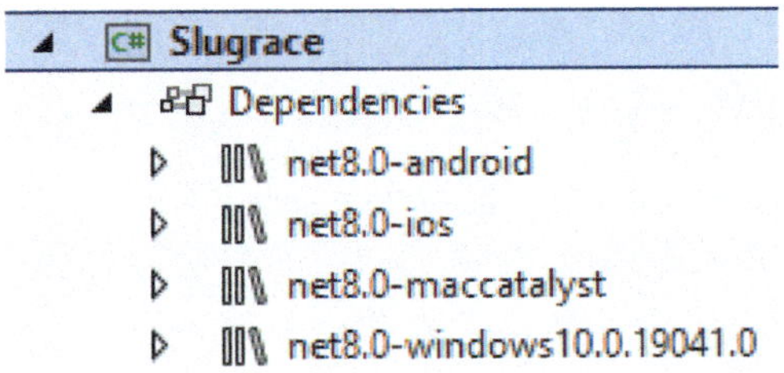

So, that would be it. This is all the code we get out of the box when we create a new .NET MAUI project. In the next chapter we'll have a look at the syntax of the XAML language.

Chapter 3 - Introduction to XAML

code: https://github.com/prospero-apps/Slugrace/tree/chapter3

In the previous chapter we were discussing the structure of the default project that is created for us when we select the .NET MAUI App template. As you saw, part of the code is written in C#, part in XAML, which is an XML-like markup language used across several technologies such as .NET MAUI, WPF, UWP or Xamarin, to mention just the most important ones.

You could create a project without XAML, with just C# code. The question is whether you should... Before we talk about the advantages and disadvantages of XAML, though, let's create a new page in our Slugrace project which we will be using throughout this book to test new stuff. This page is not going to be included in the project eventually, but I think it will be pretty helpful on the way. A good name for this page would be `TestPage`. We'll use the page to test new stuff before we implement it in the actual project. So, open the Slugrace project, right-click the project name in the Solution Explorer (Slugrace), select Add, then New Item... and in the window that opens select .NET MAUI (A), then .NET MAUI ContentPage (XAML) (B), enter the name of the page (C) and hit Add (D).

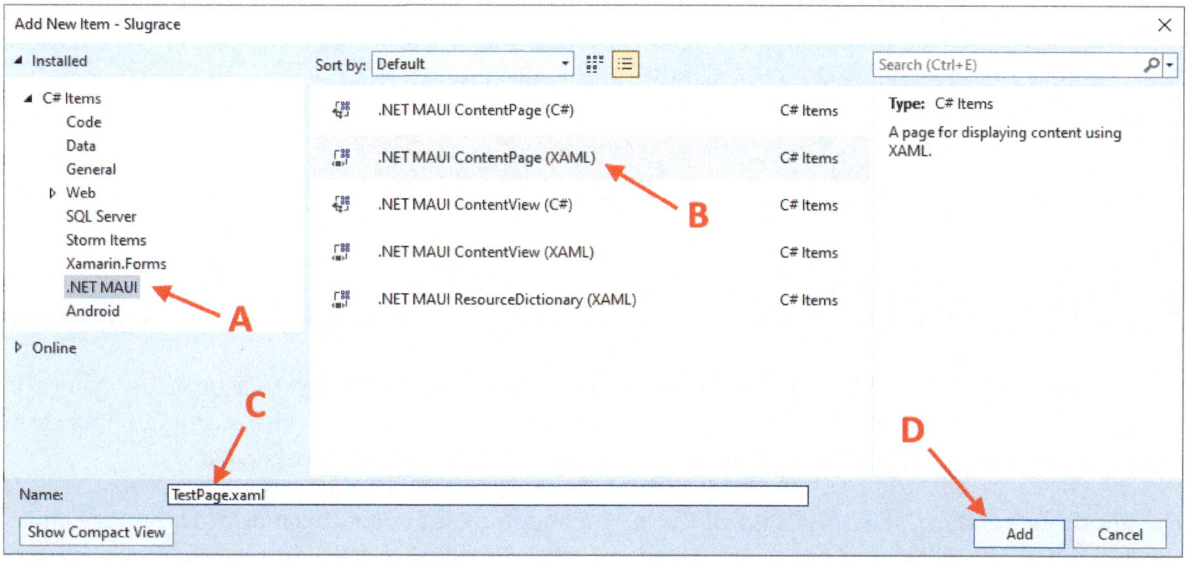

This will create two files in the root folder of the project, **TestPage.xaml** and its corresponding code-behind file, **TestPage.xaml.cs**. The XAML file should open in the editor automatically. It has some sample code that contains a `Label` element inside a `VerticalStackLayout` element. The `Text` property of the label is set to "`Welcome to .NET MAUI!`". Change it to something along the lines of "`Test Page`" so that we know which page we're on when it's displayed. The full code of the **TestPage.xaml** file should look like so:

```
<?xml version="1.0" encoding="utf-8" ?>
<ContentPage xmlns="http://schemas.microsoft.com/dotnet/2021/maui"
             xmlns:x="http://schemas.microsoft.com/winfx/2009/xaml"
             x:Class="Slugrace.TestPage"
             Title="TestPage">
    <VerticalStackLayout>
        <Label
            Text="Test Page"
            VerticalOptions="Center"
            HorizontalOptions="Center" />
    </VerticalStackLayout>
</ContentPage>
```

We also must tell the program to display this page when it's executed instead of the **MainPage**. Let's make the changes in the **AppShell.xaml** file inside the **ShellContent** element. The title of the page should be **"Test"**, the content template and route have to be changed accordingly:

```
<?xml version="1.0" encoding="UTF-8" ?>
<Shell
    ...
    <ShellContent
        Title="Test"
        ContentTemplate="{DataTemplate local:TestPage}"
        Route="TestPage" />
</Shell>
```

Let's test the app on Windows, so select Windows Machine on your Play button and hit the button. You should see the **TestPage** with the text displayed correctly. Here's the top part of the page:

Why Use XAML?

So, why should you use XAML if you don't have to? A big disadvantage that probably comes to your mind when you think about it is that if it's new to you, there's a certain learning curve. You already know C#, so why bother to learn anything new if it's not absolutely necessary?

The good news is that .NET MAUI is not the only technology that uses this markup language and if you learn it, you will be able to use it (with slight modifications) in WPF or the other technologies listed before. And besides, it's not so difficult if you know any other markup language like XML or HTML. There are lots of similarities.

So, is XAML worth learning or not? Well, I think it definitely is. Here are some reasons:

- it facilitates division of concerns: you use XAML for the UI and C# for the logic,

- it makes the graphical structure of the page clearly reflected in code,

- it's much easier and faster to create the UI of your app using a declarative markup language than C# code after you master the former,

- it makes the application easier to manage as it grows,

- it enables a UI designer to work independently of a logic developer.

We're going to see the difference between UI written with XAML and the same UI written with C# in a moment. However, before we do that, let's talk about the elements (like the label) that we place in a XAML page. They are called **views** in XAML.

Views in XAML

In XAML most of the elements inherit from the **View** class. So, the layouts are views and practically all the controls that we'll be using in our project are views. I will be using the terms 'view' and 'layout/control' interchangeably in this book. One of the most commonly used views is **Label**. Let's talk about it first.

The Label View

When we created our **TestPage**, a **Label** was added for us automatically. Let's have a look at it again:

```
<Label
    Text="Test Page"
    VerticalOptions="Center"
    HorizontalOptions="Center" />
```

As you can see, it has an opening angled bracket (**<**) and a closing one (**>**). In this particular case it's a self-closing tag, with a slash character preceding the closing bracket. We can use self-closing tags if there is no content that should go between the opening and closing tag. But even with no content, we still could use an opening and a closing tag. We can rewrite the code like so:

```
<Label
    Text="Test Page"
    VerticalOptions="Center"
    HorizontalOptions="Center">
</Label>
```

Either way will do in this case. But if there were some content, we would have to use the latter syntax. Let's remove the **Text** attribute from the opening tag and use the same string as the content of the label:

```
<Label
    VerticalOptions="Center"
    HorizontalOptions="Center">Test Page
</Label>
```

Now the closing angled bracket is required. Naturally, you could put everything on one line and it would work the same:

```
<Label VerticalOptions="Center" HorizontalOptions="Center">Test Page</Label>
```

The general rule is that if a view has some content, the content goes between the opening and closing tags of the view. The content may be a simple string like here, but it may also be a more or less complex hierarchy of other views. Like for example here - the **Label** is the content of the **VerticalStackLayout** and the **VerticalStackLayout** is the content of the **ContentPage**. Views nested inside other views are also referred to as their **children**.

Before we proceed, let's restore the original shape of the label with the **Text** attribute set inside the opening tag. As you can see, **Text** is not the only attribute here. Let's have a look at the others.

Property Attributes

Just as the elements (like **Label** or **Button**) represent class instances (we call it **Object Element Syntax**), so the attributes inside the opening tags of the elements are used to set the values of the properties of those instances. This is why we call them **property attributes**. It'll become even clearer when you see the corresponding C# code. Let's stay in the XAML file for a while, though. There are three attributes on the **Label** instance right now. Let's add some more. The order of the attributes doesn't matter. Here's the modified code:

```
<?xml version="1.0" encoding="utf-8" ?>
<ContentPage ...>
    <VerticalStackLayout>
        <Label
            Text="Test Page"
            VerticalOptions="Center"
            HorizontalOptions="Center"
            TextColor="Red"
            FontSize="36"
            FontAttributes="Bold, Italic"
            Rotation="45"
            CharacterSpacing="5"
            TranslationY="100" />
    </VerticalStackLayout>
</ContentPage>
```

The names of the attributes are self-explanatory. Now run the app again to see the result:

One interesting thing is the **FontAttributes** attribute. There are two values assigned to it. If you want to assign more than one value to an attribute (provided it's at all possible), you separate them with a comma.

And there are more attributes that you can use with a **Label** (as well as with any other view). Use Intellisense to experiment if you like.

Now, before we proceed to the C# counterpart of the above XAML code, I'd like to draw your attention to a very useful feature available in Visual Studio that will make your life a whole lot easier.

Hot Reload

The feature I'm talking about is **Hot Reload**. When you run the code, it should be activated, but if it isn't, you can activate it manually. You will find it here:

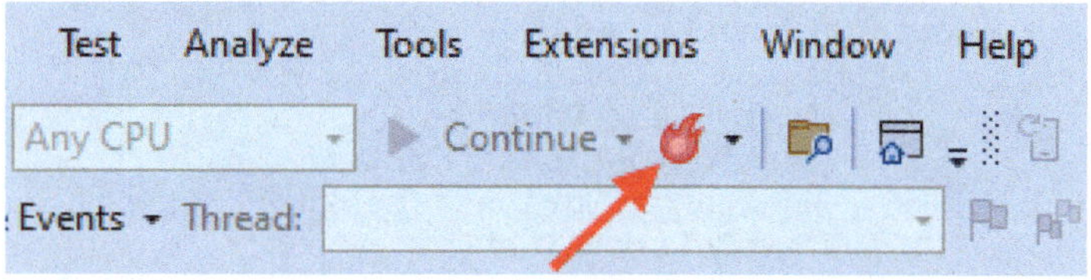

With this feature activated and your app still running, try to make some changes in the code. Let's change the values of some of the properties. Whenever you change a value, the change is immediately reflected in the running app. Here's what I tried:

```
...
        <Label
            Text="Test Page"
            VerticalOptions="Center"
            HorizontalOptions="Center"
            TextColor="Blue"
            FontSize="60"
            FontAttributes="Bold, Italic"
            Rotation="180"
            CharacterSpacing="20"
            TranslationY="100" />
    </VerticalStackLayout>
...
```

And here's the result after my last modification:

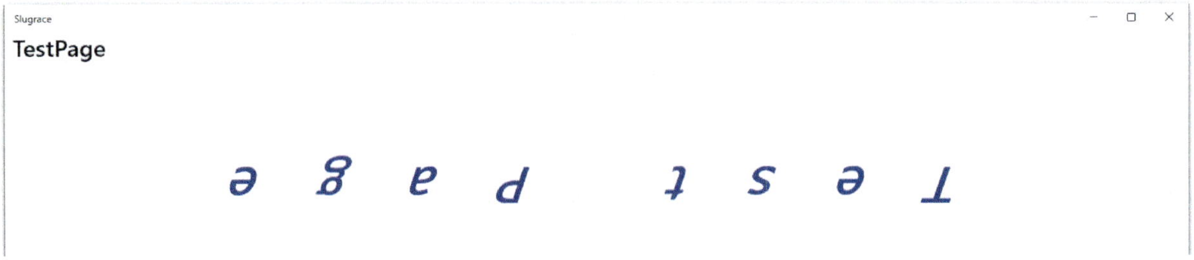

So, with Hot Reload on, you can view your changes live in the running app without having to stop and restart it every time.

XAML vs C#

And now let's finally see, what our code would look like if we decided to go with pure C#, no XAML at all. Here's the XAML code that we're going to rewrite in C#:

```
<?xml version="1.0" encoding="utf-8" ?>
<ContentPage xmlns="http://schemas.microsoft.com/dotnet/2021/maui"
             xmlns:x="http://schemas.microsoft.com/winfx/2009/xaml"
             x:Class="Slugrace.TestPage"
             Title="TestPage">
    <VerticalStackLayout>
        <Label
            Text="Test Page"
            VerticalOptions="Center"
            HorizontalOptions="Center"
            TextColor="Blue"
            FontSize="60"
            FontAttributes="Bold, Italic"
            Rotation="180"
            CharacterSpacing="20"
            TranslationY="100" />
    </VerticalStackLayout>
</ContentPage>
```

Let's delete the `TestPage` completely. Right-click the XAML file, select Delete and confirm. This will delete both the XAML file and the code-behind.

Then add a new `TestPage` like we did before, but this time select the .NET MAUI ContentPage (C#) template (A). Name the file **TestPage.cs** (B):

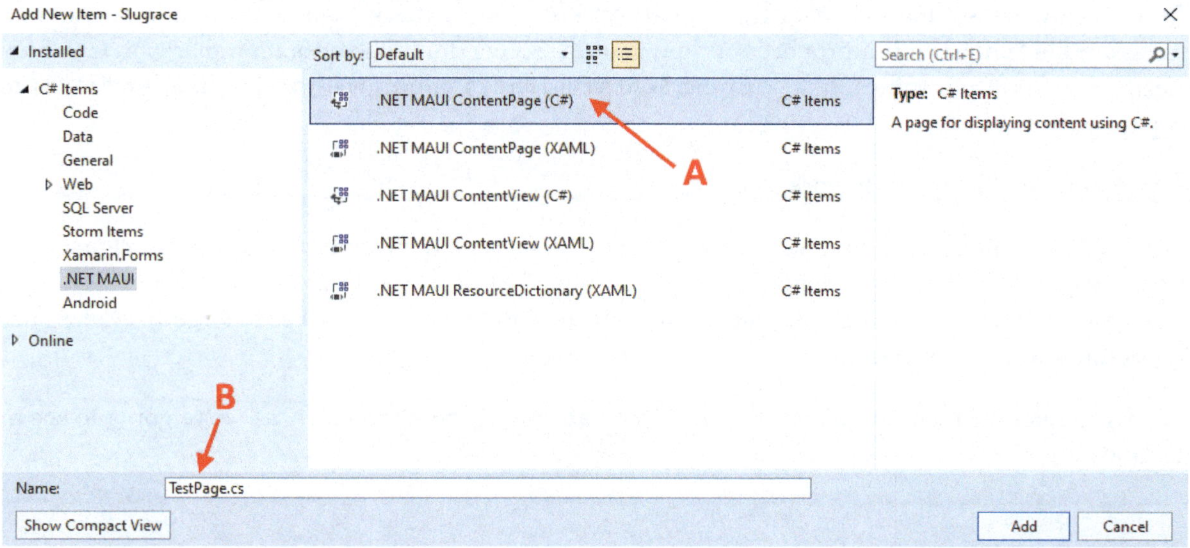

The file will open in the editor with some initial code already in it. Let's modify the code to make it the C# counterpart of the XAML code that we had before:

```
namespace Slugrace;

public class TestPage : ContentPage
{
    public TestPage()
    {
        Content = new VerticalStackLayout
        {
            Children = {
                new Label
                {
                    Text = "Test Page",
                    VerticalOptions = LayoutOptions.Center,
                    HorizontalOptions = LayoutOptions.Center,
                    TextColor = Colors.Blue,
                    FontSize = 60,
                    FontAttributes = FontAttributes.Bold | FontAttributes.Italic,
                    Rotation = 180,
                    CharacterSpacing = 20,
                    TranslationY = 100
                }
            }
        };
    }
}
```

This code is more verbose than its XAML counterpart, although at this level of complexity the difference isn't that obvious. But when our UI gets more complex, the XAML code will be much easier to read.

Look at how we set the values of the properties. We need to check their types in documentation. For example **FontSize** is a property of type **double**, so we don't use quotation marks in C#. If we need to set multiple values, like with the **FontAttributes** enum, we use the pipe symbol (**|**) to separate them.

If you now run the app, it'll work as before.

After you're done testing, remove the C# file and recreate the XAML version of the **TestPage** with its corresponding code-behind, just like we did in the first place (without the later modifications in the **Label** object except the **Text** attribute, which should be set to **"Test Page"**). Make sure everything works as expected.

In this chapter we focused on just one view, the **Label**. But there are more, as we're going to see in the next one.

Chapter 4 - Views in XAML

code: https://github.com/prospero-apps/Slugrace/tree/chapter4

In chapter 3 we were talking about the **Label** view and its property attributes. But there are lots of other views that you get out of the box. In this chapter we'll have a look at some of them, mainly the ones that we'll be using in our app. To just practice new stuff here, we'll be using the **TestPage** for that.

Let's start with the **Button** view.

Button

Open the **TestPage.xaml** file and add a button below the label:

```
<?xml version="1.0" encoding="utf-8" ?>
<ContentPage ...>
    <VerticalStackLayout>
        <Label
            ...
        <Button
            Text="Click Me!"
            BackgroundColor="Red"
            TextColor="Bisque"
            FontSize="40"
            FontAttributes="Bold"
            BorderColor="Black"
            BorderWidth="10"
            HorizontalOptions="Center" />
    </VerticalStackLayout>
</ContentPage>
```

The attributes are self-explanatory again. You can see two new attributes here, **BorderColor** and **BorderWidth**, which are defined in the **Button** class. All the other properties are derived from the **View** class.

Let's run the app on Android. Here's our fancy button.

Buttons are used instead of labels if you want add some functionality to your app. There are a couple events associated with them. Let's have a look at them now.

Button Events

The events associated with a button are **Clicked**, **Pressed** and **Released**. Let's implement them in our button. As you saw in chapter 2, the counter button implements the **Clicked** event. First it binds a method to the event:

```
<Button
    x:Name="CounterBtn"
    Text="Click me"
    SemanticProperties.Hint="Counts the number of times you click"
    Clicked="OnCounterClicked"
    HorizontalOptions="Center" />
```

And then it defines the method in the code-behind:

```
private void OnCounterClicked(object sender, EventArgs e)
{
    count++;

    if (count == 1)
        CounterBtn.Text = $"Clicked {count} time";
    else
         CounterBtn.Text = $"Clicked {count} times";

    SemanticScreenReader.Announce(CounterBtn.Text);
}
```

Here it refers to the button by its name (**CounterBtn**), which the **x:Name** attribute is set to. We'll be talking about this attribute later on, but for now we'll be referring to the button using the **sender** argument.

The **sender** argument refers to the object that fired the event, so the button in our case. As it's an **object**, we must cast it to the **Button** type. So, let's implement the **Clicked** event in our button now. Here's the XAML code in the **TestPage.xaml** file:

```
...
        <Button
            ...
            HorizontalOptions="Center"
            Clicked="Button_Clicked" />
    </VerticalStackLayout>
</ContentPage>
```

And here's the method defined in the code-behind:

```
namespace Slugrace;

public partial class TestPage : ContentPage
{
    public TestPage()
    ...
    private void Button_Clicked(object sender, EventArgs e)
    {
        var button = (Button)sender;
        button.Text = "Clicked";
        button.BorderWidth = 5;
        button.BackgroundColor = Color.FromRgba(.5, .5, .5, 1);
    }
}
```

Now run the app and click the button. You should see the text, border width and border color of the button change.

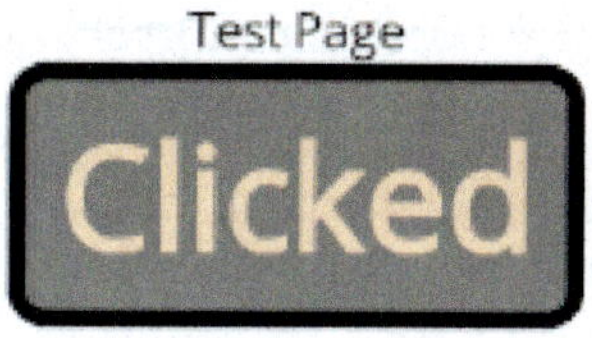

This change is only visible after you release the button. And now remove the **Clicked** event from XAML and add the **Pressed** event instead:

```
...
        <Button
            ...
            HorizontalOptions="Center"
            Pressed="Button_Pressed" />
    </VerticalStackLayout>
</ContentPage>
```

This time we'll cast the sender object to **Button** in a different way:

```
namespace Slugrace;

public partial class TestPage : ContentPage
{
    ...
    private void Button_Pressed(object sender, EventArgs e)
    {
        (sender as Button)!.Text = "Pressed";
    }
}
```

By the way, the exclamation point in the code above is the so-called null forgiving operator. We use it to tell the compiler that we know what we're doing and there is no null reference. Without it, we would get a warning.

This event will fire the moment you press the button, not only after you release it. This time only the text on the button is going to change.

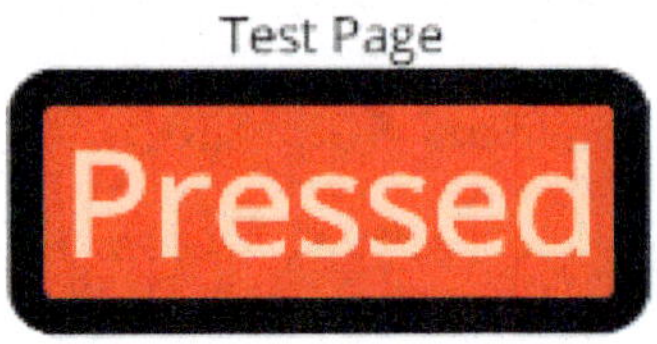

Finally, let's see how the **Released** event works. First, let's add this event in XAML:

```
...
        <Button
            ...
            Pressed="Button_Pressed"
            Released="Button_Released" />
    </VerticalStackLayout>
</ContentPage>
```

And here's the **Button_Released** method in the code-behind:

```
...
public partial class TestPage : ContentPage
{
    ...
    private void Button_Pressed(object sender, EventArgs e)
    ...
    private void Button_Released(object sender, EventArgs e)
    {
        (sender as Button)!.Text = "Click Me Again!";
    }
}
```

When you release the button, you will see the effect.

That's it as the basic functionality of the button is concerned. Now we can move on to the next view, which is the slider.

Slider

The slider can be used to set a value (of type double) between two extreme values (minimum and maximum) by dragging a thumb. You can set the minimum value, the maximum value and the current value by respectively using the **Minimum**, **Maximum** and **Value** properties.

Let's play with the **Slider** for a while. First let's remove the XAML code that creates the button and the code related to the button in the code-behind. We don't need it anymore. Instead, let's create a slider:

```
...
        <Label
            ...
        <Slider
            Minimum="-100"
            Maximum="200"
            Value="0" />
    </VerticalStackLayout>
</ContentPage>
```

As you can see, the minimum and maximum values are set to -100 and 200 respectively and the current value is 0. So the slider thumb should sit at 0 when you run the app. Let's try it out.

It would be great if we could see the current value of the slider. We have a label above it, which we can use for that. But the label must have a way to read the value from the slider. To reference a view, you just have to add the **x:Name** attribute to it. Then it will be available by name in both XAML and C# code. We're going to cover this topic in much more detail later on in the book, but for now it's enough to say that one way to do it is by setting the **BindingContext** attribute of the target view using the **x:Reference** markup extension (what's a markup extension? - more on that later on as well) to reference the view and then we use the **Binding** markup extension with the property we want to bind to. Sounds complicated, so let's have a look at the code:

```
...
        <Label
            BindingContext="{x:Reference slider1}"
            Text="{Binding Value}"
            FontSize="30"
            VerticalOptions="Center"
            HorizontalOptions="Center" />

        <Slider
            x:Name="slider1"
            Minimum="-100"
            Maximum="200"
            Value="0" />
        ...
```

So, here we name the object **slider1**. Then, in the target view, which is the label, we set **BindingContext** to the slider by its name and we set the label's **Text** property to the **Value** property of the slider. I also set the font size to make the text slightly more readable.

If you run the code now and move the slider thumb, you will see the text above it change in real time.

The initial value is 0. If you drag the thumb all the way to the left, the value will be -100. If you drag the thumb all the way to the right, the value will be 200. And the values in-between are floating-point numbers (of type double).

Let's now set some other attributes:

```
...
        <Slider
            x:Name="slider1"
            Minimum="-100"
            Maximum="200"
            Value="0"
            HeightRequest="40"
            BackgroundColor="LightBlue"
            FlowDirection="RightToLeft"
            MaximumTrackColor="Red"
            MinimumTrackColor="Green"
            ThumbColor="Black" />
        ...
```

Now the slider is thicker and has a light blue background color. Its flow direction is reversed, so the maximum value is on the left-hand side. The part of the slider with values higher than the current value is red, the part with lower values is green. And the thumb is black.

Sometimes a vertical slider is the way to go. To make your slider vertical, just set its **Rotation** property accordingly. Let's simplify the first horizontal slider and add a vertical one:

```
...
    <VerticalStackLayout>
        <Label
            BindingContext="{x:Reference slider2}"
            Text="{Binding Value}"
            ...

        <Slider
            x:Name="slider1"
            Maximum="10"
            Minimum="0"
            Value="7"
            WidthRequest="200"
            HorizontalOptions="Start" />
```

```
        <Slider
            x:Name="slider2"
            Maximum="15"
            Minimum="-15"
            WidthRequest="200"
            HorizontalOptions="End"
            TranslationY="100"
            Rotation="-90"
            Value="0" />

    </VerticalStackLayout>
</ContentPage>
```

As you can see, we specified the width of each slider to be 200. The first slider has **HorizontalOptions** set to **Start**, so it shows up on the left. The second slider has this property set to **End**, so it shows up on the right. The second slider is also translated vertically by 100 units and rotated so that the minimum value is now at the bottom. If you want the maximum value to be at the bottom, just rotate it 90 degrees instead of -90. Finally, the label now displays the current value of the second slider.

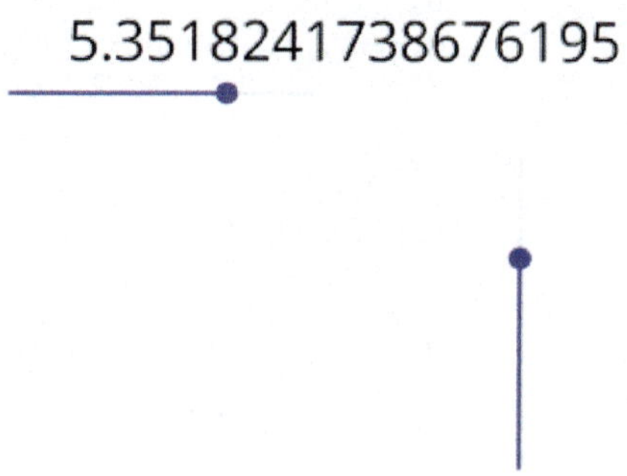

Slider Events

There are a couple interesting **Slider** events, the most obvious one being probably **ValueChanged**. It's triggered when the value changes, which isn't that hard to guess. Let's see it in action. The second slider has a range of -15 to 15. This value should be used to rotate the first slider. We could achieve this using simple binding like before:

```
...
        <Slider
            x:Name="slider1"
            BindingContext="{x:Reference slider2}"
            Rotation="{Binding Value}"
            Maximum="10"
            ...

        <Slider
            x:Name="slider2"
            ...
```

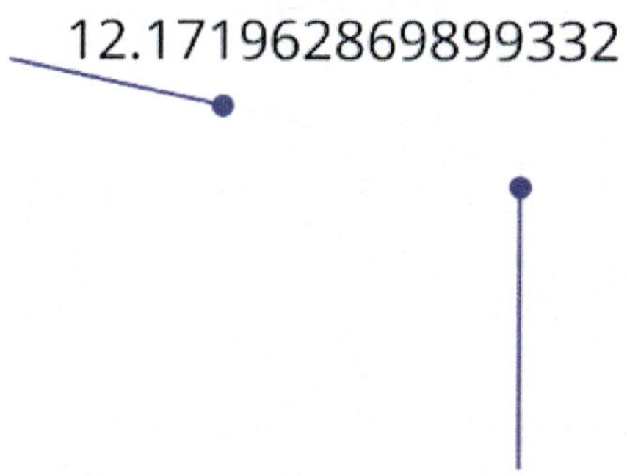

Try it out. If you drag the thumb of the second slider, the first slider rotates.

But if you're opting for a more complex scenario, the

ValueChanged event is a good solution. Have a look:

```
<?xml version="1.0" encoding="utf-8" ?>
...
    <VerticalStackLayout>
        <Label
            x:Name="label"
            Text=""
            FontSize="30"
            VerticalOptions="Center"
            HorizontalOptions="Center" />

        <Slider
            x:Name="slider1"
            Maximum="10"
            Minimum="0"
            Value="7"
            WidthRequest="200"
            HorizontalOptions="Start" />

        <Slider
            x:Name="slider2"
            Maximum="15"
            Minimum="-15"
            WidthRequest="200"
            HorizontalOptions="End"
            TranslationY="100"
            Rotation="-90"
            Value="0"
            ValueChanged="slider2_ValueChanged" />

    </VerticalStackLayout>
</ContentPage>
```

And here's the code-behind:

```
...
public partial class TestPage : ContentPage
{
    public TestPage()
    ...
    private void slider2_ValueChanged(object sender, ValueChangedEventArgs e)
    {
        if (e.NewValue > 0)
          {
                label.Text = "Rotating normally";
                slider1.Rotation = e.NewValue;
          }
          else
          {
              label.Text = "Rotating faster";
              slider1.Rotation = e.NewValue * 5;
         }
     }
}
```

I removed the binding from the label. Instead I set its **x:Name** attribute so that we can reference it in code. Now if you drag the thumb of the second slider, the first slider will be rotated and the label's

`Text` property will be set. The rotation will be different for the positive and negative range of the second slider though:

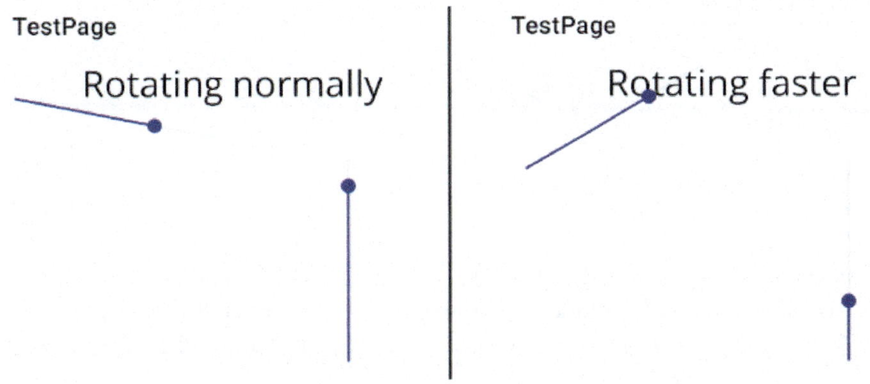

Two other events are **`DragStarted`** and **`DragCompleted`**, which are fired when you respectively start and finish dragging the slider thumb. Let's add them to the first slider:

```
...
        <Slider
            x:Name="slider1"
            Maximum="10"
            Minimum="0"
            Value="7"
            WidthRequest="200"
            HorizontalOptions="Start"
            DragStarted="slider1_DragStarted"
            DragCompleted="slider1_DragCompleted" />
        <Slider
            x:Name="slider2"
            ...
```

And here's how they are implemented in the code-behind:

```
...
public partial class TestPage : ContentPage
{
    public TestPage()
    ...
    private void slider2_ValueChanged(object sender, ValueChangedEventArgs e)
    ...
    private void slider1_DragStarted(object sender, EventArgs e)
    {
        label.Text = "Dragging started";
    }

    private void slider1_DragCompleted(object sender, EventArgs e)
    {
        label.Text = "Dragging completed";
    }
}
```

Now run the app and start dragging the first slider.

As soon as you stop dragging the slider thumb, the label text will change to "Dragging Completed." Fine, let's move on to the next view, the check box.

CheckBox

A **CheckBox** is a two-state button that can be either checked or unchecked.

Let's remove the slider-related code in both XAML and C# code and add two check boxes. We use the **IsChecked** property to set the check box's state in code. It's **False** by default. Our first check box is unchecked, but we set the **IsChecked** property of the second one to **True**:

```
...
    <VerticalStackLayout>
        <Label
            x:Name="label"
            Text=""
            FontSize="30"
            VerticalOptions="Center"
            HorizontalOptions="Center" />

        <CheckBox />
        <CheckBox IsChecked="True" />
    </VerticalStackLayout>
</ContentPage>
```

This is how they look.

You can now check or uncheck them by clicking on them. Try it out.

You can change the color of your check box if you want:

```
...
        <CheckBox Color="Red"/>
        <CheckBox IsChecked="True" Color="Green" />
    ...
```

Now they look a little bit different.

CheckBox Events

As for the **CheckBox** events, there's actually only one if you exclude those that are inherited from the **Element**, **VisualElement** or **BindableObject** classes. It's **CheckedChanged**.

Here's an example where you can see how to use it. First, the XAML file:

```
...
    <VerticalStackLayout>
        <Label
            ...
        <CheckBox
            Color="Red"
            CheckedChanged="CheckBox_CheckedChanged" />
        <CheckBox
            IsChecked="True"
            Color="Green"
            CheckedChanged="CheckBox_CheckedChanged" />
    </VerticalStackLayout>
</ContentPage>
```

And now the code-behind:

```
...
public partial class TestPage : ContentPage
{
    public TestPage()
    ...
    private void CheckBox_CheckedChanged(object sender, CheckedChangedEventArgs e)
    {
        string labelText = $"Color: {(sender as CheckBox)!.Color.ToHex()} - ";

        if (e.Value)
        {
            labelText += "checked";
        }
        else
        {
            labelText += "unchecked";
        }

        label.Text = labelText;
    }
}
```

As you can see, we're using the label here to display information about which check box has been clicked and how its state has changed. This is what you should see after unchecking the green check box.

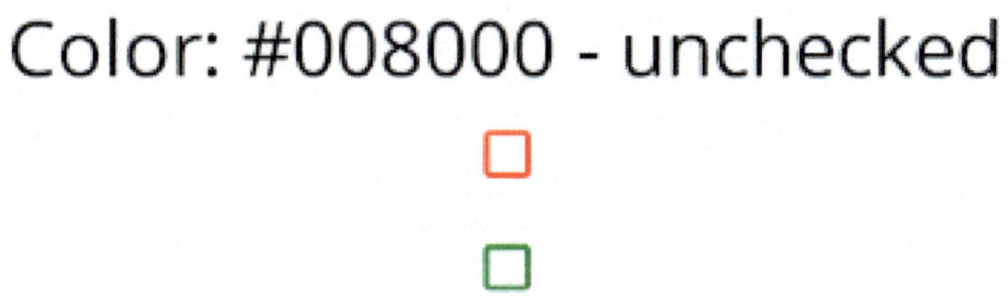

The next view we're going to have a look at is **`RadioButton`**.

RadioButton

A **RadioButton** is also a type of button, just like **CheckBox**, but it's used if only one option out of many should be selected. We also use the **IsChecked** property to set the value of a radio button's state. There are a couple other properties that we often use with radio buttons.

One of them is **Content**. We use it to set the string or view that is to be displayed in the radio button.

Another important property is **GroupName**. All radio buttons sharing the same group name are mutually exclusive, so only one of them can be selected at any given time. If you need more sets of radio buttons, just use different group names for them.

Yet another property is **Value**. You can use it to store an optional unique value associated with the radio button.

Let's have a look at all these properties in action. Remove the check boxes from XAML and the corresponding C# code from the code-behind and create the following two groups of radio buttons:

```
...
    <VerticalStackLayout>
        <Label
            ...
            FontSize="20"
            ...
        <VerticalStackLayout>
            <Label Text="Pick your prize:" />
            <RadioButton
                GroupName="prizes"
                Content="A houseplant"
                Value="45" />
            <RadioButton
                GroupName="prizes"
                Content="An antique chair"
                Value="900" />
            <RadioButton
                GroupName="prizes"
                Content="A pair of gloves"
                Value="68" />
        </VerticalStackLayout>

        <VerticalStackLayout>
            <Label Text="Where do you want it to be delivered?" />
            <RadioButton
                GroupName="delivery"
                Content="New York"
                IsChecked="True"
                Value="25" />
            <RadioButton
                GroupName="delivery"
                Content="Atlanta"
                Value="35" />
```

```
            <RadioButton
                GroupName="delivery"
                Content="Boston"
                Value="30" />
        </VerticalStackLayout>

    </VerticalStackLayout>
</ContentPage>
```

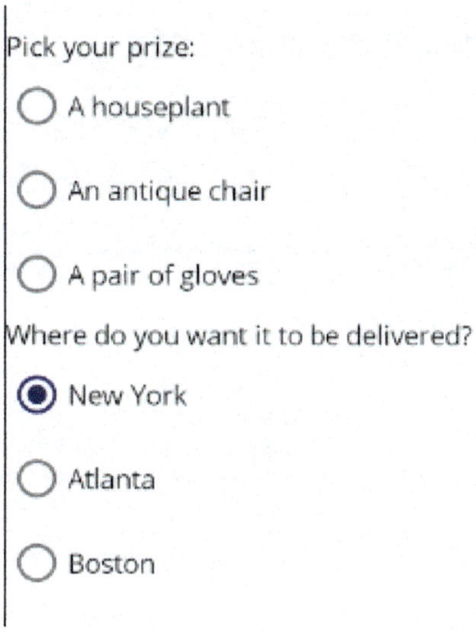

This should look like so on Android.

Now you can select one radio button in each group.

You can group the radio buttons also in a different way, by setting the **RadioButtonGroup.GroupName** attached property (we're going to talk about attached properties soon) on the parent view, so in our case on the **VerticalStackLayout**.

So, we could rewrite the code above like so:

```
...
        <Label
            ...
        <VerticalStackLayout RadioButtonGroup.GroupName="prizes">
            <Label Text="Pick your prize:" />
            <RadioButton
                Content="A houseplant"
                Value="45" />
            <RadioButton
                Content="An antique chair"
                Value="900" />
            <RadioButton
                Content="A pair of gloves"
                Value="68" />
        </VerticalStackLayout>

        <VerticalStackLayout RadioButtonGroup.GroupName="delivery">
            <Label Text="Where do you want it to be delivered?" />
            <RadioButton
                Content="New York"
                IsChecked="True"
                Value="25" />
            <RadioButton
                Content="Atlanta"
                Value="35" />
            <RadioButton
                Content="Boston"
                Value="30" />
        </VerticalStackLayout>
    </VerticalStackLayout>
</ContentPage>
```

It still works like before.

RadioButton Events

If you want to react to a state change of a radio button, you have to implement the **CheckedChanged** event. Here's how to do it. First, the XAML code:

```
<?xml version="1.0" encoding="utf-8" ?>
<ContentPage xmlns="http://schemas.microsoft.com/dotnet/2021/maui"
             ...
    <VerticalStackLayout>
        <Label
            x:Name="label1"
            FontSize="20"
            VerticalOptions="Center"
            HorizontalOptions="Center" />

        <Label
            x:Name="label2"
            FontSize="15"
            VerticalOptions="Center"
            HorizontalOptions="Center" />

        <VerticalStackLayout RadioButtonGroup.GroupName="prizes">
            <Label Text="Pick your prize:" />
            <RadioButton
                Content="A houseplant"
                Value="45"
                CheckedChanged="RadioButton_CheckedChanged" />
            <RadioButton
                Content="An antique chair"
                Value="900"
                CheckedChanged="RadioButton_CheckedChanged" />
            <RadioButton
                Content="A pair of gloves"
                Value="68"
                CheckedChanged="RadioButton_CheckedChanged" />
        </VerticalStackLayout>

        <VerticalStackLayout RadioButtonGroup.GroupName="delivery">
            <Label Text="Where do you want it to be delivered?" />
            <RadioButton
                Content="New York"
                IsChecked="True"
                Value="25"
                CheckedChanged="RadioButton_CheckedChanged_1" />
            <RadioButton
                Content="Atlanta"
                Value="35"
                CheckedChanged="RadioButton_CheckedChanged_1" />


            <RadioButton
                Content="Boston"
                Value="30"
                CheckedChanged="RadioButton_CheckedChanged_1" />
        </VerticalStackLayout>

    </VerticalStackLayout>
</ContentPage>
```

As you can see, I added another label here. And now the code-behind:

```
...
public partial class TestPage : ContentPage
{
    public TestPage()
    ...
    private void RadioButton_CheckedChanged(object sender, CheckedChangedEventArgs e)
    {
        var rb = sender as RadioButton;
        string labelText = $"Your award: {rb!.Content}\nValue: ${rb.Value}\n";
        label1.Text = labelText;
    }

    private void RadioButton_CheckedChanged_1(object sender, CheckedChangedEventArgs e)
    {
        var rb = sender as RadioButton;
        string labelText = $"Delivery: {rb!.Content}, Delivery Cost: ${rb.Value}";
        label2.Text = labelText;
    }
}
```

Here's what you can expect after making some selections.

As you can see, we leveraged the **Value** property here.

Naturally, there's more to radio buttons, but here we're covering just the basics, so let's now move on to the next view, which is the **Entry**.

Entry

We'll need some controls in our app to enter text. If this is to be a single line of text, the **Entry** view is best suited for that. For multiple lines of text we need an **Editor**, which we discuss next.

The **Entry** has lots of useful properties. Let's create an entry then and see some of them in action. As usual, remove all the **RadioButton** - related code from the XAML and C# files first. In the XAML file leave the first label only and set its **x:Name** attribute back to "**label**". Then add an entry like so:

```
...
    <VerticalStackLayout>
        <Label
            x:Name="label"
            FontSize="20"
            VerticalOptions="Center"
            HorizontalOptions="Center" />
```

```
        <Entry
            x:Name="entry"
            Text="hey"
            Placeholder="So empty here..." />

    </VerticalStackLayout>
</ContentPage>
```

Here's what it looks like.

Here we set the initial text value to "**hey**". If you delete this text, you will see the placeholder text.

Boring. Let's make the entry just a tad fancier:

```
...
        <Label
            ...
        <Entry
            x:Name="entry"
            Text="hey"
            Placeholder="So empty here..."
            CharacterSpacing="10"
            ClearButtonVisibility="WhileEditing"
            FontAttributes="Bold"
            FontSize="30"
            HorizontalTextAlignment="Center"
            TextColor="Coral"
            PlaceholderColor="BlanchedAlmond" />
    </VerticalStackLayout>
</ContentPage>
```

So, the fancier version looks like this.

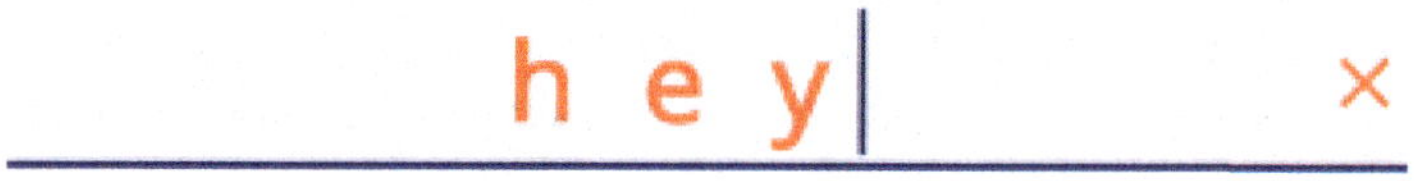

Thanks to the **ClearButtonVisibility** property, we can now clear the entry while editing by clicking on the clear button.

You can also use an entry for entering a password. All you need to do is set the **IsPassword** property to **True**:

```
...
        <Entry
            ...
            PlaceholderColor="BlanchedAlmond"
            IsPassword="True" />
    ...
```

Now the text is obscured. But let's remove this attribute now.

Entry Events

As with the other views before, there are quite a few events that you can use with an entry. Let's focus on two, **`TextChanged`** and **`Completed`**. The former is fired every time you type or delete a character, the latter only after you hit Enter to finalize the text. Let's implement them for our entry. Here's the XAML code (with the **`Entry`** view considerably simplified):

```
...
        <Entry
            FontSize="20"
            TextChanged="Entry_TextChanged"
            Completed="Entry_Completed" />
    </VerticalStackLayout>
</ContentPage>
```

And here's the code-behind:

```
...
public partial class TestPage : ContentPage
{
    public TestPage()
    ...
    private void Entry_TextChanged(object sender, TextChangedEventArgs e)
    {
        var entry = (sender as Entry);
        label.Text = $"{entry!.Text.Length} characters";
    }

    private void Entry_Completed(object sender, EventArgs e)
    {
        label.Text = $"You wrote: \"{(sender as Entry)!.Text}\"";
    }
}
```

Now run the app and start typing something in the entry. The label text above will display the length of your text.

Now hit the Enter key and the label text will change.

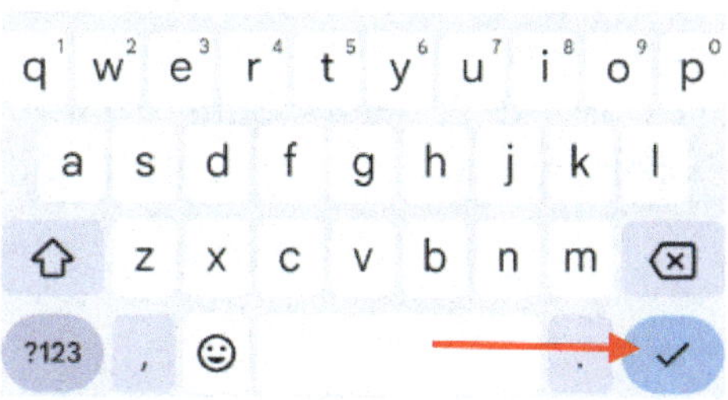

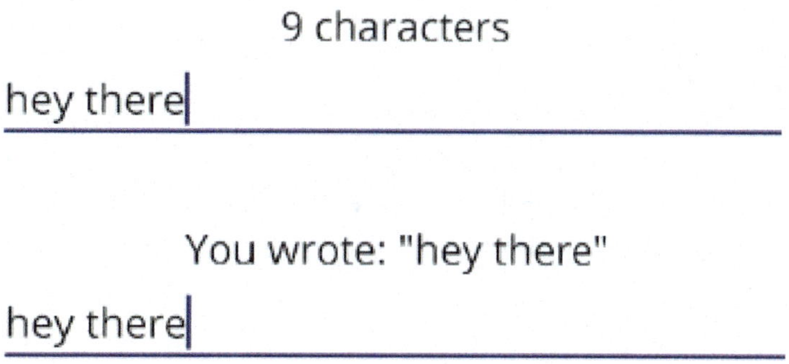

There are two more events you might want to use with an **Entry** from time to time, **Focused** and **Unfocused**. They derive from the **VisualElement** class. Let's add them to our entry:

```
...
        <Entry
            TextChanged="Entry_TextChanged"
            Completed="Entry_Completed"
            Focused="Entry_Focused"
            Unfocused="Entry_Unfocused" />
    ...
```

And here's the code-behind:

```
...
public partial class TestPage : ContentPage
{
    ...
    private void Entry_Completed(object sender, EventArgs e)
    ...
    private void Entry_Focused(object sender, FocusEventArgs e)
    {
        (sender as Entry)!.FontSize = 20;
    }

    private void Entry_Unfocused(object sender, FocusEventArgs e)
    {
        (sender as Entry)!.FontSize = 10;
    }
}
```

Now run the app and click on the entry so that it gets focus. Type something. The font size is 20 now.

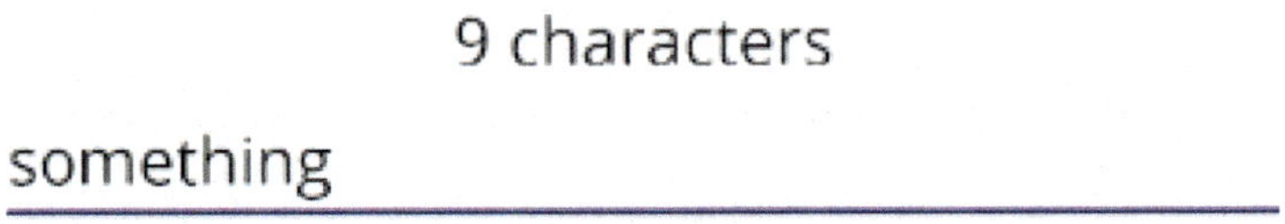

Hit the Tab key on your keyboard so that the entry loses focus. Now the text is much smaller.

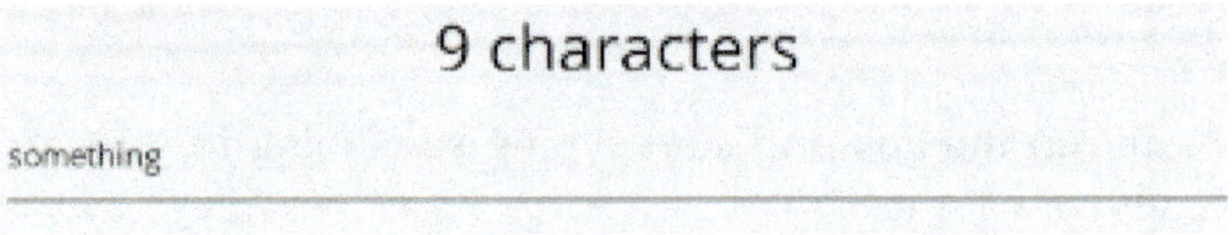

Fine. But what if we need multiline text? Well, here comes the **Editor** view to the rescue.

Editor

The **Editor** is a view that allows you to enter multiple lines of text. It shares quite a lot of properties and events with the **Entry** class. Let's remove the **Entry**-related code from XAML and C# and create an editor:

```
...
    <VerticalStackLayout>
        <Label
            ...

        <Editor
            Placeholder="Type something..."
            HeightRequest="100" />
    </VerticalStackLayout>
</ContentPage>
```

Run the app and type something in the editor. If the text you enter doesn't fit in the editor, you can scroll it, just like here.

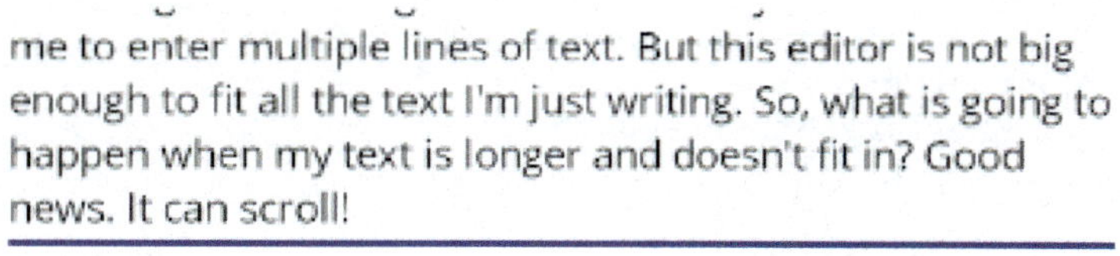

You can also set the **AutoSize** property to accommodate your input. Let's remove the **HeightRequest** property and set the **AutoSize** property:

```
...
        <Editor
            Placeholder="Type something..."
            AutoSize="TextChanges" />
    ...
```

Now the editor grows as you type.

We can use the same events as with the **Entry**, so I'm not going to demonstrate them here again.

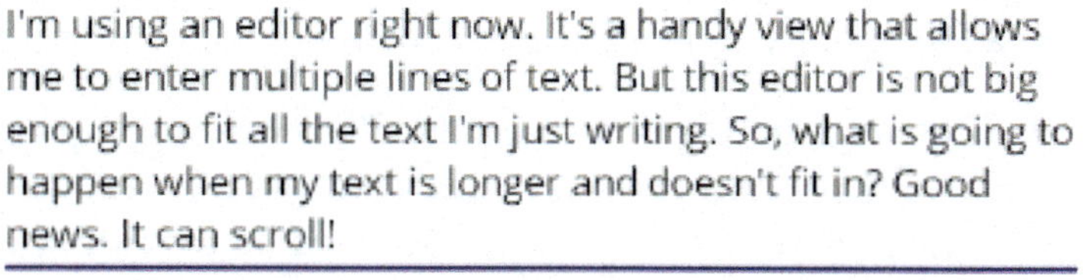

There are lots of other views that we could talk about, but you can easily check them out in the documentation if you need them. All the views we've covered so far are used to display a single item, like a label, a button or a slider, to mention just a few.

But there are also views that allow you to display multiple items in a list or in another form. The two most important ones are **ListView** and **CollectionView**. They share a lot of similarities, but the **CollectionView** is preferred over the **ListView** in modern apps. Unlike **ListView**, it allows for laying out the elements both vertically and horizontally, and also it supports single or multiple selection. We'll have a look at the **CollectionView** later in the book and in the next chapter we'll be talking about layouts.

Chapter 5 - Layouts

code: https://github.com/prospero-apps/Slugrace/tree/chapter5

In chapter 4 we were creating views like buttons, check boxes, sliders, entries and others. You might have noticed that they all were enclosed within a **VerticalStackLayout** element. Open the **TestPage.xaml** file. This is where we left off:

```
<?xml version="1.0" encoding="utf-8" ?>
<ContentPage ...>
    <VerticalStackLayout>
        <Label
            ... />
        <Editor
            ... />
    </VerticalStackLayout>
</ContentPage>
```

As you can see, there are two elements in the **VerticalStackLayout**. But what is the **VerticalStackLayout** in the first place? Well, it's one of the layouts that you can use to arrange your views. In this particular case, the elements are stacked vertically. Let's have a closer look at this layout and the other layouts that you can use. We're still going to use the **TestPage** because this is all temporary code that we're eventually not going to use in the app.

Layouts enable you to arrange the elements on the screen in almost any imaginable way. This is because they can be nested in any way you like so that you get what you want. But working with layouts requires from you some knowledge regarding child positioning and sizing. By children I mean the elements that are inside the layout, so, for example, in the code above the **Label** and the **Editor** are children of the **VerticalStackLayout**.

So, to begin with, let's have a look at three closely-related layouts: **StackLayout**, **VerticalStackLayout** and **HorizontalStackLayout**.

StackLayout, VerticalStackLayout, HorizontalStackLayout

The **StackLayout** is the layout that organizes the children in a one-dimentional stack. You can set its **Orientation** property to determine whether the elements should be arranged horizontally or vertically. Let's remove the editor from our **VerticalStackLayout**, add some buttons and change the layout itself to **StackLayout** and set the **Orientation** property to **Vertical**. Let's set **FontSize** to 30 on each button so that we can see the text better. Let's also add some margin around the whole layout and some spacing between its children.

```
<?xml version="1.0" encoding="utf-8" ?>
<ContentPage ...>
    <StackLayout Orientation="Vertical" Margin="40" Spacing="10">
        <Button Text="1" FontSize="30" />
        <Button Text="2" FontSize="30" />
        <Button Text="3" FontSize="30" />
        <Button Text="4" FontSize="30" />
        <Button Text="5" FontSize="30" />
    </StackLayout>
</ContentPage>
```

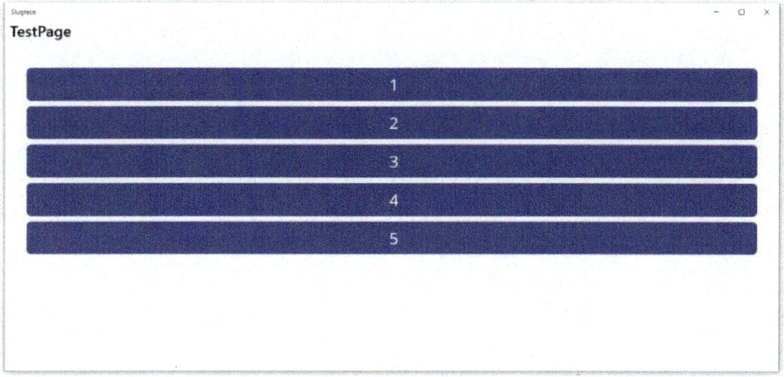

Let's test it on Windows this time.

As you can see, the elements are stacked vertically and stretched horizontally to occupy the whole available width. This is how it works if the sizes of the elements are not set explicitly.

And now let's set **Orientation** to **Horizontal**:

```
...
    <StackLayout Orientation="Horizontal" Margin="40" Spacing="10">
        ...
```

This is what we get (look right).

This time the buttons occupy the whole height, even if you resize the window (try it out). And now let's set the children's sizes to make them smaller:

```
...
<ContentPage ...>
    <StackLayout Orientation="Horizontal" Margin="40" Spacing="10">
        <Button Text="1" FontSize="80" WidthRequest="100" HeightRequest="100" />
        <Button Text="2" FontSize="80" WidthRequest="100" HeightRequest="100" />
        <Button Text="3" FontSize="80" WidthRequest="100" HeightRequest="100" />
        <Button Text="4" FontSize="80" WidthRequest="100" HeightRequest="100" />
        <Button Text="5" FontSize="80" WidthRequest="100" HeightRequest="100" />
    </StackLayout>
</ContentPage>
```

I also changed the font size to make the numbers even more visible. This code is pretty repetitive and, yes, it could be done in a better, more concise way, but don't worry about it for now.

Now the buttons look like here on the right.

The buttons are vertically centered inside their parent element (which is the **StackLayout**). This is the default behavior, but you can change it by setting the **VerticalOptions** property to a different value, for example:

```
...
    <StackLayout
        Orientation="Horizontal"
        Margin="40"
        Spacing="10"
        VerticalOptions="Start">
        <Button Text="1" FontSize="80" WidthRequest="100" HeightRequest="100"/>
        ...
```

Now the children are at the top of the layout.

In a similar way you can change their horizontal alignment:

```
...
    <StackLayout
        Orientation="Horizontal"
        Margin="40"
        Spacing="10"
        VerticalOptions="Start"
        HorizontalOptions="Center">
        <Button Text="1" FontSize="80" WidthRequest="100" HeightRequest="100"/>
        ...
```

Now they are horizontally centered.

More performant alternatives to a **StackLayout** with its **Orientation** property set are the **HorizontalStackLayout** and the **VerticalStackLayout**.

You already saw the latter in action. This time let's replace the **StackLayout** with a **HorizontalStackLayout**. We can leave all the properties (except **Orientation**) untouched:

```
...
    <HorizontalStackLayout
        Margin="40"
        Spacing="10"
        VerticalOptions="Start"
        HorizontalOptions="Center">
        <Button Text="1" FontSize="80" WidthRequest="100" HeightRequest="100"/>
        ...
```

You should still see the same output in your app window. And now let's have a look at another layout, the **Grid**.

Grid

While the layouts we've covered so far arrange their children in one dimension (vertical or horizontal), the **Grid** arranges them in two dimensions, in rows and columns. We use the **RowDefinitions** and **ColumnDefinitions** properties to define the rows and columns respectively. The rows and columns may have absolute or proportional sizes.

By default, a **Grid** contains one row and one column. Let's rewrite our XAML code to use such a basic **Grid**. Besides, we're going to put a **BoxView** inside the grid as its only child. A **BoxView** is a simple view that consists of a rectangle of a specified size and color.

So, here's the code:

```
...
<ContentPage ...>
    <Grid Margin="40">
        <BoxView HeightRequest="100" WidthRequest="100" Color="LightSeaGreen" />
    </Grid>
</ContentPage>
```

Here it is, sitting in the center of the only row and column.

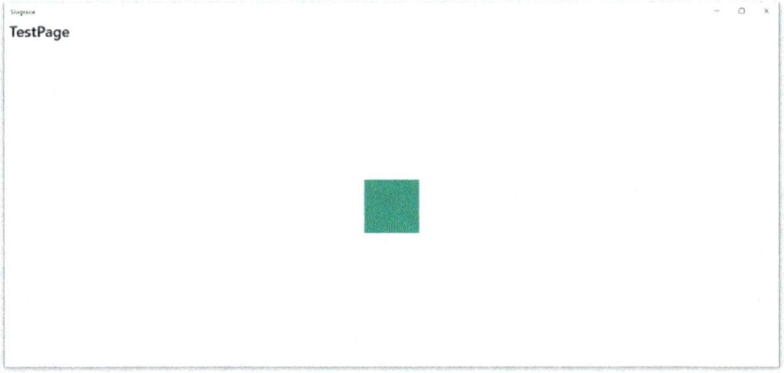

Now let's define some more rows and columns. Let's say four rows and three columns. We'll also put some more **BoxView**s in the cells.

To place an element in a specific cell in the **Grid**, you specify its row by setting the **Grid.Row** attached property and its column by setting the **Grid.Column** attached property. We're going to talk about attached properties a bit later in the book, but for short these are properties of an element that are set on another element, like here where we set the row and column of the **Grid** parent element on its children. Besides, you don't have to specify the first row and column, so whether you set **Grid.Row="0"** or you omit this altogether, the effect will be the same. The same is true for the columns.

So, how do we add more rows and columns? Well, we can do it like so:

```
...
<ContentPage ...>
    <Grid Margin="40">
        <Grid.RowDefinitions>
            <RowDefinition />
            <RowDefinition />
            <RowDefinition />
            <RowDefinition />
        </Grid.RowDefinitions>
        <Grid.ColumnDefinitions>
            <ColumnDefinition />
            <ColumnDefinition />
            <ColumnDefinition />
        </Grid.ColumnDefinitions>
        <BoxView
            HeightRequest="100"
            WidthRequest="100"
            Color="LightSeaGreen" />
        <BoxView
            Grid.Row="0"
            Grid.Column="1"
            HeightRequest="100"
            WidthRequest="100"
            Color="LightSeaGreen" />
        <BoxView
            Grid.Column="2"
            HeightRequest="100"
            WidthRequest="100"
            Color="LightSeaGreen" />
```

```
        <BoxView
            Grid.Row="1"
            HeightRequest="100"
            WidthRequest="100"
            Color="LightSeaGreen" />
        <BoxView
            Grid.Row="1"
            Grid.Column="1"
            HeightRequest="100"
            WidthRequest="100"
            Color="LightSeaGreen" />
        <BoxView
            Grid.Row="1"
            Grid.Column="2"
            HeightRequest="100"
            WidthRequest="100"
            Color="LightSeaGreen" />
        <BoxView
            Grid.Row="2"
            HeightRequest="100"
            WidthRequest="100"
            Color="LightSeaGreen" />
        <BoxView
            Grid.Row="2"
            Grid.Column="1"
            HeightRequest="100"
            WidthRequest="100"
            Color="LightSeaGreen" />
        <BoxView
            Grid.Row="2"
            Grid.Column="2"
            HeightRequest="100"
            WidthRequest="100"
            Color="LightSeaGreen" />
        <BoxView
            Grid.Row="3"
            HeightRequest="100"
            WidthRequest="100"
            Color="LightSeaGreen" />
        <BoxView
            Grid.Row="3"
            Grid.Column="1"
            HeightRequest="100"
            WidthRequest="100"
            Color="LightSeaGreen" />
        <BoxView
            Grid.Row="3"
            Grid.Column="2"
            HeightRequest="100"
            WidthRequest="100"
            Color="LightSeaGreen" />
    </Grid>
</ContentPage>
```

As you can see in the code above, I skipped all the **Grid.Row** and **Grid.Column** properties with the value of 0 because this is the default value.

If you now run the app, you will see the **BoxViews** arranged in four rows and three columns.

What if we didn't specify the **BoxViews**' sizes? Let's try it out. Here's the code:

```
...
    <Grid Margin="40">
        ...
        <BoxView
            Color="LightSeaGreen" />
        <BoxView
            Grid.Row="0"
            Grid.Column="1"
            Color="LightSeaGreen" />
        <BoxView
            Grid.Column="2"
            Color="LightSeaGreen" />
        <BoxView
            Grid.Row="1"
            Color="LightSeaGreen" />
        <BoxView
            Grid.Row="1"
            Grid.Column="1"
            Color="LightSeaGreen" />
        <BoxView
            Grid.Row="1"
            Grid.Column="2"
            Color="LightSeaGreen" />
        <BoxView
            Grid.Row="2"
            Color="LightSeaGreen" />
        <BoxView
            Grid.Row="2"
            Grid.Column="1"
            Color="LightSeaGreen" />
        <BoxView
            Grid.Row="2"
            Grid.Column="2"
            Color="LightSeaGreen" />
        <BoxView
            Grid.Row="3"
            Color="LightSeaGreen" />
```

```
        <BoxView
            Grid.Row="3"
            Grid.Column="1"
            Color="LightSeaGreen" />
        <BoxView
            Grid.Row="3"
            Grid.Column="2"
            Color="LightSeaGreen" />
    </Grid>
</ContentPage>
```

Now the children occupy all the available space inside their cells.

Well, do we still have 12 separate **BoxViews** or just one big **BoxView**? We definitely have 12, which is hard to tell, though. It would be easier to tell them apart if we changed the colors of some of them:

```
...
        <BoxView
            Color="LightSeaGreen" />
        <BoxView
            Grid.Row="0"
            Grid.Column="1"
            Color="LightCyan" />
        <BoxView
            Grid.Column="2"
            Color="LightCoral" />
        <BoxView
            Grid.Row="1"
            Color="LightCyan" />
        <BoxView
            Grid.Row="1"
            Grid.Column="1"
            Color="LightCoral" />
        <BoxView
            Grid.Row="1"
            Grid.Column="2"
            Color="LightSeaGreen" />
        <BoxView
            Grid.Row="2"
            Color="LightCoral" />
        <BoxView
            Grid.Row="2"
            Grid.Column="1"
            Color="LightSeaGreen" />
```

```
        <BoxView
            Grid.Row="2"
            Grid.Column="2"
            Color="LightCyan" />
        <BoxView
            Grid.Row="3"
            Color="LightCyan" />
        <BoxView
            Grid.Row="3"
            Grid.Column="1"
            Color="LightCoral" />
        <BoxView
            Grid.Row="3"
            Grid.Column="2"
            Color="LightSeaGreen" />
    </Grid>
</ContentPage>
```

Now we can tell them apart.

Or, let's set the colors back to original and add some spaces between the rows and columns instead. We can do it by setting the **RowSpacing** and **ColumnSpacing** properties:

```
...
    <Grid Margin="40" RowSpacing="10" ColumnSpacing="10">
        <Grid.RowDefinitions>
            ...
```

This looks pretty decent.

Naturally, you don't have to put elements in each and every cell. Let's remove some of the children:

```
...
        <BoxView
            Color="LightSeaGreen" />
        <BoxView
            Grid.Column="2"
            Color="LightSeaGreen" />
        <BoxView
            Grid.Row="1"
            Color="LightSeaGreen" />
        <BoxView
            Grid.Row="1"
            Grid.Column="1"
            Color="LightSeaGreen" />
        <BoxView
            Grid.Row="1"
            Grid.Column="2"
            Color="LightSeaGreen" />
        <BoxView
            Grid.Row="2"
            Color="LightSeaGreen" />
        <BoxView
            Grid.Row="2"
            Grid.Column="1"
            Color="LightSeaGreen" />
        <BoxView
            Grid.Row="2"
            Grid.Column="2"
            Color="LightSeaGreen" />
        <BoxView
            Grid.Row="3"
            Color="LightSeaGreen" />
        <BoxView
            Grid.Row="3"
            Grid.Column="2"
            Color="LightSeaGreen" />
    </Grid>
</ContentPage>
```

I removed two elements in the middle column.

Also, you can put more than one element inside each cell. Have a look:

```
...
        <BoxView
            Color="LightSeaGreen" />
        <Label
            Text="[0,0]"
            FontSize="80"
            FontAttributes="Bold"
            TextColor="White"
            HorizontalOptions="Center"
            VerticalOptions="Center" />
        <BoxView
            Grid.Column="2"
            Color="LightSeaGreen" />
        <BoxView
            Grid.Row="1"
            Color="LightSeaGreen" />
        <BoxView
            Grid.Row="1"
            Grid.Column="1"
            Color="LightSeaGreen" />
        <Button
            Grid.Row="1"
            Grid.Column="1"
            WidthRequest="200"
            HeightRequest="100"
            BackgroundColor="Black"
            Text="Don't click"
            FontSize="30" />
        <BoxView
            Grid.Row="1"
            Grid.Column="2"
            Color="LightSeaGreen" />
        <BoxView
            Grid.Row="2"
            Color="LightSeaGreen" />
        <BoxView
            Grid.Row="2"
            Grid.Column="1"
            Color="LightSeaGreen" />
        <BoxView
            Grid.Row="2"
            Grid.Column="2"
            Color="LightSeaGreen" />
        <BoxView
            Grid.Row="2"
            Grid.Column="2"
            HeightRequest="100"
            WidthRequest="100"
            Color="OrangeRed"
            HorizontalOptions="Start" />
```

```
        <Label
            Grid.Row="2"
            Grid.Column="2"
            Text="[2,2]"
            FontSize="80"
            FontAttributes="Bold"
            TextColor="White"
            HorizontalOptions="Center"
            VerticalOptions="Center" />
        <BoxView
            Grid.Row="2"
            Grid.Column="2"
            HeightRequest="100"
            WidthRequest="100"
            Color="OrangeRed"
            HorizontalOptions="End" />
        <BoxView
            Grid.Row="3"
            Color="LightSeaGreen" />
        <BoxView
            Grid.Row="3"
            Grid.Column="2"
            Color="LightSeaGreen" />
    </Grid>
</ContentPage>
```

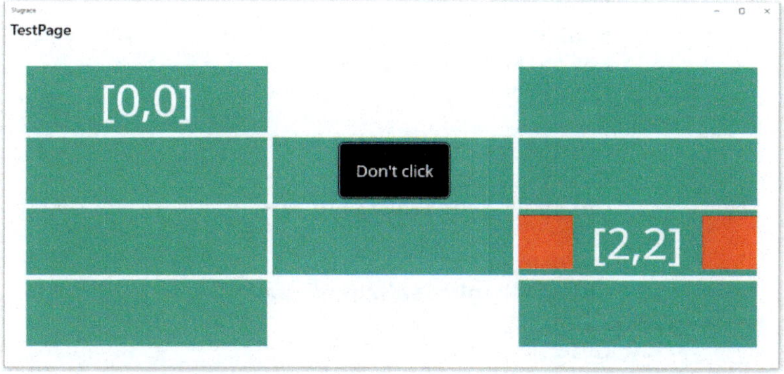

Here we additionally have a label in the first cell, a button in one of the middle cells and three elements inside one of the cells in the third column.

Now, the rows and columns are all very uniform. They have the same heights and widths, which often isn't going to be the case in a real-life scenario. So, let's differentiate them a bit. Also, for simplicity's sake, let's remove the elements we just added to the cells. We're going to use both absolute and proportional sizing:

```
...
<ContentPage ...>
    <Grid Margin="40" RowSpacing="10" ColumnSpacing="10">
        <Grid.RowDefinitions>
            <RowDefinition Height="50" />
            <RowDefinition Height="3*" />
            <RowDefinition Height="Auto" />
            <RowDefinition Height="*" />
        </Grid.RowDefinitions>
        <Grid.ColumnDefinitions>
            <ColumnDefinition Width="*" />
            <ColumnDefinition Width="Auto" />
            <ColumnDefinition Width="200" />
```

```
        </Grid.ColumnDefinitions>
        <BoxView
            Color="LightSeaGreen" />
        <BoxView
            Grid.Column="2"
            Color="LightSeaGreen" />
        <BoxView
            Grid.Row="1"
            Color="LightSeaGreen" />
        <BoxView
            Grid.Row="1"
            Grid.Column="1"
            WidthRequest="240"
            HeightRequest="80"
            Color="Red" />
        <BoxView
            Grid.Row="1"
            Grid.Column="2"
            Color="LightSeaGreen" />
        <BoxView
            Grid.Row="2"
            Color="LightSeaGreen" />
        <BoxView
            Grid.Row="2"
            Grid.Column="1"
            WidthRequest="150"
            HeightRequest="300"
            Color="Red" />
        <BoxView
            Grid.Row="2"
            Grid.Column="2"
            Color="LightSeaGreen" />
        <BoxView
            Grid.Row="3"
            Color="LightSeaGreen" />
        <BoxView
            Grid.Row="3"
            Grid.Column="2"
            Color="LightSeaGreen" />
    </Grid>
</ContentPage>
```

To make things more visible, I changed the color of the two **BoxViews** in the middle column and I set their sizes. Now, let's analyze how we defined the row heights and column widths. Here's the portion of the code where we did it:

```
...
        <Grid.RowDefinitions>
            <RowDefinition Height="50" />
            <RowDefinition Height="3*" />
            <RowDefinition Height="Auto" />
            <RowDefinition Height="*" />
        </Grid.RowDefinitions>
```

```
<Grid.ColumnDefinitions>
    <ColumnDefinition Width="*"/>
    <ColumnDefinition Width="Auto"/>
    <ColumnDefinition Width="200"/>
</Grid.ColumnDefinitions>
...
```

Let's start with the rows. We used absolute sizing for the first row. Its height is set to 50 device-independent units, so it stays the same even if you resize the window (try it out).

The third row's height is set to **Auto**. This means it autosizes based on the size of its children. The tallest child in the third row is the red **BoxView** in the middle column, so the whole row adjusts to it.

The second and fourth rows have heights set to **3*** and ***** (which is the same as **1***) respectively. The star notation is used for proportional sizing. It just means that the leftover height (so without taking the rows with heights set to an absolute value or **Auto** into account) is allocated proportionally. Here the second row takes three times as much of it as the fourth row. This proportion will be retained if you resize the window as well.

Now the columns. We use absolute sizing for the third column. It just means the third column will always be 200 device-independent units wide.

The width of the middle column is set to **Auto**, so it takes the width of its widest child, which is the red **BoxView** in the second row.

Finally, the first column takes all the remaining width.

Here's the result on the right.

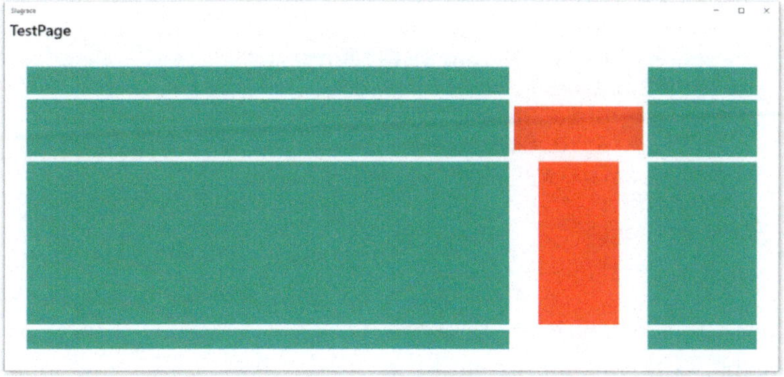

The **RowDefinitions** and **ColumnDefinitions** seem very verbose. Fortunately, this can be simplified. Let's rewrite our code using this simplified notation:

```
...
    <Grid
        Margin="40"
        RowSpacing="10"
        ColumnSpacing="10"
        RowDefinitions="50, 3*, Auto, *"
        ColumnDefinitions="*, Auto, 200">
        <BoxView
            Color="LightSeaGreen" />
        ...
```

Much more concise, isn't it?

Sometimes you may want an element to span multiple rows or columns. This is possible by setting the **Grid.RowSpan** and **Grid.ColumnSpan** properties. Let's remove some of the **BoxView**s to make some room and see how spanning multiple rows and columns may be implemented:

```
...
    <Grid
        ...
        <BoxView
            Color="LightSeaGreen"
            Grid.ColumnSpan="3" />
        <BoxView
            Grid.Row="1"
            Grid.Column="1"
            WidthRequest="240"
            HeightRequest="80"
            Color="Red" />
        <BoxView
            Grid.Row="1"
            Grid.Column="2"
            Color="LightSeaGreen"
            Grid.RowSpan="2" />
        <BoxView
            Grid.Row="2"
            Color="LightSeaGreen" />
        <BoxView
            Grid.Row="2"
            Grid.Column="1"
            WidthRequest="150"
            HeightRequest="300"
            Color="Red" />
        <BoxView
            Grid.Row="3"
            Color="LightSeaGreen" />
        <BoxView
            Grid.Row="3"
            Grid.Column="2"
            Color="LightSeaGreen" />
    </Grid>
</ContentPage>
```

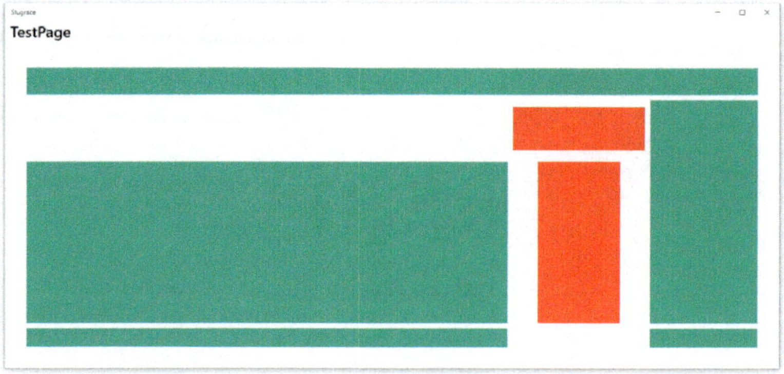

Now the element in the first cell spans all three columns and the element in the last column of the second row span two rows.

That's basically all you have to know about the **Grid** layout for now. Let's move on to the next layout.

FlexLayout

The next layout I'd like to talk about is the **FlexLayout**. It's similar to the **StackLayout** in that it also arranges its children in a horizontal or vertical stack, but it also combines the functionality available in the CSS flex display mode, if you have some CSS background.

Let's remove the **Grid** and create a simple **FlexLayout** instead. We use the **Direction** property to define how the children are to be arranged. It can be set to **Row**, **RowReverse**, **Column** or **ColumnReverse**.

Here's the code:

```
...
<ContentPage ...>
    <FlexLayout>
        <Button
            Text="1"
            FontSize="100"
            Margin="2"
            WidthRequest="150"
            HeightRequest="150" />
        <Button
            Text="2"
            FontSize="100"
            Margin="2"
            WidthRequest="150"
            HeightRequest="150" />
        <Button
            Text="3"
            FontSize="100"
            Margin="2"
            WidthRequest="150"
            HeightRequest="150" />
        <Button
            Text="4"
            FontSize="100"
            Margin="2"
            WidthRequest="150"
            HeightRequest="150" />
        <Button
            Text="5"
            FontSize="100"
            Margin="2"
            WidthRequest="150"
            HeightRequest="150" />
```

```
        <Button
            Text="6"
            FontSize="100"
            Margin="2"
            WidthRequest="150"
            HeightRequest="150" />
        <Button
            Text="7"
            FontSize="100"
            Margin="2"
            WidthRequest="150"
            HeightRequest="150" />
        <Button
            Text="8"
            FontSize="100"
            Margin="2"
            WidthRequest="150"
            HeightRequest="150" />
    </FlexLayout>
</ContentPage>
```

I used buttons with numbers on them to make it clear what order the elements are arranged in. Here's what it looks like.

As you can see, we didn't set the **`Direction`** attribute here, so the default value of **`Row`** is used. Let's change it to **`RowReverse`**:

```
...
    <FlexLayout Direction="RowReverse">
        <Button
            ...
```

Now the elements are arranged like this.

For vertical arrangement we use **Column**:

```
...
    <FlexLayout Direction="Column">
        <Button
            ...
```

which looks like so:

or **ColumnReverse**:

```
...
    <FlexLayout Direction="ColumnReverse">
        <Button
            ...
```

which looks like so:

Yes, I know, now the elements don't fit in the column. This is where the **Wrap** property comes in really handy. If set to **Wrap**, the elements that don't fit in a single row or column are wrapped. Have a look:

```
...
    <FlexLayout Direction="Column" Wrap="Wrap" >
        <Button
            ...
```

Here I set **Direction** back to **Column**. Now all elements are displayed on the screen.

And if the window is resized, they will react accordingly.

You can also set **Wrap** to **Reverse** if you want the children to wrap in the other direction:

```
...
    <FlexLayout Direction="Column" Wrap="Reverse" >
        <Button
            ...
```

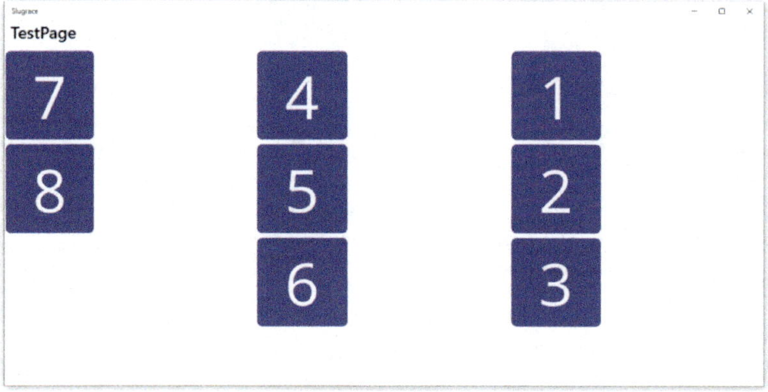

And here's the result on the right.

It works the same for the rows. Make sure to try it out.

And now let's test some other properties. First let's remove some buttons and arrange them in a row. Then let's justify them using the **JustifyContent** property. The default value of the property is **Start**, so the elements begin on the left if **Direction** is set to **Row**, on the right if **Direction** is set to **RowReverse**, at the top if **Direction** is set to **Column** and at the bottom if **Direction** is set to **ColumnReverse**.

What matters is, as you can see, where the elements actually start. This rule applies to all values of **JustifyContent**. Anyway, as **Start** is the default value, let's try **End**:

```
...
    <FlexLayout Direction="Row" JustifyContent="End">
        <Button
            Text="1"
            ...
        <Button
            Text="2"
            ...
        <Button
            Text="3"
            ...
        <Button
            Text="4"
            ...
        <Button
            Text="5"
            ...
    </FlexLayout>
</ContentPage>
```

Now the buttons stick to the end of the row.

Here are the other values you can set **JustifyContent** to (provided **Direction** is set to **Row**):

Center

SpaceBetween

SpaceAround

SpaceEvenly

JustifyContent works for the main axis the elements are arranged in. Here it's the horizontal axis, but if **Direction** were set to **Column** or **ColumnReverse**, it would be the vertical axis.

For the other axis we use the **AlignItems** property. So, if **Direction** is set to **Row** like here, this property will be used to align the items vertically. The possible values are: **Start**, **End**, **Center** and **Stretch**. Let's center the buttons both horizontally (with **JustifyContent**) and vertically (with **AlignItems**):

```
...
    <FlexLayout
        Direction="Row"
        JustifyContent="Center"
        AlignItems="Center">
        <Button
            ...
```

This is what it looks like.

There are quite a few other properties you can use with **FlexLayout**, but for now this will do. Let's move on to the next layout now, which is **AbsoluteLayout**.

AbsoluteLayout

In an **AbsoluteLayout** you position and size elements using explicit values or values relative to the layout's position and size. The position is specified by the top-left corner of the child relative to the top-left corner of the parent (which is the **AbsoluteLayout**).

Let's remove the **FlexLayout** with the buttons and create an **AbsoluteLayout** with **BoxView**s. Let's also set the background color of the **AbsoluteLayout** so that we can see it better. We use the **AbsoluteLayout.LayoutBounds** property to position and size the children. The value of this property consists of four numbers in a string. The first two numbers determine the position, the other two are for sizing. Have a look:

```
...
<ContentPage ...>
    <AbsoluteLayout Margin="40" BackgroundColor="Beige">
        <BoxView
            Color="Green"
            AbsoluteLayout.LayoutBounds="100, 60, 100, 50" />
        <BoxView
            Color="Red"
            AbsoluteLayout.LayoutBounds="400, 380, 200, 100" />
        <BoxView
            Color="Blue"
            AbsoluteLayout.LayoutBounds="750, 30, 400, 400" />
    </AbsoluteLayout>
</ContentPage>
```

Here we have three **BoxView**s. The first one is green. It's positioned 100 units from the left (which means its top-left corner is 100 units from the left), 60 units from the top and its size is 100 by 50 units. The same rules apply to the other elements. You can see the result on the right.

We used absolute values to position and size the elements. But we can also use proportional values for the position or size. We can also mix absolute and proportional values.

To enable proportional positioning, we need to set the **AbsoluteLayout.LayoutFlags** attached property to **PositionProportional**. Similarly, we use **SizeProportional** for proportional sizing. With proportional positioning and sizing we use the values from 0 to 1. Have a look:

```
...
    <AbsoluteLayout Margin="40" BackgroundColor="Beige">
        <BoxView
            Color="Green"
            AbsoluteLayout.LayoutBounds=".5, .5, 200, 200"
            AbsoluteLayout.LayoutFlags="PositionProportional" />
        <BoxView
            Color="Red"
            AbsoluteLayout.LayoutBounds="100, 400, .2, .1"
            AbsoluteLayout.LayoutFlags="SizeProportional" />
        <BoxView
            Color="Blue"
            AbsoluteLayout.LayoutBounds="1, 1, .25, .5"
            AbsoluteLayout.LayoutFlags="PositionProportional,SizeProportional" />
    </AbsoluteLayout>
</ContentPage>
```

The elements are positioned and sized in the following way:

BoxView	**Position**	**Size**
Green	proportional (**.5, .5**) - centered	absolute (**200, 200**) - 200 x 200 units
Red	absolute (**100, 400**) - 100 units from the left and 400 units from the top	proportional (**.2, .1**) - 20% of the width of the **AbsoluteLayout** and 10% of its height
Blue	proportional (**1, 1**) - all the way to the right and all the way to the bottom	proportional (**.25, .5**) - a quarter of the layout's width and half its height

And this is how they look.

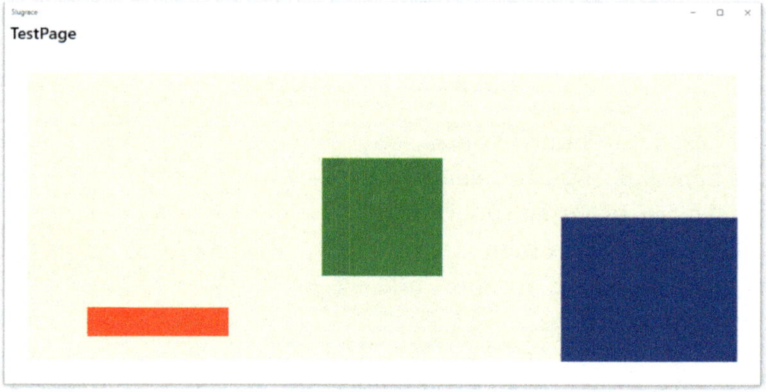

There are more options the **`AbsoluteLayout.LayoutFlags`** property can be set to, so feel free to check them out.

Well, these are all the basic layouts we should be familiar with for now.

Nested Layouts

Layouts can be nested. The example we're going to build isn't particularly useful. It's just to demonstrate how layouts can be nested. The code is pretty lengthy, but it should be pretty easy to read and understand:

```
...
<ContentPage ...>
    <FlexLayout
        BackgroundColor="Beige"
        Direction="Column">

        <HorizontalStackLayout
            BackgroundColor="Black"
            Spacing="50"
            Padding="10">
            <Label
                Text="File"
                TextColor="White"
                FontSize="20"
                FontAttributes="Bold" />
            <Label
                Text="Edit"
                TextColor="White"
                FontSize="20"
                FontAttributes="Bold" />
            <Label
                Text="View"
                TextColor="White"
                FontSize="20"
                FontAttributes="Bold" />
            <Label
                Text="Help"
                TextColor="White"
                FontSize="20"
                FontAttributes="Bold" />
        </HorizontalStackLayout>
```

```
        <Grid
            Margin="40"
            Padding="10"
            BackgroundColor="Bisque"
            RowDefinitions="100, *, 100"
            ColumnDefinitions="100, *, 100"
            RowSpacing="10"
            ColumnSpacing="10">
            <Label
                Text="Start"
                FontSize="30"
                TextColor="Firebrick" />

            <AbsoluteLayout
                Grid.Column="1"
                BackgroundColor="Beige">
                <Button
                    Text="1"
                    FontSize="40"
                    AbsoluteLayout.LayoutBounds=".1, .5, .3, .5"
                    AbsoluteLayout.LayoutFlags="PositionProportional, SizeProportional" />
                <Button
                    Text="2"
                    FontSize="40"
                    AbsoluteLayout.LayoutBounds=".9, .5, .3, .5"
                    AbsoluteLayout.LayoutFlags="PositionProportional, SizeProportional" />
            </AbsoluteLayout>

            <BoxView
                Grid.Column="2"
                Grid.RowSpan="3"
                Color="Firebrick" />

            <BoxView
                Grid.Row="1"
                Grid.Column="0"
                Grid.RowSpan="2"
                Grid.ColumnSpan="2"
                Color="Firebrick" />
        </Grid>

    </FlexLayout>
</ContentPage>
```

The result is spectacular.

In the next chapter we'll be talking about properties in XAML.

We'll clarify some property-related terms that you can often come across like property elements, content properties or attached properties.

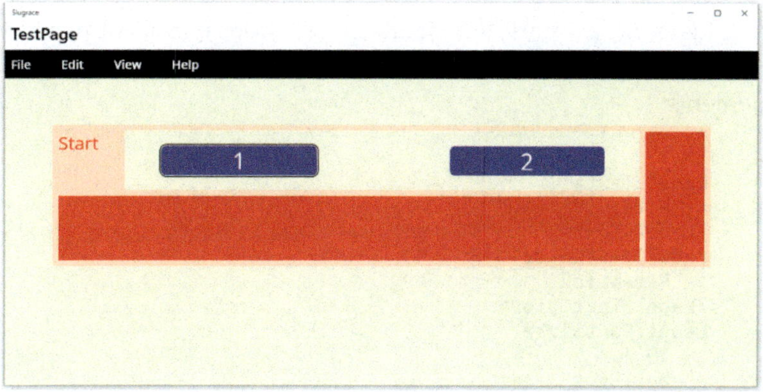

Chapter 6 - Properties in XAML

code: https://github.com/prospero-apps/Slugrace/tree/chapter6

Throughout the book we've been using properties a lot, practically all XAML objects had one or more properties set. In this chapter we'll have a look at properties in .NET MAUI in more detail. In particular, we'll clarify terms like property elements, content properties and attached properties. But first, let's recap on what we already know about properties.

Property Attributes

Most of the XAML objects so far had some properties set. Here's a **Label** with a couple properties:

```
<Label
    Text="File"
    TextColor="Firebrick"
    FontSize="20" />
```

Text, **TextColor** and **FontSize** are so-called **property attributes**, because these are attributes that we use to set the properties of an object. So here we have a **Label** object with three properties set. This is how we've been using properties in XAML so far and this is how we usually use them if they are set to a simple value like a string or integer. If we must set them to a more complex value, like another object for example, this syntax isn't very useful. Instead we should use so-called property elements. Actually, we can use property elements as an alternative to property attributes even for simple types, which will make the code a little more verbose, but it's up to you which syntax you choose. Let's have a look at property elements then.

Property Elements

As I just said, **property elements** can be used instead of property attributes even if we want to set them to simple values. Let's change all the property attributes in the example above to property elements:

```
<Label>
    <Label.Text>
        File
    </Label.Text>
    <Label.TextColor>
        Firebrick
    </Label.TextColor>
    <Label.FontSize>
        20
    </Label.FontSize>
</Label>
```

So, the value of each property is placed between the property element's opening and closing tags and it constitutes its content.

You can also mix and match:

```
<Label
    Text="File"
    TextColor="Firebrick">
    <Label.FontSize>
        20
    </Label.FontSize>
</Label>
```

Generally, you will usually use property attributes for simple values like that. But sometimes it's not so easy. This is the case if the value of the property is too complex to be written as a string. You saw an example in the previous chapter where we were discussing the **Grid** layout. The **Grid** has the **RowDefinitions** and **ColumnDefinitions** properties. These are collections of **RowDefinition** and **ColumnDefinition** objects respectively. Here's how we use the property element syntax to set these two properties:

```
<Grid>
    <Grid.RowDefinitions>
        <RowDefinition Height="50" />
        <RowDefinition Height="3*" />
        <RowDefinition Height="Auto" />
        <RowDefinition Height="*" />
    </Grid.RowDefinitions>
    <Grid.ColumnDefinitions>
        <ColumnDefinition Width="*"/>
        <ColumnDefinition Width="Auto"/>
        <ColumnDefinition Width="200"/>
    </Grid.ColumnDefinitions>
</Grid>
```

You may also remember that in this particular case we can also use property attributes to simplify the code:

```
<Grid
    RowDefinitions="50, 3*, Auto, *"
    ColumnDefinitions="*, Auto, 200">>
</Grid>
```

But it's not always possible. We'll be using property elements a lot throughout this book.

Attached Properties

Our next topic is **attached properties**. I've used this term several times so far. These are properties that are defined in one class and attached to objects of another class. Have a look at the following definition of a **Grid** and its children, similar to the one from the previous chapter, here abbreviated to include just the attached properties:

```
<Grid>
    ...
    <BoxView
        Grid.Row="1"
        Grid.Column="1" />
    <BoxView
        Grid.Row="1"
        Grid.Column="2"
        Grid.RowSpan="2"
        Grid.ColumnSpan="3" />
</Grid>
```

Here, **Grid.Row**, **Grid.Column**, **Grid.RowSpan** and **Grid.ColumnSpan** are properties of the **Grid** class, but they are set on the children of the **Grid**.

You saw another example of attached properties when we were talking about the **AbsoluteLayout**. Have a look at the code again:

```
...
    <AbsoluteLayout Margin="40" BackgroundColor="Beige">
        <BoxView
            Color="Green"
            AbsoluteLayout.LayoutBounds=".5, .5, 200, 200"
            AbsoluteLayout.LayoutFlags="PositionProportional"/>
        <BoxView
            Color="Red"
            AbsoluteLayout.LayoutBounds="100, 400, .2, .1"
            AbsoluteLayout.LayoutFlags="SizeProportional" />
        <BoxView
            Color="Blue"
            AbsoluteLayout.LayoutBounds="1, 1, .25, .5"
            AbsoluteLayout.LayoutFlags="PositionProportional,SizeProportional" />
    </AbsoluteLayout>
</ContentPage>
```

Can you spot the attached properties right away? I'm sure you can.

Here **AbsoluteLayout.LayoutBounds** and **AbsoluteLayout.LayoutFlags** are properties of the **AbsoluteLayout** class, but they are set on the **BoxView** objects.

Content Properties

Finally, there's one more term worth mentioning as far as properties in XAML are concerned, **content properties**.

Let's define a simple label in the **TestPage**:

```
<?xml version="1.0" encoding="utf-8" ?>
<ContentPage xmlns="http://schemas.microsoft.com/dotnet/2021/maui"
             xmlns:x="http://schemas.microsoft.com/winfx/2009/xaml"
             x:Class="Slugrace.TestPage"
             Title="TestPage">
    <VerticalStackLayout>
        <Label
            TextColor="Firebrick"
            FontSize="100"
            Text="Hey there">
        </Label>
    </VerticalStackLayout>
</ContentPage>
```

We could use the property element syntax as well. Let's use it for the **Text** property:

```
...
<ContentPage ...>
    <VerticalStackLayout>
        <Label
            TextColor="Firebrick"
            FontSize="100">
            <Label.Text>
                Hey there
            </Label.Text>
        </Label>
    </VerticalStackLayout>
</ContentPage>
```

If you run the code, you will see this.

We set three properties on the **Label**: **TextColor**, **FontSize** and **Text**. In case of the **Label** class, the **Text** property has a special status. It's a so-called content property.

Each class defines its own content property, it doesn't have to be **Text**, but in case of **Label** it's **Text**. A content property is a property that is not required in XAML. Anything that appears between the opening and closing tags of the object is assigned to that property.

So, we could place the string "**Hey there**" directly between the **Label** tags:

```
...
    <VerticalStackLayout>
        <Label
            TextColor="Firebrick"
            FontSize="100">
            Hey there
        </Label>
    </VerticalStackLayout>
</ContentPage>
```

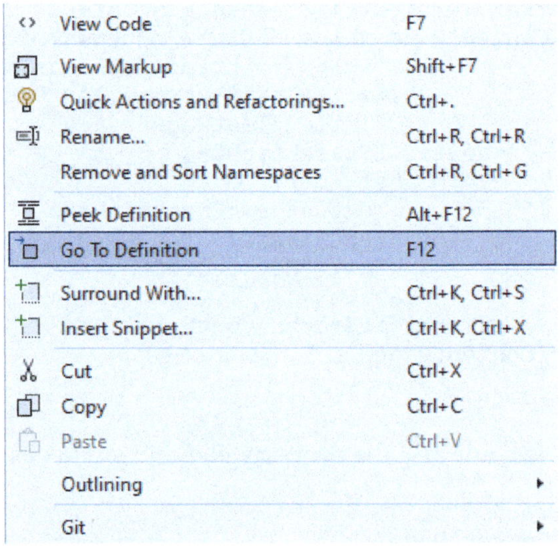

And it still works the same. But how do you know which property is the content property of a given class? Right-click on the **Label** object in Visual Studio and select Go To Definition.

You will see the definition of the **Label** class. Here's the first part of it:

```
[ContentProperty("Text")]
public class Label : View, IFontElement, ITextElement, ...
```

As you can see, the class is decorated with the **ContentProperty** attribute with the name of the content property passed to it.

Actually, there are more objects defined in our code snippet above. There's also **ContentPage** and **VerticalStackLayout**. What are their content properties? Let's check it out. Right-click on the **ContentPage** object and select Go To Definition. As you can see, **Content** is the content property:

```
[ContentProperty("Content")]
public class ContentPage : TemplatedPage, IContentView, ...
```

And you can't see the **Content** property in the XAML code. This is exactly because it's the content property, which can be omitted. If so, anything between the opening and closing tags of **ContentPage** is its content. But we could still use it, if we wanted to, like so:

```
...
<ContentPage ...>
    <ContentPage.Content>
        <VerticalStackLayout>
            <Label
                TextColor="Firebrick"
                FontSize="100">
                Hey there
            </Label>
        </VerticalStackLayout>
    </ContentPage.Content>
</ContentPage>
```

What about **VerticalStackLayout**? It turns out, its content property is **Children**:

```
[ContentProperty(nameof(Children))]
public class VerticalStackLayout : StackBase
...
```

So, let's add the content property explicitly to the code as well:

```
...
    <ContentPage.Content>
        <VerticalStackLayout>
            <VerticalStackLayout.Children>
                <Label
                    TextColor="Firebrick"
                    FontSize="100">
                    Hey there
                </Label>
            </VerticalStackLayout.Children>
        </VerticalStackLayout>
    </ContentPage.Content>
</ContentPage>
```

And remember, there's only one content property for each class.

Good, I think some of the XAML terminology has been clarified, so let's take a break from XAML for a while. As you know, you can write all your code in C#. In the next chapter we'll see how to create objects and properties in C#.

Chapter 7 - Objects and Properties in C# Code

code: https://github.com/prospero-apps/Slugrace/tree/chapter7

So far in the book we've been creating objects and properties mostly in XAML. But sometimes you may have to create an object in C# code. Or maybe you don't want to use XAML at all… This is also possible. In this chapter we'll be creating objects, like views and layouts, in C# and we'll be setting their properties in C#.

Creating objects in C# requires from you that you know what type the properties are. You can figure it out from documentation. To make things clearer, we'll be comparing XAML code with C# code so that you can immediately see what corresponds to what. Actually, we'll still be using some XAML here, because we can easily mix and match. So, open your **TestPage.xaml** and **TestPage.xaml.cs** pages and get ready.

Creating Views in C#

To start with, let's rewrite the **TestPage.xaml** file to look like so:

```
<?xml version="1.0" encoding="utf-8" ?>
<ContentPage xmlns="http://schemas.microsoft.com/dotnet/2021/maui"
             xmlns:x="http://schemas.microsoft.com/winfx/2009/xaml"
             x:Class="Slugrace.TestPage"
             Title="TestPage">
    <VerticalStackLayout x:Name="layout">
        <Label
            Text="Hey"
            VerticalOptions="Center"
            HorizontalOptions="Center"
            TextColor="Blue"
            FontSize="60"
            FontAttributes="Bold, Italic"
            Rotation="180"
            CharacterSpacing="20"
            TranslationY="100" />
    </VerticalStackLayout>
</ContentPage>
```

If you run it on Android, you will see a fancy label.

And now let's remove the label from the XAML file (still leaving the **`VerticalStackLayout`** in place):

```
...
<ContentPage ...>
    <VerticalStackLayout x:Name="layout" />
</ContentPage>
```

Now we'll create it in C#. We'll also add it to the **VerticalStackLayout** in C# code. So, open your **TestPage.xaml.cs** file and make sure it looks like this:

```
namespace Slugrace;

public partial class TestPage : ContentPage
{
    public TestPage()
    {
        InitializeComponent();

        Label label = new()
        {
            Text = "Hey",
            HorizontalOptions = LayoutOptions.Center,
            TextColor = Colors.Blue,
            FontSize = 60,
            FontAttributes = FontAttributes.Bold | FontAttributes.Italic,
            Rotation = 180,
            CharacterSpacing = 10,
            TranslationY = 100
        };

        layout.Add(label);
    }
}
```

If you run the app now, it will look the same. And now let's remove the label-related code and create a button with a click event. First, let's do it in XAML:

```
...
<ContentPage ...>
    <VerticalStackLayout x:Name="layout">
        <Button
            Text="Click"
            FontSize="24"
            WidthRequest="200"
            Margin="50"
            BorderColor="Black"
            BorderWidth="5"
            BackgroundColor="DarkGoldenrod"
            TextTransform="Uppercase"
            FontAttributes="Bold"
            CornerRadius="50"
            Clicked="Button_Clicked" />
    </VerticalStackLayout>
</ContentPage>
```

There's a **Clicked** event that we implement like this in the code-behind:

```
public partial class TestPage : ContentPage
{
    public TestPage()
    {
        InitializeComponent();
    }

    private void Button_Clicked(object sender, EventArgs e)
    {
        (sender as Button)!.Text = "Clicked";
    }
}
```

This will produce the following button.

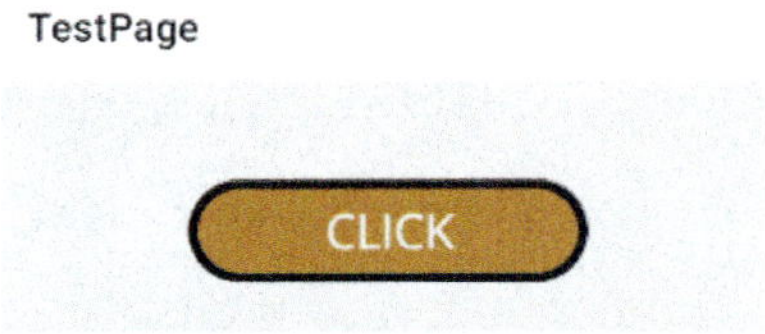

If you click the button, the text on it will change. So, here you can see some properties and an event. Let's remove the button from the XAML file, this time along with the **VerticalStackLayout**, and we'll recreate both the layout and the view in C#. The XAML file should look like so:

```
<?xml version="1.0" encoding="utf-8" ?>
<ContentPage xmlns="http://schemas.microsoft.com/dotnet/2021/maui"
             xmlns:x="http://schemas.microsoft.com/winfx/2009/xaml"
             x:Class="Slugrace.TestPage"
             Title="TestPage">
</ContentPage>
```

And here's the C# file:

```
namespace Slugrace;

public partial class TestPage : ContentPage
{
    public TestPage()
    {
        InitializeComponent();

        // create layout
        VerticalStackLayout layout = new();

        // create view
        Button button = new()
        {
            Text = "Click",
            FontSize = 24,
            WidthRequest = 200,
            Margin = 50,
            BorderColor = Colors.Black,
            BorderWidth = 5,
            BackgroundColor = Colors.DarkGoldenrod,
            TextTransform = TextTransform.Uppercase,
            FontAttributes = FontAttributes.Bold,
            CornerRadius = 50
        };
```

```
        // add event
        button.Clicked += Button_Clicked!;

        // add view to layout
        layout.Add(button);

        // set layout as the page's content
        Content = layout;
    }

    private void Button_Clicked(object sender, EventArgs e)
    {
        (sender as Button)!.Text = "Clicked";
    }
}
```

So far we've been creating simple objects and adding them to the layout. We also created a layout in C# code and set it as the page's content. Next, let's create a more complex layout with some children that use attached properties and see how to recreate it in C# code.

Creating Layouts and Attached Properties in C#

A good example of a more complex layout that we can use to demonstrate how attached properties are defined in C# code is the **Grid**. So, let's define a **Grid** in XAML and add some children to it. Remove all the button-related code from both test files and create the **Grid** in the XAML file like so:

```
...
<ContentPage ...>
    <Grid
        Margin="40"
        BackgroundColor="OldLace"
        RowSpacing="10"
        ColumnSpacing="10"
        RowDefinitions="100, *"
        ColumnDefinitions="*, 2*" >
        <BoxView Color="Red" />
        <BoxView Grid.Column="1" Color="Green" />
        <BoxView
            Grid.Row="1"
            Grid.ColumnSpan="2"
            Color="Blue" />
    </Grid>
</ContentPage>
```

Run the app and you will see three **BoxViews**.

Next, remove the **Grid** from the XAML file and define it in C# code. The XAML file should now contain just the **ContentPage**.

Watch how the **`Grid.Row`**, **`Grid.Column`** and **`Grid.ColumnSpan`** attached properties are set in C#. Also watch how the rows and columns are defined:

```
namespace Slugrace;

public partial class TestPage : ContentPage
{
    public TestPage()
    {
        InitializeComponent();

        // create grid
        Grid grid = new()
        {
            Margin = 40,
            BackgroundColor = Colors.OldLace,
            RowSpacing = 10,
            ColumnSpacing = 10,
            RowDefinitions =
            {
                new RowDefinition { Height = new GridLength(100) },
                new RowDefinition { Height = new GridLength(1, GridUnitType.Star) }
            },
            ColumnDefinitions =
            {
                new ColumnDefinition { Width = new GridLength(1, GridUnitType.Star) },
                new ColumnDefinition { Width = new GridLength(2, GridUnitType.Star) }
            }
        };

        // add children to grid

        // Row 0 and Column 0 are the default values, so we can leave them out.
        grid.Add(new BoxView
        {
            Color = Colors.Red
        });

        // We can pass the column (1) and the row (0) as arguments to the Add method.
        grid.Add(new BoxView
        {
            Color = Colors.Green
        }, 1, 0);

        // Alternatively, we can position the child with the Grid.SetRow and
        // Grid.SetColumn methods (we don't need the latter in this example
        // because the default value of 0 is used). There are also the Grid.RowSpan
        // (not used here) and Grid.ColumnSpan methods.
        BoxView blueBox = new BoxView { Color = Colors.Blue };
        Grid.SetRow(blueBox, 1);
        Grid.SetColumnSpan(blueBox, 2);
        grid.Add(blueBox);

        // set page content
        Content = grid;
    }
}
```

If you work with other attached properties, just check out in the documentation how to use them in code.

Naturally, there's much more to XAML. What we've covered so far is just a tiny fraction of what there is, but we are now ready to design the pages for our Slugrace project, so let's leverage the knowledge we just gained to do right that. And no worries… We'll be learning lots of new XAML concepts on the way.

Chapter 8 - Content Pages and Content Views

code: https://github.com/prospero-apps/Slugrace/tree/chapter8

In this chapter we'll create the pages that we need for the Slugrace project. We'll also create some content views, which are sort of reusable components. Let's start by explaining the difference between content pages and content views.

ContentPage vs ContentView

The **ContentPage** is the most common page type in .NET MAUI apps. It displays a single child, which usually is a layout with all sorts of controls as its children. In this chapter we're going to create the first rough versions of the pages that will be included in the app. These pages won't be stylized for now, nor will they have any functionality for the time being. Styling and data binding will be discussed a bit later in the book. In particular, we're going to create the following pages in this chapter:

- **SettingsPage**

- **RacePage**

- **GameOverPage**

We're not going to create the **InstructionsPage** for now because we need screenshots of the app there, which we will only have when the remaining pages are fully styled and functional.

As we haven't implemented page navigation yet, for the time being we'll be just setting **ContentTemplate** to each page one by one in the **AppShell.xaml** file. At this moment it's set to the **TestPage**:

```
<?xml version="1.0" encoding="UTF-8" ?>
<Shell
    x:Class="Slugrace.AppShell"
    xmlns="http://schemas.microsoft.com/dotnet/2021/maui"
    xmlns:x="http://schemas.microsoft.com/winfx/2009/xaml"
    xmlns:local="clr-namespace:Slugrace"
    xmlns:views="clr-namespace:Slugrace.Views"
    Shell.FlyoutBehavior="Disabled"
    Title="Slugrace">
```

```
    <ShellContent
        Title="Test"
        ContentTemplate="{DataTemplate local:TestPage}"
        Route="TestPage" />
</Shell>
```

This is why we see the **TestPage** each time we run the app. This solution is temporary and will be changed as soon as we cover page navigation.

In the **SettingsPage** and in the **RacePage** some elements will be repeated (but with different data bound to them). In the **RacePage** we'll also have two elements (the Bets panel and the Results panel) that will never be displayed at the same time. Instead, they will swap after each race. We'll implement these repeated and swappable elements as **ContentView**s.

A **ContentView** is a control that enables the creation of custom reusable controls. Well, there's a lot of work to do, so let's get started.

SettingsPage

Eventually, we're going to implement the MVVM pattern in our app, so all our pages will be saved in the **Views** folder. But we don't have the folder yet, so go ahead and create it in the root of your app (A). Then right-click it and select Add -> New Item… In the window that pops up select .NET MAUI on the left (B) - it should be there because you already used it before, but if it isn't, just use the search box on the right. Then select >NET MAUI ContentPage (XAML) (C), set the name of the page to **SettingsPage.xaml** (D) and hit Add (E).

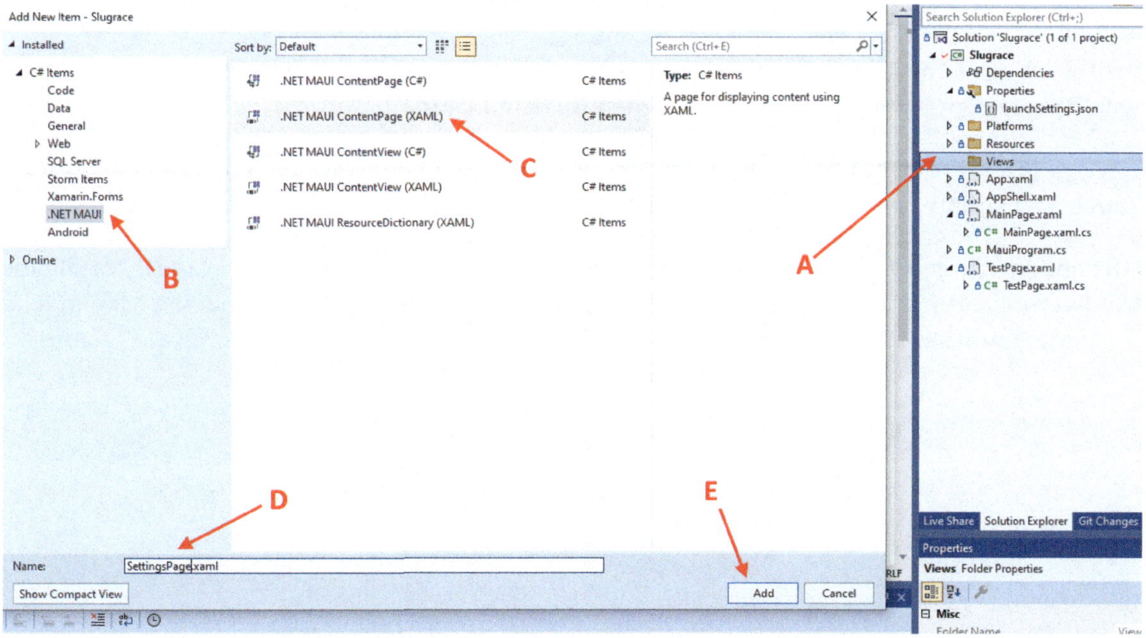

The new page, like any new page you add to the project, contains some initial code:

```
<?xml version="1.0" encoding="utf-8" ?>
<ContentPage xmlns="http://schemas.microsoft.com/dotnet/2021/maui"
             xmlns:x="http://schemas.microsoft.com/winfx/2009/xaml"
             x:Class="Slugrace.Views.SettingsPage"
             Title="SettingsPage">
    <VerticalStackLayout>
        <Label
            Text="Welcome to .NET MAUI!"
            VerticalOptions="Center"
            HorizontalOptions="Center" />
    </VerticalStackLayout>
</ContentPage>
```

In order to test the page, let's modify the **AppShell.xaml** file:

```
<?xml version="1.0" encoding="UTF-8" ?>
<Shell
    x:Class="Slugrace.AppShell"
    xmlns="http://schemas.microsoft.com/dotnet/2021/maui"
    xmlns:x="http://schemas.microsoft.com/winfx/2009/xaml"
    xmlns:local="clr-namespace:Slugrace"
    xmlns:views="clr-namespace:Slugrace.Views"
    Shell.FlyoutBehavior="Disabled"
    Title="Slugrace">

    <ShellContent
        Title="Test"
        ContentTemplate="{DataTemplate views:SettingsPage}"
        Route="SettingsPage" />
</Shell>
```

So, first of all, we added a new namespace to refer to the **Views** folder where the page sits. We're going to discuss namespaces in XAML in much more detail later on.

Then we changed the **DataTemplate** to actually use the new page when the app starts. Changing the **Route** isn't strictly necessary for now for the app to work, but let's do it for consistency's sake.

Run the app in Windows. We'll be testing all the pages in Windows now and later we'll handle the Android versions. As you might expect, there are going to be some differences that we have to take into account. You'll see the **SettingsPage** as it looks now:

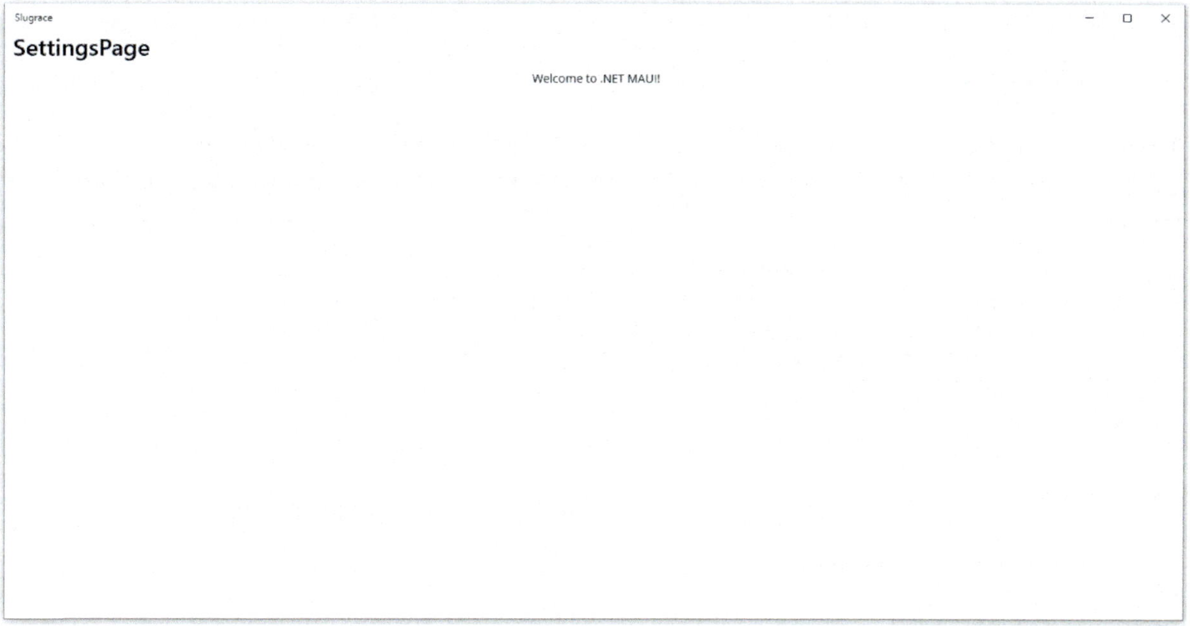

And this is what it's eventually going to look like:

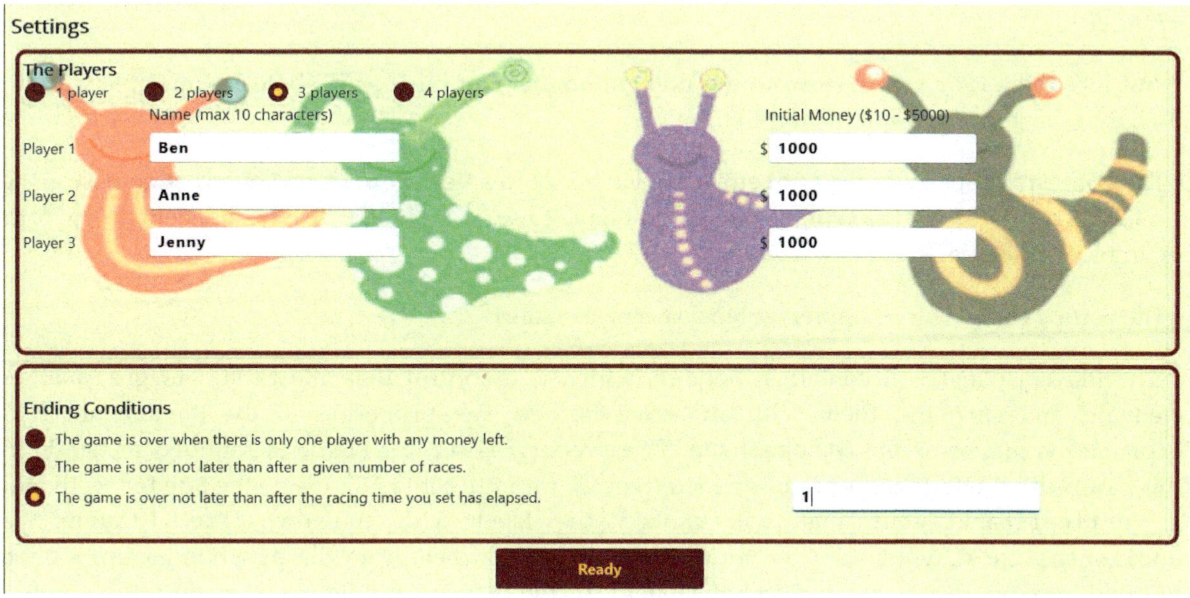

This page consists of several parts. These parts are visually separated from one another. They include:

- the label with the **`Text`** property set to **`Settings`**,

- the Players panel,

- the Ending Conditions panel,

- the Ready button.

The first thing we can do is remove the title bar near the top of the page. We won't need it. To do that, we have to set the **Title** property of the **ContentPage** to an empty string or remove it completely:

```
<?xml version="1.0" encoding="utf-8" ?>
<ContentPage xmlns="http://schemas.microsoft.com/dotnet/2021/maui"
             xmlns:x="http://schemas.microsoft.com/winfx/2009/xaml"
             x:Class="Slugrace.Views.SettingsPage">
    <VerticalStackLayout>
        ...
```

We also have to remove the **Title** property from **ShellContent** in **AppShell.xaml**:

```
<?xml version="1.0" encoding="UTF-8" ?>
<Shell
    ...
    <ShellContent
        ContentTemplate="{DataTemplate views:SettingsPage}"
        Route="SettingsPage" />
</Shell>
```

Now, let's think for a while: How are we going to implement this page? There are multiple ways to do it, but I'm going to implement it like so:

- The **Content** property of the **ContentPage** will be set to a **VerticalStackLayout** (**Content** is the content property of **ContentPage**, so you don't have to set it explicitly), which will contain the four main parts of the page.

- The Settings label will be implemented as a simple **Label**.

- The Players panel will contain a **Border**, which is a control that allows you to group other elements and surround them with an actual border. The properties of the **Border** are self-explanatory, maybe except **StrokeShape**. This property is set to a shape (a rounded rectangle in this case) with the four corner radii defined (here all four are set to 10). Inside the **Border** we'll add a **VerticalStackLayout** that will contain the label with the text "**The Players**", a **HorizontalStackLayout** with the four radio buttons that belong to the **players** group, a **Grid** with the headers (for Name and Initial Money) for the players settings and, temporarily, another **Grid** with a **BoxView** and **Label** inside. This **BoxView** will serve as a placeholder for now. Later we'll replace it with reusable controls that we must first create. Each of these reusable controls will contain controls related to a particular player.

- For the Ending Conditions panel, we'll use another **Border** control. Inside the **Border** we'll create a **VerticalStackLayout** with a **Label** and a **Grid**. In the **Grid** we'll put the ending conditions radio buttons and entries.

Here's the code in the **SettingsPage.xaml** file:

```
<?xml version="1.0" encoding="utf-8" ?>
<ContentPage xmlns="http://schemas.microsoft.com/dotnet/2021/maui"
             xmlns:x="http://schemas.microsoft.com/winfx/2009/xaml"
             x:Class="Slugrace.Views.SettingsPage">
    <VerticalStackLayout Margin="10">

        <!--the Settings label-->
        <Label
            Text="Settings"
            VerticalOptions="Center"
            FontSize="18" />

        <!--the Players panel-->
        <Border
            Stroke="brown"
            StrokeShape="RoundRectangle 10, 10, 10, 10"
            StrokeThickness="5"
            Padding="5">
            <VerticalStackLayout>
                <Label
                    Text="The Players"
                    FontSize="16" />
                <HorizontalStackLayout>
                    <RadioButton
                        Content="1 player"
                        GroupName="players" />
                    <RadioButton
                        Content="2 players"
                        GroupName="players" />
                    <RadioButton
                        Content="3 players"
                        GroupName="players" />
                    <RadioButton
                        Content="4 players"
                        GroupName="players" />
                </HorizontalStackLayout>

                <Grid
                    RowDefinitions="*"
                    ColumnDefinitions="100, 3*, 2*">
                    <Label
                        Grid.Column="1"
                        Text="Name (max 10 characters)" />
                    <Label
                        Grid.Column="2"
                        Text="Initial Money ($10 - $5000)" />
                </Grid>
                <Grid>
                    <BoxView
                        Color="Beige"
                        HorizontalOptions="FillAndExpand"
                        HeightRequest="300" />
```

```
                    <Label
                        Text="Player Settings"
                        FontSize="50"
                        FontAttributes="Italic"
                        HorizontalOptions="Center"
                        VerticalOptions="Center"/>
                </Grid>
            </VerticalStackLayout>
        </Border>

        <!--the Ending Conditions panel-->
        <Border
            Stroke="brown"
            StrokeShape="RoundRectangle 10, 10, 10, 10"
            StrokeThickness="5"
            Padding="5">
            <VerticalStackLayout>
                <Label
                    Text="Ending Conditions"
                    FontSize="16" />
                <Grid
                    RowDefinitions="*, *, *"
                    ColumnDefinitions="3*, 2*" >
                    <RadioButton
                        Content="The game is over when there is only one player with any money left."
                        GroupName="endingConditions" />
                    <RadioButton
                        Grid.Row="1"
                        Content="The game is over not later than after a given number of races."
                        GroupName="endingConditions" />
                    <Entry
                        Grid.Row="1"
                        Grid.Column="1" />
                    <Entry
                        Grid.Row="2"
                        Grid.Column="1" />
                    <RadioButton
                        Grid.Row="2"
                        Content="The game is over not later than after the racing time you set has elapsed."
                        GroupName="endingConditions" />
                </Grid>
            </VerticalStackLayout>
        </Border>

        <!--the Ready button-->
        <Button
            Text="Ready"
            WidthRequest="200"
            VerticalOptions="Center"
            FontSize="18" />
    </VerticalStackLayout>
</ContentPage>
```

Let's run the app now. You should see something more similar to what we are aiming at:

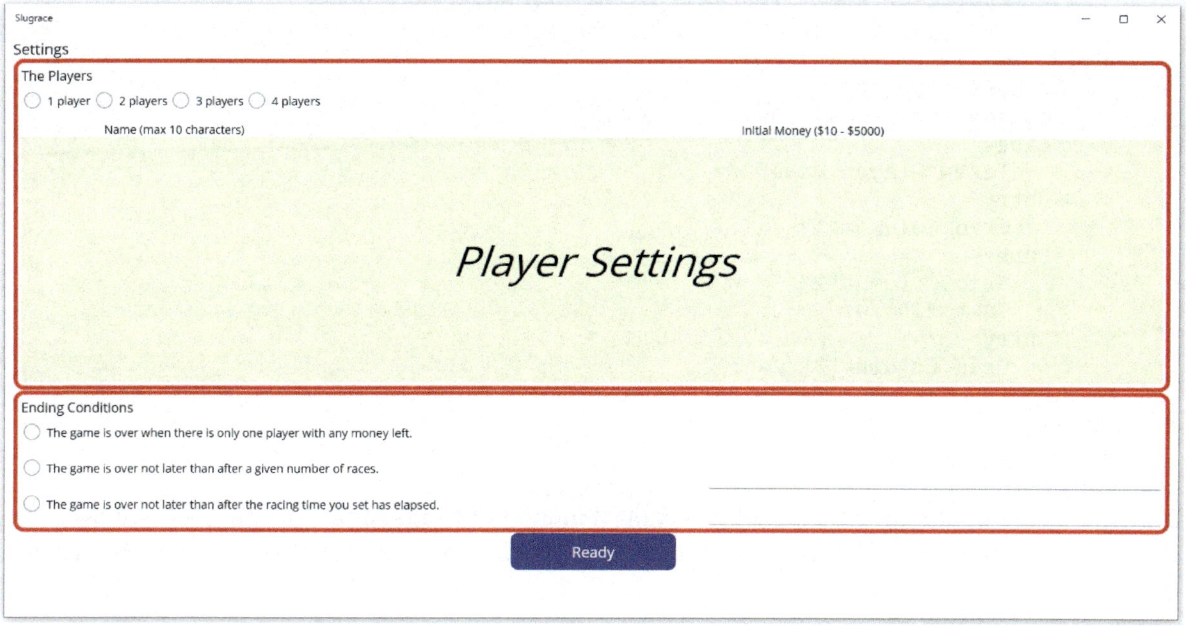

And now let's create the **PlayerSettings** content view that we can then use instead of the placeholder **BoxView**.

The PlayerSettings ContentView

We'll put our content views in a **Controls** folder, so add this folder to the root of the app. But how do we create a content view? Well, right-click the **Controls** folder and select Add -> New Item… Then select the .NET MAUI ContentView (XAML) template, name it **PlayerSettings.xaml** and hit Add.

If you open the code-behind files of the **SettingsPage** and **PlayerSettings** classes, you will notice that the former inherits from **ContentPage**, whereas the latter from **ContentView**.

Now, what do we need in the view? Have a look at it one more time:

Well, there are: a label, an entry, another label and another entry. Let's put these elements in a one-row **Grid** to make it easier to align with the headers. Make sure your **PlayerSettings.xaml** file contains the following code:

```
<?xml version="1.0" encoding="utf-8" ?>
<ContentView xmlns="http://schemas.microsoft.com/dotnet/2021/maui"
             xmlns:x="http://schemas.microsoft.com/winfx/2009/xaml"
             x:Class="Slugrace.Controls.PlayerSettings">
    <Grid
        RowDefinitions="*"
        ColumnDefinitions="100, 3*, 10, 2*">
        <Label
            Text="Player Name" />
        <Entry
            Grid.Column="1" />
        <Label
            Grid.Column="2"
            Text="$" />
        <Entry
            Grid.Column="3" />
    </Grid>
</ContentView>
```

Now we have to put four instances of this control in the **SettingsPage**. This number will then vary depending on how many players are supposed to play (which you will set by checking a radio button).

This requires two steps on our part: First, we have to add the namespace to the namespaces section of the page and then we have to add the controls just like any ordinary controls. One difference is that we have to prefix the controls with the namespace prefix defined in the namespaces section, which is **controls** (we defined it like so: **xmlns:controls** - this will become clearer when we talk about namespaces). We'll also remove the placeholder code that consists of the **Grid** with the **BoxView** and **Label**. Here's the code in the **SettingsPage.xaml** file:

```
<?xml version="1.0" encoding="utf-8" ?>
<ContentPage xmlns="http://schemas.microsoft.com/dotnet/2021/maui"
             xmlns:x="http://schemas.microsoft.com/winfx/2009/xaml"
             xmlns:controls="clr-namespace:Slugrace.Controls"
             x:Class="Slugrace.Views.SettingsPage">
    <VerticalStackLayout Margin="10">
        <!--the Settings label-->
        ...
        <!--the Players panel-->
        <Border
            ...
                <Grid
                    ...
                    <Label
                        Grid.Column="2"
                        Text="Initial Money ($10 - $5000)" />
                </Grid>
                <VerticalStackLayout>
                    <controls:PlayerSettings />
                    <controls:PlayerSettings />
                    <controls:PlayerSettings />
```

```
                <controls:PlayerSettings />
            </VerticalStackLayout>
        </VerticalStackLayout>
    </Border>

    <!--the Ending Conditions panel-->
    ...
```

Now the page looks like so:

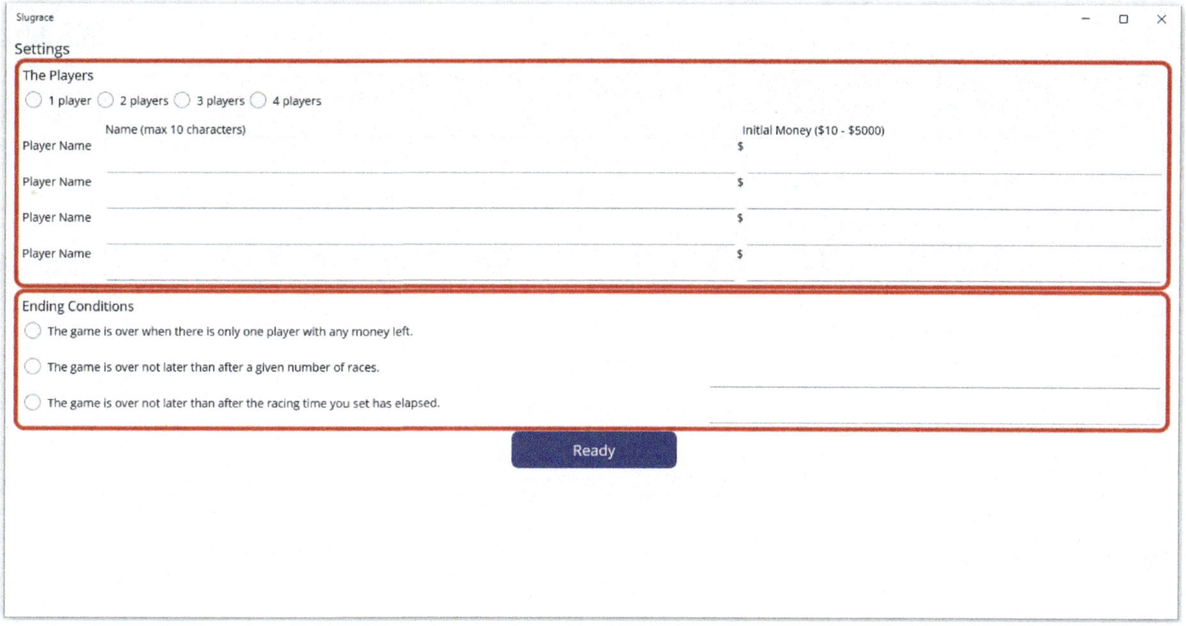

Sure, it needs styling, but all the main elements are there.

RacePage

Now it's time to create the **RacePage**, which is the most important page of the app. You will spend most of the time right there. This is where the actual game will be played. So, add a **RacePage.xaml** file to the **Views** folder and, in order to be able to display this page when you run your app, modify the code in **AppShell.xaml** to look like so:

```
<?xml version="1.0" encoding="UTF-8" ?>
<Shell
    ...
    <ShellContent
        ContentTemplate="{DataTemplate views:RacePage}"
        Route="RacePage" />
</Shell>
```

Well, what is this page going to look like? This page is going to be more dynamic than the **SettingsPage**. We'll have animations here, the data displayed will be constantly changing as we proceed and also the lower part of the page will be different before a race begins and after it finishes.

So, before a race the page should look like this:

We can distinguish some sections here. There are four smaller sections at the top:

- Game Info,

- Slugs' Stats,

- Players' Stats,

- the buttons

Let's have a closer look at them before we move on to discuss the other sections:

- Game Info - here you will see the information about the game in general, so current race number, number of races that are finished and races that are still to go, time elapsed and so on. What is displayed here will depend on what ending condition you set in the **SettingsPage**.

So, if you selected the first ending condition (the game is over when there is only one player with any money left), you will see just the current race number in this panel.

If you selected the second ending condition (the game is over not later than after a given number of races), you will see the following info displayed:

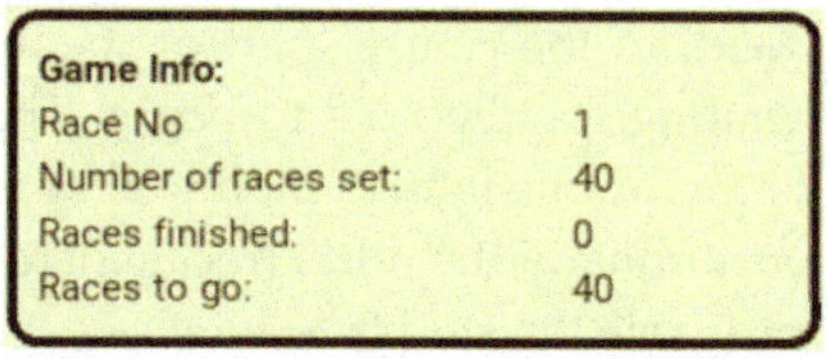

If you selected the third ending condition (the game is over not later than after the racing time you set has elapsed), you will see something like this:

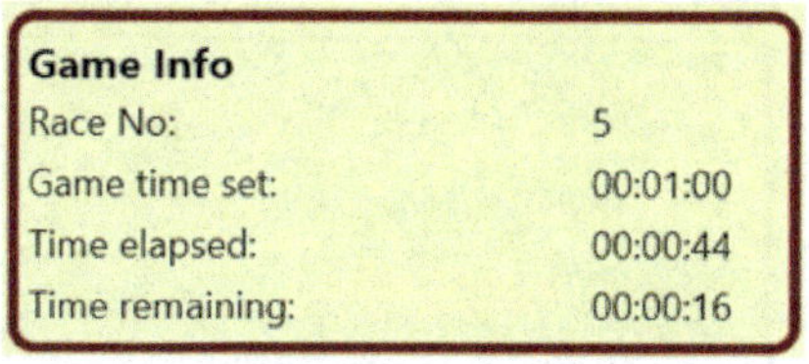

We will implement the version for the second ending condition now, and later in the book we'll implement a mechanism for displaying the correct data.

- Slugs' Stats - here the statistics related to the slugs will be displayed. There are going to be four slugs in the game. Their names are Speedster, Trusty, Iffy and Slowpoke. In this panel you will see how many races each of them has won, expressed both as an actual number of wins and as a percentage.

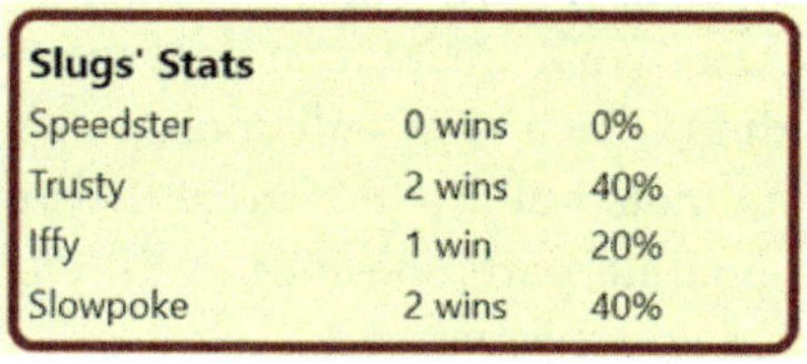

As you can see, here we have four lines with the same type of data, so we'll create a content view for a single row (which corresponds to a single slug).

- Players' Stats - here you will see statistics related to the players. Each player bets an amount of money on a slug before each race. If their slug wins, they win money. If their slug doesn't win, they lose money. In this panel the current amount of money each player has will be displayed. Depending on which option you selected in the **SettingsPage**, there may be one, two, three or four players in the game. Here's what it looks like if there are three:

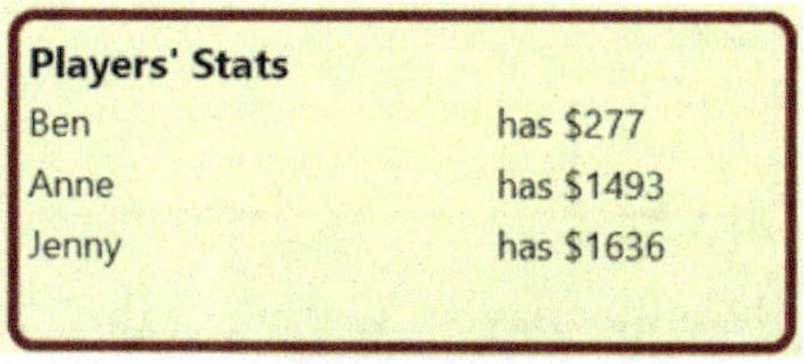

Again, we'll create a content view for a single row representing a single player.

- the buttons - there will be three buttons in the top-right corner of the app window (in the Windows version).

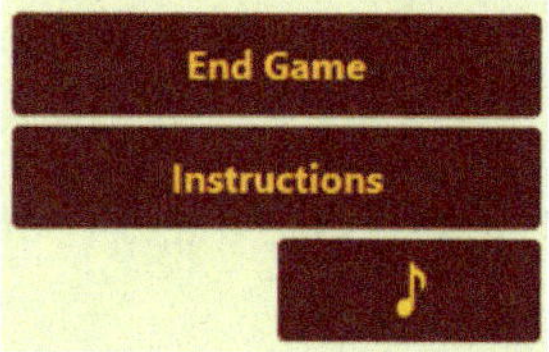

The first one will enable you to end the game any time you want, without waiting for the ending condition to be fulfilled. The second button will be used for navigation to the **InstructionsPage**. The third button will be used to mute/unmute the sounds. These buttons will be enclosed in a **VerticalStackLayout**.

Next, in the central part of the app window, you will see the racetrack with the four slugs on it waiting for the race to begin. There will also be some information about each slug on the track. Some of this information will be the same as in the Slugs' Stats panel (name, number of wins), but additionally the odds (recalculated after each race) will be displayed. The higher the odds, the less probable the slug is to win.

In order to implement this part of the UI, we'll have to add the graphical game assets to the game. Also, we'll create a content view for a single slug because it's not just a slug image as you might think. Each slug will consist of three parts: the body and the two tentacles. The tentacles will be animated and will change their position and rotation with respect to the body, so they have to be separate parts. Besides, we'll create a content view for the information that is displayed for each slug on the racetrack.

Finally, let's have a look at the bottom part of the page. It's the Bets panel:

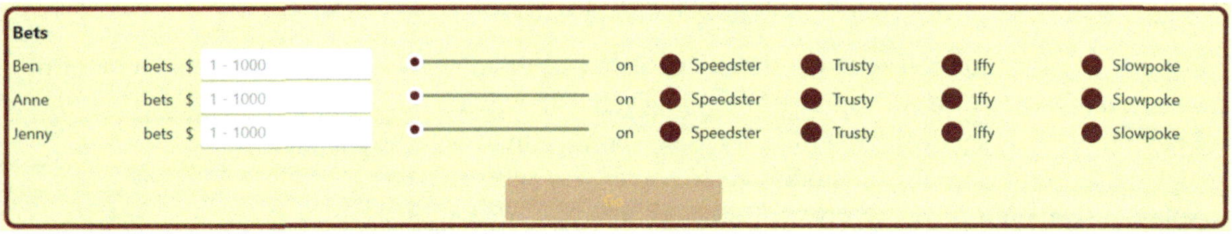

Here the players will place their bets before each race. The amount of money a player wants to bet may be typed in in an entry or set using a slider. Then the player must select the slug they want to place their bet on. As you can see, there's a lot of repetitive stuff here, so we'll create another content view for a single player.

There's also the Go button that will be used to start the race.

Now, after the race is over, almost all the parts of the page will change.

The Game Info, Slugs' Stats and Players' Stats will be updated.

In the middle part of the page, the slugs will be near the end part of the racetrack and the image of the slug that won will be displayed.

In the bottom part of the page the Bets panel will be replaced by the Results panel. The Results panel will display information on how each player did in the last race. We'll create another content view for that. There will also be a Next Race button that will reset the page to display the Bets panel again and change the racetrack part of the UI.

As the Bets and Results panels will be swapped after and before each race, we'll implement them as content views as well.

OK, this looks like a lot of work. So, let's first create an outline of the page with all the basic parts of the UI replaced by placeholders. Then we'll start implementing each part one by one. Make sure your code in the **RacePage.xaml** file looks like so:

```
<?xml version="1.0" encoding="utf-8" ?>
<ContentPage xmlns="http://schemas.microsoft.com/dotnet/2021/maui"
             xmlns:x="http://schemas.microsoft.com/winfx/2009/xaml"
             x:Class="Slugrace.Views.RacePage">
    <Grid
        RowDefinitions="1.3*, 2*, 2*"
        ColumnDefinitions="3*, 3*, 3*, 2*">

        <!--Game Info-->
        <Border
```

```
    Stroke="brown"
    StrokeShape="RoundRectangle 10, 10, 10, 10"
    StrokeThickness="5"
    Padding="5">
    <Label
        Text="Game Info"
        FontSize="36"
        FontAttributes="Italic"
        HorizontalOptions="Center"
        VerticalOptions="Center" />
</Border>

<!--Slugs' Stats-->
<Border
    Grid.Column="1"
    Stroke="brown"
    StrokeShape="RoundRectangle 10, 10, 10, 10"
    StrokeThickness="5"
    Padding="5">
    <Label
        Text="Slugs' Stats"
        FontSize="36"
        FontAttributes="Italic"
        HorizontalOptions="Center"
        VerticalOptions="Center" />
</Border>

<!--Players' Stats-->
<Border
    Grid.Column="2"
    Stroke="brown"
    StrokeShape="RoundRectangle 10, 10, 10, 10"
    StrokeThickness="5"
    Padding="5">
    <Label
        Text="Players' Stats"
        FontSize="36"
        FontAttributes="Italic"
        HorizontalOptions="Center"
        VerticalOptions="Center" />
</Border>

<!--the buttons-->
<VerticalStackLayout
    Grid.Column="3"
    Padding="5"
    Spacing="3">
    <Button
        Text="End Game" />
    <Button
        Text="Instructions" />
    <Button
        Text="Sound" />
</VerticalStackLayout>
```

```
        <!--Racetrack-->
        <Border
            Grid.Row="1"
            Grid.ColumnSpan="4"
            Stroke="brown"
            StrokeShape="RoundRectangle 10, 10, 10, 10"
            StrokeThickness="5"
            Padding="5">
            <Label
                Text="Racetrack"
                FontSize="36"
                FontAttributes="Italic"
                HorizontalOptions="Center"
                VerticalOptions="Center" />
        </Border>

        <!--Bets/Results panel-->
        <Border
            Grid.Row="2"
            Grid.ColumnSpan="4"
            Stroke="brown"
            StrokeShape="RoundRectangle 10, 10, 10, 10"
            StrokeThickness="5"
            Padding="5">
            <Label
                Text="Bets / Results"
                FontSize="36"
                FontAttributes="Italic"
                HorizontalOptions="Center"
                VerticalOptions="Center" />
        </Border>
    </Grid>
</ContentPage>
```

Run the app and you will see the placeholders:

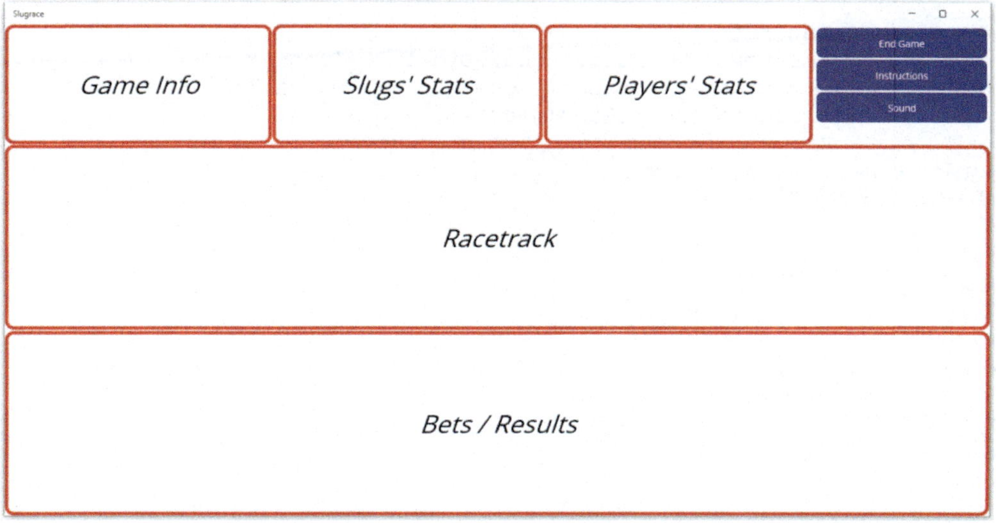

As you can see, we had to write quite a lot of XAML code to obtain just the placeholders. If we now implement the particular UI areas in full, the code will become really lengthy. We could do that, but to keep things clean and tidy, let's implement each part as a separate content view. Then we'll put just the content views in the page. So, we're going to implement the following content views:

- **`GameInfo`**,

- **`SlugsStats`**,

- **`PlayersStats`**,

- **`Racetrack`**,

- **`Bets`**

- **`Results`**

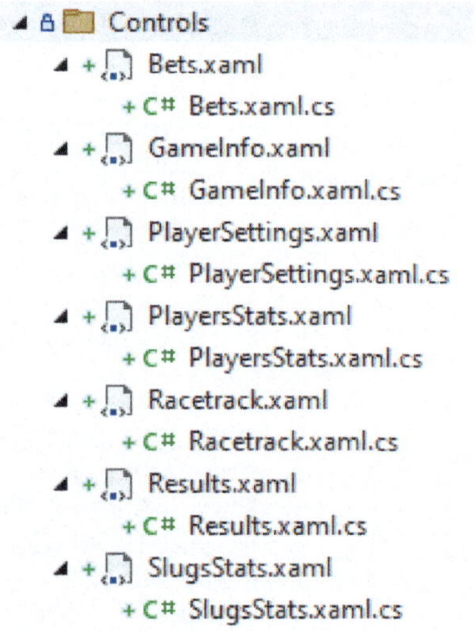

Add content view files using the .NET MAUI ContentView (XAML) template to the **Controls** folder.

The folder should now look like here on the right.

The buttons will be added directly to the page. Let's implement the content views one by one. We'll also create other content views on the way that will be nested in them. So, let's start with the **`GameInfo`** control.

The GameInfo ContentView

The **`GameInfo`** content view is the easiest one to implement. It's not going to contain any nested content views. Here's the code in the **GameInfo.xaml** file:

```
<?xml version="1.0" encoding="utf-8" ?>
<ContentView xmlns="http://schemas.microsoft.com/dotnet/2021/maui"
             xmlns:x="http://schemas.microsoft.com/winfx/2009/xaml"
             x:Class="Slugrace.Controls.GameInfo">
    <Grid
        RowDefinitions="*, *, *, *, *"
        ColumnDefinitions="3*, *">
        <Label
            Text="Game Info"
            FontAttributes="Bold" />
        <Label
            Grid.Row="1"
            Text="Race No:" />
        <Label
            Grid.Row="1"
            Grid.Column="1"
            Text="3" />
```

```
        <Label
            Grid.Row="2"
            Text="Number of races set:" />
        <Label
            Grid.Row="2"
            Grid.Column="1"
            Text="20" />
        <Label
            Grid.Row="3"
            Text="Races finished:" />
        <Label
            Grid.Row="3"
            Grid.Column="1"
            Text="2" />
        <Label
            Grid.Row="4"
            Text="Races to go:" />
        <Label
            Grid.Row="4"
            Grid.Column="1"
            Text="18" />
    </Grid>
</ContentView>
```

As you can see, it's just a simple **Grid** with labels displaying some dummy data. Let's add this view to the **RacePage**. Don't forget to add the namespace in the top section of the page. Here's the code:

```
<?xml version="1.0" encoding="utf-8" ?>
<ContentPage xmlns="http://schemas.microsoft.com/dotnet/2021/maui"
             xmlns:x="http://schemas.microsoft.com/winfx/2009/xaml"
             xmlns:controls="clr-namespace:Slugrace.Controls"
             x:Class="Slugrace.Views.RacePage">
    <Grid
        ...
        <!--Game Info-->
        <Border
            Stroke="brown"
            StrokeShape="RoundRectangle 10, 10, 10, 10"
            StrokeThickness="5"
            Padding="5">
            <controls:GameInfo />
        </Border>

        <!--Slugs' Stats-->
        ...
```

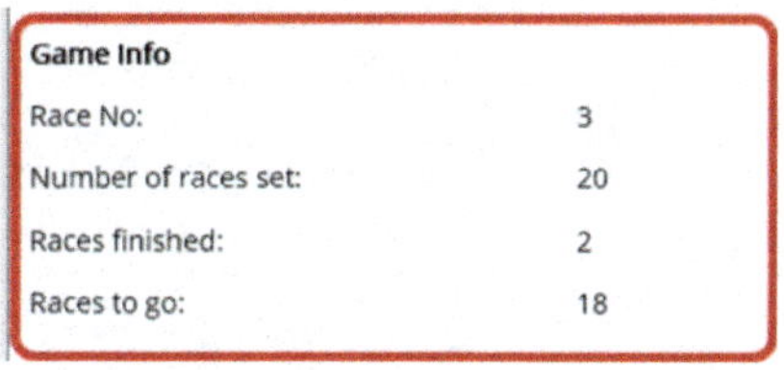

That's it. Run the app and watch the Game Info panel.

Let's take care of the Slugs' Stats panel next.

The SlugsStats and SlugStats ContentViews

The **SlugsStats** content view is a bit more complicated than **GameInfo** in that it will contain nested content views. I named the view **SlugsStats** (with the plural form *Slugs* at the beginning) because this view will display data for all the slugs. The nested view will display data for just one slug, so let's name it **SlugStats** (with the singular form *Slug* at the beginning). For easy alignment, we'll implement the **SlugStats** view as a one-row grid. Actually, let's start with the nested view. So, add a new content view file to the **Controls** folder and name it **SlugStats.xaml**. Then implement the code in this file like this:

```
<?xml version="1.0" encoding="utf-8" ?>
<ContentView xmlns="http://schemas.microsoft.com/dotnet/2021/maui"
             xmlns:x="http://schemas.microsoft.com/winfx/2009/xaml"
             x:Class="Slugrace.Controls.SlugStats">
    <Grid
        RowDefinitions="*"
        ColumnDefinitions="2*, *, *">
        <Label
            Text="Slug Name" />
        <Label
            Grid.Column="1"
            Text="4 wins" />
        <Label
            Grid.Column="2"
            Text="46%" />
    </Grid>
</ContentView>
```

To add this control to the **SlugsStats** view, we have to add its namespace in the latter. Here's the implementation of the **SlugsStats** content view:

```
<?xml version="1.0" encoding="utf-8" ?>
<ContentView xmlns="http://schemas.microsoft.com/dotnet/2021/maui"
             xmlns:x="http://schemas.microsoft.com/winfx/2009/xaml"
             xmlns:controls="clr-namespace:Slugrace.Controls"
             x:Class="Slugrace.Controls.SlugsStats">
    <Grid
        RowDefinitions="*, *, *, *, *"
        ColumnDefinitions="*">
        <Label
            Text="Slugs' Stats"
            FontAttributes="Bold" />
        <controls:SlugStats
            Grid.Row="1" />
        <controls:SlugStats
            Grid.Row="2" />
```

```
        <controls:SlugStats
            Grid.Row="3" />
        <controls:SlugStats
            Grid.Row="4" />
    </Grid>
</ContentView>
```

Finally, we can add the **SlugsStats** view to the **RacePage**:

```
...
<ContentPage ...>
    ...
        <!--Slugs' Stats-->
        <Border
            ...>
            <controls:SlugsStats />
        </Border>

        <!--Players' Stats-->
        ...
```

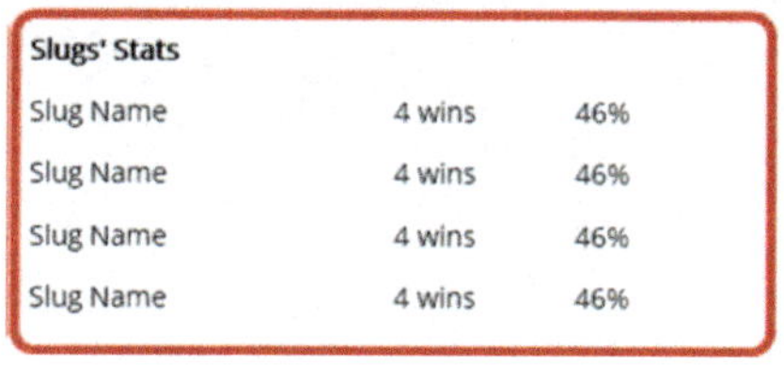

Run the app and watch the control (with dummy data for now) in action.

Next, let's implement the **PlayersStats** and **PlayerStats** content views.

The PlayersStats and PlayerStats ContentViews

We'll implement the **PlayersStats** view in a very similar way as the **SlugsStats** view. It will also contain nested views. The nested view will be named **PlayerStats**. Add a content view file named **PlayerStats.xaml** to the **Controls** folder and implement the code like this:

```
<?xml version="1.0" encoding="utf-8" ?>
<ContentView xmlns="http://schemas.microsoft.com/dotnet/2021/maui"
             xmlns:x="http://schemas.microsoft.com/winfx/2009/xaml"
             x:Class="Slugrace.Controls.PlayerStats">
    <Grid
        RowDefinitions="*"
        ColumnDefinitions="2.5*, 1.5*">
        <Label
            Text="Player Name" />
        <Label
            Grid.Column="1"
            Text="has $1000" />
    </Grid>
</ContentView>
```

Next, let's implement the **PlayersStats** like this:

```
<?xml version="1.0" encoding="utf-8" ?>
<ContentView xmlns="http://schemas.microsoft.com/dotnet/2021/maui"
             xmlns:x="http://schemas.microsoft.com/winfx/2009/xaml"
             xmlns:controls="clr-namespace:Slugrace.Controls"
             x:Class="Slugrace.Controls.PlayersStats">
    <Grid
        RowDefinitions="*, *, *, *, *"
        ColumnDefinitions="*">
        <Label
            Text="Players' Stats"
            FontAttributes="Bold" />
        <controls:PlayerStats
            Grid.Row="1" />
        <controls:PlayerStats
            Grid.Row="2" />
        <controls:PlayerStats
            Grid.Row="3" />
        <controls:PlayerStats
            Grid.Row="4" />
    </Grid>
</ContentView>
```

And finally, let's add the **PlayersStats** control to the **RacePage**:

```
...
<ContentPage ...>
    ...
        <!--Players' Stats-->
        <Border
            ...>
            <controls:PlayersStats />
        </Border>

        <!--the buttons-->
        ...
```

Run the app and watch the Players' Stats panel.

We're done with the upper part of the UI. Now let's take care of the part in the middle, which is the racetrack. In order to implement the racetrack, we'll need the graphical assets representing the slugs in top view, their tentacles in top view, their silhouettes and the image of the track. Let's add the assets to the app first.

The Graphical Assets

We'll need a couple of images. First, let's add the image of the slimy track. It's saved as **racetrack.png**. The dimensions of the image are 1000 x 200 px. It looks like this:

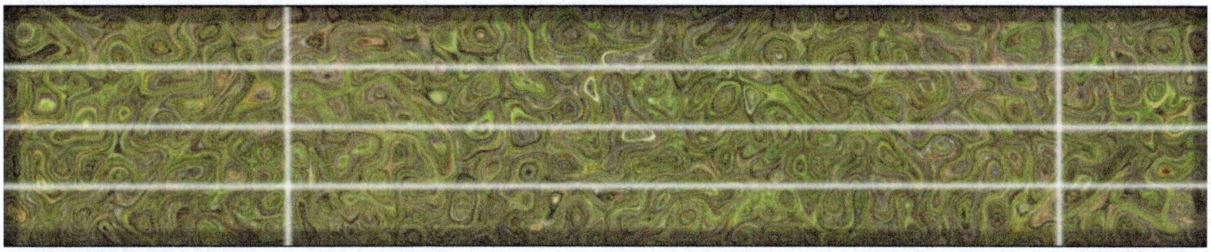

Next, we'll need the top-view images of the slugs, separately their bodies and tentacles. These images look like so:

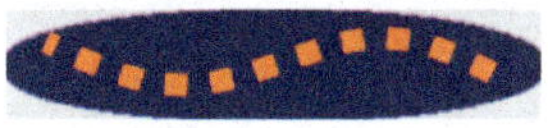

speedster_body.png

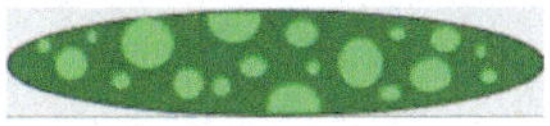

trusty_body.png

iffy_body.png

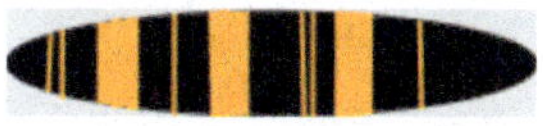

slowpoke_body.png

speedster_eye.png

trusty_eye.png

iffy_eye.png

slowpoke_eye.png

Finally, we'll need the silhouette images of the slugs. They will be displayed in the **WinnerInfo** panel (that we are about to create) after each race. These images look like this:

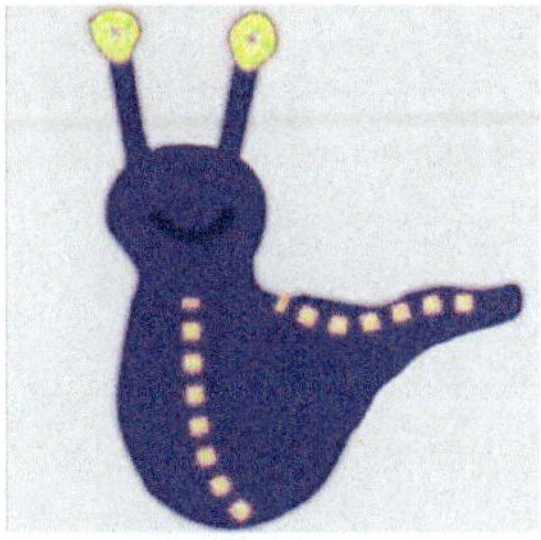

speedster.png

trusty.png

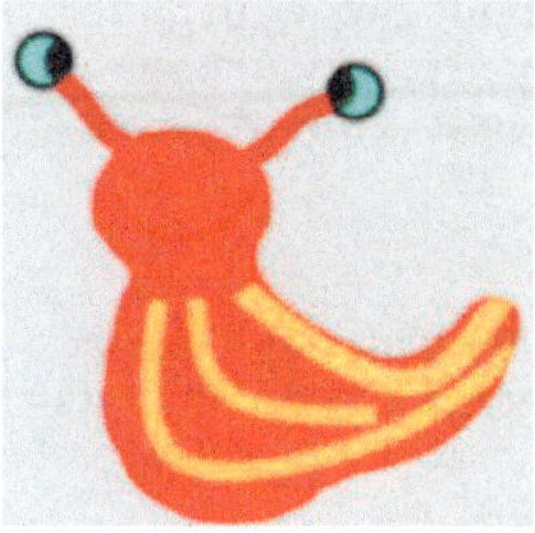

iffy.png

slowpoke.png

You will find the images in the Github repository for the project. Download them from there and add to the **Images** folder inside the **Resources** folder.

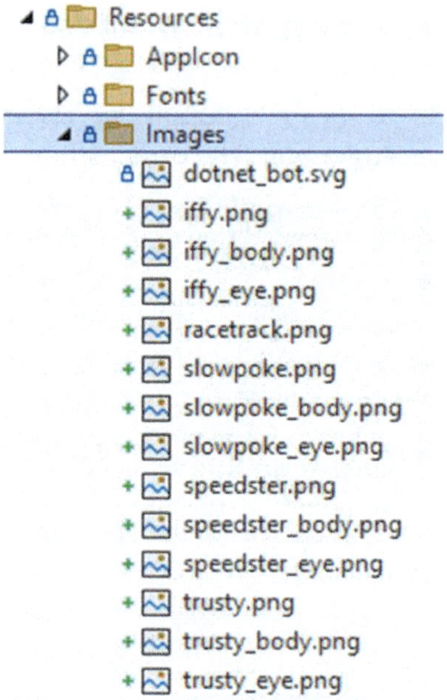

Now we can use the images in our content views.

The Racetrack, SlugImage, TrackImage, SlugInfo and WinnerInfo ContentViews

The **`Racetrack`** will be implemented as a content view that consists of several other content views. Let's start by adding the following content views to the **Controls** folder:

- **`SlugImage`**,

- **`TrackImage`**,

- **`SlugInfo`**,

- **`WinnerInfo`**.

Let's create the **`SlugImage`** view first. This is a purely graphical view. Here's the code in the **SlugImage.xaml** file:

```
<?xml version="1.0" encoding="utf-8" ?>
<ContentView xmlns="http://schemas.microsoft.com/dotnet/2021/maui"
             xmlns:x="http://schemas.microsoft.com/winfx/2009/xaml"
             x:Class="Slugrace.Controls.SlugImage">
    <AbsoluteLayout>
        <Image
            Source="speedster_eye.png"
            AbsoluteLayout.LayoutBounds="1.2, .35, .25, .23"
            AbsoluteLayout.LayoutFlags="All"
            Rotation="-30"
            AnchorX="0"/>
        <Image
            Source="speedster_eye.png"
            AbsoluteLayout.LayoutBounds="1.2, .65, .25, .23"
            AbsoluteLayout.LayoutFlags="All"
            Rotation="30"
            AnchorX="0"/>
        <Image
            Source="speedster_body.png"
            AbsoluteLayout.LayoutBounds="0, 0, 1, 1"
            AbsoluteLayout.LayoutFlags="All"
            Aspect="Fill"/>
    </AbsoluteLayout>
</ContentView>
```

The view contains an **AbsoluteLayout** with three children, which are images that together form the slug character. This type of layout enables us to position and size the elements relative to their parent. This is important because we don't want the particular parts of the image to fall apart when the size of the app window changes. We're using proportional positioning and sizing here.

One thing that may be new to you in the code above is the **AnchorX** property in the **Image** class. **AnchorX** and **AnchorY** are used to set the center of a transformation. In this case the eye images are rotated -30 and 30 degrees. If we don't set the **AnchorX** and **AnchorY** properties, the default values will be used, which means the image will be rotated around its central point.

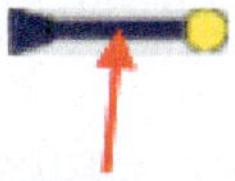

So, if we didn't set the **AnchorX** property on the eye images, the slug would end up looking like here.

This slug doesn't look healthy. The **AnchorX** and **AnchorY** properties can be set to values between 0 and 1. If we set **AnchorX** to 1, the image would be rotated around the point which is the farthest to the right horizontally and in the center vertically.

And the slug would look even less healthy than before.

We want the tentacles with the eyes to be rotated around the central point of the tentacle's base, which is on the far left of the image.

This is why we set **AnchorX** to 0 and we left **AnchorY** out, allowing for its default value of 0.5. Now the slug looks good.

Another new property that we set on the image of the slug's body is **Aspect**. There are a couple options you can set this property to. The property is used to indicate how the image will fit into the display area. If you set it to **Fill**, the image will be stretched to completely fill the display area. This way the eyes won't get detached from the body no matter how much you stretch or squeeze the image:

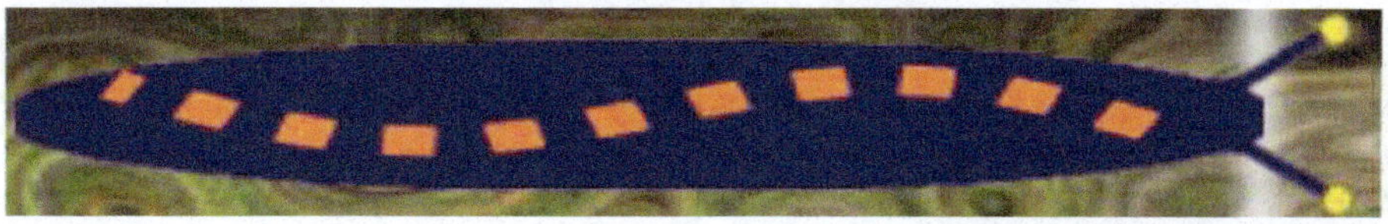

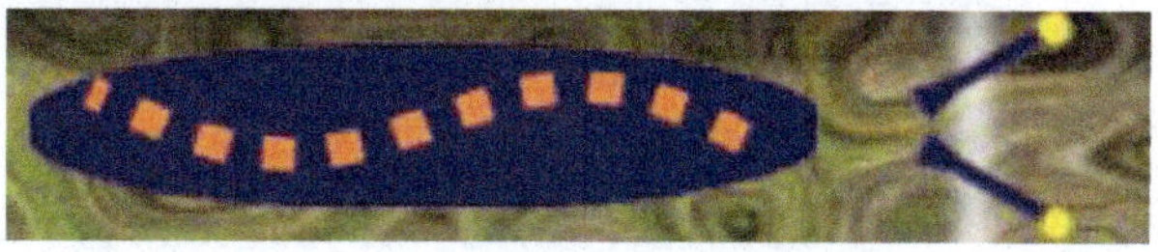

Stretching wouldn't look so good if you set **Aspect** to a different value. For example, if you set it to **AspectFit**, everything looks fine until the image is stretched. Then it turns into something like here - Poor kid.

This is why this property is set to **Fill**.

Next, let's implement the **SlugInfo** view. This view will be used inside the **TrackImage** view along with the **SlugImage** views. The **SlugInfo** view will contain information about a particular slug. We'll implement it as a **Grid**. The **Text** properties of the labels will be hardcoded for now. Here's the code:

```
<?xml version="1.0" encoding="utf-8" ?>
<ContentView xmlns="http://schemas.microsoft.com/dotnet/2021/maui"
             xmlns:x="http://schemas.microsoft.com/winfx/2009/xaml"
             x:Class="Slugrace.Controls.SlugInfo">
    <Grid
        Padding="5, 2, 0, 2"
        RowDefinitions="*, *"
        ColumnDefinitions="6.8*, 2.2*">
        <Label
            Text="Speedster"
            FontSize="18"
            FontAttributes="Bold"
            TextColor="White"/>
        <Label
            Grid.Row="1"
            Text="0 wins"
            FontSize="14"
            TextColor="White"/>
        <Label
            Grid.Column="1"
            Grid.RowSpan="2"
            VerticalOptions="Center"
            Text="1.40"
            FontSize="40"
            FontAttributes="Bold"
            TextColor="White"/>
    </Grid>
</ContentView>
```

With the **SlugImage** and **SlugInfo** views in place, we can now create the **TrackImage** content view. This view will contain the image of the track and on it will be the images of the slugs along with the information enclosed in the **SlugInfo** view. Here's the code:

```
<?xml version="1.0" encoding="utf-8" ?>
<ContentView xmlns="http://schemas.microsoft.com/dotnet/2021/maui"
             xmlns:x="http://schemas.microsoft.com/winfx/2009/xaml"
             xmlns:controls="clr-namespace:Slugrace.Controls"
             x:Class="Slugrace.Controls.TrackImage">
    <AbsoluteLayout>
        <!--Racetrack-->
        <Image
            Source="racetrack.png"
            AbsoluteLayout.LayoutBounds="0, 0, 1, 1"
            AbsoluteLayout.LayoutFlags="All"
            Aspect="Fill"/>
```

```
        <!--Speedster-->
        <controls:SlugImage
            AbsoluteLayout.LayoutBounds=".1, .05, .15, .15"
            AbsoluteLayout.LayoutFlags="All"/>
        <controls:SlugInfo
            AbsoluteLayout.LayoutBounds="0, 0, 1, .25"
            AbsoluteLayout.LayoutFlags="All"/>

        <!--Trusty-->
        <controls:SlugImage
            AbsoluteLayout.LayoutBounds=".1, .35, .15, .15"
            AbsoluteLayout.LayoutFlags="All"/>
        <controls:SlugInfo
            AbsoluteLayout.LayoutBounds="0, .35, 1, .25"
            AbsoluteLayout.LayoutFlags="All"/>

        <!--Iffy-->
        <controls:SlugImage
            AbsoluteLayout.LayoutBounds=".1, .65, .15, .15"
            AbsoluteLayout.LayoutFlags="All"/>
        <controls:SlugInfo
            AbsoluteLayout.LayoutBounds="0, .68, 1, .25"
            AbsoluteLayout.LayoutFlags="All"/>

        <!--Slowpoke-->
        <controls:SlugImage
            AbsoluteLayout.LayoutBounds=".1, .95, .15, .15"
            AbsoluteLayout.LayoutFlags="All"/>
        <controls:SlugInfo
            AbsoluteLayout.LayoutBounds="0, 1.02, 1, .25"
            AbsoluteLayout.LayoutFlags="All"/>
    </AbsoluteLayout>
</ContentView>
```

Next, let's implement the **WinnerInfo** view. It's going to be a **Grid** with two labels and an image. The labels will inform us which slug has won a race and we will see the silhouette of this slug in the image. Here's the code:

```
<?xml version="1.0" encoding="utf-8" ?>
<ContentView xmlns="http://schemas.microsoft.com/dotnet/2021/maui"
             xmlns:x="http://schemas.microsoft.com/winfx/2009/xaml"
             x:Class="Slugrace.Controls.WinnerInfo">
    <Grid
        RowDefinitions=".6*, *, 3*">
        <Label
            Text="The winner is"
            FontSize="30"
            HorizontalOptions="Center"
            FontAttributes="Bold" />
```

```
        <Label
            Grid.Row="1"
            Text="Speedster"
            FontSize="40"
            HorizontalOptions="Center"
            FontAttributes="Bold" />
        <Image
            Grid.Row="2"
            Source="speedster.png" />
    </Grid>
</ContentView>
```

Now we have all the building blocks in place. Let's create the **Racetrack** view, which consists of the **TrackImage** on the left and the **WinnerInfo** on the right:

```
<?xml version="1.0" encoding="utf-8" ?>
<ContentView xmlns="http://schemas.microsoft.com/dotnet/2021/maui"
             xmlns:x="http://schemas.microsoft.com/winfx/2009/xaml"
             xmlns:controls="clr-namespace:Slugrace.Controls"
             x:Class="Slugrace.Controls.Racetrack">
    <Grid
        ColumnDefinitions="9*, 2*">
        <controls:TrackImage
            Margin="20, 0, 0, 0" />
        <controls:WinnerInfo
            Grid.Column="1" />
    </Grid>
</ContentView>
```

Finally, we can place the whole big and complex **Racetrack** content view in the **RacePage**:

```
...
<ContentPage ...>
    ...
        <!--Racetrack-->
        <Border
            ...>
            <controls:Racetrack />
        </Border>

        <!--Bets/Results panel-->
        ...
```

If you now run the app, you should see something like this:

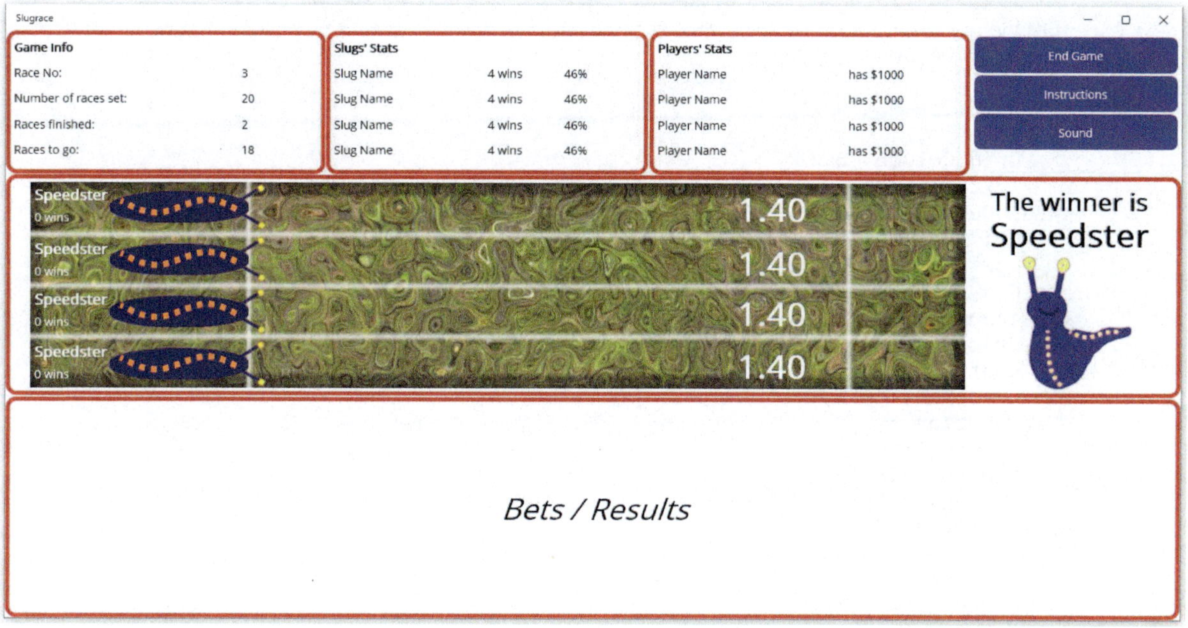

Not bad at all. Last but not least, let's implement the **Bets** and **Results** views.

The Bets and PlayerBet ContentViews

We already created the **Bets.xaml** file. Inside the **Bets** view we'll embed controls that will enable the players to place their bets. There will be one such control for each player. We haven't created it yet, so go ahead and add a new **ContentView** to the **Controls** folder. Name it **PlayerBet**. It will contain the player's name, an entry and a slider for setting the amount of money the player wants to bet and four radio buttons, one for each slug, so that the player can check the slug they want to bet on.

Here's the code in the **PlayerBet.xaml** file:

```
<?xml version="1.0" encoding="utf-8" ?>
<ContentView xmlns="http://schemas.microsoft.com/dotnet/2021/maui"
             xmlns:x="http://schemas.microsoft.com/winfx/2009/xaml"
             x:Class="Slugrace.Controls.PlayerBet">
    <Grid
        ColumnDefinitions="*, .7*, .1*, .7*, 1.5*, .3*, *, *, *, *">
        <Label
            Text="Player 1" />
        <Label
            Grid.Column="1"
            Text="bets" />
```

```
        <Label
            Grid.Column="2"
            Text="$" />
        <Entry
            Grid.Column="3" />
        <Slider
            Grid.Column="4"/>
        <Label
            Grid.Column="5"
            Text="on" />
        <RadioButton
            Grid.Column="6"
            Content="Speedster"
            GroupName="player1" />
        <RadioButton
            Grid.Column="7"
            Content="Trusty"
            GroupName="player1" />
        <RadioButton
            Grid.Column="8"
            Content="Iffy"
            GroupName="player1" />
        <RadioButton
            Grid.Column="9"
            Content="Slowpoke"
            GroupName="player1" />
    </Grid>
</ContentView>
```

Now let's put four instances of this control inside the **Bets** view. Here's the **Bets.xaml** file:

```
<?xml version="1.0" encoding="utf-8" ?>
<ContentView xmlns="http://schemas.microsoft.com/dotnet/2021/maui"
             xmlns:x="http://schemas.microsoft.com/winfx/2009/xaml"
             xmlns:controls="clr-namespace:Slugrace.Controls"
             x:Class="Slugrace.Controls.Bets">
    <Grid
        RowDefinitions="*, 4*, *">
        <Label
            Text="Bets"
            FontAttributes="Bold"/>
        <VerticalStackLayout
            Grid.Row="1">
            <controls:PlayerBet />
            <controls:PlayerBet />
            <controls:PlayerBet />
            <controls:PlayerBet />
        </VerticalStackLayout>

        <Button
            Grid.Row="2"
            Text="Go"
            HorizontalOptions="Center" />
    </Grid>
</ContentView>
```

Finally, let's add the **Bets** view to the **RacePage**:

```
<?xml version="1.0" encoding="utf-8" ?>
<ContentPage xmlns="http://schemas.microsoft.com/dotnet/2021/maui"
             ...>
    ...
        <!--Bets/Results panel-->
        <Border
            ...>
            <controls:Bets />
        </Border>
    </Grid>
</ContentPage>
```

Run the app and watch the Bets panel:

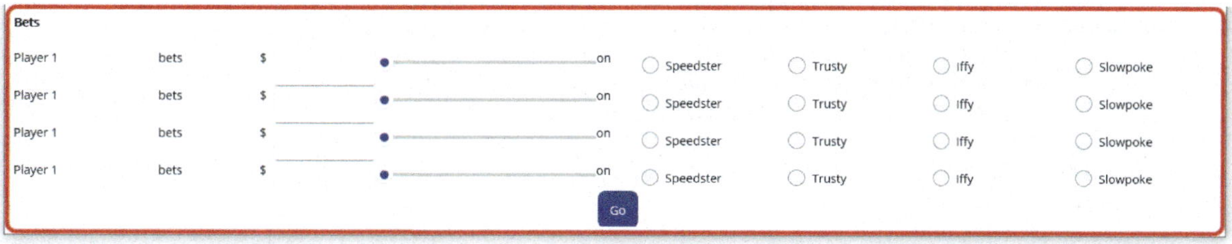

After each race, the **Bets** view will be replaced by the **Results** view. So, let's create it next.

The Results and PlayerResult ContentViews

The **Results** view will look very much like the **Bets** view. We'll also embed in it other views that will present the results of the particular players. To this end, let's create a new **ContentView** and name it **PlayerResult**. The **PlayerResult.xaml** file should contain the following code:

```
<?xml version="1.0" encoding="utf-8" ?>
<ContentView xmlns="http://schemas.microsoft.com/dotnet/2021/maui"
             xmlns:x="http://schemas.microsoft.com/winfx/2009/xaml"
             x:Class="Slugrace.Controls.PlayerResult">
    <Grid
        ColumnDefinitions="*, *, *, *, *, *, *">
        <Label
            Text="Player 1" />
        <Label
            Grid.Column="1"
            Text="had $1000," />
        <Label
            Grid.Column="2"
            Text="bet $250" />
        <Label
            Grid.Column="3"
            Text="on Speedster,"/>
```

```
        <Label
            Grid.Column="4"
            Text="lost $250,"/>
        <Label
            Grid.Column="5"
            Text="now has $750. " />
        <Label
            Grid.Column="6"
            Text="The odds were 1.64." />
    </Grid>
</ContentView>
```

Instances of this control will be embedded in the **Results** view. Here's the **Results.xaml** file:

```
<?xml version="1.0" encoding="utf-8" ?>
<ContentView xmlns="http://schemas.microsoft.com/dotnet/2021/maui"
             xmlns:x="http://schemas.microsoft.com/winfx/2009/xaml"
             xmlns:controls="clr-namespace:Slugrace.Controls"
             x:Class="Slugrace.Controls.Results">
    <Grid
        RowDefinitions="*, 4*, *">
        <Label
            Text="Results"
            FontAttributes="Bold"/>
        <VerticalStackLayout
            Grid.Row="1">
            <controls:PlayerResult />
            <controls:PlayerResult />
            <controls:PlayerResult />
            <controls:PlayerResult />
        </VerticalStackLayout>

        <Button
            Grid.Row="2"
            Text="Next Race"
            HorizontalOptions="Center" />
    </Grid>
</ContentView>
```

And now replace the **Bets** view in the **RacePage** by the **Results** view to see what it looks like:

```
...
<ContentPage ...>
    ...
        <!--Bets/Results panel-->
        <Border
            ...>
            <controls:Results />
        </Border>

    </Grid>
</ContentPage>
```

Run the app and you'll see the Results panel now:

Looks like we're done with the **RacePage**. There's one more page to implement for now, the **GameOverPage**. This one is going to be pretty easy. Let's implement it with some dummy data.

GameOverPage

We have to create the **GameOverPage** first, so right-click the **Views** folder and add a new **ContentPage**. Make sure you select .NET MAUI ContentPage (XAML) and not .NET MAUI ContentView (XAML). Then change the **ContentTemplate** in the **AppShell.xaml** file:

```
<?xml version="1.0" encoding="UTF-8" ?>
<Shell...>

    <ShellContent
        ContentTemplate="{DataTemplate views:GameOverPage}"
        Route="GameOverPage" />
</Shell>
```

This page is only going to display some labels and buttons. The **GameOverPage.xaml** file should look like this:

```
<?xml version="1.0" encoding="utf-8" ?>
<ContentPage xmlns="http://schemas.microsoft.com/dotnet/2021/maui"
             xmlns:x="http://schemas.microsoft.com/winfx/2009/xaml"
             x:Class="Slugrace.Views.GameOverPage">
    <Grid
        RowDefinitions="2*, 2*, 2*, *">
        <Label
            Text="Game Over"
            FontSize="120"
            FontAttributes="Bold"
            HorizontalOptions="Center" />
        <Label
            Grid.Row="1"
            Text="There's only one player with any money left."
            FontSize="40"
            FontAttributes="Bold"
            HorizontalOptions="Center" />
```

```
        <Label
            Grid.Row="2"
            Text="The winner is Player 2, having started at $1000, winning at $396."
            FontSize="40"
            FontAttributes="Bold"
            HorizontalOptions="Center" />
        <FlexLayout
            Grid.Row="3"
            JustifyContent="Center">
            <Button
                Text="Play Again"
                FontSize="30"
                WidthRequest="300"
                Margin="0, 0, 50, 20" />
            <Button
                Text="Quit"
                FontSize="30"
                WidthRequest="300"
                Margin="0, 0, 50, 20" />
        </FlexLayout>
    </Grid>
</ContentPage>
```

As you can see, we're using a **FlexLayout** to center the buttons. Run the app. The **GameOverPage** should look something like this:

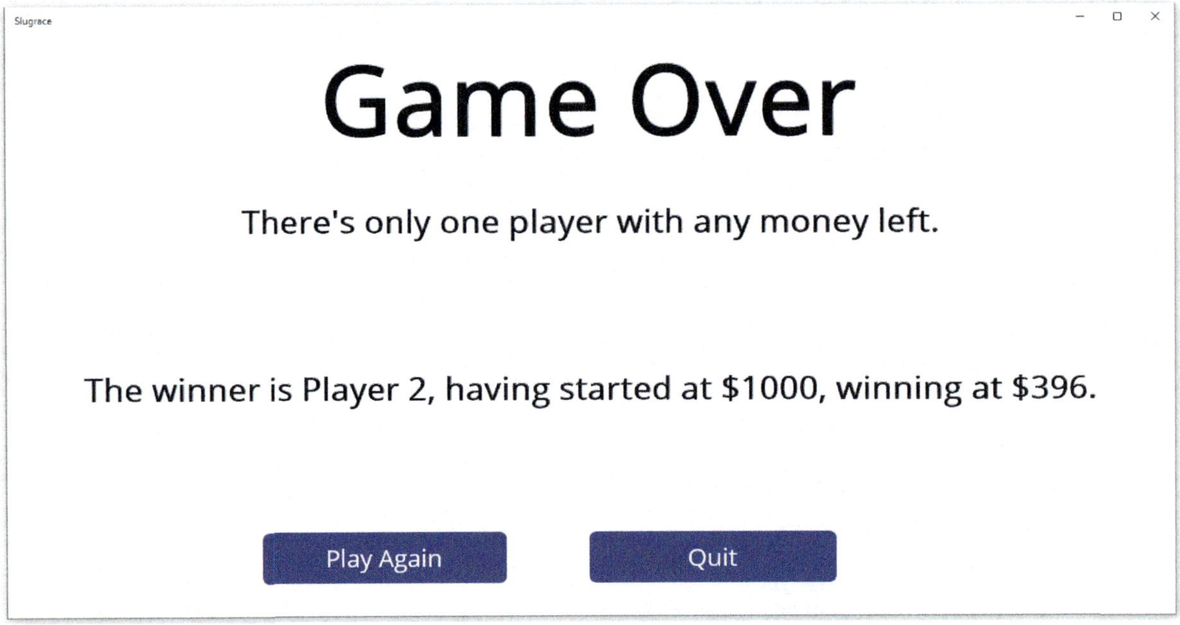

We're done. All our most important pages are in place. Of course, they aren't functional and contain dummy data, which we will fix soon. They don't look pretty, either. In the next chapter we'll be styling them so that they really shine.

Chapter 9 - Styles in XAML

code: https://github.com/prospero-apps/Slugrace/tree/chapter9

In the previous chapter we created all the major pages and content views. But we didn't care so much about how the particular elements look. We'll fix this in this chapter by adding styles.

When you run your app, all the views already have some default styles applied. These styles are defined in the **Styles.xaml** file in the **Resources** → **Styles** folder. But usually you will want to define your own styles, so let's see how to do it.

About Styles

If you look at the screenshots from the previous chapter, you will notice two things. On one hand, there's a lot of repetitive code that determines how the particular views should look. Here's an example from the **GameOverPage**:

```
...
<ContentPage ...>
    ...
            <Button
                Text="Play Again"
                FontSize="30"
                WidthRequest="300"
                Margin="0, 0, 50, 20" />
            <Button
                Text="Quit"
                FontSize="30"
                WidthRequest="300"
                Margin="0, 0, 50, 20" />
        </FlexLayout>
    ...
```

The two buttons have some properties set to identical values, like **FontSize**, **WidthRequest** or **Margin**. And there are lots of examples like this throughout the application. This means repetitive code. Lots of repetitive code. Imagine you decide to change the **FontSize** property to 40 on all buttons. You would have to do it for every button individually, which is time-consuming and error-prone. What if there were 75 buttons altogether?

On the other hand, if we're at buttons, have a look at how they differ across the pages:

Different sizes, different font sizes, etc. Maybe they would look better if they had a more uniform look and feel.

These two issues can be easily addressed by defining styles in one place and applying them to all the views that should share them. Naturally, sometimes you may want to make one or two views look different than all the others. It's also possible, because styles in XAML can be defined for particular views, layouts, pages or globally, for the entire app.

Style Object and ResourceDictionary

To create a style in XAML we use the **Style** object. The **Style** object contains a collection of property values. You can assign the object to any number of visual elements (which are objects that inherit from **VisualElement**, so the views, layouts, and so on).

Let's have a look at the buttons in the **GameOverPage** again. Which property values do they share? They have the same **FontSize**, **WidthRequest** and **Margin**. So, instead of duplicating the code, let's create a style and apply it to them. In order to do that, we have to add a **ResourceDictionary** to the page.

A **ResourceDictionary** is an object in which we define one or more styles. It's the content property of the **ContentPage.Resources** object, so it may be omitted.

Each style contains one or more **Setter** objects. Each **Setter** object has two properties: **Property** and **Value**. The **Property** property (awkward as it sounds) is set to the name of the property of the object to which the style is to be applied. The **Value** property is the value we want that property to be set to.

If this sounds complicated to you, then don't worry. Let's create a **ResourceDictionary** in the **GameOverPage** with one style that we will apply to the buttons. Here's the code:

```
...
<ContentPage ...>

    <ContentPage.Resources>
        <ResourceDictionary>
            <Style TargetType="Button">
                <Setter Property="FontSize" Value="30" />
                <Setter Property="WidthRequest" Value="300" />
                <Setter Property="Margin" Value="0, 0, 50, 20" />
            </Style>
        </ResourceDictionary>
    </ContentPage.Resources>

    <Grid
        ...
        <FlexLayout
            Grid.Row="3"
            JustifyContent="Center">
            <Button
                Text="Play Again" />
            <Button
                Text="Quit" />
        </FlexLayout>
    ...
```

As I mentioned before, we can omit the **ResourceDictionary** because it's the content property of **ContentPage.Resources**. The following code will work just as fine:

```
...
<ContentPage ...>

    <ContentPage.Resources>
        <Style TargetType="Button">
            <Setter Property="FontSize" Value="30" />
            <Setter Property="WidthRequest" Value="300" />
            <Setter Property="Margin" Value="0, 0, 50, 20" />
        </Style>
    </ContentPage.Resources>

    <Grid
        ...
```

Anyway, here we have one style. One thing to keep in mind is that we always have to set the **TargetType** property of the **Style** object to the name of the **VisualElement** that the style will be applied to. Here we're going to apply it to the **Button** objects.

Have a look at the two buttons inside the **FlexLayout** again. We removed all the properties that are defined in the style and only left those that differ for each instance. So, the style we defined in the **ResourceDictionary** applies to both the buttons and if there were more buttons, it would apply to all of them. Let's now change the style to look like so:

```
...
<ContentPage ...>

    <ContentPage.Resources>
        <Style TargetType="Button">
            <Setter Property="FontSize" Value="40" />
            <Setter Property="WidthRequest" Value="300" />
            <Setter Property="Margin" Value="0, 0, 50, 20" />
            <Setter Property="HeightRequest" Value="100" />
            <Setter Property="BackgroundColor" Value="Black" />
            <Setter Property="TextColor" Value="White" />
            <Setter Property="CornerRadius" Value="50" />
        </Style>
    </ContentPage.Resources>

    <Grid
        ...
```

So, we changed the value of the **FontSize** property from 30 to 40 and we added some more properties. You have to write this code only once, right here in the **ResourceDictionary**, and the style will be applied to all the buttons on the page. If you run the app (with the **GameOverPage** set in **AppShell.xaml**), the two buttons will look like so:

Fine, but what if we wanted to apply the style only to some elements of a particular type and another style to the others? Well, this is where implicit and explicit styles come into play.

Implicit vs Explicit Styles

The styles defined above are so-called implicit styles. **Implicit styles** are applied to all elements of the type defined in the **TargetType** property.

We can also define **explicit types** and then apply them only to those instances of the type defined in the **TargetType** property that we want to. To do that, we must specify an **x:Key** attribute in the **Style** object and then explicitly apply the styles using the value assigned to that attribute.

Again, things will get clearer when you see it in action. Still in the **GameOverPage**, have a look at the three labels:

```
...
<ContentPage ...>
...
    <Grid
        RowDefinitions="2*, 2*, 2*, *">
        <Label
            Text="Game Over"
            FontSize="120"
            FontAttributes="Bold"
            HorizontalOptions="Center" />
        <Label
            Grid.Row="1"
            Text="There's only one player with any money left."
            FontSize="40"
            FontAttributes="Bold"
            HorizontalOptions="Center" />
        <Label
            Grid.Row="2"
            Text="The winner is Player 2, having started at $1000, winning at $396."
            FontSize="40"
            FontAttributes="Bold"
            HorizontalOptions="Center" />
        <FlexLayout
            ...
```

They all share the values of the **FontAttributes** and **HorizontalOptions** properties, but the **FontSize** property of the first label is set to 120, whereas the **FontSize** of the other two is set to 40. So, let's create two styles for the labels. These are going to be explicit styles, so we need to specify the **x:Key** attribute for them. We can use any value for that attribute we want. A descriptive one wouldn't be that bad. So, let's add the two styles to the **ResourceDictionary** and then apply them to the particular labels:

```
...
<ContentPage ...>

    <ContentPage.Resources>
        <Style TargetType="Button">
            ...
        </Style>

        <Style x:Key="labelBaseStyle" TargetType="Label">
            <Setter Property="FontAttributes" Value="Bold" />
            <Setter Property="HorizontalOptions" Value="Center" />
            <Setter Property="FontSize" Value="40" />
        </Style>

        <Style x:Key="labelLargeStyle" TargetType="Label">
            <Setter Property="FontAttributes" Value="Bold" />
            <Setter Property="HorizontalOptions" Value="Center" />
            <Setter Property="FontSize" Value="120" />
        </Style>
    </ContentPage.Resources>
```

```
<Grid
    RowDefinitions="2*, 2*, 2*, *">
    <Label
        Text="Game Over"
        Style="{StaticResource labelLargeStyle}" />
    <Label
        Grid.Row="1"
        Text="There's only one player with any money left."
        Style="{StaticResource labelBaseStyle}" />
    <Label
        Grid.Row="2"
        Text="The winner is Player 2, having started at $1000, winning at $396."
        Style="{StaticResource labelBaseStyle}" />
    <FlexLayout
        ...
```

The **labelLargeStyle** is applied only to the first label. The **labelBaseStyle** is applied to the other two. Watch the syntax that we use to apply a style to an object. We use the **Style** property and set it to something that looks weird. You will run into syntax like that quite often in XAML. The curly braces mean that we have a so-called markup extension here. We're not going to go into details here because markup extensions will be the topic of one of the following chapters. Just remember that we use the **StaticResource** (for styles that remain unchanged for the duration of the application) or **DynamicResource** (if the style may change) markup extension with the key specified in the **ResourceDictionary** to apply a style.

You may have noticed that the two label styles in the **ResourceDictionary** still share some values. They both have the same values of **FontAttributes** and **HorizontalOptions**. This can be simplified even further. Styles can inherit from other styles.

Style Inheritance

In order to reduce code duplication, styles can inherit from other styles that share some of the property values. For example, you could create a base style for all labels that will only contain the properties shared by all labels and then derive other styles from it. To derive a style from another style, we use the **BasedOn** property and set it to a **StaticResource** markup extension that references the base style. Let's see how it works on the example of our three labels.

The **labelLargeStyle** will inherit from **labelBaseStyle** and only define those properties that were not defined in the base style:

```
...
    <ContentPage.Resources>
        ...
        <Style x:Key="labelLargeStyle"
               TargetType="Label"
               BasedOn="{StaticResource labelBaseStyle}">
            <Setter Property="FontAttributes" Value="Bold" />
            <Setter Property="HorizontalOptions" Value="Center" />
```

```
            <Setter Property="FontSize" Value="120" />
        </Style>
    </ContentPage.Resources>
    ...
```

That's much more concise. OK, but what if we wanted to create a style that can be applied to both labels and buttons. Let's say we want the labels and buttons to share the same value of the **Rotation** property.

Styles Applicable to Multiple Types

You can apply a style to objects of different types like **Label** and **Button** if they inherit from a common type. Let's create a style that will define the **Rotation** property and then use it for both the labels and the buttons. To do that, we set the **TargetType** property to a type that both **Label** and **Button** derive from. This could be **View** or **VisualElement**. **Label** and **Button** inherit from **View** and **View** inherits from **VisualElement**. Have a look:

```
...
    <ContentPage.Resources>
        <Style x:Key="baseStyle" TargetType="View">
            <Setter Property="Rotation" Value="5" />
        </Style>

        <Style TargetType="Button"
               BasedOn="{StaticResource baseStyle}">
            <Setter Property="FontSize" Value="40" />
            ...
        </Style>

        <Style x:Key="labelBaseStyle" TargetType="Label"
               BasedOn="{StaticResource baseStyle}">
            <Setter Property="FontAttributes" Value="Bold" />
            ...
        </Style>
        ...
```

Now all **View** instances are rotated by 5 degrees.

It would work the same if you set the **TargetType** property of **baseStyle** to **VisualElement**.

By the way, in the code there's style inheritance on multiple levels: **labelLargeStyle** inherits from **labelBaseStyle**, which, in turn, inherits from **baseStyle**.

Well, we know how to define styles. All the styles we've created so far were defined on page level, but is this the only place where you can define styles? And what does it have to do with style scopes?

Style scopes

We defined all our styles on page level. This means they are available everywhere within that page. This is where we usually define styles if we need them on that page only. But this isn't the only place where you can define styles. You can define styles anywhere in the hierarchy. Where you define them, determines their scope. They are always available for the element they are defined on and all its children.

Let's set the **ContentTemplate** and **Route** properties in **AppShell.xaml** to **SettingsPage** so that we can see this page when we launch the app. Also, open the **SettingsPage.xaml** file so that we can define some styles in it.

This time we'll create a style on layout level, not on page level. Find the **Grid** layout where the header labels are defined. It looks like so:

```
...
        <!--the Players panel-->
        ...
                <Grid
                    RowDefinitions="*"
                    ColumnDefinitions="100, 3*, 2*"
                    >
                    <Label
                        Grid.Column="1"
                        Text="Name (max 10 characters)" />
                    <Label
                        Grid.Column="2"
                        Text="Initial Money ($10 - $5000)" />
                </Grid>

                <VerticalStackLayout>
                    ...
```

If we define the styles inside the **Grid**, they will be accessible only to the **Grid** and its children, but not anywhere else on the page. Let's define an implicit style:

```
...
                <Grid
                    RowDefinitions="*"
                    ColumnDefinitions="100, 3*, 2*">
```

```
                <Grid.Resources>
                    <Style TargetType="Label">
                        <Setter Property="TextColor" Value="Green" />
                        <Setter Property="FontSize" Value="30" />
                    </Style>
                </Grid.Resources>

                <Label
                    ...
```

Here, the style is defined in the **ResourceDictionary** that is the content property of the **Grid.Resources** object. Run the app and you will see that only the labels inside the **Grid** have been styled:

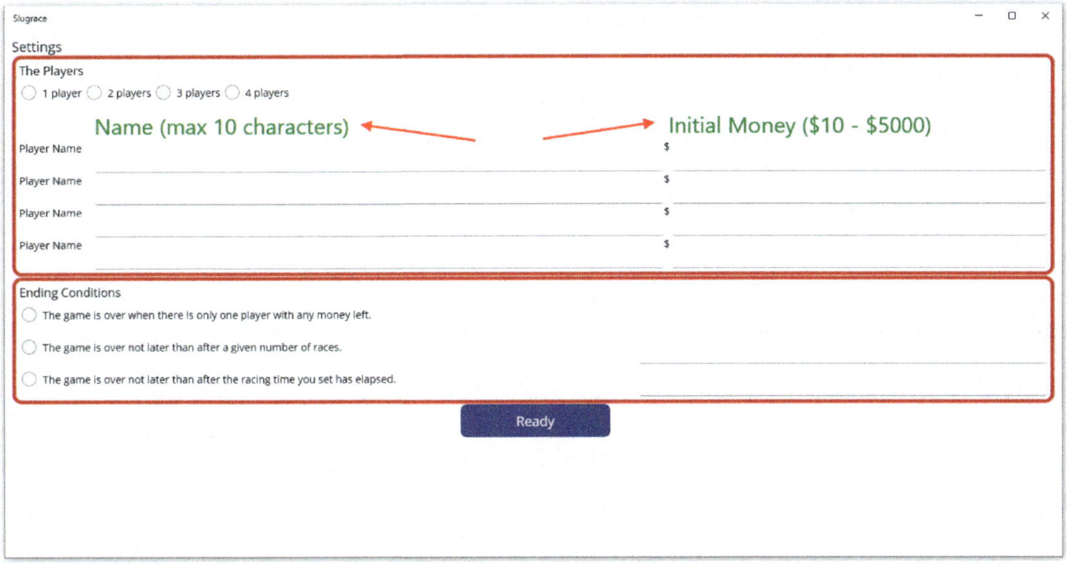

Now remove the style you just created and let's try to define a style on a view level. This definitely isn't something you're going to be doing frequently, but it is possible. Let's define the style inside the first label with the **Text** property set to **"Settings"**:

```
...
        <!--the Settings label-->
        <Label
            Text="Settings"
            VerticalOptions="Center"
            FontSize="18">

            <Label.Resources>
                <Style TargetType="Label">
                    <Setter Property="TextDecorations" Value="Underline" />
                    <Setter Property="TextColor" Value="Red" />
                </Style>
            </Label.Resources>

        </Label>
        ...
```

As you can see, we can't use self-closing tags for the label anymore. If you run the app, you'll see that only this one label has been styled:

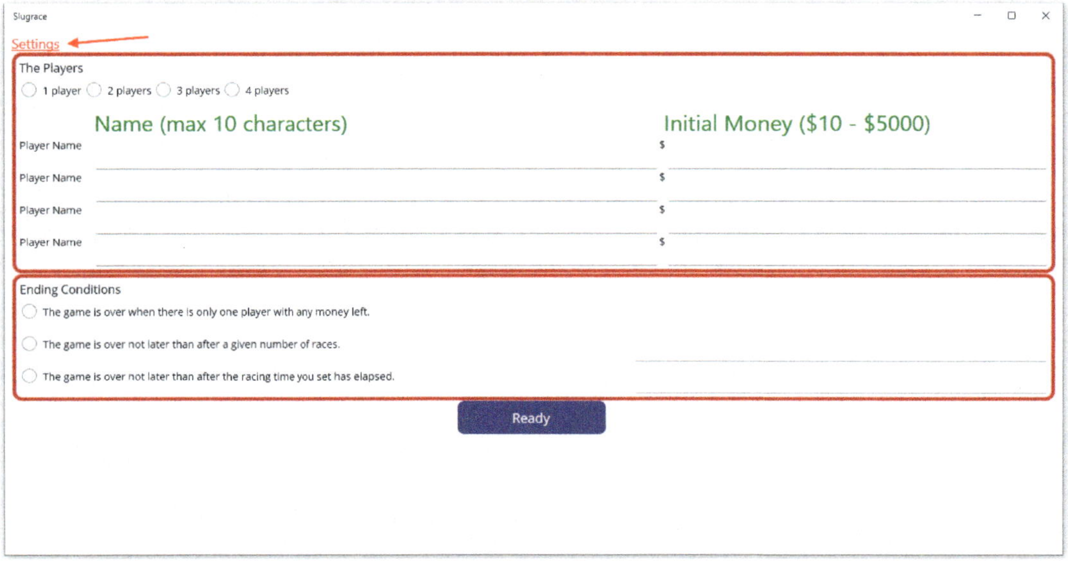

To achieve the same effect, you could just have set the properties directly on the **Label** object like we did before.

Remove the style from the **Label** view. We set it there just for demonstrational purposes. OK, we know how to define styles with different scopes within a page, but what if we want to create a style that can be used globally, everywhere in the app. For example, let's say we want all the buttons across all the pages to have the same look and feel.

Global styles are defined in the app's resource dictionary, in the **App.xaml** file. They can be implicit or explicit. Let's define an implicit style for the **Button**. Here's the code:

```
<?xml version = "1.0" encoding = "UTF-8" ?>
<Application ...>
    <Application.Resources>
        <ResourceDictionary>
            <ResourceDictionary.MergedDictionaries>
                ...
            </ResourceDictionary.MergedDictionaries>

            <Style TargetType="Button">
                <Setter Property="BackgroundColor" Value="Red" />
                <Setter Property="TextColor" Value="Yellow" />
                <Setter Property="FontSize" Value="30" />
                <Setter Property="FontAttributes" Value="Bold, Italic" />
            </Style>
        </ResourceDictionary>
    ...
```

Now the style should be applied to all the buttons across the app. But is it? Let's check it out. We should see a red button with a yellow text. You have to manually change the page in the **AppShell.xaml** file to test it. Here's the **`SettingsPage`**:

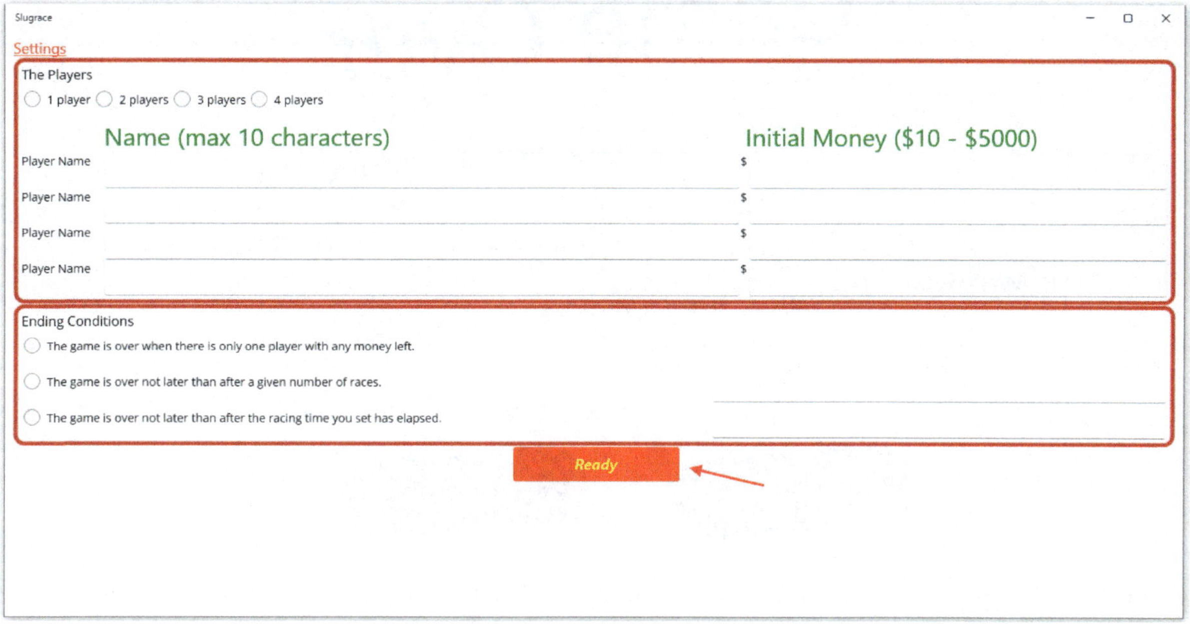

The style has been applied correctly. Let's now run the **`RacePage`**:

Here it works too. What about the **GameOverPage**? Lest check it out:

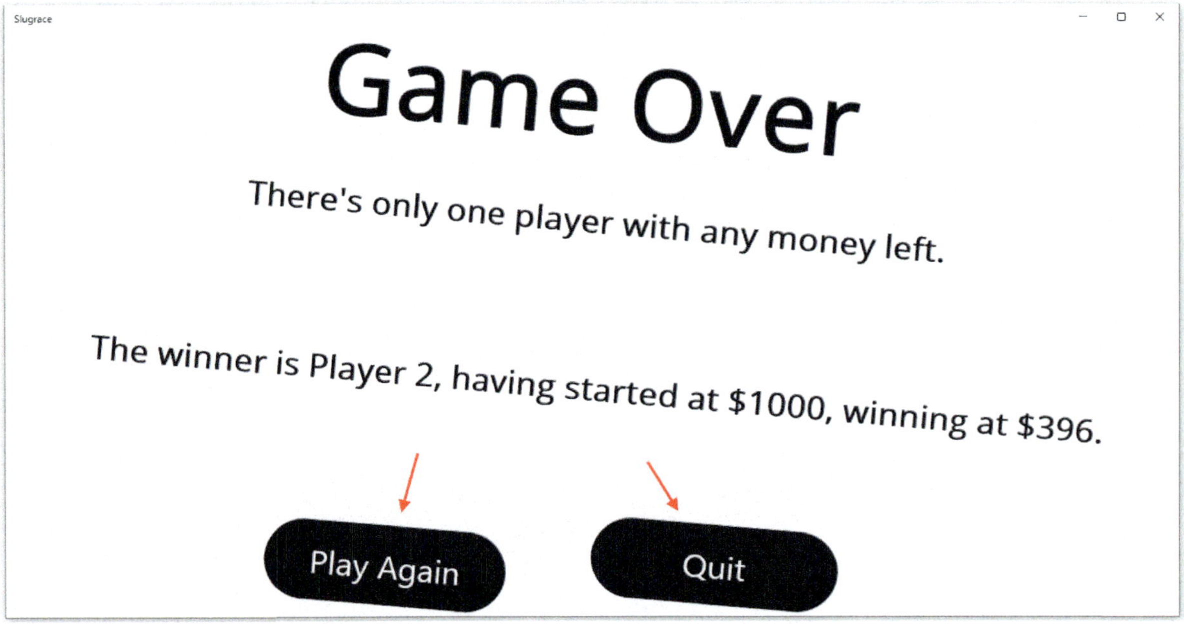

Well, here it doesn't look that good. What happened? Well, a conflict happened. The styles for the button are defined in two places: on page level and globally in **App.xaml**. Looks like the style defined in the **GameOverPage**'s **ResourceDictionary** wins. The font size is 40, because this is what we set in the page-level style. But the background color is black, which is what we set on page level too, and so on. In order to understand why it is like that, we have to talk about precedence of styles.

Precedence of Styles

If you have ever worked with CSS, you know that styles can be overridden by styles defined lower in the hierarchy. In XAML it works exactly the same. App-level styles are overridden by page-level styles and control-level styles. Page-level styles are overridden by control-level styles, etc. All styles are overridden by properties set directly on a control. And this is why the buttons in the **GameOverPage** looked different than those in the other pages. But let's have a closer look at what exactly happened.

Let's start at the app level. Do we have any styles defined here that are applied to buttons? Turns out we do:

```
...
<Application ...>
    <Application.Resources>
        <ResourceDictionary>
            ...
```

```
            <Style TargetType="Button">
                <Setter Property="BackgroundColor" Value="Red" />
                <Setter Property="TextColor" Value="Yellow" />
                <Setter Property="FontSize" Value="30" />
                <Setter Property="FontAttributes" Value="Bold, Italic" />
            </Style>
        </ResourceDictionary>
    </Application.Resources>
</Application>
```

The **BackgroundColor**, **TextColor**, **FontSize** and **FontAttributes** properties are set here. At this level all the buttons across the app are red, with a yellow text with **FontSize** set to 30 and the **FontAttributes** set to **Bold** and **Italic**.

Let's move down the hierarchy. We're interested in the **GameOverPage**, so let's see if there are any styles defined on page level:

```
<?xml version="1.0" encoding="utf-8" ?>
<ContentPage ...>

    <ContentPage.Resources>
        <Style x:Key="baseStyle" TargetType="View">
            <Setter Property="Rotation" Value="5" />
        </Style>

        <Style TargetType="Button"
               BasedOn="{StaticResource baseStyle}">
            <Setter Property="FontSize" Value="40" />
            <Setter Property="WidthRequest" Value="300" />
            <Setter Property="Margin" Value="0, 0, 50, 20" />
            <Setter Property="HeightRequest" Value="100" />
            <Setter Property="BackgroundColor" Value="Black" />
            <Setter Property="CornerRadius" Value="50" />
        </Style>

        ...
    </ContentPage.Resources>
    ...
```

Here we have an implicit style that is applied to all buttons on this page. The following properties are set here: **FontSize**, **WidthRequest**, **Margin**, **HeightRequest**, **BackgroundColor**, **CornerRadius** and **Rotation**, which is inherited from **baseStyle**. As you can see, two of the properties, **FontSize** and **BackgroundColor** are set again. They will take precedence and override the same properties set on app level. This is why the font size is 40 and the background color is black. The other properties were not defined on app level, so they are set here for the first time.

Let's move down the hierarchy to see if any styles for the buttons are defined there. Well, there are no styles defined in the **Grid** that encloses the **FlexLayout** where the buttons are defined, nor in the **FlexLayout** itself. Let's see if any properties were set on the **Button** objects themselves:

```
...
<ContentPage ...>
    ...
        <FlexLayout
            ...>
            <Button
                Text="Play Again" />
            <Button
                Text="Quit" />
        </FlexLayout>
    ...
```

Well, just the **Text** property. The **Text** property could also be set higher up in the hierarchy, even in global styles if for some reason you wanted to have the same text on all buttons. But here it's defined directly on the buttons, so this value will be applied. No other properties are set directly on the buttons. We're done. The properties that were set lower in the hierarchy overrode the ones set higher up.

If you want to set a different value for, let's say, the **BackgroundColor** property on just one of the buttons, all you have to do is set it directly on that button:

```
...
<ContentPage ...>
    ...
        <FlexLayout
            ...
            <Button
                Text="Play Again" />
            <Button
                Text="Quit"
                BackgroundColor="Green" />
        </FlexLayout>
    </Grid>
</ContentPage>
```

This value will override the one defined on page level:

Styles in the Slugrace Project

Now that we know how to use styles in .NET MAUI, let's implement them in our Slugrace project. As we want the styles to be consistent across the entire app, we'll define most of the styles globally, in the **App.xaml** file. If a different style should be applied to a particular control, we'll define it lower in the hierarchy.

ContentPages

Let's start by setting the background color of the **ContentPage**s to a shade of yellow. We'll use hex values to set the color this time, not a named color.

First, remove the style we created for the buttons in the **App.xaml** file and set the **SettingsPage** in **AppShell.xaml** as the page you want to see when you run the app. Then add the following code to the app's resource dictionary:

```
...
<Application ...>
    <Application.Resources>
        <ResourceDictionary>
            <ResourceDictionary.MergedDictionaries>
                ...
            </ResourceDictionary.MergedDictionaries>

            <Style TargetType="ContentPage"
                   ApplyToDerivedTypes="True">
                <Setter Property="BackgroundColor" Value="#FFFBDB" />
            </Style>
        </ResourceDictionary>
    </Application.Resources>
</Application>
```

For this to work, we also have to set the **ApplyToDerivedTypes** property to **True**. Normally, this property is set to **True** to enable a style to be applied to controls that derive from a base type assigned to the **TargetType** property, but sometimes it must be used, like here, even if the style is to be applied to the base type.

Anyway, if you run the app now, the **SettingsPage** will look like this:

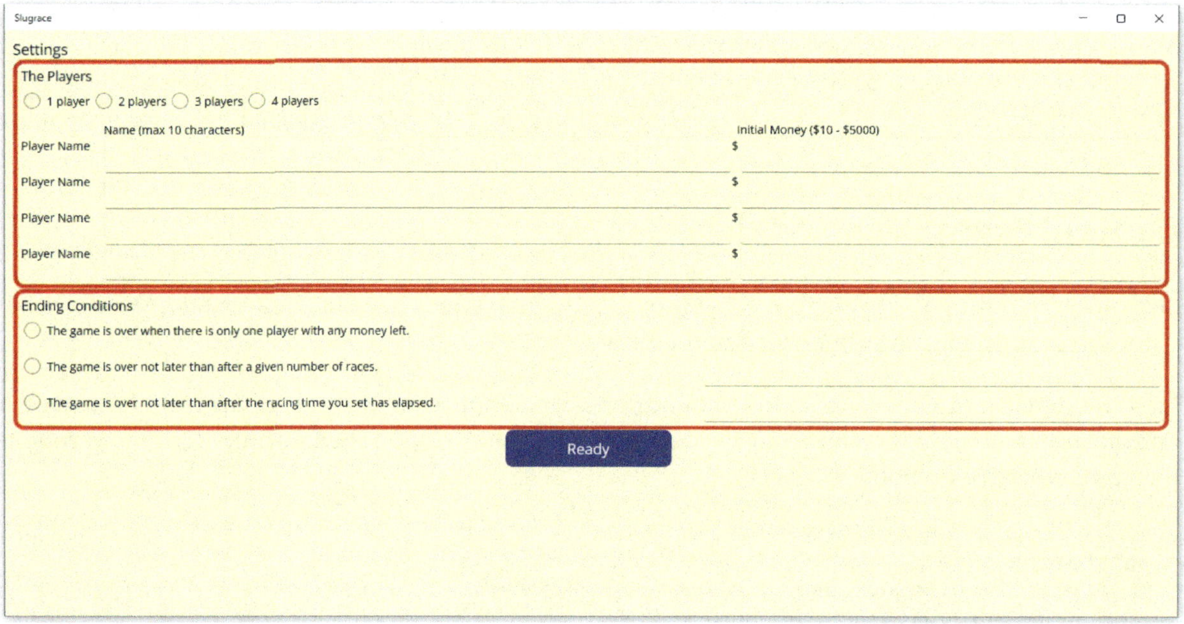

Let's not only define the styles that will be used in our app, but also let's take care of the other visual aspects. Assuming we're still in the **SettingsPage.xaml** file, you can see that the main elements on this page are placed inside a **VerticalStackLayout**, but I think a **Grid** would be a better choice. Fortunately, this is very easy to change. Make sure your code in the **SettingsPage.xaml** file looks like this:

```
<?xml version="1.0" encoding="utf-8" ?>
<ContentPage ...>
    <Grid
        Margin="10"
        RowDefinitions="50, 2.5*, 1.5*, 50">

        <!--the Settings label-->
        <Label
            Text="Settings"
            ... />

        <!--the Players panel-->
        <Border
            Grid.Row="1"
            Stroke="brown"
            ...
        </Border>

        <!--the Ending Conditions panel-->
        <Border
            Grid.Row="2"
            Stroke="brown"
            ...
        </Border>
```

```
        <!--the Ready button-->
        <Button
            Grid.Row="3"
            Text="Ready"
            ... />
    </Grid>
</ContentPage>
```

Now the page should look like so:

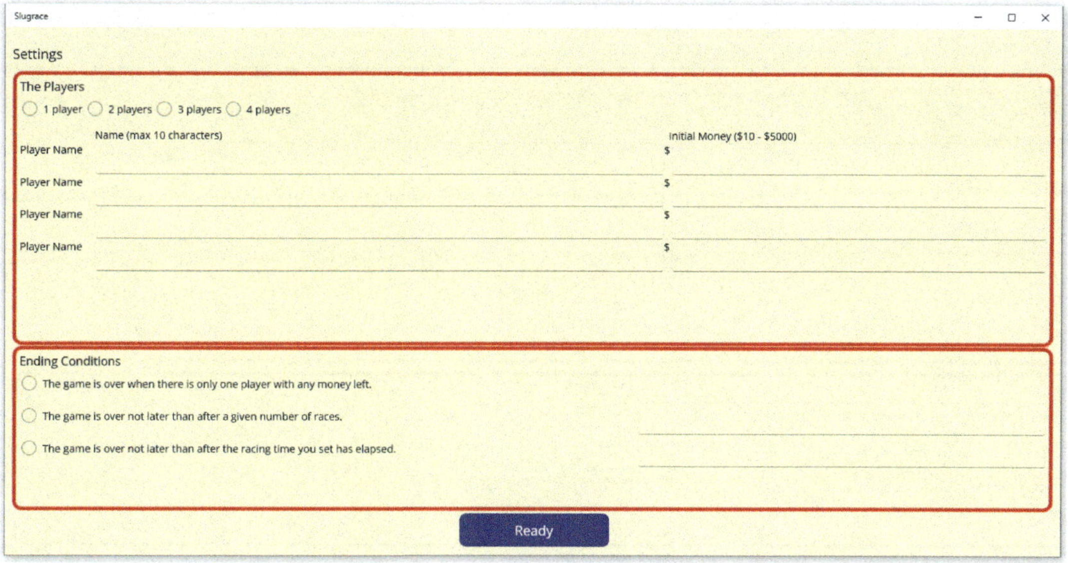

Borders

Next, let's define a style for the **Borders**. As there are **Borders** in the **RacePage** as well, let's put the code in the **App.xaml** file. An implicit style will do because we want to apply the style to all the **Borders**:

```
<?xml version = "1.0" encoding = "UTF-8" ?>
<Application ...>
    <Application.Resources>
        <ResourceDictionary>
            ...
            <Style TargetType="ContentPage"
                ...
            <Style TargetType="Border">
                <Setter Property="Stroke" Value="#331A00" />
                <Setter Property="StrokeShape" Value="RoundRectangle 10, 10, 10, 10" />
                <Setter Property="StrokeThickness" Value="5" />
                <Setter Property="Padding" Value="5" />
                <Setter Property="Margin" Value="5" />
            </Style>
        </ResourceDictionary>
    ...
```

As you can see, I used the same values as were originally set on the **Border** objects, except for the **Stroke** property, which is now set to a darker shade of brown. I also added the **Margin** property to add some room around the borders.

Also, remove all the properties except **Grid.Row**, **Grid.Column** and **Grid.ColumnSpan** from the **Border** objects in the **SettingsPage** and in the **RacePage**. Now the **SettingsPage** should look like this:

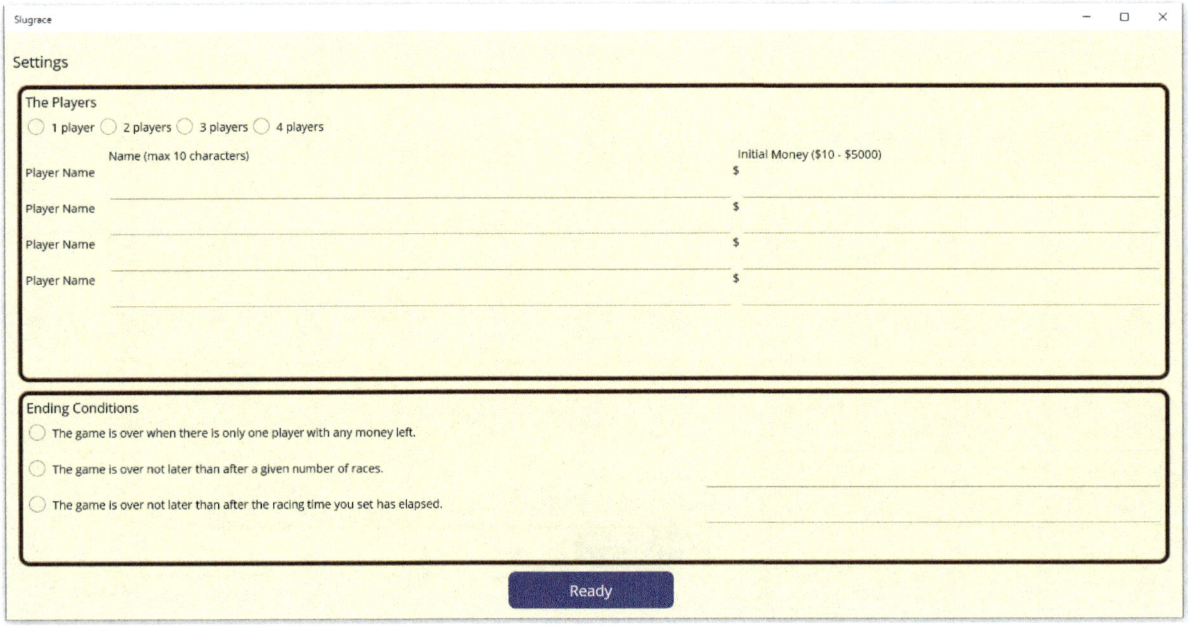

In the **RacePage** I added some padding directly on the **ContentPage** object:

```
<?xml version="1.0" encoding="utf-8" ?>
<ContentPage ...
             x:Class="Slugrace.Views.RacePage"
             Padding="5">
    <Grid
        ...
```

If you run the **RacePage**, you should see the following:

Buttons

The next element I'd like to style is the **Button**. There are buttons on each of the three pages, and they all (except the Sound button) should look the same, so, again, let's define a global style in **App.xaml**:

```
...
<Application ...>
    ...
            <Style TargetType="Border">
                ...
            </Style>

            <Style TargetType="Button">
                <Setter Property="BackgroundColor" Value="#520000" />
                <Setter Property="TextColor" Value="#FFCC1A" />
                <Setter Property="FontSize" Value="18" />
                <Setter Property="FontAttributes" Value="Bold" />
                <Setter Property="HorizontalOptions" Value="Center" />
                <Setter Property="VerticalOptions" Value="Center" />
                <Setter Property="WidthRequest" Value="250" />
                <Setter Property="HeightRequest" Value="50" />
            </Style>

        </ResourceDictionary>
    ...
```

Now remove all the **Button** styles from the three pages as well as the properties set directly on the buttons in all the pages and content views that were defined in the resource dictionary. An exception is the Sound button in the **RacePage**, which is supposed to be shorter and right-aligned. Besides, we want a note image to be displayed on this button instead of the text. Actually two note images will be needed, one to indicate the sound is on and another to indicate the sound is off. You can grab the images from the Github repository. Their names are **sound_on.png** and **sound_off.png**. Download them from there and place them in the **Images** folder like before. We can place an image on the button using the **ImageSource** property.

The sound button should be defined like this in the **RacePage**:

```
...
<ContentPage ...>
    ...
        <!--the buttons-->
        <VerticalStackLayout
            ...
            <Button
                Text="Instructions" />
            <Button
                ImageSource="sound_on.png"
                WidthRequest="125"
                HorizontalOptions="End" />
        </VerticalStackLayout>
        ...
```

Now the **RacePage** should look like this:

The buttons on the other pages look pretty much the same. Check it out.

The Other Controls

Next, let's take care of the other controls. I'm not going to discuss each and every detail because this would take too long. I'll just show you the code and will only discuss those things that need an explanation. On the way I'm also going to tweak some of the values I set before in order to adjust the general look to the new styles. I'm going to tweak some layouts and controls as well, so make sure you compare the version of code you have with the newer one, which is available on Github.

Some controls are used on multiple pages, so I'll define the styles for them globally. Those controls that are used only in one location, will be styled locally. I'll try to keep the code clean and simple.

So, let's first define some global styles in the **App.xaml** file:

```
...
<Application ...>
    ...
            <Style TargetType="Button">
                ...
            </Style>

            <Style x:Key="labelBaseStyle" TargetType="Label">
                <Setter Property="FontSize" Value="18" />
                <Setter Property="VerticalOptions" Value="Center" />
            </Style>

            <Style x:Key="labelSectionTitleStyle"
                   TargetType="Label"
                   BasedOn="{StaticResource labelBaseStyle}">
                <Setter Property="FontSize" Value="20" />
                <Setter Property="FontAttributes" Value="Bold" />
            </Style>

            <Style TargetType="Entry">
                <Setter Property="BackgroundColor" Value="White" />
                <Setter Property="FontSize" Value="18" />
                <Setter Property="CharacterSpacing" Value="1.5" />
                <Setter Property="HorizontalOptions" Value="Start" />
            </Style>

            <Style TargetType="RadioButton">
                <Setter Property="FontSize" Value="18" />
                <Setter Property="VerticalOptions" Value="Center" />
            </Style>

        </ResourceDictionary>
    </Application.Resources>
</Application>
```

Here we have a base style for the `Label` and another `Label` style that inherits from it. We don't need any more styles on app level because these are the two styles that occur over and over again throughout the entire application. There are some labels that are styled differently, but we'll define the styles for them locally.

Let's have a look at the pages and content views one by one where these styles are applied. You will find the full code base in my Github repository, so if something is not clear, make sure to check it out right there. Here's how the XAML code in the **SettingsPage.xaml** file ended up looking:

```
<?xml version="1.0" encoding="utf-8" ?>
<ContentPage xmlns="http://schemas.microsoft.com/dotnet/2021/maui"
             xmlns:x="http://schemas.microsoft.com/winfx/2009/xaml"
             xmlns:controls="clr-namespace:Slugrace.Controls"
             x:Class="Slugrace.Views.SettingsPage">

    <ContentPage.Resources>
        <Style TargetType="RadioButton">
            <Setter Property="Margin" Value="0, 0, 0, 10" />
        </Style>
    </ContentPage.Resources>

    <Grid
        Margin="10"
        RowDefinitions="40, 2.5*, 1.5*, 50">

        <!--the Settings label-->
        <Label
            Text="Settings"
            FontAttributes="Bold"
            FontSize="24" />

        <!--the Players panel-->
        <Border
            Grid.Row="1">

            <Grid>
                <Image
                    Source="all_slugs.png"
                    Aspect="Fill"
                    Opacity=".5"/>

                <VerticalStackLayout VerticalOptions="Center">
                    <Label
                        Text="The Players"
                        Style="{StaticResource labelSectionTitleStyle}" />
                    <HorizontalStackLayout>
                        <RadioButton
                            Content="1 player"
                            GroupName="players" />
                        <RadioButton
                            Content="2 players"
                            GroupName="players" />
                        <RadioButton
                            Content="3 players"
                            GroupName="players" />
                        <RadioButton
                            Content="4 players"
                            GroupName="players" />
                    </HorizontalStackLayout>
```

```
            <Grid
                RowDefinitions="*"
                ColumnDefinitions="150, 3*, 2*">

                <Label
                    Grid.Column="1"
                    Text="Name (max 10 characters)"
                    Style="{StaticResource labelBaseStyle}"/>
                <Label
                    Grid.Column="2"
                    Text="Initial Money ($10 - $5000)"
                    Style="{StaticResource labelBaseStyle}"/>
            </Grid>

            <VerticalStackLayout>
                <controls:PlayerSettings />
                <controls:PlayerSettings />
                <controls:PlayerSettings />
                <controls:PlayerSettings />
            </VerticalStackLayout>
        </VerticalStackLayout>

    </Grid>
</Border>

<!--the Ending Conditions panel-->
<Border
    Grid.Row="2">
    <VerticalStackLayout VerticalOptions="Center">
        <Label
            Text="Ending Conditions"
            Style="{StaticResource labelSectionTitleStyle}"
            Margin="0, 0, 0, 10"/>
        <Grid
            RowDefinitions="*, *, *"
            ColumnDefinitions="4*, 2*">
            <RadioButton
                Content="The game is over when there is only one player with any money left."
                GroupName="endingConditions" />
            <RadioButton
                Grid.Row="1"
                Content="The game is over not later than after a given number of races."
                GroupName="endingConditions" />
            <Entry
                Grid.Row="1"
                Grid.Column="1"
                WidthRequest="200"
                HorizontalOptions="Start" />
            <Entry
                Grid.Row="2"
                Grid.Column="1"
                WidthRequest="200"
                HorizontalOptions="Start" />
            <RadioButton
                Grid.Row="2"
                Content="The game is over not later than after the racing time you set has elapsed."
                GroupName="endingConditions" />
        </Grid>
    </VerticalStackLayout>
</Border>
```

```
        <!--the Ready button-->
        <Button
            Grid.Row="3"
            Text="Ready" />
    </Grid>
</ContentPage>
```

There's one thing worth mentioning here. I added a background image to the Players panel. To do that, I wrapped the **VerticalStackLayout** that was there in a **Grid** and added the image in the first cell. I set its **Aspect** property to **Fill** and **Opacity** to 0.5.

The **SettingsPage** contains four instances of the **PlayerSettings** content view. The **PlayerSettings.xaml** view should now look like so:

```
<?xml version="1.0" encoding="utf-8" ?>
<ContentView xmlns="http://schemas.microsoft.com/dotnet/2021/maui"
             xmlns:x="http://schemas.microsoft.com/winfx/2009/xaml"
             x:Class="Slugrace.Controls.PlayerSettings">

    <ContentView.Resources>
        <Style TargetType="Label"
               BasedOn="{StaticResource labelBaseStyle}" />
    </ContentView.Resources>

    <Grid
        RowDefinitions="*"
        ColumnDefinitions="150, 3*, 10, 2*"
        Margin="0, 10">
        <Label
            Text="Player Name" />
        <Entry
            Grid.Column="1"
            WidthRequest="300"/>
        <Label
            Grid.Column="2"
            Text="$" />
        <Entry
            Grid.Column="3"
            WidthRequest="250" />
    </Grid>
</ContentView>
```

In the **ResourceDictionary** of the view we defined a new style for the **Label** that inherits from **labelBaseStyle** and doesn't define any new properties. So, the new style is actually a copy of the original one. However, as this is an implicit style, we don't have to set the style individually on each and every label. There are also some minor changes in the values of some properties.

I also changed the color of the **Border** in the **App.xaml** file to match the color of the buttons. I also want to fill the circles in the radio buttons with that color, but for now we're quite limited as far as styling radio buttons is concerned. This is possible and we'll do it in the next chapter where we'll be talking about visual states and control templates. For now let's leave the radio buttons as is.

Now the **SettingsPage** should look like this:

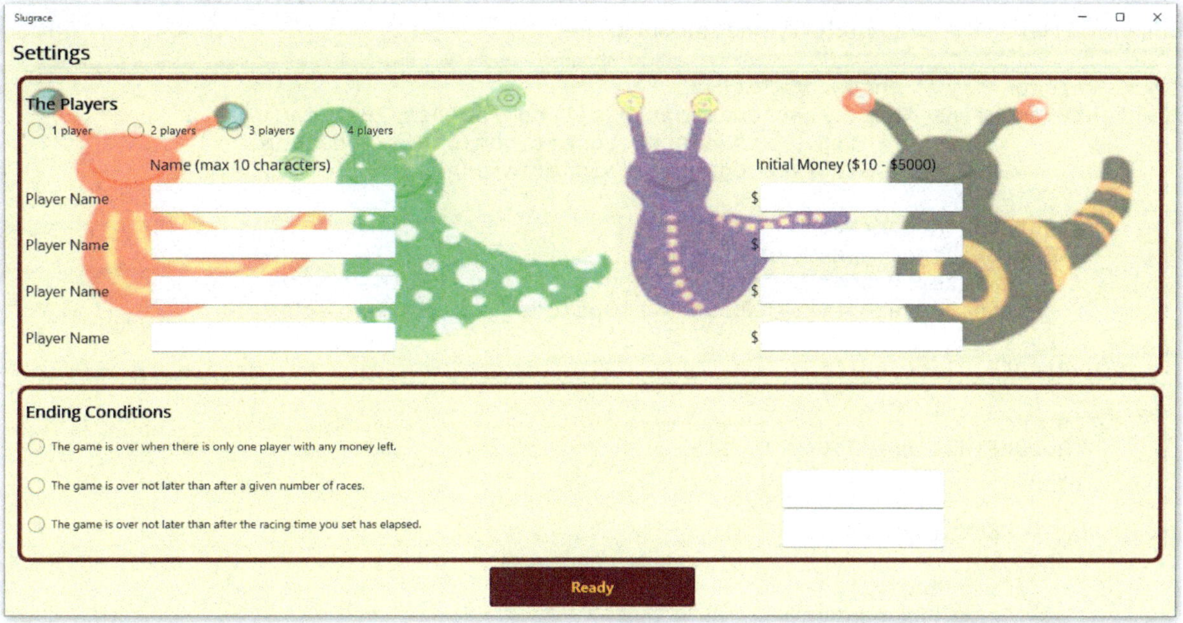

Next, let's set the **RacePage** as the starting page in **AppShell.xaml**. This page contains several content views, so let's have a look at the particular views one by one. The first three content views are very similar. The first one is **GameInfo**. Here's the code in the **GameInfo.xaml** file:

```
<?xml version="1.0" encoding="utf-8" ?>
<ContentView xmlns="http://schemas.microsoft.com/dotnet/2021/maui"
             xmlns:x="http://schemas.microsoft.com/winfx/2009/xaml"
             x:Class="Slugrace.Controls.GameInfo">

    <ContentView.Resources>
        <Style TargetType="Label" BasedOn="{StaticResource labelBaseStyle}" />
    </ContentView.Resources>

    <Grid
        RowDefinitions="*, *, *, *, *"
        ColumnDefinitions="3*, *">
        <Label
            Text="Game Info"
            Style="{StaticResource labelSectionTitleStyle}" />
        <Label
            ...
```

Again, I copied the style in the **ResourceDictionary** and so don't have to set the style individually on each label. The code in the **SlugsStats.xaml** and **PlayersStats.xaml** files looks very similar. In the

SlugInfo content view there are white labels, but I didn't create a style for them. The properties are still set directly on the objects.

I made some minor changes in the **WinnerInfo** content view. I also defined a style for the labels in this view. Here's the code in the **WinnerInfo.xaml** file:

```
<?xml version="1.0" encoding="utf-8" ?>
<ContentView xmlns="http://schemas.microsoft.com/dotnet/2021/maui"
             xmlns:x="http://schemas.microsoft.com/winfx/2009/xaml"
             x:Class="Slugrace.Controls.WinnerInfo">

    <ContentView.Resources>
        <Style TargetType="Label">
            <Setter Property="FontAttributes" Value="Bold" />
            <Setter Property="HorizontalOptions" Value="Center" />
        </Style>
    </ContentView.Resources>

    <Grid
        RowDefinitions=".6*, *, 3*">
        <Label
            Text="The winner is"
            FontSize="28" />
        <Label
            Grid.Row="1"
            Text="Speedster"
            FontSize="36" />
        <Image
            Grid.Row="2"
            Source="speedster.png" />
    </Grid>
</ContentView>
```

In the **Bets** content view I created a style for the sliders. The style is defined for the content view, so it's also available for its children all the way down in the hierarchy. The sliders are actually inside the **PlayerBet** views. The same works for the labels. I created a copy of **labelBaseStyle**, which will be used on the labels in the **PlayerBet** views. Here's the code of the **Bets.xaml** file:

```
<?xml version="1.0" encoding="utf-8" ?>
<ContentView xmlns="http://schemas.microsoft.com/dotnet/2021/maui"
             xmlns:x="http://schemas.microsoft.com/winfx/2009/xaml"
             xmlns:controls="clr-namespace:Slugrace.Controls"
             x:Class="Slugrace.Controls.Bets">

    <ContentView.Resources>
        <Style TargetType="Label" BasedOn="{StaticResource labelBaseStyle}" />
        <Style TargetType="Slider">
            <Setter Property="ThumbColor" Value="#520000" />
            <Setter Property="MinimumTrackColor" Value="#520000" />
        </Style>
    </ContentView.Resources>
```

```
    <Grid
        RowDefinitions="*, 4*, *">
        <Label
            Text="Bets"
            Style="{StaticResource labelSectionTitleStyle}" />
        <VerticalStackLayout
            Grid.Row="1">
            <controls:PlayerBet />
            <controls:PlayerBet />
            <controls:PlayerBet />
            <controls:PlayerBet />
        </VerticalStackLayout>

        <Button
            Grid.Row="2"
            Text="Go"
            Margin="0, 0, 0, 5"/>
    </Grid>
</ContentView>
```

The **Results** content view is styled in a similar way. If you now run the app, the **RacePage** will look like so:

As far as the **GameOverPage** is concerned, I created an implicit style for the labels there, with the **FontSize** property overridden on the first label:

```
<?xml version="1.0" encoding="utf-8" ?>
<ContentPage xmlns="http://schemas.microsoft.com/dotnet/2021/maui"
             xmlns:x="http://schemas.microsoft.com/winfx/2009/xaml"
             x:Class="Slugrace.Views.GameOverPage">

    <ContentPage.Resources>
        <Style TargetType="Label">
            <Setter Property="FontAttributes" Value="Bold" />
```

```
            <Setter Property="HorizontalOptions" Value="Center" />
            <Setter Property="FontSize" Value="40" />
        </Style>

    </ContentPage.Resources>

    <Grid
        RowDefinitions="2*, 2*, 2*, *">
        <Label
            Text="Game Over"
            FontSize="120" />
        <Label
            Grid.Row="1"
            Text="There's only one player with any money left." />
        <Label
            Grid.Row="2"
            Text="The winner is Player 2, having started at $1000, winning at $396." />
        <FlexLayout
            Grid.Row="3"
            JustifyContent="SpaceEvenly">

            <Button
                Text="Play Again" />
            <Button
                Text="Quit" />
        </FlexLayout>
    </Grid>
</ContentPage>
```

As you can see, the buttons are spaced a bit differently now. Here's the effect:

We're almost, although not entirely, done with styles. As I mentioned before, in the next chapter we'll be talking about visual states and control templates.

Chapter 10 - Visual States and Control Templates

code: https://github.com/prospero-apps/Slugrace/tree/chapter10

In the previous chapter we created styles and applied them to the particular elements in our app. We aren't completely done with the styles yet, though.

First of all, some controls, even if they look OK, don't look exactly the way we want. Here I mean the radio buttons, for example. What if I wanted to fill the circles with a color or modify another aspect of their visual representation?

Secondly, some controls should change their visual appearance if something happens, like here - there are two entries in the **SettingsPage**. The first one got focus and changed slightly its visual representation:

But what if you wanted it to change in a different way? Or what if you wanted to disable this change? Or what if you wanted to change the appearance when you hover your mouse cursor over the entry?

In our app, as of now, if you hover your mouse over a button, or even if you click the button, there is no difference, it looks the same. For some controls this functionality has been implemented, to a certain extent, by defining a couple visual states in the **Styles.xaml** file. But we need to define more visual states.

So, let's try to address these two kinds of issues.

Visual States Terminology

Controls can be in different states. A button can be disabled or pressed, a radio button can be checked or unchecked, a switch can be on or off, and so on. In .NET MAUI we use **visual states** to cater to it. Visual states come with their own terminology, let's start with that.

Visual states can be defined on a particular view or in a style. This determines their scope. But how do we define visual states in the first place?

Well, visual states are handled by the **Visual State Manager**. They are placed inside **visual state groups**. There may be one or more such groups and they are identified by name, just like the visual states themselves. The Visual State Manager defines a visual state group called **`CommonStates`** that contains the most frequently used states. The **`CommonStates`** group contains the following visual states:

- **`Normal`**,

- **`Disabled`**,

- **`Focused`**,

- **`PointerOver`**

These states are supported by all types that derive from **`VisualElement`**. What you should keep in mind is that all states within one visual state group are mutually exclusive, so if the current state changes to, let's say, **`Focused`**, all the settings for the previous state are cleared.

You get all the above visual states in the **`CommonStates`** group out of the box, but you can define your own groups with other visual states, which we are going to do in a while. But first let's see how it works on an example. We're going to use just the states from the **`CommonStates`** group for now.

To set the visual states we use **`Setter`** objects that are grouped inside the **`Setters`** property of the **`VisualState`** object.

CommonStates

Without further ado, let's demonstrate how visual states can be implemented and how they work on the example of the **`Button`** view. At first, we'll set the visual states on one particular view, which is the Ready button in the **`SettingsPage`**, and then we'll move it to a style so that it can be used by all the buttons in the app. Here's the **SettingsPage.xaml** file:

```
...
<ContentPage ...>
    ...
        <!--the Ready button-->
        <Button
            Grid.Row="3"
            Text="Ready">

            <VisualStateManager.VisualStateGroups>
                <VisualStateGroup x:Name="CommonStates">
```

```
                    <VisualState x:Name="Normal" />

                    <VisualState x:Name="Disabled">
                        <VisualState.Setters>
                            <Setter Property="BackgroundColor" Value="Gray" />
                        </VisualState.Setters>
                    </VisualState>

                    <VisualState x:Name="PointerOver">
                        <VisualState.Setters>
                            <Setter Property="Scale" Value="1.1" />
                            <Setter Property="Rotation" Value="180" />
                            <Setter Property="FontSize" Value="30" />
                            <Setter Property="TextColor" Value="White" />
                        </VisualState.Setters>
                    </VisualState>
                </VisualStateGroup>
            </VisualStateManager.VisualStateGroups>

        </Button>
    </Grid>
</ContentPage>
```

As you can see, we defined three visual states for the button. The first one, **Normal**, is an empty state. We must still include it because otherwise the button wouldn't revert from another state to its **Normal** state. For the **Disabled** state we defined one **Setter**. In order to see this state in action, we would have to make the button disabled. You can do it manually by setting its **IsEnabled** property to **False**:

```
<?xml version="1.0" encoding="utf-8" ?>
<ContentPage ...>
    ...
        <!--the Ready button-->
        <Button
            Grid.Row="3"
            Text="Ready"
            IsEnabled="False">
            <VisualStateManager.VisualStateGroups>
                ...
```

If you now run the app, the button will be in the **Disabled** state and its background color will change:

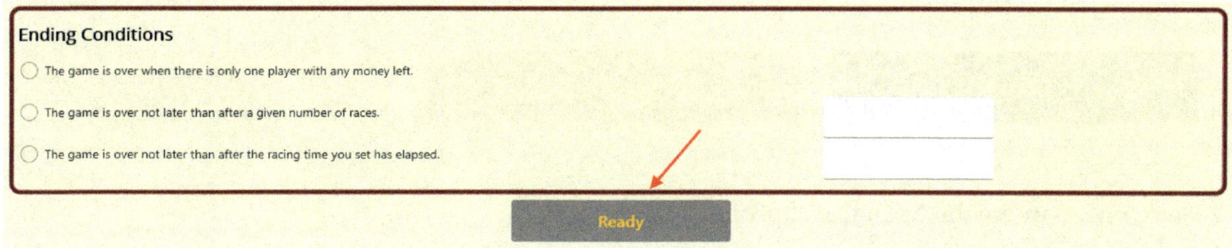

Remove the **IsEnabled** property from the code. And now let's test the third state we defined, **PointerOver**. Just hover your mouse pointer over the button and you should notice that the four properties defined in the **Setters** property have changed:

Well, maybe we don't want the changes to be so extreme, so let's modify the code a bit. We'll just change the background color to a slightly brighter shade for the **PointerOver** state and we'll reduce the button's opacity for the **Disabled** state:

```
...
        <!--the Ready button-->
        <Button
            ...
            <VisualStateManager.VisualStateGroups>
                <VisualStateGroup x:Name="CommonStates">
                    <VisualState x:Name="Normal" />

                    <VisualState x:Name="Disabled">
                        <VisualState.Setters>
                            <Setter Property="Opacity" Value=".3" />
                        </VisualState.Setters>
                    </VisualState>

                    <VisualState x:Name="PointerOver">
                        <VisualState.Setters>
                            <Setter Property="BackgroundColor" Value="#891C20" />
                        </VisualState.Setters>
                    ...
```

Hover your mouse cursor over the button, then temporarily disable it by setting the **IsEnabled** property like you did before and compare the three states:

When done, remove the **IsEnabled** property again.

Well, we just handled the visual states of the Ready button in the **SettingsPage**, but what about the other buttons? Can we define visual states that will be shared by all the buttons? Well, we can easily accomplish this by moving the visual states to a style.

Visual States in a Style

As you know, we can define styles on different levels. We usually define them on page level or globally in the **App.xaml** file. As we want the visual states to apply to all the buttons throughout the entire app, let's define them in a global style. We already have an implicit style there that applies to all buttons:

```
...
<Application ...>
    <Application.Resources>
        <ResourceDictionary>
            ...
            <Style TargetType="Button">
                <Setter Property="BackgroundColor" Value="#520000" />
                <Setter Property="TextColor" Value="#FFCC1A" />
                <Setter Property="FontSize" Value="18" />
                <Setter Property="FontAttributes" Value="Bold" />
                <Setter Property="HorizontalOptions" Value="Center" />
                <Setter Property="VerticalOptions" Value="Center" />
                <Setter Property="WidthRequest" Value="250" />
                <Setter Property="HeightRequest" Value="50" />
            </Style>

            <Style x:Key="labelBaseStyle" TargetType="Label">
                ...
```

To add visual states to this style, we have to set the **VisualStateManager.VisualStateGroups** property, which we can do by adding a new **Setter** object. The **VisualStateGroups** property is of type **VisualStateGroupList**. As the **Value** property of the **Setter** object is the content property, we can define the **VisualStateGroupList** object as its child. So, let's move the visual states code to the style:

```
...
<Application ...>
    <Application.Resources>
        <ResourceDictionary>
            ...
            <Style TargetType="Button">
                ...
                <Setter Property="HeightRequest" Value="50" />
                <Setter Property="VisualStateManager.VisualStateGroups">
                    <VisualStateGroupList>
                        <VisualStateGroup x:Name="CommonStates">
                            <VisualState x:Name="Normal" />

                            <VisualState x:Name="Disabled">
```

```
                                <VisualState.Setters>
                                    <Setter Property="Opacity" Value=".3" />
                                </VisualState.Setters>
                            </VisualState>

                            <VisualState x:Name="PointerOver">
                                <VisualState.Setters>
                                    <Setter Property="BackgroundColor" Value="#891C20" />
                                </VisualState.Setters>
                            </VisualState>
                        </VisualStateGroup>
                    </VisualStateGroupList>
                </Setter>
            </Style>

            <Style x:Key="labelBaseStyle" TargetType="Label">
                ...
```

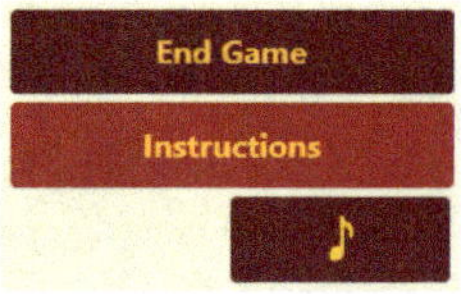

Don't forget to remove this code from the Ready button in the **SettingsPage**. It should be defined only once, in the style. If you run the app now, it will work the same. But this time it should work for all the buttons. Let's set the **RacePage** as the starting page and check it out.

As you can see, it works. We're hovering the mouse pointer over the Instructions button. But how do we set the visual state for when the button is pressed? Turns out, there are control-specific states that we can use.

Specific Visual States

The visual states described above, like **Normal**, **Disabled**, **Focused** and **PointerOver** can be defined for any **VisualElement**. But there are also visual states specific to just one particular state. For example, there's the **IsChecked** visual state for the **CheckBox**, there's **On** and **Off** for the **Switch**, **Selected** for the **CollectionView**, or **Checked** and **Unchecked** for the **RadionButton**. We do have some radio buttons in our app and we will use visual states with them, but first let's take care of the **Button** objects. There's the **Pressed** visual state that we are going to implement.

So, let's add the **Pressed** visual state to the **CommonStates** group in the **App.xaml** file:

```
...
<Application ...>
    ...
            <Style TargetType="Button">
                ...
                <Setter Property="VisualStateManager.VisualStateGroups">
                    <VisualStateGroupList>
                        <VisualStateGroup x:Name="CommonStates">
                            ...
                            <VisualState x:Name="PointerOver">
                                ...
```

```
                        <VisualState x:Name="Pressed">
                            <VisualState.Setters>
                                <Setter Property="Scale" Value=".98" />
                                <Setter Property="BackgroundColor" Value="#891C20" />
                            </VisualState.Setters>
                        </VisualState>
                    </VisualStateGroup>
                ...
```

If you now press the button, it will both shrink and change color.

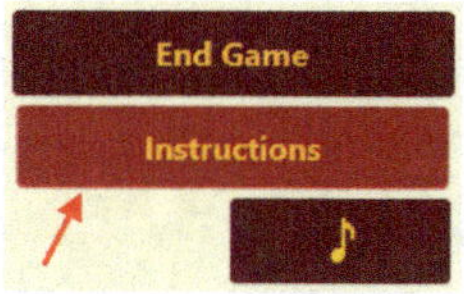

We're done with the **Button**. Next, let's say we want to change the appearance of the radio buttons. Well, it's not that easy using just styles. But don't worry, this is where visual states and control templates come to the rescue.

ControlTemplates

Control templates is a tool that enables you to define the visual structure of controls. We're not going to discuss them here in great detail, but we'll use them to modify the appearance of our radio buttons. We'll do it in **App.xaml** because we want uniform radio buttons all throughout the app.

We want the circles of the radio buttons to be filled with the same shade of red or brown - depending on how you perceive this color - as the buttons in **Normal** state. When checked, a yellow circle will appear inside. It's always easier to understand if you see it, so this is how the radio buttons should look:

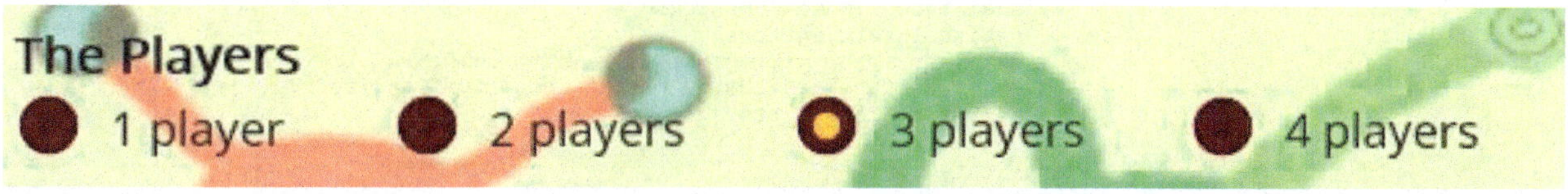

These are the radio buttons in the Players section of the **SettingsPage**. As you can see, I also added some space between the particular radio buttons. The third button is checked, so a little yellow circle can be seen in it. By the way, it's the same shade of yellow as the text color on the buttons.

Now, how does it look in code? We're going to modify the part of the **App.xaml** file where the style for the **RadioButton** is defined, which is right after the definition of the **Entry** style. The code should look like this:

```
...
<Application ...>
    <Application.Resources>
        <ResourceDictionary>
            ...
            <Style TargetType="Entry">
                ...
```

```
            <ControlTemplate x:Key="RadioButtonTemplate">
                <FlexLayout JustifyContent="Start">
                    <FlexLayout.Resources>
                        <Style TargetType="Label">
                            <Setter Property="FontSize" Value="18"/>
                            <Setter Property="VerticalOptions" Value="Center" />
                            <Setter Property="Margin" Value="0, 0, 40, 0" />
                        </Style>
                    </FlexLayout.Resources>
                    <Grid
                        Margin="0, 0, 5, 0"
                        WidthRequest="28"
                        HeightRequest="28"
                        HorizontalOptions="Center"
                        VerticalOptions="Center">
                        <Ellipse
                                Fill="#520000"
                                HeightRequest="24"
                                WidthRequest="24"
                                HorizontalOptions="Center"
                                VerticalOptions="Center" />
                        <Ellipse
                                x:Name="check"
                                Fill="#FFCC1A"
                                Background="Transparent"
                                HeightRequest="12"
                                WidthRequest="12"
                                HorizontalOptions="Center"
                                VerticalOptions="Center" />
                    </Grid>
                    <ContentPresenter />

                    <VisualStateManager.VisualStateGroups>
                        <VisualStateGroupList>
                            <VisualStateGroup x:Name="CommonStates">
                                <VisualState x:Name="Checked">
                                    <VisualState.Setters>
                                        <Setter TargetName="check" Property="Opacity" Value="1" />
                                    </VisualState.Setters>
                                </VisualState>
                                <VisualState x:Name="Unchecked">
                                    <VisualState.Setters>
                                        <Setter TargetName="check" Property="BackgroundColor" Value="#F3F2F1" />
                                        <Setter TargetName="check" Property="Opacity" Value="0" />
                                    </VisualState.Setters>
                                </VisualState>
                            </VisualStateGroup>
                        </VisualStateGroupList>
                    </VisualStateManager.VisualStateGroups>

                </FlexLayout>
            </ControlTemplate>

            <Style TargetType="RadioButton">
                <Setter Property="ControlTemplate" Value="{StaticResource RadioButtonTemplate}" />
            </Style>

        </ResourceDictionary>
    </Application.Resources>
</Application>
```

It's pretty daunting, so let's analyze it piece by piece. At first we define a **ContentTemplate** and give it a name, which in this case is **RadioButtonTemplate**. Then we define the visual representation of the control using XAML markup. In our case the template will be structured as a **FlexLayout** with a **Grid** inside, which in turn will contain two **Ellipse** objects. **Ellipse** is a type that you can use to draw an ellipse and we'll use it to draw the bigger outer circle and the smaller inner circle. The names of the properties inside the **Grid** and the two ellipses are self-explanatory.

We also define a style that will be applied to all labels inside our radio button. We only have one - this is the content of the radio button, which you can see next to it. This content will be placed inside the **ContentPresenter** object. If you put the object before the **Grid**, the label would precede the circle, but we want it to follow it, hence the position of the **ContentPresenter** after the **Grid**.

Next, we define two visual states for the **RadioButton**, **Checked** and **Unchecked**. We use the **Opacity** property to make the inner circle fully opaque in the **Checked** state and fully transparent in the **Unchecked** state.

We also use the **TargetName** property in the code above to reference the smaller **Ellipse** object. If you look at the second ellipse, you'll see that we set its name to **check**. This very name is used here in the **Setter** object.

Finally, we assign the **RadioButtonTemplate** to the **ControlTemplate** property in the style for the **RadioButton**. I also removed the two **Setter** objects for the content label (setting the **FontSize** and **VerticalOptions** properties) because they are now defined inside the control template.

If you now run the app, all radio buttons will look the same. We already saw the top row of radio buttons in the **SettingsPage**. Let's try out the radio buttons in the Bets panel of the **RacePage**:

At this moment we can only select one radio button in total, which isn't the behavior we want, but don't worry, we're going to fix this in due time.

The states we've been using so far were the common states that we can define for all or some of the controls. But we can also create custom visual states. This is what we're going to do next.

Custom Visual States

As I just mentioned, we can create custom visual states. I'll demonstrate it on the example of the entries in the Players section of the **SettingsPage**. We're going to use visual states for user input validation.

But before we start, let's slightly modify the style defined for the **Entry** control in **App.xaml**. We want the text to be in bold type and the placeholder text to be a nice shade of gray:

```
...
<Application ...>
    <...
            <Style TargetType="Entry">
                <Setter Property="BackgroundColor" Value="White" />
                <Setter Property="FontSize" Value="18" />
                <Setter Property="CharacterSpacing" Value="1.5" />
                <Setter Property="HorizontalOptions" Value="Start" />
                <Setter Property="FontAttributes" Value="Bold" />
                <Setter Property="PlaceholderColor" Value="#A0A0A0" />
            </Style>
            ...
```

And now let's create the visual states for our **Entry** controls. As you look at the code of the **SettingsPage**, you'll see that the entries are not used directly there. They are inside the **PlayerSettings** content view that we created before. So, let's define the visual states inside this content view.

We're going to create two custom states for the entries where the names of the players will be entered: **NameValid** and **NameInvalid**. They will be inside a visual state group called **NameValidityStates**.

For the entries where the initial amount of money each player starts the game with is entered, we'll create a visual state group called **InitialMoneyValidityStates** with three visual states: **InitialMoneyValid**, **InitialMoneyInvalid** and **InitialMoneyEmpty**.

Let's have a look at the code and then we'll discuss what's new. So, here's the code in the **PlayerSettings.xaml** file:

```
...
<ContentView ...>
    ...
    <Grid
        ...
        <Entry
            x:Name="nameEntry"
            Grid.Column="1"
            WidthRequest="300"
            TextChanged="OnNameTextChanged">
            <VisualStateManager.VisualStateGroups>
                <VisualStateGroup x:Name="NameValidityStates">
                    <VisualState x:Name="NameValid">
                        <VisualState.Setters>
                            <Setter Property="BackgroundColor" Value="White" />
                            <Setter Property="TextColor" Value="Black" />
                        </VisualState.Setters>
                    </VisualState>
                    <VisualState x:Name="NameInvalid">
                        <VisualState.Setters>
                            <Setter Property="BackgroundColor" Value="#FFDDEE" />
```

```
                        <Setter Property="TextColor" Value="Red" />
                    </VisualState.Setters>
                </VisualState>
            </VisualStateGroup>
        </VisualStateManager.VisualStateGroups>
    </Entry>
    <Label
        .../>
    <Entry
        x:Name="initialMoneyEntry"
        Placeholder="1000"
        Grid.Column="3"
        WidthRequest="250"
        TextChanged="OnInitialMoneyTextChanged">
        <VisualStateManager.VisualStateGroups>
            <VisualStateGroup x:Name="InitialMoneyValidityStates">
                <VisualState x:Name="InitialMoneyValid">
                    <VisualState.Setters>
                        <Setter Property="BackgroundColor" Value="White" />
                        <Setter Property="TextColor" Value="Black" />
                    </VisualState.Setters>
                </VisualState>
                <VisualState x:Name="InitialMoneyInvalid">
                    <VisualState.Setters>
                        <Setter Property="BackgroundColor" Value="#FFDDEE" />
                        <Setter Property="TextColor" Value="Red" />
                    </VisualState.Setters>
                </VisualState>
                <VisualState x:Name="InitialMoneyEmpty">
                    <VisualState.Setters>
                        <Setter Property="BackgroundColor" Value="White" />
                        <Setter Property="TextColor" Value="White" />
                        <Setter Property="FontAttributes" Value="None" />
                    </VisualState.Setters>
                </VisualState>
            </VisualStateGroup>
        </VisualStateManager.VisualStateGroups>
    </Entry>
...
```

As you can see, we gave names to the entries because we'll have to reference them in the code-behind. We also added the **TextChanged** events that we'll also handle in the code-behind. We're going to validate the text as it's being entered, so these events are necessary. Additionally, I set the **Placeholder** property to 1000, which seems a reasonable initial money amount for the game. And then we have the visual states with the custom names we mentioned above. There's nothing special or new about them.

Now, the states should change depending on the current text in the entries. This functionality is handled in the code-behind.

To use a state, we must call the static **VisualStateManager.GoToState** method. This method takes two arguments: the name of the object on which the state should be set and the state itself. Have a look yourself, here's the code in the **PlayerSettings.xaml.cs** file:

```
namespace Slugrace.Controls;

public partial class PlayerSettings : ContentView
{
    public PlayerSettings()
    {
        InitializeComponent();
        GoToNameState(true);
        GoToInitialMoneyState(true, true);
    }

    private void OnNameTextChanged(object sender, TextChangedEventArgs e)
    {
        bool nameValid = e.NewTextValue.Length <= 10;
        GoToNameState(nameValid);
    }

    private void OnInitialMoneyTextChanged(object sender, TextChangedEventArgs e)
    {
        bool isNumeric = int.TryParse(e.NewTextValue, out int enteredInitialMoney);
        bool isInRange = isNumeric && enteredInitialMoney >= 10 && enteredInitialMoney <= 5000;
        bool initialMoneyValid = isInRange;
        bool initialMoneyEmpty = e.NewTextValue == string.Empty;
        GoToInitialMoneyState(initialMoneyValid, initialMoneyEmpty);
    }

    void GoToNameState(bool nameValid)
    {
        string visualState = nameValid ? "NameValid" : "NameInvalid";
        VisualStateManager.GoToState(nameEntry, visualState);
    }

    void GoToInitialMoneyState(bool initialMoneyValid, bool initialMoneyEmpty)
    {
        string visualState = initialMoneyValid ? "InitialMoneyValid" : "InitialMoneyInvalid";

        if (initialMoneyEmpty)
        {
            visualState = "InitialMoneyEmpty";
        }

        VisualStateManager.GoToState(initialMoneyEntry, visualState);
    }
}
```

As you can see, we created two methods here, **GoToNameState** and **GoToInitialMoneyState**. Each of the methods calls the static **VisualStateManager.GoToState** method on the respective **Entry** object (referenced by name) and passes to it as the second argument the appropriate visual state.

As you type the players' names and initial amounts of money in the entries, the **OnNameTextChanged** and **OnInitialMoneyTextChanged** methods are fired and the input is validated.

Name validation is very simple: The name is valid as long as it's not longer than 10 characters. The initial money amount is valid if a numeric value from a specified range is entered. We treated the case when the input is empty separately. This enables us to define three states for the entries.

And now let's see how it works. Run your app with the **SettingsPage** set as the starting page and enter all kinds of text in the entries. Some values should be valid, some should be invalid and one of the initial money entries should be empty. Here's what I got:

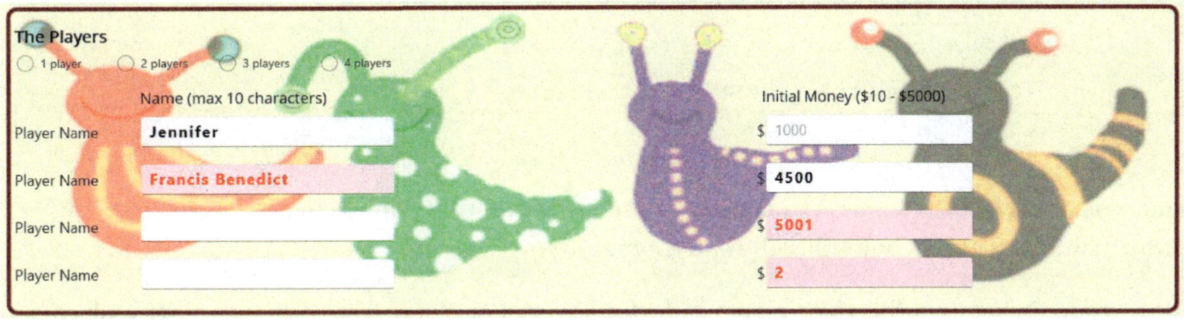

The first name entry has valid input, so it's in the **NameValid** visual state. The name in the second one is too long, so the entry is in the **NameInvalid** state.

The first initial money entry is empty, so it's in the **InitialMoneyEmpty** state. The second one has valid input, so it's in the **InitialMoneyValid** state. The third and fourth entries have input from outside the range (which is 10-5000), so they're in the **InitialMoneyInvalid** state.

In a similar way, we can define custom visual states for the other entries in our app. We also have two **Entry** object in the Ending Conditions section of the **SettingsPage** and four in the Bets panel in the **RacePage**. Let's take care of the former first. But, wait a minute... If we use entries in multiple places, why not move the visual states to the **App.xaml** file. All entries will be able to use three visual states: **Valid**, **Invalid** and **Empty**. So, the code in the **App.xaml** file should look like so:

```
<?xml version = "1.0" encoding = "UTF-8" ?>
<Application ...>
    ...
            <Style TargetType="Entry">
                ...
                <Setter Property="PlaceholderColor" Value="#A0A0A0" />
                <Setter Property="VisualStateManager.VisualStateGroups">
                    <VisualStateGroupList>
                        <VisualStateGroup x:Name="ValidityStates">
                            <VisualState x:Name="Valid">
                                <VisualState.Setters>
                                    <Setter Property="BackgroundColor" Value="White" />
                                    <Setter Property="TextColor" Value="Black" />
                                </VisualState.Setters>
                            </VisualState>
                            <VisualState x:Name="Invalid">
                                <VisualState.Setters>
                                    <Setter Property="BackgroundColor" Value="#FFDDEE" />
                                    <Setter Property="TextColor" Value="Red" />
```

```
                    </VisualState.Setters>
                </VisualState>
                <VisualState x:Name="Empty">
                    <VisualState.Setters>
                        <Setter Property="BackgroundColor" Value="White" />
                        <Setter Property="TextColor" Value="White" />
                        <Setter Property="FontAttributes" Value="None" />
                    </VisualState.Setters>
                </VisualState>
            </VisualStateGroup>
        </VisualStateGroupList>
    </Setter>
</Style>

<ControlTemplate x:Key="RadioButtonTemplate">
    ...
```

Here, the names of the states are more general than before because they're not associated with any particular **Entry** object, but rather the entire type.

Now you can remove the code responsible for the visual states from the two **Entry** objects in **PlayerSettings.xaml**. But leave the names of the entries and the **TextChanged** events. As the states for particular entries will require different conditions to be met, we'll implement the state change logic in the code-behind files. Let's modify the code in the **PlayerSettings.xaml.cs** file first. It's the same code as before except for the names of the visual states:

```
...
public partial class PlayerSettings : ContentView
{
    ...
    void GoToNameState(bool nameValid)
    {
        string visualState = nameValid ? "Valid" : "Invalid";
        VisualStateManager.GoToState(nameEntry, visualState);
    }

    void GoToInitialMoneyState(bool initialMoneyValid, bool initialMoneyEmpty)
    {
        string visualState = initialMoneyValid ? "Valid" : "Invalid";

        if (initialMoneyEmpty)
        {
            visualState = "Empty";
        }

        VisualStateManager.GoToState(initialMoneyEntry, visualState);
    }
}
```

The validation should work as before. But don't take my word for it.

How about the other entries? Well, the other entries should all accept numeric input in a certain range, so, if we implement the code like before we'll get a lot of almost identical repetitive code scattered all around the code-behind files. In order to keep our code dry (DRY = Don't Repeat Yourself - often used to describe code that is not repetitive), we'll create a static class with a helper method that we can use to validate the user input in the entries. So, in the root of the project add a class and name it **Helpers**. Make it static and add a method to it. This static method could be named **ValidateNumericInputAndSetState** and it should combine the functionality of the **OnInitialMoneyTextChanged** method and the **GoToInitialMoneyState** method defined in the **PlayerSettings.xaml.cs** file. Here's the **Helpers** class:

```
namespace Slugrace;

public static class Helpers
{
    public static void ValidateNumericInputAndSetState(
        string enteredText,
        int min,
        int max,
        VisualElement control)
    {
        bool isNumeric = int.TryParse(enteredText, out int numericValue);
        bool isInRange = isNumeric && numericValue >= min && numericValue <= max;
        bool isValid = isInRange;
        bool isEmpty = enteredText == string.Empty;

        string visualState = isValid ? "Valid" : "Invalid";

        if (isEmpty)
        {
            visualState = "Empty";
        }

        VisualStateManager.GoToState(control, visualState);
    }
}
```

As you can see, we pass all the data it needs as arguments. We have the text entered in the entry, the minimum and maximum limits of the range we want to check, and the control whose input should be validated.

With that in place, we can modify the code in **PlayerSettings.xaml.cs**:

```
...
public partial class PlayerSettings : ContentView
{
    public PlayerSettings()
    {
        InitializeComponent();
        GoToNameState(true);
        VisualStateManager.GoToState(initialMoneyEntry, "Empty");
    }
```

```
private void OnNameTextChanged(object sender, TextChangedEventArgs e)
...
private void OnInitialMoneyTextChanged(object sender, TextChangedEventArgs e)
{
    Helpers.ValidateNumericInputAndSetState(e.NewTextValue, 10, 5000, initialMoneyEntry);
}

void GoToNameState(bool nameValid)
...
```

So, we use the **Helpers.ValidateNumericInputAndSetState** method here. We got rid of the **GoToInitialMoneyState** method. In order for the initial money entries to be in the **Empty** state when the app starts, we moved the code responsible for that from the **GoToInitialMoneyState** method directly to the constructor. We didn't change anything about the code that validates the input in the name entries because it's different and it's used only in this one place.

And now let's take care of the two entries in the Ending Conditions section. The first one will be used for entering the maximum number of races after which the game is over. This should be a number between 1 and 100. In the final version of the app this entry will be visible only if the second ending condition is selected. If the third condition is selected, the second entry will become visible and you'll be able to enter the maximum number of minutes the game should last. This number should be between 1 and 120.

Our validation code must pick the correct visual state depending on what text we enter. The **Valid** state will be chosen if the text is a number between 1 and 100 in the first entry or between 1 and 120 in the second one. We'll also give names to the entries and add events to them.

The two entries are defined directly in the **SettingsPage**, so let's add the following code in the SettingsPage.xaml and **SettingsPage.xaml.cs** files, starting with the former:

```
...
<ContentPage ...>
    ...
        <!--the Ending Conditions panel-->
        ...
                    <RadioButton
                        ...
                    <Entry
                        x:Name="maxRacesEntry"
                        Grid.Row="1"
                        Grid.Column="1"
                        Placeholder="Set max number of races (1-100)"
                        WidthRequest="300"
                        HorizontalOptions="Start"
                        TextChanged="OnMaxRacesTextChanged" />
                    <RadioButton
                        ...
                    <Entry
                        x:Name="maxTimeEntry"
                        Grid.Row="2"
                        Grid.Column="1"
```

```
                Placeholder="Set max game time (1-120 min)"
                WidthRequest="300"
                HorizontalOptions="Start"
                TextChanged="OnMaxTimeTextChanged" />
        </Grid>
    ...
```

Here I also changed the value of the **WidthRequest** property to accommodate the entire placeholder text.

And here's the code-behind:

```
namespace Slugrace.Views;

public partial class SettingsPage : ContentPage
{
    public SettingsPage()
    {
        InitializeComponent();
        VisualStateManager.GoToState(maxRacesEntry, "Empty");
        VisualStateManager.GoToState(maxTimeEntry, "Empty");
    }

    private void OnMaxRacesTextChanged(object sender, TextChangedEventArgs e)
    {
        Helpers.ValidateNumericInputAndSetState(e.NewTextValue, 1, 100, maxRacesEntry);
    }

    private void OnMaxTimeTextChanged(object sender, TextChangedEventArgs e)
    {
        Helpers.ValidateNumericInputAndSetState(e.NewTextValue, 1, 120, maxTimeEntry);
    }
}
```

This code doesn't really differ much from that in the **PlayerSettings.xaml.cs** file. You can now run the app and check whether the validation works:

As you can see, the first entry is in **Invalid** state whereas the second one is in **Empty** state.

And finally, let's take care of the entries in the Bets panel in **RacePage**, or, to be precise, in the **PlayerBet** control where the entry actually sits. This is going to be quick and easy, so here's the **PlayerBet.xaml** file:

```
<?xml version="1.0" encoding="utf-8" ?>
<ContentView ...>
    <Grid
```

```
    ...
    <Entry
        x:Name="betAmountEntry"
        Grid.Column="3"
        WidthRequest="200"
        Placeholder="1 - 1000"
        TextChanged="OnBetAmountTextChanged" />
    <Slider
        ...
```

And here's the code-behind file (**PlayerBet.xaml.cs**):

```
namespace Slugrace.Controls;

public partial class PlayerBet : ContentView
{
    public PlayerBet()
    {
        InitializeComponent();
        VisualStateManager.GoToState(betAmountEntry, "Empty");
    }

    private void OnBetAmountTextChanged(object sender, TextChangedEventArgs e)
    {
        Helpers.ValidateNumericInputAndSetState(e.NewTextValue, 1, 1000, betAmountEntry);
    }
}
```

If you now run the **RacePage**, you can see that the text you enter is validated:

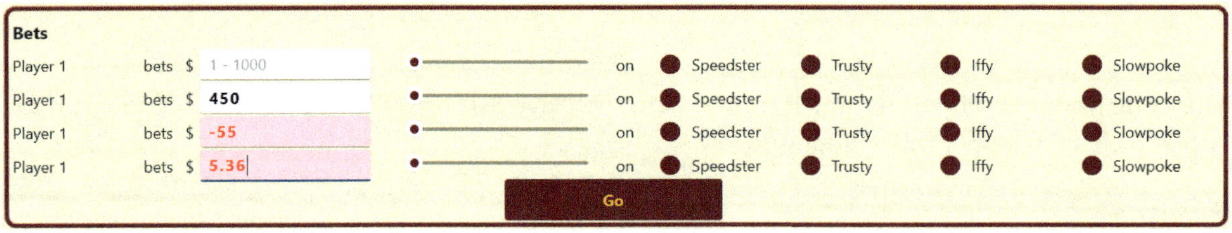

By the way, the placeholder text is hardcoded for now. In the final version of the game, the fixed value of 1000 will be replaced by the actual amount of money the player currently has and can bet.

Good, now we can create custom visual states. But what if we want to see the entries in the Ending Conditions section of the **SettingsPage** only if a corresponding radio button is checked? To implement this, we would have to be able to attach visual states to an element and let them set properties on other elements. And, yes, this is possible.

Setting States on Other Objects

Let's start with the radio buttons and entries in the Ending Conditions section of the

SettingsPage. The two entries should be by default invisible and disabled. To ensure that, we have to set **Opacity** to 0 and **IsEnabled** to **False** on each of them. Let's do it then. Here's the code in the **SettingsPage.xaml** page:

```
<?xml version="1.0" encoding="utf-8" ?>
<ContentPage ...>
    ...
        <!--the Ending Conditions panel-->
        ...
                    <RadioButton
                        ...
                    <RadioButton
                        ...
                    <Entry
                        x:Name="maxRacesEntry"
                        Grid.Row="1"
                        Grid.Column="1"
                        Placeholder="Set max number of races (1-100)"
                        WidthRequest="300"
                        HorizontalOptions="Start"
                        Opacity="0"
                        IsEnabled="False"
                        TextChanged="OnMaxRacesTextChanged"/>
                    <RadioButton
                        ...
                    <Entry
                        x:Name="maxTimeEntry"
                        Grid.Row="2"
                        Grid.Column="1"
                        Placeholder="Set max game time (1-120 min)"
                        WidthRequest="300"
                        HorizontalOptions="Start"
                        Opacity="0"
                        IsEnabled="False"
                        TextChanged="OnMaxTimeTextChanged"/>
                </Grid>
            ...
```

Then we'll add visual states to the radio buttons that will change the state not of themselves, but of the entries. Look how it's done:

```
<?xml version="1.0" encoding="utf-8" ?>
<ContentPage ...>
    ...
        <!--the Ending Conditions panel-->
        ...
                <Grid
                    ...
                    <RadioButton
                        ...
                    <RadioButton
                        Grid.Row="1"
                        Content="The game is over not later than after a given number of races."
                        GroupName="endingConditions">

                        <VisualStateManager.VisualStateGroups>
                            <VisualStateGroup x:Name="CommonStates">
                                <VisualState x:Name="Unchecked" />
                                <VisualState x:Name="Checked">
                                    <VisualState.Setters>
```

```
                        <Setter TargetName="maxRacesEntry" Property="Opacity" Value="1" />
                        <Setter TargetName="maxRacesEntry" Property="IsEnabled" Value="True" />
                    </VisualState.Setters>
                </VisualState>
            </VisualStateGroup>
        </VisualStateManager.VisualStateGroups>
    </RadioButton>
    <Entry
        x:Name="maxRacesEntry"
        ...
    <RadioButton
        Grid.Row="2"
        Content="The game is over not later than after the racing time you set has elapsed."
        GroupName="endingConditions">
        <VisualStateManager.VisualStateGroups>
            <VisualStateGroup x:Name="CommonStates">
                <VisualState x:Name="Unchecked" />
                <VisualState x:Name="Checked">
                    <VisualState.Setters>
                        <Setter TargetName="maxTimeEntry" Property="Opacity" Value="1" />
                        <Setter TargetName="maxTimeEntry" Property="IsEnabled" Value="True" />
                    </VisualState.Setters>
                </VisualState>
            </VisualStateGroup>
        </VisualStateManager.VisualStateGroups>
    </RadioButton>
    <Entry
        x:Name="maxTimeEntry"
        ...
```

There are a couple things worth mentioning here. First, we're using the **Unchecked** state as an empty state, which means the default values (the ones set on the respective **Entry** object) will be used when the radio button is unchecked. Next, in the **Checked** state we set **Opacity** to 1 and **IsEnabled** to **True**, so the entry will be visible and you will be able to enter text in it when the radio button is checked.

Now, if you attach visual states to an object, which is not the object on which the properties are supposed to be set, you must somehow reference the other object. You do it by setting the **TargetName** property to its name, like here. The visual states are attached to the radio buttons, but the properties are set on the entries. The entries are referenced by their names.

Let's also check the first radio button by setting its **IsChecked** property to **True**. This will make the first ending condition the default one:

```
...
<ContentPage ...>
    ...
        <!--the Ending Conditions panel-->
        ...

                    <RadioButton
                        Content="The game is over when there is only one player with any money left."
                        IsChecked="True"
                        GroupName="endingConditions" />
                    <RadioButton
                        ...
```

Before we proceed, we must make sure there aren't any styles defined for the **RadioButton** in the **SettingsPage**. If there are, they will take precedence. Earlier, we set the **Margin** property in the page-level resources:

```
...
<ContentPage ...>

    <ContentPage.Resources>
        <Style TargetType="RadioButton">
            <Setter Property="Margin" Value="0, 0, 0, 10" />
        </Style>
    </ContentPage.Resources>

    <Grid
        ...
```

Just remove this piece of code and it will work as expected. Now if you run the app (with the **SettingsPage** as the starting page), the first ending will be checked and you won't see any of the two entries:

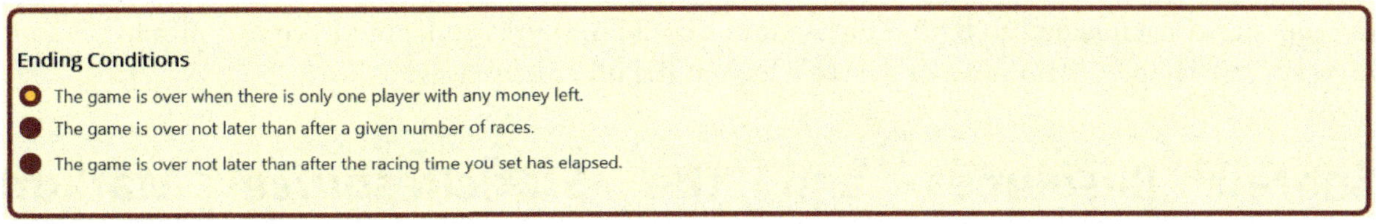

If you select one of the other two radio buttons, their corresponding entry will show up:

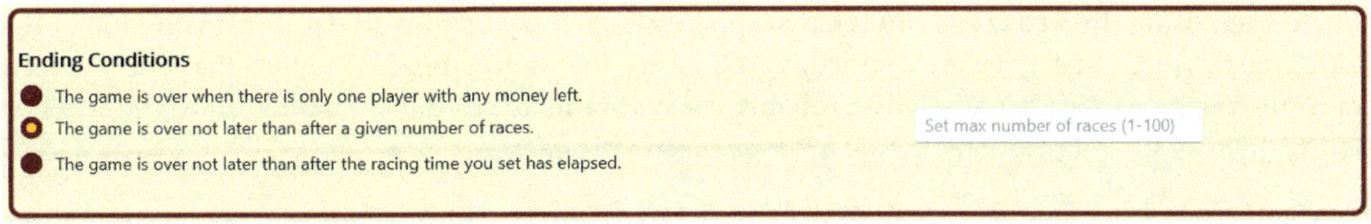

Good. That's it. We've covered the basics of visual states and control templates. You might have noticed that some of the values in the styles were repeated multiple times. For example, we used the same color value for the background color of the **Button**, the color of the **Border** and the color of the outer circle of the **RadioButton**. If we wanted to change the color now, we would have to do it in multiple places, which is tedious and error-prone. But there is a way to solve this problem - we can use markup extensions. And there are many other use cases for markup extensions, so let's talk about them in the next chapter.

Chapter 11 - Markup Extensions

code: https://github.com/prospero-apps/Slugrace/tree/chapter11

In the preceding chapters of the book we were already using markup extensions. You can easily spot them because with most of them (but not all) we use curly braces. Here's an example from the **SettingsPage.xaml** file:

```
Style="{StaticResource labelSectionTitleStyle}"
```

This is the **StaticResource** markup extension. We use it here to set the **Style** property. **StaticResource** is just one example of markup extensions. In this chapter we're going to see some more.

So, what are **markup extensions** and what do we use them for? Well, we use them to set properties to objects or values defined somewhere else, like in the example above, where the **labelSectionTitleStyle** is referenced. Markup extensions are used to share objects and values, to reference constants and to bind data. As far as data binding is concerned, we're going to see to it in a separate chapter. And now let's have a look at the other use cases.

Shared Resources and the StaticResource Markup Extension

We've been using the **StaticResource** markup extension to set styles so far. But if you look at the XAML code where the styles are defined, you'll notice that there are some values that are repeated multiple times. In C# code we would probably use constants to store these values. In XAML we can define them as shared resources inside a **ResourceDictionary**.

Let's start with the colors. Here's how the colors are defined inside the implicit **Entry** style in the **App.xaml** file:

```
...
<Application ...>
    <Application.Resources>
        <ResourceDictionary>
            ...
            <Style TargetType="Entry">
                <Setter Property="BackgroundColor" Value="White" />
                ...
                <Setter Property="PlaceholderColor" Value="#A0A0A0" />
                <Setter Property="VisualStateManager.VisualStateGroups">
                    <VisualStateGroupList>
                        <VisualStateGroup x:Name="ValidityStates">
                            <VisualState x:Name="Valid">
                                <VisualState.Setters>
```

```
                        <Setter Property="BackgroundColor" Value="White" />
                        <Setter Property="TextColor" Value="Black" />
                    </VisualState.Setters>
                </VisualState>
                <VisualState x:Name="Invalid">
                    <VisualState.Setters>
                        <Setter Property="BackgroundColor" Value="#FFDDEE" />
                        <Setter Property="TextColor" Value="Red" />
                    </VisualState.Setters>
                </VisualState>
                <VisualState x:Name="Empty">
                    <VisualState.Setters>
                        <Setter Property="BackgroundColor" Value="White" />
                        <Setter Property="TextColor" Value="White" />
                        ...
                    </VisualState.Setters>
                </VisualState>
            </VisualStateGroup>
        </VisualStateGroupList>
    </Setter>
</Style>
...
```

Here we can see colors assigned to different properties, like **BackgroundColor** or **TextColor**. Some of the values are repeated, like the named color **White**. This is just a small portion of the code, but there are more repeated values throughout the entire file. If we now wanted to change all white elements to blue ones, we would have to set the properties one by one. We should avoid such situations, so let's define a color resource that we can share. Actually, let's define color resources for all repeated colors in the **ResourceDictionary**:

```
<?xml version = "1.0" encoding = "UTF-8" ?>
<Application ...>
    <Application.Resources>
        <ResourceDictionary>
            <ResourceDictionary.MergedDictionaries>
                ...
            </ResourceDictionary.MergedDictionaries>

            <!--Colors-->
            <Color x:Key="mainButtonColor">#520000</Color>
            <Color x:Key="buttonTextColor">#FFCC1A</Color>
            <Color x:Key="pressedButtonColor">#891C20</Color>
            <Color x:Key="normalEntryColor">White</Color>

            <Style TargetType="ContentPage"
                   ...
```

Then we can set the colors using the **StaticResource** markup extension and the names defined in the **ResourceDictionary**:

```
<?xml version = "1.0" encoding = "UTF-8" ?>
<Application ...>
    ...
            <Style TargetType="Border">
                <Setter Property="Stroke" Value="{StaticResource mainButtonColor}" />
                ...
            <Style TargetType="Button">
                <Setter Property="BackgroundColor" Value="{StaticResource mainButtonColor}" />
                <Setter Property="TextColor" Value="{StaticResource buttonTextColor}" />
                ...
                    <VisualStateGroupList>
                        ...
                            <VisualState x:Name="PointerOver">
                                <VisualState.Setters>
                                    <Setter Property="BackgroundColor" Value="{StaticResource pressedButtonColor}" />
                                </VisualState.Setters>
                            </VisualState>

                            <VisualState x:Name="Pressed">
                                <VisualState.Setters>
                                    ...
                                    <Setter Property="BackgroundColor" Value="{StaticResource pressedButtonColor}" />
                                </VisualState.Setters>
                            </VisualState>
                        </VisualStateGroup>
                    </VisualStateGroupList>
                ...
            <Style TargetType="Entry">
                <Setter Property="BackgroundColor" Value="{StaticResource normalEntryColor}" />
                ...
                    <VisualStateGroupList>
                        <VisualStateGroup x:Name="ValidityStates">
                            <VisualState x:Name="Valid">
                                <VisualState.Setters>
                                    <Setter Property="BackgroundColor" Value="{StaticResource normalEntryColor}" />
                                    ...
                                </VisualState.Setters>
                            </VisualState>
                            ...
                            <VisualState x:Name="Empty">
                                <VisualState.Setters>
                                    <Setter Property="BackgroundColor" Value="{StaticResource normalEntryColor}" />
                                    <Setter Property="TextColor" Value="{StaticResource normalEntryColor}" />
                                    ...
                                </VisualState.Setters>
                            </VisualState>
                        </VisualStateGroup>
                    </VisualStateGroupList>
                ...
            <ControlTemplate x:Key="RadioButtonTemplate">
                ...
                        <Ellipse
                                Fill="{StaticResource mainButtonColor}"
                                ...
                        <Ellipse
                                ...
                                Fill="{StaticResource buttonTextColor}"
                                ...
                    </Grid>
                    ...
```

We could put all the colors in the **ResourceDictionary** to keep them centralized, but here I limited myself to the colors that are repeated at least twice in the code.

So, this is how we can share color values across the app. But we can also share other values, like layout options or numeric values, for example. For the latter we can use tags like **<x:Double>** or

<x:Int32>. Let's now put all repeated values in the **ResourceDictionary** and then reference them using the **StaticResource** markup extension and their names:

```
...
<Application ...>
    <Application.Resources>
        <ResourceDictionary>
            ...
            <!--Colors-->
            ...
            <!--Layout options-->
            <LayoutOptions x:Key="defaultLayoutOptions" Alignment="Center" />

            <!--Numeric values-->
            <x:Double x:Key="defaultFontSize">18</x:Double>

            <!--Other values-->
            <FontAttributes x:Key="emphasized">Bold</FontAttributes>

            <Style TargetType="ContentPage"
                   ...
            <Style TargetType="Button">
                ...
                <Setter Property="FontSize" Value="{StaticResource defaultFontSize}" />
                <Setter Property="FontAttributes" Value="{StaticResource emphasized}" />
                <Setter Property="HorizontalOptions" Value="{StaticResource defaultLayoutOptions}" />
                ...
            <Style x:Key="labelBaseStyle" TargetType="Label">
                <Setter Property="FontSize" Value="{StaticResource defaultFontSize}" />
                <Setter Property="VerticalOptions" Value="{StaticResource defaultLayoutOptions}" />
            </Style>

            <Style x:Key="labelSectionTitleStyle"
                   TargetType="Label"
                   BasedOn="{StaticResource labelBaseStyle}">
                <Setter Property="FontSize" Value="20" />
                <Setter Property="FontAttributes" Value="{StaticResource emphasized}" />
            </Style>

            <Style TargetType="Entry">
                ...
                <Setter Property="FontSize" Value="{StaticResource defaultFontSize}" />
                ...
                <Setter Property="FontAttributes" Value="{StaticResource emphasized}" />
                ...
            <ControlTemplate x:Key="RadioButtonTemplate">
                <FlexLayout JustifyContent="Start">
                    <FlexLayout.Resources>
                        <Style TargetType="Label">
                            <Setter Property="FontSize" Value="{StaticResource defaultFontSize}" />
                            <Setter Property="VerticalOptions" Value="{StaticResource defaultLayoutOptions}" />
                            ...
                        </Style>
                    </FlexLayout.Resources>
                    <Grid
                        ...
                        HorizontalOptions="{StaticResource defaultLayoutOptions}"
                        VerticalOptions="{StaticResource defaultLayoutOptions}">
                        <Ellipse
                                ...
                                HorizontalOptions="{StaticResource defaultLayoutOptions}"
                                VerticalOptions="{StaticResource defaultLayoutOptions}" />
                        <Ellipse
                                ...
                                HorizontalOptions="{StaticResource defaultLayoutOptions}"
                                VerticalOptions="{StaticResource defaultLayoutOptions}" />
                    </Grid>
                    ...
```

Again, we could put all the values in the **ResourceDictionary** and then reference them, but I only put there those that are repeated throughout the code. If you run the code now, everything will look exactly as before.

The resources defined in the **App.xaml** file are available everywhere throughout the app. So, for example, the **ThumbColor** and **MinimumTrackColor** properties in the **Bets** content view are set to the same value as the buttons and borders. We defined the color as **mainButtonColor**, so let's use it now. Here's the **Bets.xaml** file:

```
...
<ContentView ...>

    <ContentView.Resources>
        ...
        <Style TargetType="Slider">
            <Setter Property="ThumbColor" Value="{StaticResource mainButtonColor}" />
            <Setter Property="MinimumTrackColor" Value="{StaticResource mainButtonColor}" />
        </Style>
    ...
```

We can also use some of the other resources that we defined in **App.xaml** in other pages and content views. For example, in the **GameOverPage** we can set the **FontSize** and **HorizontalOptions** properties like so:

```
...
<ContentPage ...>

    <ContentPage.Resources>

        <Style TargetType="Label">
            <Setter Property="FontAttributes" Value="{StaticResource emphasized}" />
            <Setter Property="HorizontalOptions" Value="{StaticResource defaultLayoutOptions}" />
            ...
```

Or, in the **SettingsPage**, we can set **FontAttributes** and **VerticalOptions** like this:

```
<?xml version="1.0" encoding="utf-8" ?>
<ContentPage ...>
    ...
        <!--the Settings label-->
        <Label
            Text="Settings"
            FontAttributes="{StaticResource emphasized}"
            FontSize="24" />

        <!--the Players panel-->
        ...
                <VerticalStackLayout VerticalOptions="{StaticResource defaultLayoutOptions}">
                    <Label
                        Text="The Players"
                        Style="{StaticResource labelSectionTitleStyle}" />
                    ...
```

```
<!--the Ending Conditions panel-->
<Border
    Grid.Row="2">
    <VerticalStackLayout VerticalOptions="{StaticResource defaultLayoutOptions}">
        ...
```

There are also values that are repeated inside one particular page or content view. In such cases, we can define the resources locally in the **ResourceDectionary** inside that page or view. As we're at the **SettingsPage** now, let's start there. A couple values are repeated, like for example **WidthRequest**, which is set to 300, and **Opacity**, which is set to 0. Let's turn them into resources and then reference them:

```
...
<ContentPage ...>

    <ContentPage.Resources>
        <x:Double x:Key="entryWidth">300</x:Double>
        <x:Double x:Key="invisible">0</x:Double>
    </ContentPage.Resources>
    ...
        <!--the Ending Conditions panel-->
        ...
                    <Entry
                        ...
                        WidthRequest="{StaticResource entryWidth}"
                        HorizontalOptions="Start"
                        Opacity="{StaticResource invisible}"
                        .../>
                    ...
                    <Entry
                        ...
                        WidthRequest="{StaticResource entryWidth}"
                        HorizontalOptions="Start"
                        Opacity="{StaticResource invisible}"
                        .../>
                </Grid>
            ...
```

In the **SlugInfo** content view we both define a view-scoped resource and reuse some resources defined globally:

```
...
<ContentView ...>

    <ContentView.Resources>
        <Color x:Key="infoTextColor">White</Color>
    </ContentView.Resources>

    <Grid
        ...
```

```
        <Label
            ...
            FontAttributes="{StaticResource emphasized}"
            TextColor="{StaticResource infoTextColor}" />
        <Label
            ...
            TextColor="{StaticResource infoTextColor}" />
        <Label
            ...
            VerticalOptions="{StaticResource defaultLayoutOptions}"
            ...
            FontAttributes="{StaticResource emphasized}"
            TextColor="{StaticResource infoTextColor}" />
    </Grid>
</ContentView>
```

In all the examples above we were using the **StaticResource** markup extension. Let's now have a look at some others. Let's start with the **x:Static** markup extension.

The x:Static Markup Extension

The **x:Static** markup extension is used to reference a public static field, a public static property, a public constant field or an enumeration member that are defined somewhere in the code. We're not going to use it in our app, so let's use the **TestPage** to demonstrate it. But first of all, move the **TestPage.xaml** and **TestPage.xaml.cs** files into the **Views** folder so that we can use it as the starting page in **AppShell.xaml** without any additional modifications. This will require a few changes in the files so that the correct namespaces are defined.

Now make sure the **TestPage** is the starting page. Then open the **TestPage.xaml** file and make sure it looks like this:

```
<?xml version="1.0" encoding="utf-8" ?>
<ContentPage xmlns="http://schemas.microsoft.com/dotnet/2021/maui"
             xmlns:x="http://schemas.microsoft.com/winfx/2009/xaml"
             x:Class="Slugrace.Views.TestPage"
             Title="TestPage">
    <Grid>
        <BoxView
            Color="Red"
            WidthRequest="600"
            HeightRequest="600" />
    </Grid>
</ContentPage>
```

So, here we have a **BoxView** control with some basic settings. Now open the code-behind and make sure it looks like this:

```
namespace Slugrace.Views;

public partial class TestPage : ContentPage
{
    public TestPage()
    {
        InitializeComponent();
    }
}
```

Watch the namespace. It's **Slugrace.Views**, not **Slugrace** like before, because we moved the file into the **Views** folder.

If you run the app, you will see a red box:

We set three properties on the view using literal values. Instead, we could create some resources and reference them using the **StaticResource** markup extension. But we can also define some static fields or properties somewhere in the code and then reference them using the **x:Static** extension. Let's temporarily add a field and a property to the **Helpers** class that we defined before:

```
namespace Slugrace
{
    public static class Helpers
    {
        public static readonly double BoxSize = 600;
        public static Color BoxColor { get; set; } = Colors.Red;

        public static void ValidateNumericInputAndSetState(...)
        ...
```

In order to be able to reference these static values in the **TestPage**, we must add a namespace with a prefix there:

```
...
<ContentPage xmlns="http://schemas.microsoft.com/dotnet/2021/maui"
             xmlns:x="http://schemas.microsoft.com/winfx/2009/xaml"
             xmlns:local="clr-namespace:Slugrace"
             x:Class="Slugrace.Views.TestPage"
             Title="TestPage">
    <Grid>
        ...
```

This way the program will know where to look for the values. Don't worry if you don't understand how it works. We're going to discuss namespaces in XAML in one of the following chapters.

Anyway, now we can reference the field and property like so:

```
<?xml version="1.0" encoding="utf-8" ?>
<ContentPage ...>
    <Grid>
        <BoxView
            Color="{x:Static local:Helpers.BoxColor}"
            WidthRequest="{x:Static local:Helpers.BoxSize}"
            HeightRequest="{x:Static local:Helpers.BoxSize}" />
    </Grid>
</ContentPage>
```

If you run the app, it will work like before.

And now let's see how we can use enumeration members. Modify the XAML code so that it looks like this:

```
...
<ContentPage ...>
    <Grid>
        <BoxView
            Color="{x:Static Colors.Red}"
            WidthRequest="400"
            HeightRequest="400"
            VerticalOptions="{x:Static LayoutOptions.Start}"
            HorizontalOptions="{x:Static LayoutOptions.Center}" />
    </Grid>
</ContentPage>
```

As you can see, we're using the **x:Static** markup extension to set the **Color**, **VerticalOptions** and **HorizontalOptions** properties.

When you're done experimenting, remove the field and property from the **Helpers** class because we don't want to clutter it with stuff we won't be using in the app. And now let's move on to the next markup extensions.

Markup Extension Properties

Markup extensions can have properties. If there are more than one, they're separated with commas. We assign values to the properties using equals signs and we don't use quotation marks inside the curly braces. Here's an example of the **x:Static** markup extension that we used in our code:

```
Color="{x:Static local:Helpers.BoxColor}"
```

We don't clearly see the property name here, just the value. This is because it's the value of the content property, and the name of a content property can be omitted provided it's the first or the only property. The content property of the **x:Static** markup extension is **Member**, so we could rewrite the code like this:

```
Color="{x:Static Member=local:Helpers.BoxColor}"
```

There may be only one content property.

CollectionView, the x:Array and x:Type Markup Extensions

Unlike our Slugrace application, many apps display data retrieved from a list or other collection, sometimes from the disk, sometimes from an API, sometimes the data is hardcoded in the program. In .NET MAUI we have a couple controls that we can use to display such data. One of them is **ListView**. The recommended one, however, is **CollectionView**. It's more flexible and performant than **ListView**.

We're going to use the **TestPage.xaml** file again, because the collection that we are about to see will not be part of our app. To create a **CollectionView**, we must provide two pieces of information to the object: the collection itself and the template for a single item in the collection. We use the **ItemsSource** property to populate the view. To define the appearance of each item in the collection, we set the **ItemTemplate** property to **DataTemplate**.

Let's create a **CollectionView** in the **TestPage.xaml** file then so that we have something to look at as we discuss the details. Make sure your code looks like this:

```
...
<ContentPage ...>
    <CollectionView Margin="50">
        <CollectionView.ItemsSource>
            <x:Array Type="{x:Type x:Int32}">
                <x:Int32>128</x:Int32>
                <x:Int32>526</x:Int32>
                <x:Int32>311</x:Int32>
                <x:Int32>781</x:Int32>
                <x:Int32>982</x:Int32>
            </x:Array>
        </CollectionView.ItemsSource>
```

```
        <CollectionView.ItemTemplate>
            <DataTemplate>
                <Border HeightRequest="80" WidthRequest="500">
                    <Grid>
                        <Image
                            Source="racetrack.png"
                            Scale="1"/>
                        <Button
                            Text="{Binding}"
                            FontSize="20" />
                    </Grid>
                </Border>
            </DataTemplate>
        </CollectionView.ItemTemplate>
    </CollectionView>
</ContentPage>
```

You can clearly see the two properties in the code. First, we set the **ItemsSource** property to an array of integer numbers and then we set the **ItemTemplate** property to a **DataTemplate** which defines each individual item in the array. Let's start with the **ItemsSource** property.

In the example above we hardcoded the items of the array. We use the **x:Array** markup extension to define an array in XAML. Unlike with all the other markup extensions that we discussed before, with the **x:Array** extension we don't use curly braces, but rather the items are listed between the opening and closing tags.

And there's the **x:Type**, another markup extension that we often use with the **x:Array** extension. This one is used with curly braces. Here it's used to define the type of the items. So, our **CollectionView** contains five integer numbers. These could be strings, colors, images or any other objects.

Next, we must define the template for a single item. This is what **DataTemplate** is for. We could present the data as labels, as images with text, as custom content views, or anything else. Here each item is displayed inside a border and consists of an image with a button on it. The **Text** property of the button is set to the appropriate number from the array. As you can see, we're using yet another markup extension to set the **Text** property, **Binding**. It just binds the **Text** property to each item from the collection one by one. We're not going to discuss it in more detail here, because there's going to be a separate chapter about data binding.

Now let's run the app (with the **TestPage** set as the starting page) and we should see the five items displayed like this:

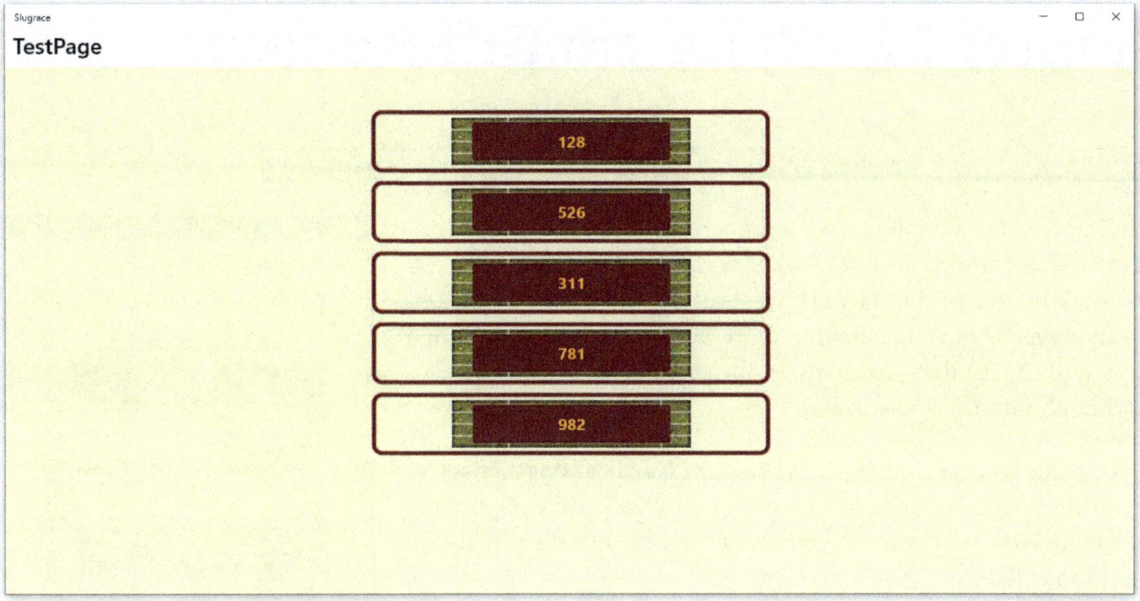

Naturally, there are more markup extensions, but we've covered the most important ones. Now that our app looks so great… But wait, does it? That's the problem. We've been running it exclusively on Windows, but what about Android? Does it look as great on your cell phone? And if not, what can we do about it? In the next chapter we'll be talking about platform differences.

Chapter 12 - Platform Differences

code: https://github.com/prospero-apps/Slugrace/tree/chapter12

In the preceding chapters we were creating the GUI for our Slugrace application and it looks pretty decent. At least on Windows. In the previous part we created a **CollectionView** that displayed items consisting of a border, an image and a button with a number taken from the collection. It looked OK. But what about other platforms?

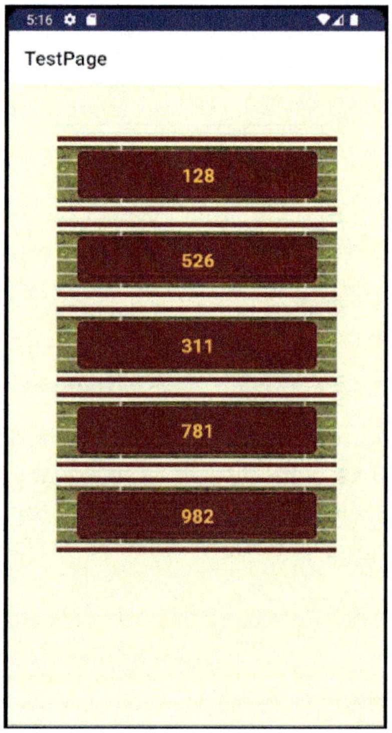

Let's test the app on Android. Make sure the **TestPage** is set as the starting page because we're going to check this page first. Also, make sure you run the app on Android. Look right to see what it looks like.

It doesn't look bad, but it's not perfect. For example, the borders have been cut off at both ends. This is because we set their **WidthRequest** property to 500, which is too much to fit on the screen. We could set it to a different value, like 300, but then it would look too small on Windows.

Fortunately, we don't have to pick just one platform to look good and neglect the others. We can set the properties to different values depending on which platform we're using. To do that, we use the **OnPlatform** markup extension.

There is one more markup extension that may come in handy, **OnIdiom**. This one enables us to set the properties to different values depending on the device idiom (whether it's a phone, a tablet, a desktop, and so on). Let's have a look at the **OnPlatform** markup extension first.

The OnPlatform Markup Extension

We use the **OnPlatform** markup extension to define different values for different platforms. This markup extension has a couple properties that we use to set values for particular platforms. The most important properties are: **Android**, **iOS**, **MacCatalyst** and **WinUI**. You set them to values that are to be applied on the particular platforms. So, let's say we want the **WidthRequest** property to be set to 500 like before, but only on Windows. On Android devices it should be set to 300. This is how we do it:

```
...
<ContentPage ...>
    <CollectionView Margin="50">
        <CollectionView.ItemsSource>
            ...
        </CollectionView.ItemsSource>
        <CollectionView.ItemTemplate>
            <DataTemplate>
                <Border
                    HeightRequest="80"
                    WidthRequest="{OnPlatform WinUI=500, Android=280}">
                    <Grid>
                        ...
```

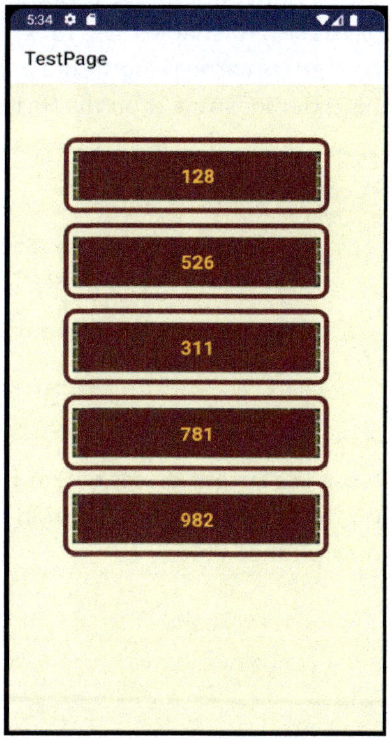

Now, if you run the app on Windows, it looks like before. But on Android devices the borders are narrower.

There is one more property that we're going to use a lot, **`Default`**.

As the name suggests, it's used to set a default value for all platforms except those which are explicitly specified.

Our app is going to be deployed to Windows and Android, so we can use the **`Default`** property for Windows and explicitly specify the values for Android.

Let's rewrite the code then:

```
...
<ContentPage ...>
    ...
                <Border
                    HeightRequest="100"
                    WidthRequest="{OnPlatform Default=500, Android=300}">
                    <Grid>
                        ...
```

As **`Default`** is the content property and it's the first property, we can skip the name:

```
...
<ContentPage ...>
    ...
                <Border
                    HeightRequest="100"
                    WidthRequest="{OnPlatform 500, Android=300}">
                    <Grid>
                        ...
```

This notation is more concise and I'm going to use it in the app. So, the default property will be used for Windows.

Before we actually start using the **OnPlatform** markup extension in our app, let's have a look at a slightly different approach.

The OnIdiom Markup Extension

We're not going to use it in our app, but it's good to know that there is another markup extension, **OnIdiom**. It enables us to specify different values for different idioms. The most important properties correspond to the available idioms, so we have: **Phone**, **Tablet**, **Desktop**, **TV** and **Watch**. Let's demonstrate it on the **HeightRequest** property:

```
...
<ContentPage ...>
    ...
        <CollectionView.ItemTemplate>
            <DataTemplate>
                <Border
                    HeightRequest="{OnIdiom Desktop=80, Phone=70}"
                    ...
                    <Grid>
                        ...
```

Now the height of each item in the **CollectionView** will be 80 on desktop devices and 70 on phones. Here's what it looks like on a phone.

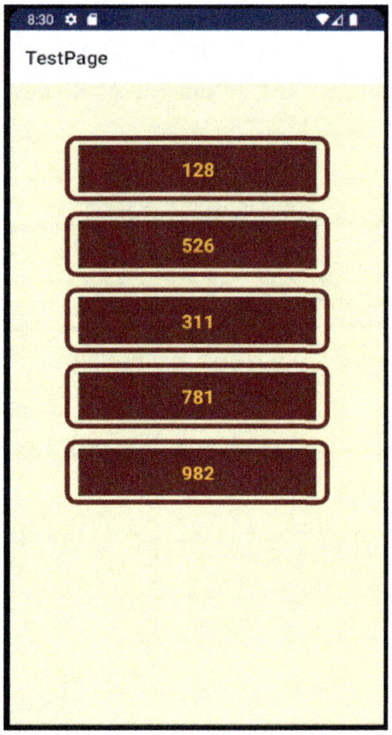

There's also the **Default** property, which works the same way as with the **OnPlatform** extension, so we could rewrite the code like this:

```
...
<ContentPage ...>
    ...
        <CollectionView.ItemTemplate>
            <DataTemplate>
                <Border
                    HeightRequest="{OnIdiom 80, Phone=70}"
                    ...
```

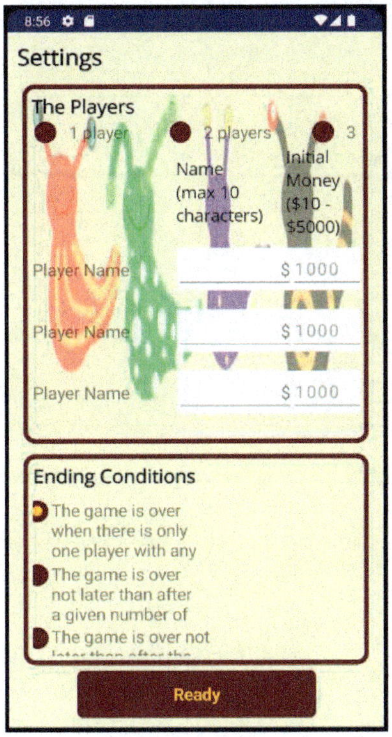

And now we can start to use the **OnPlatform** markup extension in our app to modify the appearance of the pages and content views on Android. We assume the values we set before are the default ones, so the ones that will be applied to Windows.

SettingsPage on Android

Let's start with the **SettingsPage** and the **PlayerSettings** content view. It looks OK on Windows, but if you run it on Android (look left), you may be disappointed.

Half the stuff we should see here is missing. Let's fix this. We're going to modify three files, **SettingsPage.xaml**, **PlayerSettings.xaml** and **App.xaml**. Actually, let's start with the last one. In **App.xaml** our global styles are defined.

Let's think about the styles that we apply to the particular elements in the **SettingsPage** and elsewhere. We're not going to change the **FontSize** property of the labels because we're going to change the text, but let's reduce the **FontSize** property of the **Entry** objects. The text should be smaller on Android:

```
...
<Application ...>
    ...
            <Style TargetType="Entry">
                <Setter Property="BackgroundColor" Value="{StaticResource normalEntryColor}" />
                <Setter Property="FontSize"
                        Value="{OnPlatform {StaticResource defaultFontSize}, Android=12}" />
                <Setter Property="CharacterSpacing" Value="1.5" />
                ...
```

On Windows the default value of 18 will be used.

Next, let's have a look at the **PlayerSettings.xaml** file. We'll make some modifications there:

```
...
<ContentView ...>
    ...
    <Grid
        RowDefinitions="*"
        Margin="0, 10">
        <Grid.ColumnDefinitions>
            <ColumnDefinition Width="{OnPlatform 150, Android=80}" />
            <ColumnDefinition Width="{OnPlatform 3*, Android=2.5*}" />
            <ColumnDefinition Width="10" />
            <ColumnDefinition Width="2*" />
```

```
        </Grid.ColumnDefinitions>

        <Label>
            <Label.Text>
                <OnPlatform x:TypeArguments="x:String">
                    <On Platform="WinUI" Value="Player Name" />
                    <On Platform="Android" Value="Player X" />
                </OnPlatform>
            </Label.Text>
        </Label>

        <Entry
            x:Name="nameEntry"
            Grid.Column="1"
            WidthRequest="{OnPlatform 300, Android=130}"
            TextChanged="OnNameTextChanged">
        </Entry>

        <Label
            ...
        <Entry
            x:Name="initialMoneyEntry"
            Placeholder="1000"
            Grid.Column="3"
            WidthRequest="{OnPlatform 250, Android=100}"
            TextChanged="OnInitialMoneyTextChanged">
        </Entry>
    </Grid>
</ContentView>
```

We can see some interesting changes here. Let's have a look at them going from top to bottom.

So, we defined **ColumnDefinitions** using property elements and setting different widths to the first two columns on Android. The last two columns will be the same on both platforms.

We also used property element syntax for the label below to set the **Text** property. Here you can see a different syntax for specifying platform-dependent values. We use the **OnPlatform** and **On** objects where we set the values for Windows and Android. As you remember, we don't use quotation marks inside curly braces, so we must do it like this. We mustn't forget to set the **x:TypeArguments** property to the type of the data.

Finally, we made the two entries narrower on Android by setting their **WidthRequest** property to platform-specific values.

And now let's have a look at a fragment of the **SettingsPage.xaml** file:

```
...
<ContentPage ...>
    ...
    <Grid
        Margin="{OnPlatform 10, Android=2}">
```

```
<Grid.RowDefinitions>
    <RowDefinition Height="{OnPlatform 40, Android=30}" />
    <RowDefinition Height="2.5*" />
    <RowDefinition Height="1.5*" />
    <RowDefinition Height="50" />
</Grid.RowDefinitions>

<!--the Settings label-->
<Label
    ...
    FontSize="{OnPlatform 24, Android=20}" />

<!--the Players panel-->
...
    <Grid>
        <Image
            Source="all_slugs.png"
            Aspect="{OnPlatform Fill, Android=AspectFill}"
            Opacity=".5"/>
        <VerticalStackLayout VerticalOptions="{StaticResource defaultLayoutOptions}">
            <Label
                Style="{StaticResource labelSectionTitleStyle}">
                <Label.Text>
                    <OnPlatform x:TypeArguments="x:String">
                        <On Platform="WinUI" Value="The Players" />
                        <On Platform="Android" Value="How many players?" />
                    </OnPlatform>
                </Label.Text>
            </Label>

            <HorizontalStackLayout>
                <RadioButton
                    GroupName="players">
                    <RadioButton.Content>
                        <Label>
                            <Label.Text>
                                <OnPlatform x:TypeArguments="x:String">
                                    <On Platform="WinUI" Value="1 player" />
                                    <On Platform="Android" Value="1" />
                                </OnPlatform>
                            </Label.Text>
                        </Label>
                    </RadioButton.Content>
                </RadioButton>
                ...
            </HorizontalStackLayout>

            <Grid
                RowDefinitions="*"
                ColumnDefinitions="150, 3*, 2*">

                <Label
                    Grid.Column="1"
                    Style="{StaticResource labelBaseStyle}">
                    <Label.Text>
                        <OnPlatform x:TypeArguments="x:String">
                            <On Platform="WinUI" Value="Name (max 10 characters)" />
                            <On Platform="Android" Value="Name" />
                        </OnPlatform>
                    </Label.Text>
                </Label>
```

```
                        <Label
                            Grid.Column="2"
                            Style="{StaticResource labelBaseStyle}">
                            <Label.Text>
                                <OnPlatform x:TypeArguments="x:String">
                                    <On Platform="WinUI" Value="Initial Money ($10 - $5000)" />
                                    <On Platform="Android" Value="Money" />
                                </OnPlatform>
                            </Label.Text>
                        </Label>
                    </Grid>
                    ...
        <!--the Ending Conditions panel-->
        <Border
            Grid.Row="2">
            <VerticalStackLayout VerticalOptions="{StaticResource defaultLayoutOptions}">
                <Label
                    Text="Ending Conditions"
                    Style="{StaticResource labelSectionTitleStyle}"
                    Margin="0, 0, 0, 10"/>
                <Grid
                    RowDefinitions="*, *, *"
                    ColumnDefinitions="4*, 2*">
                    <RadioButton
                        IsChecked="True"
                        GroupName="endingConditions">
                        <RadioButton.Content>
                            <Label>
                                <Label.Text>
                                    <OnPlatform x:TypeArguments="x:String">
                                        <On Platform="WinUI" Value="The game is over when
there is only one player with any money left." />
                                        <On Platform="Android" Value="last player left" />
                                    </OnPlatform>
                                </Label.Text>
                            </Label>
                        </RadioButton.Content>
                    </RadioButton>
                    ...
                    <Entry
                        x:Name="maxRacesEntry"
                        Grid.Row="1"
                        Grid.Column="1"
                        WidthRequest="{OnPlatform {StaticResource entryWidth}, Android=100}"
                        HorizontalOptions="Start"
                        Opacity="{StaticResource invisible}"
                        IsEnabled="False"
                        TextChanged="OnMaxRacesTextChanged">
                        <Entry.Placeholder>
                            <OnPlatform x:TypeArguments="x:String">
                                <On Platform="WinUI" Value="Set max number of races (1-100)" />
                                <On Platform="Android" Value="1-100 races" />
                            </OnPlatform>
                        </Entry.Placeholder>
                    </Entry>
                    ...
```

So, again, let's have a look at some of the changes.

First, we set platform-specific values for the **Margin** property on the main **Grid**. We also use property element notation for the **RowDefinitions** to make the first row different on each platform:

```
<Grid
    Margin="{OnPlatform 10, Android=2}">
    <Grid.RowDefinitions>
        <RowDefinition Height="{OnPlatform 40, Android=30}" />
        <RowDefinition Height="2.5*" />
        <RowDefinition Height="1.5*" />
        <RowDefinition Height="50" />
    </Grid.RowDefinitions>
```

We also want the image in the Players panel to be displayed differently:

```
<Image
    Source="all_slugs.png"
    Aspect="{OnPlatform Fill, Android=AspectFill}"
    Opacity=".5"/>
```

Also in the Players panel, we want a different text to be displayed:

```
<Label
    Style="{StaticResource labelSectionTitleStyle}">
    <Label.Text>
        <OnPlatform x:TypeArguments="x:String">
            <On Platform="WinUI" Value="The Players" />
            <On Platform="Android" Value="How many players?" />
        </OnPlatform>
    </Label.Text>
</Label>
```

This way we'll be able to put just numbers next to the radio buttons in that part of the UI. Here's the first radio button:

```
<RadioButton
    GroupName="players">
    <RadioButton.Content>
        <Label>
            <Label.Text>
                <OnPlatform x:TypeArguments="x:String">
                    <On Platform="WinUI" Value="1 player" />
                    <On Platform="Android" Value="1" />
                </OnPlatform>
            </Label.Text>
        </Label>
    </RadioButton.Content>
</RadioButton>
```

The others look almost the same, so I omitted them in the code above.

The other changes are pretty much of the same type, so I'm not going to bore you with each and every one of them. You will find the complete code on Github. And here's the final effect - the **SettingsPage** on Android.

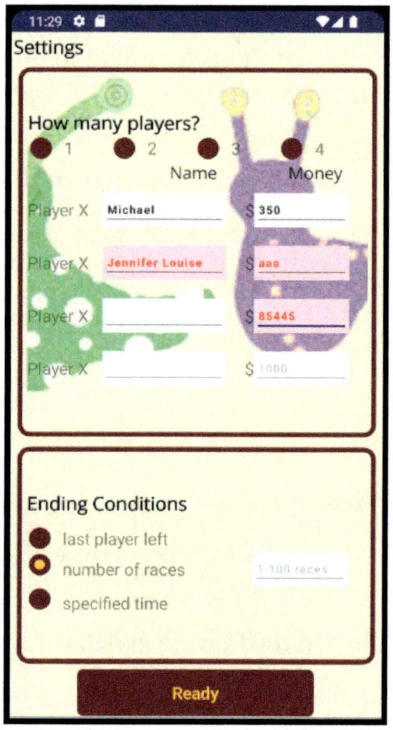

As you can see, most of the labels are slightly different. Also the placeholder text in the Ending Conditions section is shorter. You can also see that when you enter data in the entries, the validation works just like on Windows.

Styles

As far as the other pages are concerned, I'm not going to show you each and every change I made, because this would be too lengthy. You will find the entire modified code on Github, so go ahead, open each XAML file one by one and search for the occurrences of the **OnPlatform** markup extension. There also some other minor modifications.

I also made some changes in the **App.xaml** file where the global styles are defined. These changes affect the entire app. There are some new styles and some of the old ones are now platform-specific:

```
...
<Application ...>
    ...
            <!--Numeric values-->
            <x:Double x:Key="defaultFontSize">18</x:Double>
            <x:Double x:Key="androidDefaultFontSize">14</x:Double>
            ...
            <Style TargetType="Border">
                ...
                <Setter Property="StrokeThickness"
                        Value="{OnPlatform 5, Android=1}" />
                <Setter Property="Padding" Value="5" />
                <Setter Property="Margin"
                        Value="{OnPlatform 5, Android=1}" />
            </Style>

            <Style TargetType="Button">
                ...
                <Setter Property="WidthRequest"
                        Value="{OnPlatform 250, Android=150}" />
                <Setter Property="HeightRequest"
                        Value="{OnPlatform 50, Android=40}" />
                ...
            <Style x:Key="labelBaseStyle" ...
```

```
<Style x:Key="androidLabelBaseStyle" TargetType="Label">
    <Setter Property="FontSize"
            Value="{StaticResource androidDefaultFontSize}" />
    <Setter Property="VerticalOptions"
            Value="{StaticResource defaultLayoutOptions}" />
</Style>
    ...
<Style x:Key="labelSectionTitleStyle"...
<Style x:Key="androidLabelSectionTitleStyle"
       TargetType="Label"
       BasedOn="{StaticResource labelBaseStyle}">
    <Setter Property="FontSize" Value="16" />
    <Setter Property="FontAttributes" Value="{StaticResource emphasized}" />
</Style>

<Style TargetType="Entry">
    ...
    <Setter Property="FontSize"
            Value="{OnPlatform {StaticResource defaultFontSize}, Android=12}" />
    ...
<ControlTemplate x:Key="RadioButtonTemplate">
    ...
            <Ellipse
                    Fill="{OnPlatform {StaticResource mainButtonColor},
                        Android=White}"
                    Stroke="{StaticResource mainButtonColor}"
                    HeightRequest="{OnPlatform 24, Android=20}"
                    WidthRequest="{OnPlatform 24, Android=20}"
                    ...
            <Ellipse
                    x:Name="check"
                    Fill="{OnPlatform {StaticResource buttonTextColor},
                        Android={StaticResource mainButtonColor}}"
                    HeightRequest="{OnPlatform 12, Android=8}"
                    WidthRequest="{OnPlatform 12, Android=8}"
                    ...
```

For example I modified the border to be thinner on Android and the radio buttons to have different colors and sizes of the circles. This change affects also the **SettingsPage**, which eventually looks like this (look right).

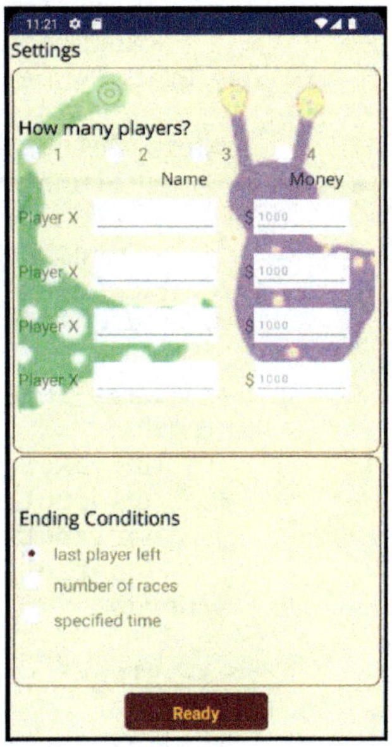

And now let's have a look at the other pages.

RacePage on Android

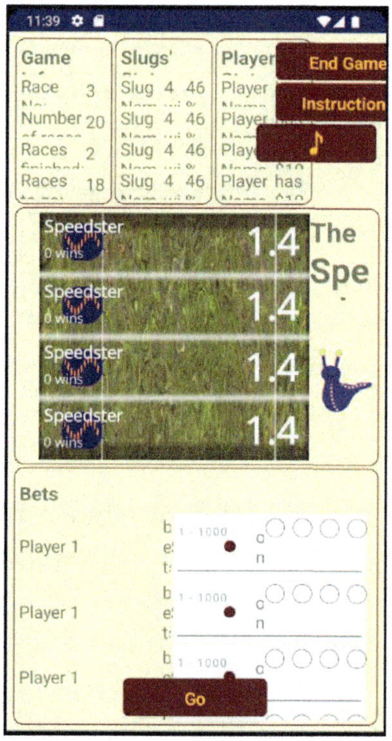

Let's have a look at the **RacePage** as it looks now.

We could do better than this, right?

First of all, let's rearrange the elements on the page. Let's move the Bets / Results panel to the top so that it doesn't get hidden behind the keyboard when you type in the values in the entries.

Let's also move the game info, the stats panels, and the buttons, to the bottom. We can easily do that by setting the **Grid.Row** and **Grid.Column** properties to different values for each platform.

Here's the **RacePage.xaml** file:

```
...
<ContentPage ...>
    <Grid>
        <Grid.RowDefinitions>
            <RowDefinition Height="{OnPlatform 1.3*, Android=2.6*}" />
            <RowDefinition Height="{OnPlatform 2*, Android=.7*}" />
            <RowDefinition Height="{OnPlatform 2*, Android=*}" />
            <RowDefinition Height="{OnPlatform 0, Android=*}" />
        </Grid.RowDefinitions>

        <Grid.ColumnDefinitions>
            <ColumnDefinition Width="{OnPlatform 3*, Android=*}" />
            <ColumnDefinition Width="{OnPlatform 3*, Android=*}" />
            <ColumnDefinition Width="{OnPlatform 3*, Android=0}" />
            <ColumnDefinition Width="{OnPlatform 2*, Android=0}" />
        </Grid.ColumnDefinitions>

        <!--Game Info-->
        <Border
            Grid.Row="{OnPlatform 0, Android=3}"
            Grid.Column="{OnPlatform 0, Android=1}"
            HorizontalOptions="{OnPlatform Android=Fill}">
            <controls:GameInfo/>
        </Border>

        <!--Slugs' Stats-->
        <Border
            Grid.Row="{OnPlatform 0, Android=2}"
            Grid.Column="{OnPlatform 1, Android=0}"
```

```
            HorizontalOptions="{OnPlatform Android=Fill}">
            <controls:SlugsStats />
        </Border>

        <!--Players' Stats-->
        <Border
            Grid.Row="{OnPlatform 0, Android=2}"
            Grid.Column="{OnPlatform 2, Android=1}"
            HorizontalOptions="{OnPlatform Android=Fill}">
            <controls:PlayersStats />
        </Border>

        <!--the buttons-->
        <VerticalStackLayout
            Grid.Row="{OnPlatform 0, Android=3}"
            Grid.Column="{OnPlatform 3, Android=0}"
            HorizontalOptions="{OnPlatform Android=Fill}"
            VerticalOptions="{OnPlatform Android=Center}"
            WidthRequest="{OnPlatform 260, Android=150}"
            Padding="5"
            Spacing="3">
            <Button
                Text="End Game" />
            <Button
                Text="Instructions" />
            <Button
                ImageSource="sound_on.png"
                WidthRequest="{OnPlatform 125, Android=150}"
                HorizontalOptions="{OnPlatform Default=End, Android=Center}"/>
        </VerticalStackLayout>

        <!--Racetrack-->
        <Border
            Grid.Row="1"
            Grid.ColumnSpan="4"
            HorizontalOptions="{OnPlatform Android=Fill}">
            <controls:Racetrack />
        </Border>

        <!--Bets/Results panel-->
        <Border
            Grid.Row="{OnPlatform 2, Android=0}"
            Grid.ColumnSpan="4"
            HorizontalOptions="{OnPlatform Android=Fill}">
            <controls:Bets />
        </Border>
    </Grid>
</ContentPage>
```

If we run the app now, we can see this new arrangement:

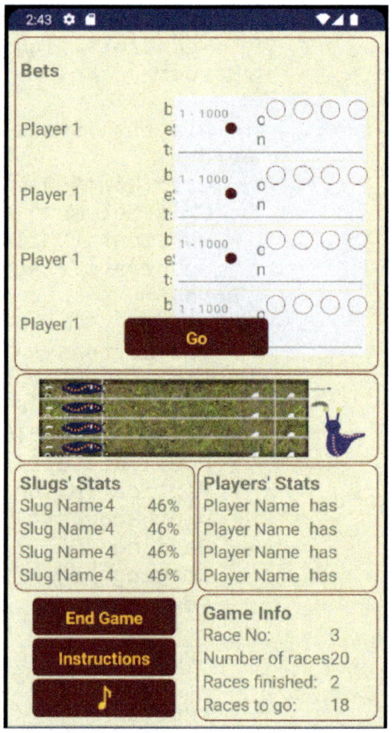

We now have to polish the individual content views. Let's start with the Bets panel. Here's the **Bets.xaml** file:

```
...
<ContentView ...>
    ...
    <Grid>
        <Grid.RowDefinitions>
            <RowDefinition Height="{OnPlatform *, Android=.3*}" />
            <RowDefinition Height="{OnPlatform 4*, Android=3*}" />
            <RowDefinition Height="{OnPlatform *, Android=.5*}" />
        </Grid.RowDefinitions>

        <Label
            Text="Bets"
            Style="{OnPlatform {StaticResource labelSectionTitleStyle},
                Android={StaticResource androidLabelSectionTitleStyle}}" />
        <VerticalStackLayout
            ...
```

For the effect to be visible, we also have to modify the **PlayerBet** content view:

```
...
<ContentView ...>

    <ContentView.Resources>
        <Color x:Key="backgroundColor">#FFF4E5</Color>
        <Style TargetType="Label"
                    BasedOn="{OnPlatform {StaticResource labelBaseStyle},
                        Android={StaticResource androidLabelBaseStyle}}" />
    </ContentView.Resources>

    <Grid
        BackgroundColor="{OnPlatform Android={StaticResource backgroundColor}}"
        Margin="0, 0, 0, 2">

        <Grid.RowDefinitions>
            <RowDefinition Height="{OnPlatform *, Android=*}" />
            <RowDefinition Height="{OnPlatform 0, Android=*}" />
        </Grid.RowDefinitions>

        <Grid.ColumnDefinitions>
            <ColumnDefinition Width="{OnPlatform 150, Android=80}" />
            <ColumnDefinition Width="{OnPlatform .3*, Android=.8*}" />
            <ColumnDefinition Width="{OnPlatform .1*, Android=.1*}" />
            <ColumnDefinition Width="{OnPlatform 1.5*, Android=1.4*}" />
            <ColumnDefinition Width="{OnPlatform 1.5*, Android=1.9*}" />
            <ColumnDefinition Width="{OnPlatform .3*, Android=.5*}" />
            <ColumnDefinition Width="{OnPlatform 4*, Android=0}" />
        </Grid.ColumnDefinitions>

        <Label
            Text="Player 1" />
        ...
        <Entry
            x:Name="betAmountEntry"
            Grid.Column="3"
            WidthRequest="{OnPlatform 200, Android=80}"
            Placeholder="1 - 1000"
            BackgroundColor="{OnPlatform Android={StaticResource backgroundColor}}"
            Keyboard="Numeric"
            TextChanged="OnBetAmountTextChanged"/>
        <Slider
            ...
        <Grid
            Grid.Row="{OnPlatform 0, Android=1}"
            Grid.Column="{OnPlatform 6, Android=0}"
            Grid.ColumnSpan="{OnPlatform Android=6}"
            RowDefinitions="*"
            ColumnDefinitions="*, *, *, *">

            <RadioButton
                GroupName="player1">
                <RadioButton.Content>
```

```
            <Label
                Text="Speedster"
                Style="{OnPlatform {StaticResource labelBaseStyle},
                    Android={StaticResource androidLabelBaseStyle}}">
                <Label.Margin>
                    <OnPlatform x:TypeArguments="Thickness">
                        <On Platform="WinUI" Value="0" />
                        <On Platform="Android" Value="-12, 0, 0, 0" />
                    </OnPlatform>
                </Label.Margin>
            </Label>
        </RadioButton.Content>
    </RadioButton>
    <RadioButton
        Grid.Column="1"
        GroupName="player1">
        <RadioButton.Content>
            <Label
                Text="Trusty"
                Style="{OnPlatform {StaticResource labelBaseStyle},
                    Android={StaticResource androidLabelBaseStyle}}">
                <Label.Margin>
                    <OnPlatform x:TypeArguments="Thickness">
                        <On Platform="WinUI" Value="0" />
                        <On Platform="Android" Value="-12, 0, 0, 0" />
                    </OnPlatform>
                </Label.Margin>
            </Label>
        </RadioButton.Content>
    </RadioButton>
    <RadioButton
        Grid.Column="2"
        GroupName="player1">
        <RadioButton.Content>
            <Label
                Text="Iffy"
                Style="{OnPlatform {StaticResource labelBaseStyle},
                    Android={StaticResource androidLabelBaseStyle}}">
                <Label.Margin>
                    <OnPlatform x:TypeArguments="Thickness">
                        <On Platform="WinUI" Value="0" />
                        <On Platform="Android" Value="-12, 0, 0, 0" />
                    </OnPlatform>
                </Label.Margin>
            </Label>
        </RadioButton.Content>
    </RadioButton>
    <RadioButton
        Grid.Column="3"
        GroupName="player1">
        <RadioButton.Content>
            <Label
                Text="Slowpoke"
                Style="{OnPlatform {StaticResource labelBaseStyle},
                    Android={StaticResource androidLabelBaseStyle}}">
```

```
                        <Label.Margin>
                            <OnPlatform x:TypeArguments="Thickness">
                                <On Platform="WinUI" Value="0" />
                                <On Platform="Android" Value="-12, 0, 0, 0" />
                            </OnPlatform>
                        </Label.Margin>
                    </Label>
                </RadioButton.Content>
            </RadioButton>
        </Grid>
    </Grid>
</ContentView>
```

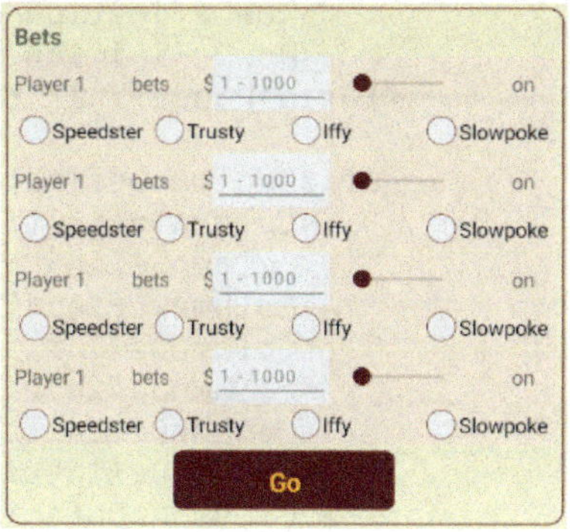

The Bets panel looks much better now.

What about the Results panel? Here's the **Results.xaml** file:

```
...
<ContentView ...>
    ...
    <Grid>
        <Grid.RowDefinitions>
            <RowDefinition Height="{OnPlatform *, Android=.3*}" />
            <RowDefinition Height="{OnPlatform 4*, Android=3*}" />
            <RowDefinition Height="{OnPlatform *, Android=.5*}" />
        </Grid.RowDefinitions>

        <Label
            Text="Results"
            Style="{OnPlatform {StaticResource labelSectionTitleStyle},
                Android={StaticResource androidLabelSectionTitleStyle}}" />
        <VerticalStackLayout
            Grid.Row="1"
            Spacing="{OnPlatform 0, Android=15}">
            <controls:PlayerResult />
            ...
        </VerticalStackLayout>
        <Button
            ...
```

And the **PlayerResult** content view:

```
...
<ContentView ...>

    <ContentView.Resources>
        <Color x:Key="backgroundColor">#FFF4E5</Color>
        <Style TargetType="Label"
                  BasedOn="{OnPlatform {StaticResource labelBaseStyle},
                      Android={StaticResource androidLabelBaseStyle}}" />
    </ContentView.Resources>

    <Grid
        BackgroundColor="{OnPlatform Android={StaticResource backgroundColor}}"
```

```
        RowSpacing="{OnPlatform 0, Android=10}"
        Margin="0, 0, 0, 5">

        <Grid.RowDefinitions>
            <RowDefinition Height="{OnPlatform *, Android=*}" />
            <RowDefinition Height="{OnPlatform 0, Android=*}" />
        </Grid.RowDefinitions>

        <Grid.ColumnDefinitions>
            <ColumnDefinition Width="{OnPlatform *, Android=1.2*}" />
            <ColumnDefinition Width="{OnPlatform *, Android=1.4*}" />
            <ColumnDefinition Width="{OnPlatform *, Android=*}" />
            <ColumnDefinition Width="{OnPlatform *, Android=1.2*}" />
            <ColumnDefinition Width="{OnPlatform *, Android=0}" />
            <ColumnDefinition Width="{OnPlatform *, Android=0}" />
            <ColumnDefinition Width="{OnPlatform *, Android=0}" />
        </Grid.ColumnDefinitions>

        <Label
            Text="Player 1" />
        ...
        <Label
            Grid.Row="{OnPlatform 0, Android=1}"
            Grid.Column="{OnPlatform 4, Android=0}"
            Text="lost $250,"/>
        <Label
            Grid.Row="{OnPlatform 0, Android=1}"
            Grid.Column="{OnPlatform 5, Android=1}" >
            <Label.Text>
                <OnPlatform x:TypeArguments="x:String">
                    <On Platform="WinUI" Value="now has $750. " />
                    <On Platform="Android" Value="has $750. " />
                </OnPlatform>
            </Label.Text>
        </Label>

        <Label
            Grid.Row="{OnPlatform 0, Android=2}"
            Grid.Column="{OnPlatform 6, Android=2}"
            Grid.ColumnSpan="{OnPlatform 1, Android=2}"
            Text="The odds were 1.64." />
    </Grid>
</ContentView>
```

The Results panel doesn't look bad either.

Let's modify the Game Info panel next. There seems to be too little space to fit all the text. Let's make the text shorter on Android. Here's the code:

```
...
<ContentView ...>

    <Grid
        RowDefinitions="*, *, *, *, *"
        ColumnDefinitions="3*, *">

        <Grid.Resources>
            <Style TargetType="Label"
                   BasedOn="{OnPlatform {StaticResource labelBaseStyle},
                       Android={StaticResource androidLabelBaseStyle}}" />
        </Grid.Resources>

        <Label
            Text="Game Info"
            Style="{OnPlatform {StaticResource labelSectionTitleStyle},
                Android={StaticResource androidLabelSectionTitleStyle}}" />
        <Label
            ...
        <Label
            Grid.Row="2">
            <Label.Text>
                <OnPlatform x:TypeArguments="x:String">
                    <On Platform="WinUI" Value="Number of races set:" />
                    <On Platform="Android" Value="Total races:" />
                </OnPlatform>
            </Label.Text>
        </Label>
        <Label
            ...
```

Here's the Android version of the Game Info panel:

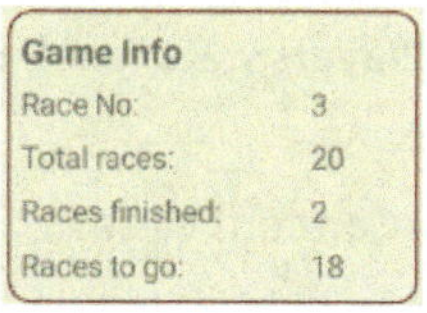

There's also too little room in the stats panels. Let's start with the Slugs' Stats panel. Here's the **SlugsStats.xaml** file:

```
...
<ContentView ...>

    <Grid
        RowDefinitions="*, *, *, *, *"
        ColumnDefinitions="*">
        <Label
            Text="Slugs' Stats"
            Style="{OnPlatform {StaticResource labelSectionTitleStyle},
                Android={StaticResource androidLabelSectionTitleStyle}}" />
        <controls:SlugStats
            ...
```

And the **SlugStats.xaml** file:

```
...
<ContentView ...>

    <ContentView.Resources>
        <Style TargetType="Label"
                      BasedOn="{OnPlatform {StaticResource labelBaseStyle},
                          Android={StaticResource androidLabelBaseStyle}}" />
    </ContentView.Resources>

    <Grid
        RowDefinitions="*">
        <Grid.ColumnDefinitions>
            <ColumnDefinition Width="{OnPlatform 2*, Android=1.8*}" />
            <ColumnDefinition Width="{OnPlatform *, Android=1.4*}" />
            <ColumnDefinition Width="*" />
        </Grid.ColumnDefinitions>
        <Label
            ...
```

Now the Slugs' Stats panel looks like so:

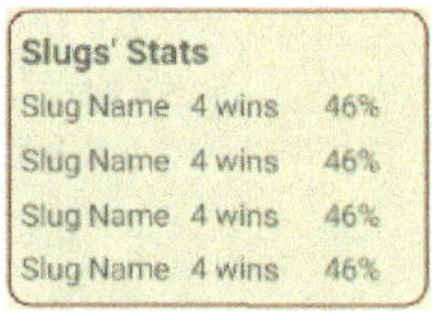

You can now see all the text. Let's take care of the Players' Stats panel then. Here's the **PlayersStatsPanel.xaml** file:

```
...
<ContentView ...>
    ...
    <Grid
        RowDefinitions="*, *, *, *, *"
        ColumnDefinitions="*">
        <Label
            Text="Players' Stats"
            Style="{OnPlatform {StaticResource labelSectionTitleStyle},
                Android={StaticResource androidLabelSectionTitleStyle}}" />
        <controls:PlayerStats
            ...
```

And the **PlayerStats.xaml** file:

```
...
<ContentView ...>

    <ContentView.Resources>
        <Style TargetType="Label"
                      BasedOn="{OnPlatform {StaticResource labelBaseStyle},
                          Android={StaticResource androidLabelBaseStyle}}" />
    </ContentView.Resources>
```

```
<Grid
        RowDefinitions="*">
        <Grid.ColumnDefinitions>
            <ColumnDefinition Width="{OnPlatform 2.5*, Android=*}" />
            <ColumnDefinition Width="{OnPlatform 1.5*, Android=*}" />
        </Grid.ColumnDefinitions>
        <Label
            ...
```

This is what it looks like now:

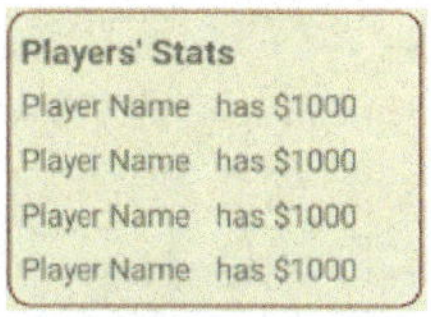

We're not going to change anything in the **Racetrack.xaml**, **TrackImage.xaml** or **SlugImage.xaml** files. But there are going to be some changes in **SlugInfo.xaml**:

```
...
<ContentView ...>
    ...
    <Grid
        Padding="5, 2, 0, 2"
        RowDefinitions="*, *"
        ColumnDefinitions="6.8*, 2.2*">
        <Label
            Text="Speedster"
            FontSize="18"
            FontAttributes="{StaticResource emphasized}"
            TextColor="{StaticResource infoTextColor}"
            Opacity="{OnPlatform 1, Android=0}" />
        <Label
            Grid.Row="1"
            Text="0 wins"
            FontSize="14"
            TextColor="{StaticResource infoTextColor}"
            Opacity="{OnPlatform 1, Android=0}" />
        <Label
            Grid.Column="1"
            Grid.RowSpan="2"
            VerticalOptions="{StaticResource defaultLayoutOptions}"
            Text="1.40"
            FontSize="{OnPlatform 40, Android=12}"
            FontAttributes="{StaticResource emphasized}"
            TextColor="{StaticResource infoTextColor}"/>
    </Grid>
</ContentView>
```

There are also going to be some changes in the **WinnerInfo.xaml** file:

```
...
<ContentView ...>
    ...
    <Grid
        RowDefinitions=".6*, *, 3*">
```

```
        <Label
            Text="The winner is"
            FontSize="{OnPlatform 28, Android=10}" />
        <Label
            Grid.Row="1"
            Text="Speedster"
            FontSize="{OnPlatform 36, Android=12}" />
        <Image
            Grid.Row="2"
            Source="speedster.png" />
    </Grid>
</ContentView>
```

The Race Track area now looks like so:

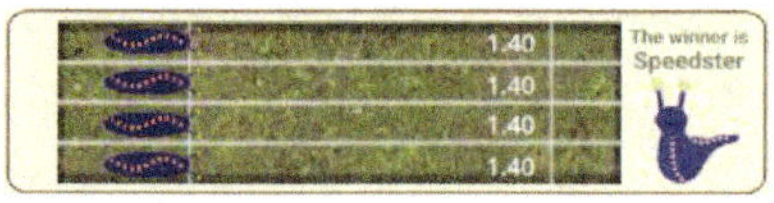

As you can see, the white labels near the slug images on the left are invisible on Android. It would be hard to read them anyway.

So, if we now run the app on Android, the RacePage looks a whole lot better than before:

WITH THE BETS PANEL	WITH THE RESULTS PANEL
	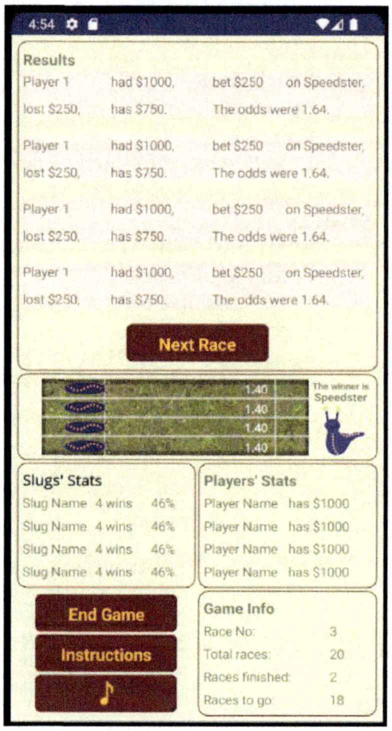

Don't worry about the Winner Info panel being visible before the race even begins. We'll handle the logic later on.

That's it as far as the **RacePage** is concerned. Let's move on to the **GameOverPage**.

GameOverPage on Android

Finally, let's take care of the **GameOverPage**. If you run it now, it's not very attractive.

Here the changes are going to be far less spectacular, though.

The **GameOverPage.xaml** file should look like so:

```
...
<ContentPage xmlns="http://schemas.microsoft.com/dotnet/2021/maui"
             xmlns:x="http://schemas.microsoft.com/winfx/2009/xaml"
             x:Class="Slugrace.Views.GameOverPage">

    <ContentPage.Resources>
        <Style TargetType="Label">
            ...
            <Setter Property="FontSize"
                    Value="{OnPlatform 40, Android=30}" />
        </Style>
    </ContentPage.Resources>

    <Grid
        RowDefinitions="2*, 2*, 2*, *">

        <Grid.Margin>
            <OnPlatform x:TypeArguments="Thickness">
                <On Platform="WinUI" Value="0" />
                <On Platform="Android" Value="20" />
            </OnPlatform>
        </Grid.Margin>

        <Label
            Text="Game Over"
            FontSize="{OnPlatform 120, Android=65}" />
        <Label
            Grid.Row="1"
            Text="There's only one player with any money left." />
        <Label
            ...
```

Now it's much more readable.

The changes in the code were made to target the two different platforms. Let's now have a look at some interesting places in the code.

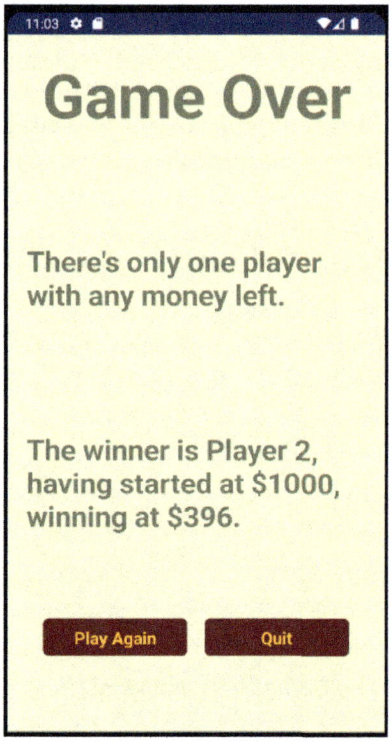

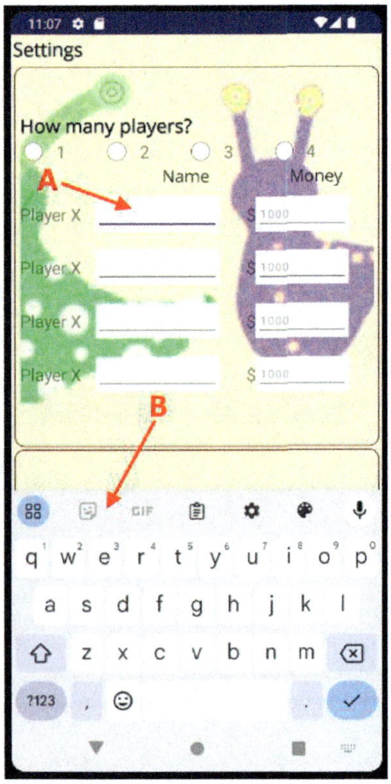

Numeric Keyboard

Let's use the **SettingsPage** for demonstrational purposes. When an entry gets focus on Android (A), a keyboard pops up (B).

This is great for the name entry where you need all alphanumeric characters. But for numeric inputs, like the initial money entry or the bet amount entry in the **RacePage**, we would either have to hold the button down for a while until the digit replaces the letter which is assigned to the same button:

or we would have to tap the **?123** button in the bottom-left corner and then use the keyboard with direct access to numeric keys:

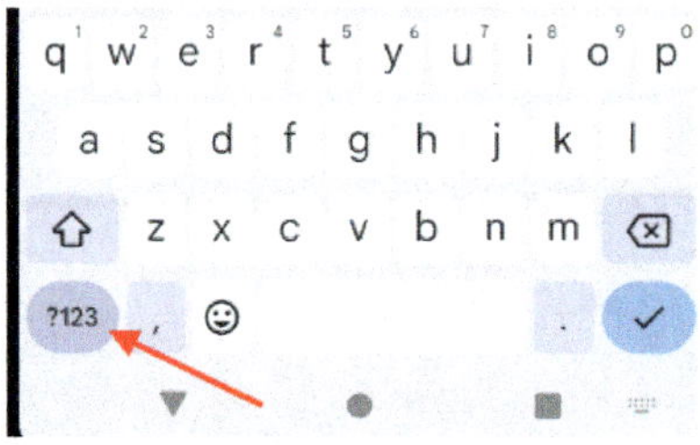

This isn't a problem if you have to do it once or twice, but in our application you will be entering numbers all the time, maybe not in the **SettingsPage**, but definitely in the Bets panel, so there must be a way to make our lives easier. And there is a very simple one. All we have to do is set the **Keyboard** property of the entries to **Numeric**. Here's the entry in the **PlayerSettings** view:

```
...
<ContentView xmlns...>
    ...
        <Entry
            x:Name="initialMoneyEntry"
            Placeholder="1000"
            Grid.Column="3"
            WidthRequest="{OnPlatform 250, Android=100}"
            Keyboard="Numeric"
            TextChanged="OnInitialMoneyTextChanged">
        ...
```

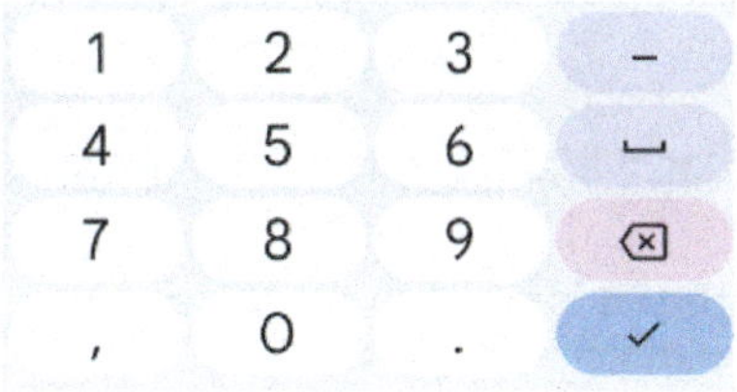

Now if the initial money entry gets focus, a numeric keyboard will show up.

The entry in the **PlayerBet** view has this property set too.

Layouts

The layouts on the two platforms differ, especially in the **RacePage**. This can be achieved by setting the row heights and column widths to different values. To keep the same number of rows and columns, we can set some of them to 0, which has the same effect as if they weren't there at all. Then we set the **Grid.Row** and **Grid.Column** attached properties to different values where needed. Here's an example from the **RacePage**:

```
...
<ContentPage ...>
    <Grid>
        <Grid.RowDefinitions>
            <RowDefinition Height="{OnPlatform 1.3*, Android=2.6*}" />
            <RowDefinition Height="{OnPlatform 2*, Android=.7*}" />
            <RowDefinition Height="{OnPlatform 2*, Android=*}" />
            <RowDefinition Height="{OnPlatform 0, Android=*}" />
        </Grid.RowDefinitions>

        <Grid.ColumnDefinitions>
            <ColumnDefinition Width="{OnPlatform 3*, Android=*}" />
            <ColumnDefinition Width="{OnPlatform 3*, Android=*}" />
            <ColumnDefinition Width="{OnPlatform 3*, Android=0}" />
            <ColumnDefinition Width="{OnPlatform 2*, Android=0}" />
        </Grid.ColumnDefinitions>

        <!--Game Info-->
        <Border
            Grid.Row="{OnPlatform 0, Android=3}"
            Grid.Column="{OnPlatform 0, Android=1}"
            HorizontalOptions="{OnPlatform Android=Fill}">
            <controls:GameInfo/>
        </Border>
        ...
```

The Game Info content view, for example, is positioned in the first row and first column on Windows, but in the fourth row and second column on Android. It works the same for the other views.

Margin and Padding

Most of the remaining code is pretty straightforward, so I don't think it's necessary to discuss it in great detail. Let's have a look at two properties, **Margin** and **Padding**, that may not be completely clear.

Well, what is actually the difference between the two?

Margin is used to set the distance between an element and its adjacent elements.

Padding is used to set the distance between and element and its child elements (its content).

Both **Margin** and **Padding** are of type **Thickness**, which is a structure. Depending on which constructor is called, we can define **Thickness** by one, two or four values.

If only one value is defined, it's applied to all sides of the element uniformly.

If two values are defined, the first value is applied to the left and right sides of the element and the second value is applied to the top and bottom sides.

If four values are defined, they're applied to the left, top, right and bottom sides of the element, in this exact order.

Here's an example of **Margin** from the **PlayerBet** content view:

```
...
<ContentView ...>
    ...
            <RadioButton
                GroupName="player1">
                <RadioButton.Content>
                    <Label
                        Text="Speedster"
                        Style="{OnPlatform {StaticResource labelBaseStyle},
                            Android={StaticResource androidLabelBaseStyle}}">
                        <Label.Margin>
                            <OnPlatform x:TypeArguments="Thickness">
                                <On Platform="WinUI" Value="0" />
                                <On Platform="Android" Value="-12, 0, 0, 0" />
                            </OnPlatform>
                        </Label.Margin>
                    </Label>
                ...
```

So, on Windows the label will have the same **`Margin`** on all four sides, on Android the distance on the left side will be decreased (hence the negative value), but it will be 0 on the other sides.

Now we have all the styles in place, our app looks good on both Windows and Android. There's just one little topic as far as the visual appearance of our app is concerned, themes. We'll be talking about themes in the next chapter.

Chapter 13 - Themes

code: https://github.com/prospero-apps/Slugrace/tree/chapter13

Mobile devices usually include light and dark **themes** which can be set manually by the user or change automatically when some conditions are met. For example, your cell phone will probably switch to dark mode when it gets dark in the evening. This way the screen will be easier on the eyes.

If you want to implement this functionality in your app, you have to set the properties that are supposed to depend on the current theme to different values, so one value for the light theme and another for the dark theme. To do that, we use the **`AppThemeBinding`** markup extension. Let's first demonstrate it using the **`TestPage`**.

Light Theme, Dark Theme

Delete the code from the **TestPage.xaml** file and implement the page like this:

```
<?xml version="1.0" encoding="utf-8" ?>
<ContentPage xmlns="http://schemas.microsoft.com/dotnet/2021/maui"
             xmlns:x="http://schemas.microsoft.com/winfx/2009/xaml"
             xmlns:local="clr-namespace:Slugrace"
             x:Class="Slugrace.Views.TestPage"
             Title="TestPage"
             Padding="20"
             BackgroundColor="DarkGoldenrod">
    <FlexLayout
        Direction="Column"
        JustifyContent="SpaceEvenly"
        AlignItems="Center"
        BackgroundColor="White">
        <Label
            Text="Hey, what a beautiful day!"
            FontSize="26" />
        <Image
            Source="Speedster.png"
            Scale=".9"/>
        <Button
            Text="Press"
            BackgroundColor="Black"
            TextColor="White" />
    </FlexLayout>
</ContentPage>
```

Now run the app on Android.

Nothing special, just a label, an image and a button inside a **FlexLayout** with a white background color and the background color of the **ContentPage** set to a shade of golden.

Let's modify the code and deliver distinct values for some of the properties.

For example the **FlexLayout** background color should be white in light theme and black in dark theme. The button should also change from black to white, and the text on it the other way around.

We'll also change the label text.

First, let's temporarily define two static properties in the **Helpers** class:

```
namespace Slugrace
{
    public static class Helpers
    {
        public static string LightThemeText { get; set; } = "Hey, what a beautiful day!";
        public static string DarkThemeText { get; set; } = "Hey, what a beautiful night!";

        public static void ValidateNumericInputAndSetState(...)
        ...
```

We're going to use them in the **TestPage**. Here's the modified code:

```
<?xml version="1.0" encoding="utf-8" ?>
<ContentPage ...>
    <FlexLayout
        ...
        BackgroundColor="{AppThemeBinding Light=White, Dark=Black}">
        <Label
            Text="{AppThemeBinding
                Light={x:Static local:Helpers.LightThemeText},
                Dark={x:Static local:Helpers.DarkThemeText}}"
            FontSize="26" />
        ...
```

```
        <Button
            Text="Press"
            BackgroundColor="{AppThemeBinding Light=Black, Dark=White}"
            TextColor="{AppThemeBinding Light=White, Dark=Black}" />
    </FlexLayout>
</ContentPage>
```

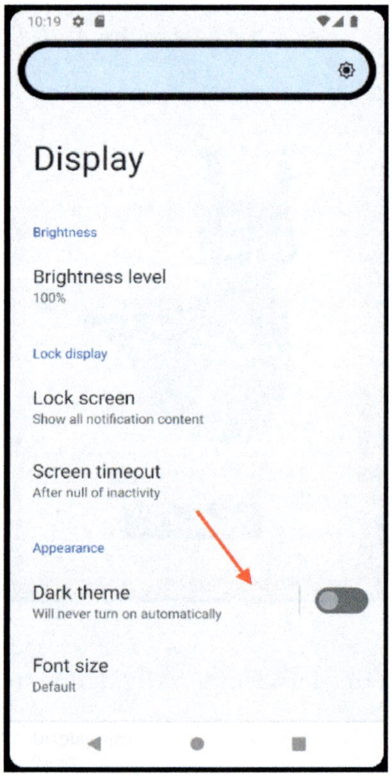

To see the themes in action, we have to pick them manually in the emulator. How to exactly do that depends on the emulator, but you will probably have to go to the settings and find it there under Display or something like that. In my emulator it looks like here on the right.

Switch to dark theme. Now our app uses the set of values defined for the dark theme (look left).

You typically change colors in the dark theme to make the text more readable, but you can change any properties you like.

Let's now implement themes in the Slugrace app. But first, remove the two static properties you just added in the **Helpers** class and set the label text in the **TestPage** manually to what it was originally.

Themes in Our Application

We're going to apply themes in our app globally and locally. Let's start with the former. Here's the **App.xaml** file with the themes implemented:

```
...
<Application ...>
    ...
            <!--Colors-->
            ...
            <Color x:Key="normalEntryColor">White</Color>
            <Color x:Key="lightPrimaryColor">#FFFFCC</Color>
            ...
```

```
<!--Other values-->
<FontAttributes x:Key="emphasized">Bold</FontAttributes>

<Style TargetType="ContentPage"
       ApplyToDerivedTypes="True">
    <Setter Property="BackgroundColor"
            Value="{AppThemeBinding Light={StaticResource lightPrimaryColor},
                Dark=Black}" />
</Style>

<Style TargetType="Border">
    <Setter Property="Stroke"
            Value="{AppThemeBinding
                Light={StaticResource mainButtonColor},
                Dark={StaticResource lightPrimaryColor}}" />
    <Setter Property="StrokeShape" Value="RoundRectangle 10, 10, 10, 10" />
    ...
<Style TargetType="Button">
    <Setter Property="BackgroundColor"
            Value="{AppThemeBinding
                Light={StaticResource mainButtonColor},
                Dark={StaticResource buttonTextColor}}" />
    <Setter Property="TextColor"
            Value="{AppThemeBinding
                Light={StaticResource buttonTextColor},
                Dark={StaticResource mainButtonColor}}" />
    <Setter Property="FontSize" Value="{StaticResource defaultFontSize}" />
    ...
                <VisualState x:Name="PointerOver">
                    <VisualState.Setters>
                        <Setter Property="BackgroundColor"
                                Value="{AppThemeBinding
                                    Light={StaticResource pressedButtonColor},
                                    Dark={StaticResource lightPrimaryColor}}" />
                    </VisualState.Setters>
                </VisualState>

                <VisualState x:Name="Pressed">
                    <VisualState.Setters>
                        <Setter Property="Scale" Value=".98" />
                        <Setter Property="BackgroundColor"
                                Value="{AppThemeBinding
                                    Light={StaticResource pressedButtonColor},
                                    Dark={StaticResource lightPrimaryColor}}" />
                    </VisualState.Setters>
                ...
```

As you can see, I extracted the background color into a resource and used it to set the background color of **ContentPage** in the light theme. In the dark theme the background color is set to black.

The colors of the **BackgroundColor** and **TextColor** properties of **Button** are switched in the two themes.

I also used the new **lightPrimaryColor** resource to set the **Stroke** property of **Border** and the background color of **Button** in the **PointerOver** and **Pressed** visual states.

And now let's have a look at some local changes.

In the **RacePage** a different image is used in dark theme for the Sound button. Otherwise it would be hardly visible in this theme. You can grab the **sound_on_dark.png** image and the other one, **sound_off_dark.png** (which we're going to need later) from my Github repository. Paste them to the **Resources/Images** folder. Here's how this is implemented in the **RacePage.xaml** file:

```
...
<ContentPage ...>
    ...
        <!--the buttons-->
        <VerticalStackLayout
            ...
            <Button
                Text="Instructions" />
            <Button
                ImageSource="{AppThemeBinding
                    Light=sound_on.png,
                    Dark=sound_on_dark.png}"
                WidthRequest="{OnPlatform 125, Android=150}"
                ...
```

In the Bets content view I modified the colors of the slider:

```
...
<ContentView ...>

    <ContentView.Resources>
        <Style TargetType="Label" BasedOn="{StaticResource labelBaseStyle}" />
        <Style TargetType="Slider">
            <Setter Property="ThumbColor"
                    Value="{AppThemeBinding
                        Light={StaticResource mainButtonColor},
                        Dark={StaticResource buttonTextColor}}" />
            <Setter Property="MinimumTrackColor"
                    Value="{AppThemeBinding
                        Light={StaticResource mainButtonColor},
                        Dark={StaticResource buttonTextColor}}" />
        </Style>
    ...
```

I also defined new color resources in the **PlayerBet** and **PlayerResult** content views. They're used to set the background color of the **Grid** and they look the same:

```
...
<ContentView ...>

    <ContentView.Resources>
        <Color x:Key="backgroundColorLight">#FFF4E5</Color>
        <Color x:Key="backgroundColorDark">Black</Color>
        <Style TargetType="Label"
                  ...
```

```
<Grid
    BackgroundColor="{OnPlatform
        Android={AppThemeBinding
            Light={StaticResource backgroundColorLight},
            Dark={StaticResource backgroundColorDark}}}"
    ...
```

And that's it. Let's now compare all the pages in light theme and dark theme:

Here's the **SettingsPage**:

LIGHT THEME

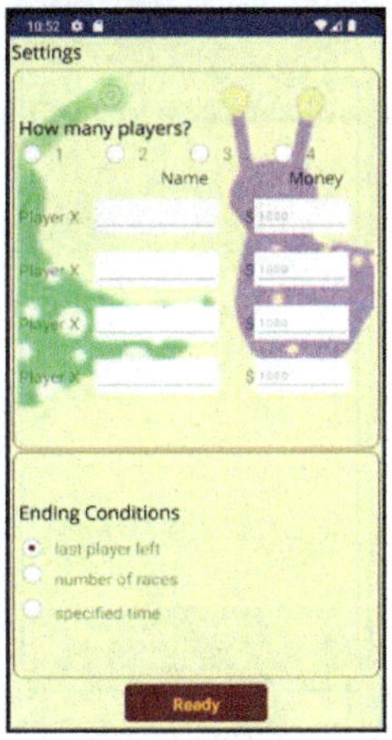

DARK THEME

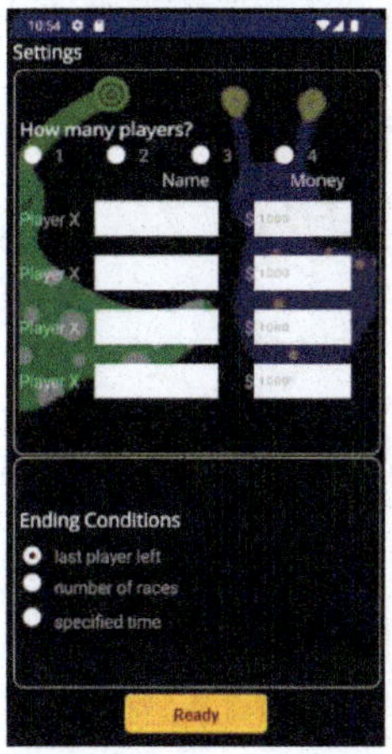

Here's the **RacePage** with the Bets panel:

LIGHT THEME

DARK THEME

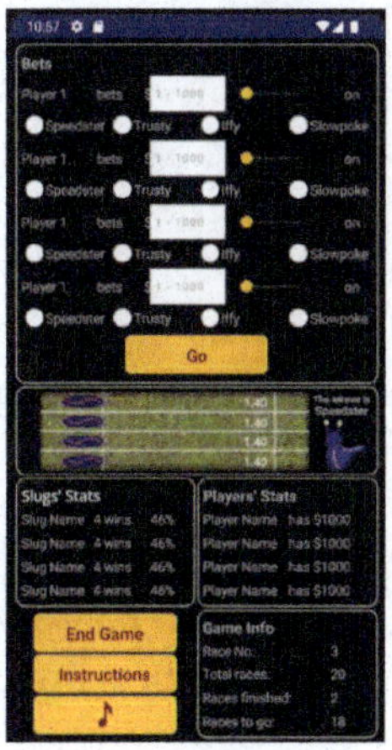

Here's the **RacePage** with the Results panel:

LIGHT THEME

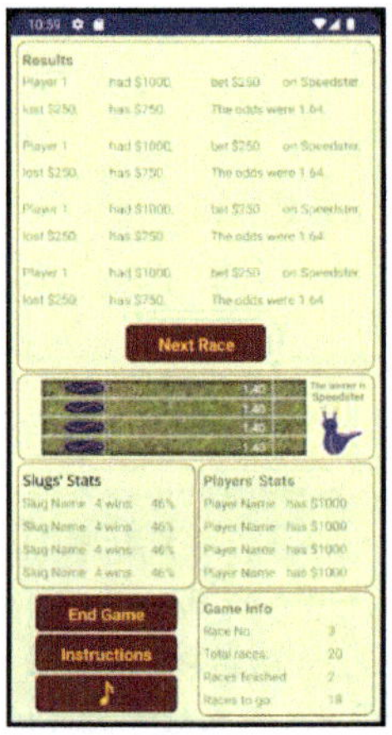

DARK THEME

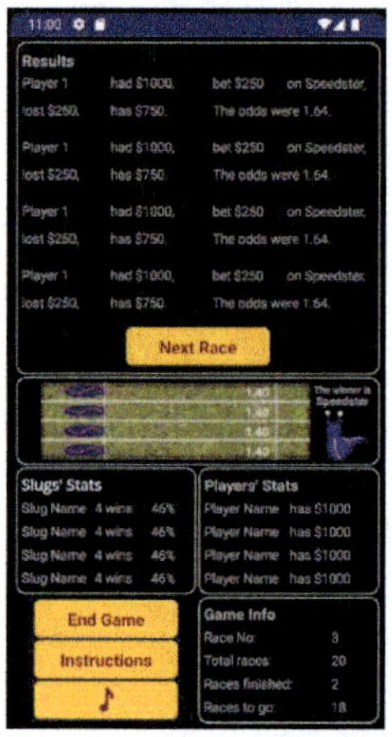

Here's the **GameOverPage**:

LIGHT THEME

DARK THEME

If you're wondering why the labels are white in the dark theme, even if we didn't define their color for that theme, this is because default values for either theme are defined in the **Resources/Styles/Style.xaml** file.

Our application is now beautifully styled, it supports the light and dark themes on Android and the only thing it lacks is data. In the next chapter we'll be briefly talking about namespaces in XAML and then, in the following chapters, we'll see how to provide data and bind to it.

Chapter 14 - Namespaces in XAML

code: https://github.com/prospero-apps/Slugrace/tree/chapter14

In the previous chapter we implemented the light and dark themes in our app. Before that, we styled the app. The next step is to start working with real data, because at this moment all the labels display hardcoded data. But before we dive into data and data binding, let's briefly discuss another topic, namespaces in XAML. It's a pretty straightforward topic, but let's systematize our knowledge of namespaces before we move on.

Default and Non-default Namespaces

You must have noticed that each page and each content view in XAML, and generally each root element, starts like this:

```
<ContentPage xmlns="http://schemas.microsoft.com/dotnet/2021/maui"
             xmlns:x="http://schemas.microsoft.com/winfx/2009/xaml"...
```

or this:

```
<ContentView xmlns="http://schemas.microsoft.com/dotnet/2021/maui"
             xmlns:x="http://schemas.microsoft.com/winfx/2009/xaml"...
```

The **App.xaml** file starts like this:

```
<Application xmlns="http://schemas.microsoft.com/dotnet/2021/maui"
             xmlns:x="http://schemas.microsoft.com/winfx/2009/xaml"...
```

And the **Styles.xaml** file in the **Resources** folder also starts in a similar way:

```
<ResourceDictionary
    xmlns="http://schemas.microsoft.com/dotnet/2021/maui"
    xmlns:x="http://schemas.microsoft.com/winfx/2009/xaml">
```

Whatever the root element is, it always contains these two lines of code. At least these two, but there may be more. So, what are these lines of code actually for?

Well, these are **namespace declarations**. The first line defines the **default namespace**. All elements in the XAML file that are used without any prefix are instances of .NET MAUI classes. Here belong **`ContentPage`**, **`Label`**, **`Button`**, **`Slider`**, **`Grid`**, and many, many more. This namespace declaration enables us to use the elements in code like so:

```
<Grid>
<Label>
<ContentView>
```

and so on, so without any prefix. Any other namespaces are **non-default namespaces** and they do require a prefix. We use the prefix both in the namespace declaration and then inside the code. In the second line of each code fragment above you can see the **x** prefix. This particular namespace contains classes intrinsic to XAML, and specifically, to the 2009 XAML specification.

To reference items from this namespace in code, we must always use the **x** prefix. We've already used such objects and attributes in our app. Here are some examples:

```
<Color x:Key="mainButtonColor">#520000</Color>
```

```
<VisualState x:Name="Normal" />
```

```
<OnPlatform x:TypeArguments="Thickness">
```

```
<ContentPage xmlns="http://schemas.microsoft.com/dotnet/2021/maui"
             xmlns:x="http://schemas.microsoft.com/winfx/2009/xaml"
             xmlns:controls="clr-namespace:Slugrace.Controls"
             x:Class="Slugrace.Views.RacePage"
             Padding="5">
```

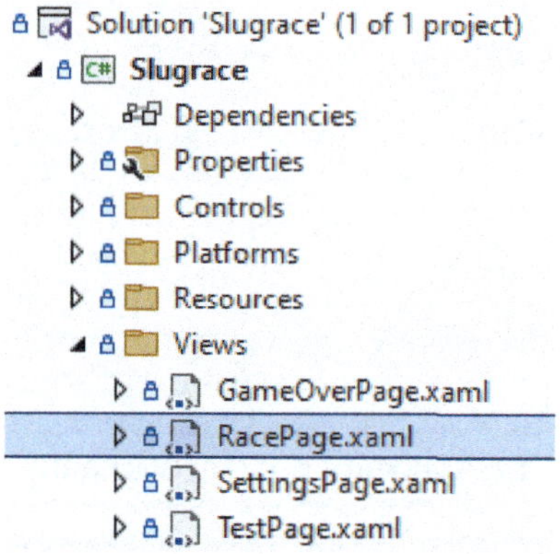

In the last example you can see that the argument is defined on the root element. This attribute specifies the namespace and class name for a class defined in XAML. In this particular case it tells us that the class's name is **RacePage** and that it's defined in the **Views** folder, which is inside the root **Slugrace** folder.

If you open the code-behind file you will see that the class name of the class defined there matches the one defined in XAML:

```
namespace Slugrace.Views;

public partial class RacePage : ContentPage
{
    ...
}
```

You can also see this exact same namespace defined in C#.

There also markup extensions that are used with the **x** prefix, like **x:Static**, **x:Array** or **x:Type** that we talked about before.

Namespaces for Types

To reference types in XAML you have to declare their namespaces with a prefix. The declaration must specify the Common Language Runtime (CLR) namespace name using the **clr-namespace** (or **using**) keyword inside the namespace declaration. If the types are in a different assembly, the assembly name must be delivered, too.

You can use any prefixes you like, but there are some conventions, like, for example, the **local** prefix. Here you can see it in **App.xaml**:

```
xmlns:local="clr-namespace:Slugrace"
```

By convention we use the **local** prefix to reference types local to the app, so types added directly to the root. When we created the .NET MAUI project, the **MainPage.xaml** file was added to the root. We could use the prefix to reference the **MainPage** like so:

```
local:MainPage
```

Another convention is that we often use the names of the folders as prefixes. This is not mandatory, but it's pretty common. Let's have a look at the **AppShell.xaml** file:

```
<?xml version="1.0" encoding="UTF-8" ?>
<Shell
    ...
    xmlns:views="clr-namespace:Slugrace.Views"
    ...
```

Here we use the **views** prefix to declare the namespace. It corresponds to the name of the folder it references. Then, below, in the same file, we use the prefix to reference a type that we defined there, **SettingsPage**:

```
<?xml version="1.0" encoding="UTF-8" ?>
<Shell
    ...
    ...
    <ShellContent
        ContentTemplate="{DataTemplate views:SettingsPage}"
        Route="SettingsPage" />
</Shell>
```

We also used another prefix, **controls**, to reference types defined in the **Controls** folder, like for example in the **SettingsPage**:

```
...
<ContentPage ...
             xmlns:controls="clr-namespace:Slugrace.Controls"
             x:Class="Slugrace.Views.SettingsPage">
    ...
                    <VerticalStackLayout>
                        <controls:PlayerSettings />
                        <controls:PlayerSettings />
                        <controls:PlayerSettings />
                        <controls:PlayerSettings />
                    </VerticalStackLayout>
                ...
```

We're not using types from a different assembly in our app, but if we were, we would have to declare the namespace like this:

```
<ContentPage ...
             xmlns:controls="clr-namespace:Controls;assembly=ExternalLibraryName" ...>
```

That's all you need to know about namespaces in XAML, at least for now. We can finally make our app do something, not only look decent. In order for an app to do something, it must consume data that we deliver to it. So, in the next chapter we'll be talking about data and data binding.

Chapter 15 – Data Binding

code: https://github.com/prospero-apps/Slugrace/tree/chapter15

In the preceding parts of the book we created the main visual elements of our application, like pages and content views. They are filled with smaller visual elements called views or controls. This all looks good, but the app doesn't do anything. All the data it displays is hardcoded and never changes. This is not how applications work. What would an application be without data? It would be no good. So, it's time we took care of it.

Data in an application can come from different sources. It can come from properties defined in the code-behind or from a visual component. If you enter something in an entry, it becomes data that may be consumed by other elements, like for instance be displayed by a label.

How do we handle data in a .NET MAUI application? Well, one way is to use events. For example you enter something in an entry like in the example above, its **TextChanged** event fires and the **Text** property of the label is set to a new value, which is handled in the code-behind. This approach works, but if there's a lot of data, there would have to be lots of events, the code would quickly become lengthy. Fortunately, there's a more efficient approach, data binding.

If we used data binding instead of an event, the **Text** property of the label would be set automatically when you entered text in the entry. This is because in **data binding** properties of two objects are linked so that if one changes, the other changes too.

In this chapter, we'll be talking about data binding. It's a complex topic, but first things first. Let's start with some basic terminology.

In this chapter I'll be demonstrating stuff using simple code in the **TestPage**. We're going to implement data binding in the actual app when we discuss the MVVM pattern.

Data Binding Terminology

It'll be easier to talk about basic terminology if we have an example to work on. Actually, let's implement the example we discussed above, with an entry and a label. Make sure your code in the **TestPage.xaml** file looks like this:

```
<?xml version="1.0" encoding="utf-8" ?>
<ContentPage xmlns="http://schemas.microsoft.com/dotnet/2021/maui"
             xmlns:x="http://schemas.microsoft.com/winfx/2009/xaml"
             x:Class="Slugrace.Views.TestPage"
             Title="TestPage"
             Padding="50">
```

```
    <VerticalStackLayout>
        <Entry
            x:Name="entry"
            FontSize="30" />
        <Label
            BindingContext="{x:Reference Name=entry}"
            Text="{Binding Path=Text}"
            FontSize="30" />
    </VerticalStackLayout>
</ContentPage>
```

If you run the app (on Windows or Android, it doesn't matter), you will see just an empty entry. The label is there too, but its **Text** property is set to an empty string, so we don't see anything. This is because it's linked to the **Text** property of the entry, which also is an empty string at this moment. But as you start typing in the entry, the exact same text will start appearing in the label.

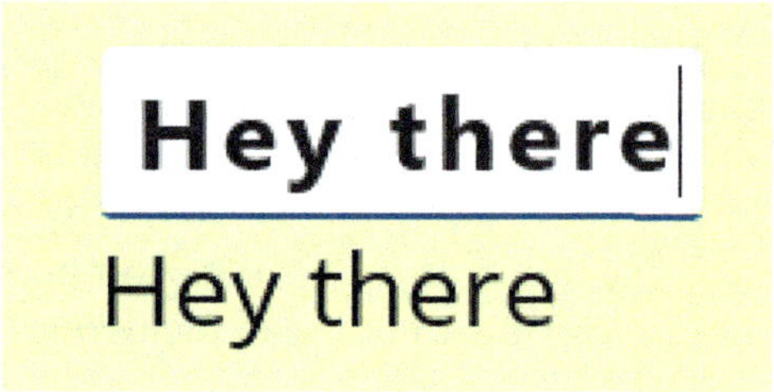

So, here we have a working data binding. The **Text** properties of the two views are linked. And now the terminology.

We have two objects here, an entry and a label. The entry is the source, the label is the target.

The **source** is the object on which data binding is set.

The **target** is the object referenced by the data binding.

The data flows from source to target, so the value of the target property is set to the value of the source property. This is how it works here, but sometimes data can flow in the opposite direction or in both directions, as we're going to see.

Then we have the binding context, another term. The **binding context** is set on the target and references the source so that the target object knows where to pull the data from.

The target property must be a **bindable property**. This means the target object must inherit from **BindableObject**. **Element**, **VisualElement**, **View** and **View** derivatives inherit from **BindableObject**. The **Text** property of the **Label** class is associated with the bindable property **TextProperty**.

We also use two markup extensions here. The first one is **x:Reference**. As its name suggests, it's used to reference an object by its name. The second one is **Binding**. Its **Path** property is set to the property of the source object we want to bind to.

The **Name** property of **x:Reference** and the **Path** property of **Binding** are content properties, so they may be omitted if they're the first properties (or the only ones like here). So, we could rewrite the code like this:

```
...
<ContentPage ...>
    ...
        <Label
            BindingContext="{x:Reference entry}"
            Text="{Binding Text}"
            ...
```

We usually set the bindings in XAML, but, naturally, we could do it in C# as well. Let's see how.

Data Binding in C# Code

Let's rewrite the code above so that the binding is set in C# code. First, let's remove the binding from the XAML file and add a name to the label so that we can reference it from the code-behind:

```
...
<ContentPage ...>
    <VerticalStackLayout>
        <Entry
            x:Name="entry"
            FontSize="30" />
        <Label
            x:Name="label"
            FontSize="30" />
    </VerticalStackLayout>
</ContentPage>
```

And now let's set the binding in the **TestPage.xaml.cs** file:

```
namespace Slugrace.Views;
public partial class TestPage : ContentPage
{
    public TestPage()
    {
        InitializeComponent();

        label.BindingContext = entry;
        label.SetBinding(Label.TextProperty, "Text");
    }
}
```

If you now run the app, it'll work just like before.

So, we use the **BindingContext** property to specify the source object and the **SetBinding** method to specify the target and source properties that should be linked. The **SetBinding** method is called on the target.

Now look how the source and target properties are specified. The target property is specified as a **BindableProperty** object, **Label.TextProperty**. The source property is specified as a string.

As I mentioned before, we're going to set our bindings primarily in XAML, so remove the two lines of code where the binding was set from the code-behind and go back to the XAML file. The example we discussed above with the **`Text`** properties of an entry and a label linked together is an example of view-to-view binding. Let's have a look at another example of that type.

View-to-view Binding

Each control can have its **`BindingContext`** set to only one source (although there is a way around it, as we're going to learn), but you can bind as many targets to the source as you wish. To keep things simple, let's bind two targets to a single source. Modify the **TestPage.xaml** file so that it looks like this:

```
...
<ContentPage ...>
    <VerticalStackLayout>
        <Slider x:Name="slider"
                Maximum="200" />
        <Label
            x:Name="label"
            FontSize="30"
            BindingContext="{x:Reference slider}"
            Text="{Binding Value}" />
        <BoxView
            x:Name="boxView"
            Color="Green"
            BindingContext="{x:Reference slider}"
            WidthRequest="{Binding Value}"
            HeightRequest="{Binding Value}" />
    </VerticalStackLayout>
</ContentPage>
```

Here the slider is the source and the label and the box view are the targets. So, both targets have the same binding context and they both bind to the same property of the source, **`Value`**. If you run the app, you will see the slider and the label, but not the box view below:

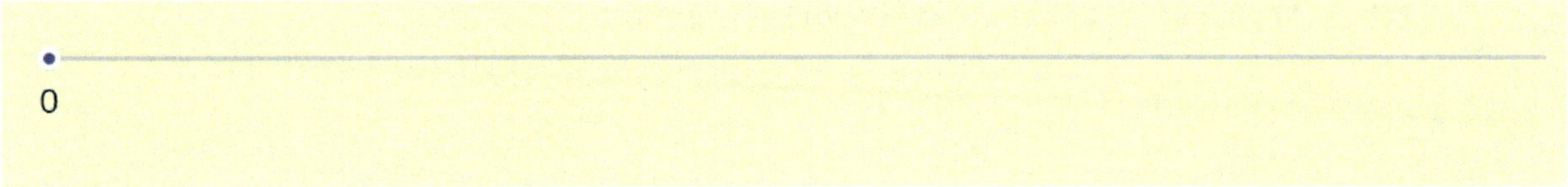

The **`Text`** property of the label is set to 0 and you can't see the box view because its **`WidthRequest`** and **`HeightRequest`** properties are set to 0. Why? Because the **`Text`** property of the label and the **`WidthRequest`** and **`HeightRequest`** properties of the box view are all bound to the **`Value`** property of the slider and the default value of the slider is 0.

Now try dragging the slider to the right. You should see the label text change and the box view grow:

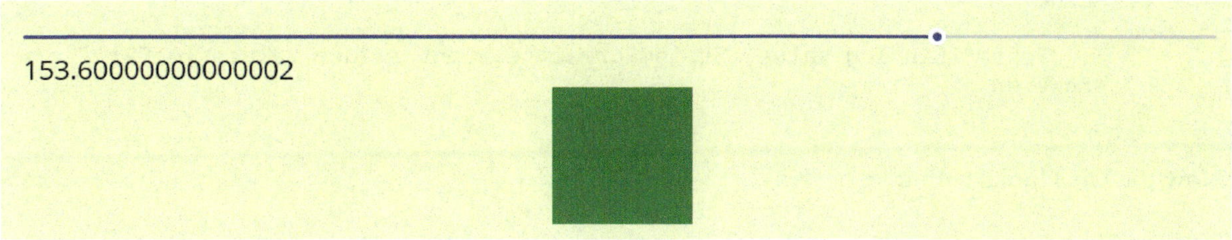

You can also bind to different properties of the source object. Let's bind the box view's **WidthRequest** property to the **Maximum** property of the slider. As the **Maximum** property doesn't change over time, the width of the box view won't change either. Here's the code:

```
...
<ContentPage ...>
    ...
        <BoxView
            ...
            WidthRequest="{Binding Maximum}"
            HeightRequest="{Binding Value}" />
    ...
```

If you now run the app, the label's **Text** property and the box view's **HeightRequest** property will change, but the **WidthRequest** property of the latter will remain constant:

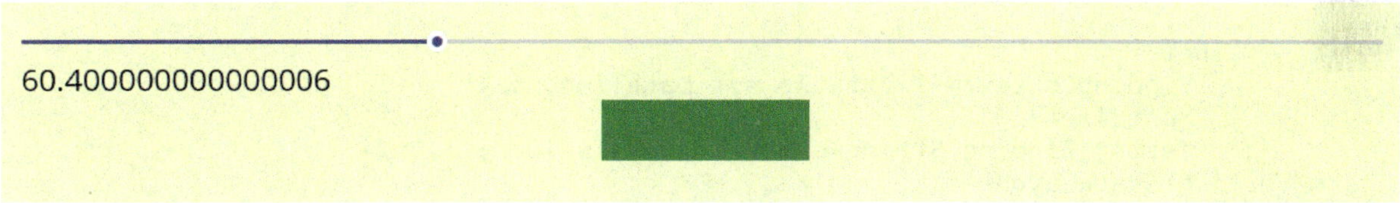

So, everything works as expected. But what if we don't like how the label text is formatted? Well, we can easily fix it.

StringFormat

You can easily format strings by setting the **StringFormat** property. This only works if the target property is a string, which is the case with the **Text** property of **Label**. Let's display the text as a number with some additional info. If you want to add additional text, you must enclose it in single quotes. The actual data is placed in curly braces and you can format it any way you want. In our case we'll format it to be a float number with two decimal places:

```
...
<ContentPage ...>
    ...
        <Label
            ...
            Text="{Binding Value, StringFormat='Current slider value: {0:F2}'}" />
        <BoxView
            ...
```

Now the label looks better:

Here's another example. Let's add another label that will display the current date:

```
...
<ContentPage xmlns="http://schemas.microsoft.com/dotnet/2021/maui"
             xmlns:x="http://schemas.microsoft.com/winfx/2009/xaml"
             xmlns:sys="clr-namespace:System;assembly=netstandard"
             x:Class="Slugrace.Views.TestPage"
             Title="TestPage"
             Padding="50">
    <VerticalStackLayout>
        ...
        <BoxView
            ...
        <Label
            BindingContext="{x:Static sys:DateTime.Now}"
            FontSize="20"
            Text="{Binding StringFormat='Today is {0:D}.'}" />
    </VerticalStackLayout>
</ContentPage>
```

In this example we're not binding to another view, but rather to the static **DateTime.Now** property. As you know, we use the **x:Static** markup extension to reference a static property. This property is defined in the **System** namespace, in a different assembly, so, as we learned in the previous chapter, we must add the appropriate namespace in the XAML code. Here we're using the **sys** prefix.

Now our **TestPage** looks like this:

In the example above we used a binding context. But is it always necessary? Turns out, it isn't.

The Source Property

Instead of defining a binding context, we can set the **Source** property of **Binding**. Let's rewrite one of the bindings in the example above:

```
...
<ContentPage ...>
    ...
        <Label
            x:Name="label"
            FontSize="30"
            Text="{Binding Value,
                           Source={x:Reference slider},
                           StringFormat='Current slider value: {0:F2}'}" />
        <BoxView
            ...
```

This is an alternative syntax. But there's yet another alternative syntax, not so common, but still worth knowing.

Object-Element Syntax

We usually use the **Binding** markup extension to set a binding, but using object elements is also possible. Let's rewrite the binding on the first label again using this notation:

```
...
<ContentPage ...>
    ...
        <Label
            x:Name="label"
            FontSize="30">
            <Label.Text>
                <Binding Path="Value"
                         Source="{x:Reference slider}"
                         StringFormat="Current slider value: {0:F2}" />
            </Label.Text>
        </Label>
        <BoxView
            ...
```

Or, even, we can express the **x:Reference** markup extension as an object element:

```
...
<ContentPage ...>
    ...
```

```
        <Label
            x:Name="label"
            FontSize="30">
            <Label.Text>
                <Binding Path="Value"
                         StringFormat="Current slider value: {0:F2}">
                    <Binding.Source>
                        <x:Reference Name="slider" />
                    </Binding.Source>
                </Binding>
            </Label.Text>
        ...
```

This syntax may be useful with complex objects. But in such a simple example as ours, it's not necessary. Let's modify the code so that the binding context is set again:

```
...
<ContentPage ...>
    ...
        <Label
            x:Name="label"
            FontSize="30"
            BindingContext="{x:Reference slider}"
            Text="{Binding Value,
                           StringFormat='Current slider value: {0:F2}'}" />
        <BoxView
            ...
```

The first label and the box view use the same binding context. This means we have to set it twice, on each object individually. Or do we?

Binding Context Inheritance

The **BindingContext** property value is inherited by the children of the object it's set on. So, if the first label and the box view were children of, let's say, a **VerticalStackLayout**, we could set the **BindingContext** property on the parent and it would be inherited by the children. Let's check it out.

```
...
<ContentPage ...>
    <VerticalStackLayout>
        <Slider ... />

        <VerticalStackLayout BindingContext="{x:Reference slider}">
            <Label
                x:Name="label"
                ...
            <BoxView
                x:Name="boxView"
```

```
        ...
    </VerticalStackLayout>

    <Label
        ...
```

The app still works as before.

Now, remember how I told you that each object can only have one **BindingContext** and that there is a way around it? Well, let's have a closer look at this next.

Binding Modes

A single view can have data binding on multiple properties. In our example the box view has two bindings: one set on the **WidthRequest** property and another set on the **HeightRequest** property. The former is bound to the value of the **Maximum** property of the slider and the latter is bound to its **Value** property. But still, both **Maximum** and **Value** are properties of the slider. But what if we wanted to bind the two properties of the box view to properties of two different objects? Well, we would need two binding contexts on the box view, which isn't possible because a single view can only have one **BindingContext**.

Let's modify our code slightly to illustrate the problem. Here's the code:

```
<?xml version="1.0" encoding="utf-8" ?>
<ContentPage xmlns="http://schemas.microsoft.com/dotnet/2021/maui"
             xmlns:x="http://schemas.microsoft.com/winfx/2009/xaml"
             x:Class="Slugrace.Views.TestPage"
             Title="TestPage"
             Padding="50">

    <ContentPage.Resources>
        <Style TargetType="Label">
            <Setter Property="FontSize" Value="30" />
        </Style>
    </ContentPage.Resources>

    <VerticalStackLayout>
        <Label Text="Width" />
        <Slider x:Name="slider1"
                Maximum="200" />

        <Label Text="Height" />
        <Slider x:Name="slider2"
                Maximum="200" />

        <Label Text="Rotation" />
        <Slider x:Name="slider3"
                Maximum="360" />
```

```
        <BoxView x:Name="boxView"
                 BindingContext="{x:Reference slider1}"
                 Color="Green"
                 WidthRequest="{Binding Value}"
                 HeightRequest="{Binding Value}" />

    </VerticalStackLayout>
</ContentPage>
```

Now we have three sliders with accompanying labels to inform us what each slider is meant for. We also have the box view. We now want to use the first slider to change the box view's width, the second slider to change its height and the third one to rotate it. But we can't set the **`BindingContext`** property of the box view to all three sliders, we have to pick one. Here **`slider1`** was picked to set the width, but what about the others? Run the app and try dragging the sliders. Only the first one does anything:

So, what can we do? Well, we can't set more binding contexts, but we could use another feature of data binding, which is modes. Let's first rewrite the code so that it works as intended and then let's think about how it works:

```
...
<ContentPage ...>
    ...
    <VerticalStackLayout>
        <Label Text="Width" />
        <Slider x:Name="slider1"
                Maximum="200"
                BindingContext="{x:Reference boxView}"
                Value="{Binding WidthRequest, Mode=OneWayToSource}" />

        <Label Text="Height" />
        <Slider x:Name="slider2"
                Maximum="200"
                BindingContext="{x:Reference boxView}"
                Value="{Binding HeightRequest, Mode=OneWayToSource}" />

        <Label Text="Rotation" />
```

```
        <Slider x:Name="slider3"
                Maximum="360"
                BindingContext="{x:Reference boxView}"
                Value="{Binding Rotation, Mode=OneWayToSource}" />

        <BoxView x:Name="boxView"
                 Color="Green" />

    </VerticalStackLayout>
</ContentPage>
```

Looks as if everything had been reversed. Now the binding context is no longer set on the box view to reference a slider, but rather the box view is set as the binding context for each slider. The bindings are set on the **Value** properties of the sliders. We also set the **Mode** property to **OneWayToSource**. This is one of a couple possible values (we're going to discuss them in a while). As the name of this binding mode suggests, the **Value** properties of the sliders set the appropriate values of the box view, so **WidthRequest**, **HeightRequest** and **Rotation** respectively. In other words, values are transferred from the target (each particular slider) to the source (the box view). Now run the app and try it out:

So, what binding modes are there? The **Mode** property can be set to a member of the **BindingMode** enumeration. And the members are:

- **Default**

- **OneWay**

- **OneWayToSource**

- **TwoWay**

- **OneTime**

The **OneWay** mode is the default mode of most bindable properties and it's used to transfer values from source to target. The **OneWayToSource** mode is used to transfer values in the opposite direction.

In the **OneTime** mode values are transferred from source to target, but only if the **BindingContext** changes. We're not going to discuss this mode in more detail.

What about **TwoWay**? Well, **TwoWay** is used to transfer values in both directions between source and target. Let's modify our code like this:

```
...
<ContentPage ...>

    <ContentPage.Resources>
        <Style TargetType="Label">
            <Setter Property="FontSize" Value="30" />
        </Style>
    </ContentPage.Resources>

    <VerticalStackLayout>
        <Label BindingContext="{x:Reference slider}"
               Text="{Binding Value, StringFormat='Width: {0:F2}'}" />

        <Slider x:Name="slider"
                BindingContext="{x:Reference boxView}"
                Minimum="50"
                Maximum="200"
                Value="{Binding WidthRequest, Mode=TwoWay}" />

        <BoxView x:Name="boxView"
                 Color="Green"
                 HeightRequest="100" />
    </VerticalStackLayout>
</ContentPage>
```

Here we have a label, a slider and a box view. The label's **Text** property is bound to the slider's **Value** property. This is a **OneWay** binding. The data flows from source (slider) to target (label).

The slider's **Value** property is bound to the box view's **WidthRequest** property. This is a **TwoWay** binding, which we explicitly specified, although we didn't have to because the default binding mode for the **Slider**'s **Value** property is **TwoWay**. So, we could leave it out:

```
<?xml version="1.0" encoding="utf-8" ?>
<ContentPage ...>
    ...
        <Slider x:Name="slider"
                ...
                Value="{Binding WidthRequest}" />

        <BoxView ...
```

Let's run the app:

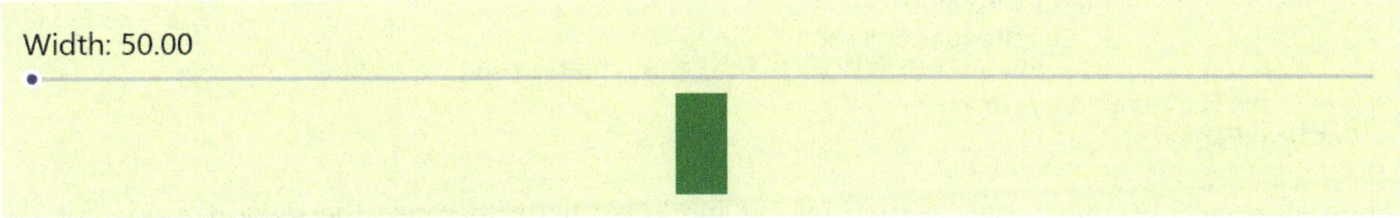

As you can see, the value of the **Slider**'s **Value** property is 50, and the width of the box view is also 50. Drag the slider in both directions and watch the label and the box view change.

Some properties, like the **Slider**'s **Value** property, are **TwoWay** by default. Some other properties like that are the **Date** property of **DatePicker**, the **Text** property of **Entry** and **Editor** and some more. But it doesn't mean we can't set a different binding mode. We can override the binding mode. Let's try it out by explicitly setting the binding mode of the slider's **Value** property to **OneWay**:

```
...
<ContentPage ...>
    ...
        <Slider x:Name="slider"
                ...
                Value="{Binding WidthRequest, Mode=OneWay}" />

        <BoxView ...
```

Run the app again. Now the box view occupies all available width because we didn't set the **WidthRequest** property on it and if you now drag the slider and thus change the **Value** property, the **WidthRequest** isn't updated because the flow now is in one direction only:

Let's change the binding mode back to **TwoWay**. As this binding works in both directions, we could set it on the other object instead:

```
...
<ContentPage ...>
    ...
        <Slider x:Name="slider"
                Minimum="50"
                Maximum="200" />
```

```
        <BoxView x:Name="boxView"
                 BindingContext="{x:Reference slider}"
                 Color="Green"
                 HeightRequest="100"
                 WidthRequest="{Binding Value, Mode=TwoWay}" />
    </VerticalStackLayout>
</ContentPage>
```

Here, however, we must specify the binding mode explicitly because the default mode for the **WidthRequest** property of **BoxView** is **OneWay**. Now it works as before.

Great. But what if we wanted the data to be used in a different way? Let's say, we want the box view to be visible only if the slider's **Value** is greater than 150? Or maybe we want the label to represent the **Value** of the slider using integer size categories like 1 for very small values, 2 for a bit greater values and so on, moving to the next category every 50 units? To implement scenarios like these, we need value converters.

Value Converters

In the examples above the values that were transferred from source to target, from target to source or in both directions were either of the same type, like the **Slider**'s **Value** and the **BoxView**'s **WidthRequest** properties, which are both of type **double**, or of different types, but with one type easily convertible to the other type using an implicit conversion, like the **Value** property of **Slider** (**double**) and the **Text** property of **Label** (**string**). But sometimes an explicit type conversion is necessary.

You can convert any type into a string using the **StringFormat** property, as we saw before. But what about other types? Well, for other type conversions we need **value converters**, also known as **binding converters**. These are classes that implement the **IValueConverter** interface. Let's see how to use them in practice.

So, suppose we want the label to represent the **Value** of the slider using integer size categories like I mentioned before. The **Value** property is of type **double** and we need categories of type **int**. What we need is a value converter that converts doubles to ints. We usually define also a method that does the conversion in the opposite direction. We wouldn't have to do it if we were sure that the converter is only going to be used in **OneWay** bindings, but you never know. You may want to reuse the converter in a different part of the app where a **TwoWay** or **OneWayToSource** conversion is required, so it's a good idea to make the converters more universal. This is why we're always going to define two methods in our converters, one for the conversion in one direction and the other for the conversion in the opposite direction. These two methods are called **Convert** and **ConvertBack** respectively.

Let's start with our example. We're going to set the **Text** property of the label. If the **Value** of the slider is between 50 and 100, the width category should be 1. Category 2 will be for widths between

100 and 150, and category 3 for widths between 150 and 200. We could use just the **StringFormat** property for that, but let's also use a value converter.

We need to convert doubles to ints, so we'll create a class named **DoubleToIntConverter**. To keep things organized, let's create a new folder in the root of our app named **Converters**. In this folder we can now create our first converter, so add the aforementioned class to it and implement the two methods in it:

```
using System.Globalization;

namespace Slugrace.Converters;

public class DoubleToIntConverter : IValueConverter
{
    public object? Convert(object? value, Type targetType, object? parameter, CultureInfo culture)
    {
        return (int)((double)value! / 50);
    }

    public object? ConvertBack(object? value, Type targetType, object? parameter, CultureInfo culture)
    {
        return (double)((int)value! * 50);
    }
}
```

Now we must instantiate the converter in the **TestPage**'s resource dictionary and then reference it by key in the XAML code. We must also remember to add the converter's namespace using a prefix:

```
...
<ContentPage xmlns="http://schemas.microsoft.com/dotnet/2021/maui"
             xmlns:x="http://schemas.microsoft.com/winfx/2009/xaml"
             xmlns:converters="clr-namespace:Slugrace.Converters"
             x:Class="Slugrace.Views.TestPage"
             Title="TestPage"
             Padding="50">

    <ContentPage.Resources>
        <Style TargetType="Label">
            <Setter Property="FontSize" Value="30" />
        </Style>
        <converters:DoubleToIntConverter x:Key="doubleToInt" />
    </ContentPage.Resources>

    <VerticalStackLayout>
        <Label BindingContext="{x:Reference slider}"
               Text="{Binding Value,
                              Converter={StaticResource doubleToInt},
                              StringFormat='Width Category: {0}'}" />

        <Slider x:Name="slider"
                ...
```

As you can see, here we have both the converter and the **StringFormat** property. In such cases, the converter is invoked first and the result is formatted as a string. If we now run the app and drag the slider, the width category will change every 50 units:

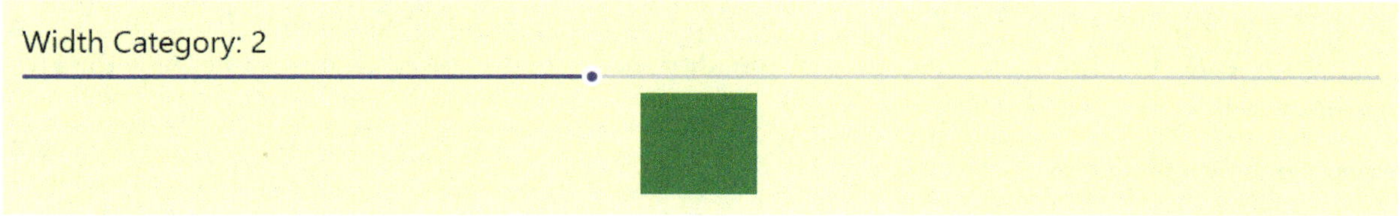

The **Convert** method takes quite a few parameters. We only used one so far, **value**, which is of type **object**. This is the object or value from the data-binding source, so, in our case, from the slider's **Value** property.

The method must return a value of the type of the data-binding target or a type that can be implicitly converted to the target's type. Here it returns an **int**, which is then converted using the **StringFormat** property.

In the example the width category changes every 50 units. But what if we wanted to make the converter more universal and let the user decide what value should be used. We can do it using the **parameter** parameter, which is of type **object**, too.

Let's modify the **Convert** method and then add another label and set the parameter to 50 on one label and 10 on the other. Here's the **Convert** method:

```
...
public class DoubleToIntConverter : IValueConverter
{
    public object? Convert(object? value, Type targetType, object? parameter, CultureInfo culture)
    {
        if (!double.TryParse(parameter as string, out double granularity))
        {
            granularity = 1;
        }

        return (int)((double)value! / granularity);
    }

    public object? ConvertBack(object? value, Type targetType, object? parameter, CultureInfo culture)
    {
        if (!double.TryParse(parameter as string, out double granularity))
        {
            granularity = 1;
        }

        return (double)((int)value! * granularity);
    }
}
```

And now let's set the parameters:

```
...
<ContentPage ...>
    ...
```

```
<VerticalStackLayout>
    <Label BindingContext="{x:Reference slider}"
           Text="{Binding Value,
                          Converter={StaticResource doubleToInt},
                          ConverterParameter=50,
                          StringFormat='Width Category (granularity 50): {0}'}" />

    <Label BindingContext="{x:Reference slider}"
           Text="{Binding Value,
                          Converter={StaticResource doubleToInt},
                          ConverterParameter=10,
                          StringFormat='Width Category (granularity 10): {0}'}" />

    <Slider ...
```

Now the categories will be different for each label:

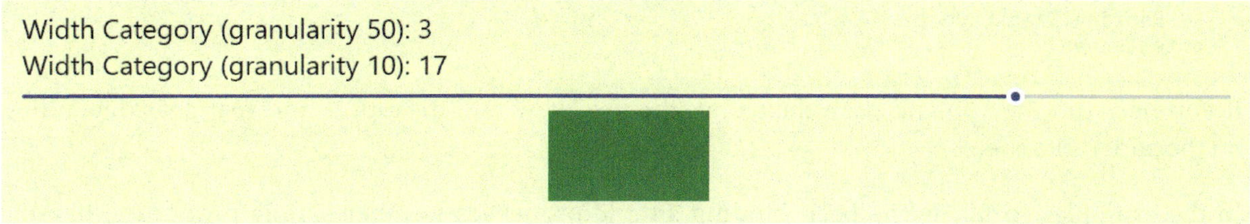

Next, let's create another converter in the **Converters** folder. This time we want to make the box view invisible if the **Value** property of the slider is greater than 150. To make the box view invisible, we have to set its **IsVisible** property to **False**, which is a boolean value. So, we need a converter that converts doubles to bools:

```
using System.Globalization;

namespace Slugrace.Converters;

public class DoubleToBoolConverter : IValueConverter
{
    public object? Convert(object? value, Type targetType, object? parameter, CultureInfo culture)
    {
        if (!double.TryParse(parameter as string, out double limit))
        {
            limit = 100;
        }

        return (double)value! < limit;
    }

    public object? ConvertBack(object? value, Type targetType, object? parameter, CultureInfo culture)
    {
        if (!double.TryParse(parameter as string, out double limit))
        {
            limit = 100;
        }

        return (bool)value! ? limit : limit + 1;
    }
}
```

Let's use it:

```
...
<ContentPage ...>

    <ContentPage.Resources>
        ...
        <converters:DoubleToIntConverter x:Key="doubleToInt" />
        <converters:DoubleToBoolConverter x:Key="doubleToBool" />
    </ContentPage.Resources>

    <VerticalStackLayout>
        ...
        <BoxView x:Name="boxView"
                 ...
                 WidthRequest="{Binding Value, Mode=TwoWay}"
                 IsVisible="{Binding Value,
                                     Converter={StaticResource doubleToBool},
                                     ConverterParameter=150}" />

    </VerticalStackLayout>
</ContentPage>
```

If you now run the app and drag the slider, the box view will disappear and reappear depending on the slider's **Value**.

In the examples so far, we've been binding simple properties to other simple properties, like the **Slider**'s **Value** property and the **Label**'s **Text** property. You know that we use the **Path** property to set a binding to a particular property. The **Path** property is the content property of **Binding** and may be omitted when it's the first property. But we haven't demonstrated more complex paths yet.

Binding Path

The **Path** property may be set to a simple property, a subproperty or to a member of a collection. Let's check it out:

```
...
<ContentPage ...
             Padding="50"
             x:Name="page">
    ...
        <BoxView x:Name="boxView"
                 ...
        <Label Text="{Binding Source={x:Reference page},
                              Path=Content.Children[0],
                              StringFormat='The first child is of type: {0}.'}" />

        <Label Text="{Binding Source={x:Reference page},
                              Path=Content.Children[1].Text.Length,
                              StringFormat='The second label contains {0} characters.'}" />

        <Label Text="{Binding Source={x:Reference page},
                              Path=Content.Children.Count,
                              StringFormat='This page contains {0} children.'}" />

    </VerticalStackLayout>
</ContentPage>
```

First we specified the name of the **ContentPage** so that we can reference it. Then we created three labels.

In the first label the **Text** property is bound to the first child of **Content**. Here **Content** is the **VerticalStackLayout**. It has 7 children: 5 labels, a slider and a box view. The first child is a label.

In the second label the **Text** property is bound to the **Length** property of **Text**, which is a property of the second child of **Content**.

In the third label the **Text** property is bound to the **Count** subproperty of **Children**, which itself is a subproperty of **Content**.

Here's the result:

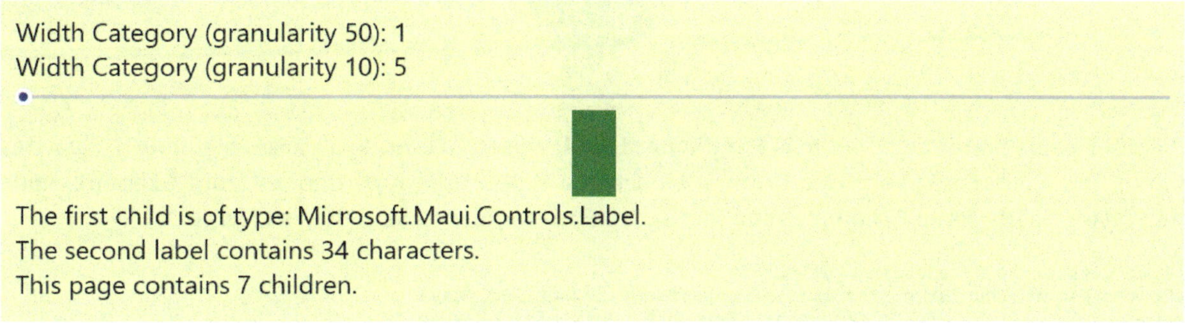

We can bind to properties of other objects that we specify by name. But we can also use relative bindings.

Relative Bindings

Relative bindings enable us to set the binding source relative to the position of the binding target. We use the **RelativeSource** markup extension to create relative bindings. The content property of **RelativeSource** is **Mode**. It can be set to a couple values, one of which is **Self**. This value is used if we want to bind one property of an object to another property of the same object. Let's simplify the **TestPage**:

```
<?xml version="1.0" encoding="utf-8" ?>
<ContentPage xmlns="http://schemas.microsoft.com/dotnet/2021/maui"
             xmlns:x="http://schemas.microsoft.com/winfx/2009/xaml"
             x:Class="Slugrace.Views.TestPage"
             Title="TestPage"
             Padding="50">
```

```
    <VerticalStackLayout>
        <BoxView x:Name="boxView"
                 Color="Green"
                 WidthRequest="120"
                 HeightRequest="{Binding Source={RelativeSource Self},
                                         Path=WidthRequest}"
                 Rotation="{Binding Source={RelativeSource Self},
                                    Path=WidthRequest}" />
    </VerticalStackLayout>
</ContentPage>
```

Here the **HeightRequest** and **Rotation** properties of the box view are bound to its **WidthRequest** property. If you run it, all three properties will have the same value:

Another value **Mode** can be set to is **FindAncestor**. It's used to bind to a parent element. To use this mode, the **AncestorType** property must be set to a type. If the type derives from **Element**, **Mode** will be implicitly set to **FindAncestor**. Let's again rewrite the code in the **TestPage**:

```
<?xml version="1.0" encoding="utf-8" ?>
<ContentPage xmlns="http://schemas.microsoft.com/dotnet/2021/maui"
             xmlns:x="http://schemas.microsoft.com/winfx/2009/xaml"
             x:Class="Slugrace.Views.TestPage"
             Title="TestPage"
             Padding="50">

    <ContentPage.Resources>
        <Style TargetType="Label">
            <Setter Property="FontSize" Value="30" />
        </Style>
    </ContentPage.Resources>

    <VerticalStackLayout Rotation="5">
        <VerticalStackLayout Rotation="-15">
            <Label Text="{Binding Source={RelativeSource AncestorType={x:Type VerticalStackLayout}},
                                  Path=Rotation,
                                  StringFormat='inner layout is rotated {0} degrees' }" />
            <Label Text="{Binding Source={RelativeSource AncestorType={x:Type VerticalStackLayout},
                                                         AncestorLevel=2},
                                  Path=Rotation,
                                  StringFormat='outer layout is rotated {0} degrees' }" />
        </VerticalStackLayout>
        <Label Text="{Binding Source={RelativeSource AncestorType={x:Type ContentPage}},
                              Path=Title}" />
    </VerticalStackLayout>
</ContentPage>
```

Here we didn't even give names to the elements because we'll be binding to their properties by type, not by name. Let's see the result first and then discuss it:

The first label's **Text** property is bound to an ancestor of type **VerticalStackLayout**. This label has a direct parent of this type and an indirect one, which is its grandparent. By default it binds its **Text** property to the direct parent, which is the **VerticalStackLayout** with **Rotation** set to -15.

If we want to bind to the outer **VerticalStackLayout**, we must set **AncestorLevel** to 2. This is what the second label does.

The third label is bound to an ancestor of type **ContentPage**. There's only one ancestor of this type.

So far, all the bindings have worked correctly, but what if a binding fails or returns a null value? Let's have a look at such situations next.

Binding Fallbacks

Sometimes we try to bind to a property that doesn't exist. How to handle this? Let's rewrite our code in the **TestPage** like so:

```
<?xml version="1.0" encoding="utf-8" ?>
<ContentPage xmlns="http://schemas.microsoft.com/dotnet/2021/maui"
             xmlns:x="http://schemas.microsoft.com/winfx/2009/xaml"
             x:Class="Slugrace.Views.TestPage"
             Title="TestPage"
             Padding="50">

    <ContentPage.Resources>
        <Style TargetType="Label">
            <Setter Property="FontSize" Value="30" />
        </Style>
    </ContentPage.Resources>

    <VerticalStackLayout>
        <Label x:Name="label1"
               Text="A Label has the Text property." />
        <Slider x:Name="slider" />
        <Label BindingContext="{x:Reference label1}"
               Text="{Binding Text}" />
        <Label BindingContext="{x:Reference slider}"
               Text="{Binding Text, FallbackValue='Text property not defined'}" />
    </VerticalStackLayout>
</ContentPage>
```

Here we have three labels and a slider. The last label's **Text** property is bound to the slider's **Text** property, which… doesn't exist. We can use the **FallbackValue** property to specify what value should be used instead. If we didn't specify this property, the last label's **Text** property would be an empty string.

If we now run the app, we'll see the fallback value in the last label:

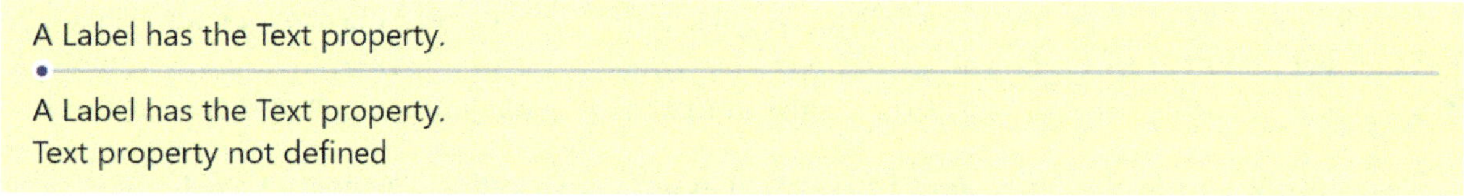

This example is pretty artificial, because we know that a **Slider** doesn't have the **Text** property and we just don't bind to it. A more realistic example would be binding to properties of heterogeneous objects in a collection where the given property may not exist on all objects.

There's just one more topic for now as far as data binding is concerned that I'd like to discuss, multi-bindings.

Multi-bindings

Multi-bindings are the way to go if you want to attach multiple **Binding** objects to one target property. Suppose we want to create a page with an entry, a stepper, a slider and a button (plus some labels with info about the main views) and the button should be enabled only if the entry isn't empty, and the **Value** properties of the stepper and the slider are greater than zero. These three conditions must be met simultaneously for the button to be enabled.

A multi-binding is created by instantiating the **MultiBinding** class. The class has a **Bindings** property that is a collection of the individual bindings. **Bindings** is the class's content property, so we don't have to use it explicitly in XAML. We also must provide an **IMultiValueConverter** instance that evaluates all the **Binding** objects inside the **Bindings** collection and returns a single value that can be used by the target property.

In our case we have a **Bindings** collection of three **Binding** objects. The target property is the **IsEnabled** property of the button, which is of type boolean. The three source properties are:

- the entry's **Text** property's **Length** property (if it's zero, the entry is empty),

- the stepper's **Value** property,

- the slider's **Value** property.

These three source properties are all of type double.

So, we must create a converter that evaluates multiple double values and returns a boolean value. Let's create an **AllGreaterThanZeroMultiConverter** class in the **Converters** folder. Its name is pretty self-explanatory. It's supposed to return **true** only if all source properties are set to a value greater than 0. Here's the code:

```
using System.Globalization;

namespace Slugrace.Converters;

public class AllGreaterThanZeroMultiConverter : IMultiValueConverter
{
    public object Convert(object[] values, Type targetType, object parameter, CultureInfo culture)
    {
        if (values == null || !targetType.IsAssignableFrom(typeof(bool)))
        {
            return false;
        }

        foreach (object value in values)
        {
            if (value is not (double or int))
            {
                return false;
            }
            else if (value is int i)
            {
                if (i <= 0)
                {
                    return false;
                }
            }
            else if (value is double d)
            {
                if (d <= 0)
                {
                    return false;
                }
            }
        }
        return true;

    }

    public object[] ConvertBack(object value, Type[] targetTypes, object parameter, CultureInfo culture)
    {
        throw new NotImplementedException();
    }
}
```

The class implements the **IMultiValueConverter** interface. We're not going to implement the **ConvertBack** method, because we don't need conversions in the opposite direction. Let's have a closer look at the **Convert** method, though.

In the first step we check whether the **values** array, which in our case contains the three values from the source properties, is not **null**. We also check if a boolean value can be assigned to the target type. If one or both of these conditions are met, the method returns **false**. In our case, however, the **values** array will contain three values and the target **IsEnabled** property can be assigned a boolean value, so the next step can begin.

In the next step we check, in a loop, whether all values that we delivered are of type double or int, and if so, whether they're less or equal to zero. If any of the values is not a double or int, or if any of the values is less than or equal to 0, the method returns **false**. Otherwise, so if all values are positive doubles or ints, the method returns **true**.

With the converter in place, let's replace the code in **TestPage.xaml** by the following:

```
<?xml version="1.0" encoding="utf-8" ?>
<ContentPage xmlns="http://schemas.microsoft.com/dotnet/2021/maui"
             xmlns:x="http://schemas.microsoft.com/winfx/2009/xaml"
             xmlns:converters="clr-namespace:Slugrace.Converters"
             x:Class="Slugrace.Views.TestPage"
             Title="TestPage"
             Padding="50">

    <ContentPage.Resources>
        <Style TargetType="Label">
            <Setter Property="FontSize" Value="30" />
        </Style>
        <converters:AllGreaterThanZeroMultiConverter x:Key="AllGreaterThanZeroConverter" />
    </ContentPage.Resources>

    <VerticalStackLayout>
        <Label Text="At least 1 character" />
        <Entry x:Name="entry" WidthRequest="100" Margin="0, 0, 0, 20" />

        <Label Text="A positive number" />
        <HorizontalStackLayout>
            <Stepper x:Name="stepper" Margin="0, 0, 0, 20" />
            <Label Text="{Binding Source={x:Reference stepper}, Path=Value}" />
        </HorizontalStackLayout>

        <Label Text="A value greater than 0" />
        <Slider x:Name="slider" Margin="0, 0, 0, 20" />

        <Button Text="Proceed">
            <Button.IsEnabled>
                <MultiBinding Converter="{StaticResource AllGreaterThanZeroConverter}">
                    <Binding Source="{x:Reference entry}" Path="Text.Length" />
                    <Binding Source="{x:Reference stepper}" Path="Value" />
                    <Binding Source="{x:Reference slider}" Path="Value" />
                </MultiBinding>
            </Button.IsEnabled>
        </Button>
    </VerticalStackLayout>
</ContentPage>
```

We instantiated the converter in the resource dictionary and referenced it to set the **MultiBinding.Converter** property. If we now run the app, the entry will be empty (which it is by default) and the two other controls will have the default value of the **Value** property, which is 0. The button should be disabled:

If you now start playing with the three controls, the button will remain disabled as long as at least one of the source properties is less than or equal to zero:

But if all three values are greater than zero, the button will be enabled:

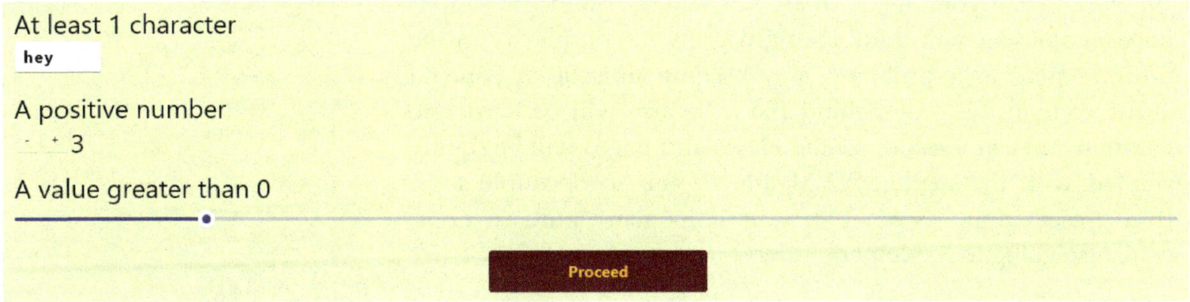

It will remain enabled until any of the three values is again set to 0. Try it out.

That's it, as far as data binding is concerned, at least for now. We've covered the basics, but where data binding really shines is in an app where the MVVM pattern is implemented. Our Slugrace application is going to be such an app, so let's start implementing the pattern now.

Chapter 16 – Introduction to MVVM

code: https://github.com/prospero-apps/Slugrace/tree/chapter16

As I mentioned in the previous chapter, we're going to structure our application using the **MVVM** pattern. This pattern is often used in XAML-based frameworks like WPF or Xamarin.Forms. It's also used in .NET MAUI.

The MVVM acronym stands for:

M - Model (used to define the basic domain classes)

V - View (used to display stuff to the user)

VM - ViewModel (used like a code-behind, but completely decoupled, to provide data for the View).

We're going to talk about all these elements in this book. But let's take it slowly.

Well, in .NET MAUI (as well as in the other aforementioned frameworks) you don't have to use the MVVM pattern in your app. You can put all the logic in the code-behind files and it will still work fine. If your app is small, this will do. But if your app is more complex or you think it might grow in complexity in the future, maintenance problems may become an issue. If you put all the code in the code-behind files, the app will be harder to maintain and test. Besides all the views and pages will be tightly coupled with the logic. MVVM allows you to decouple logic from presentation. As MVVM is used in many modern apps, we're also going to implement it in our app.

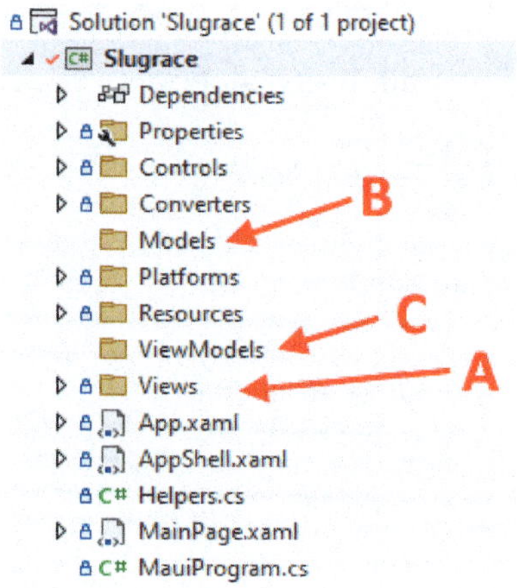

We'll need some folders to implement the pattern. We already have the **Views** folder (A). Add two more folders to the root of the project and name them **Models** (B) and **ViewModels** (C).

Before we create any models and view models, let's have a look at how MVVM actually works.

How MVVM Works

It's important to understand how the three components, model, view and view model, relate to one another. Have a look at this diagram:

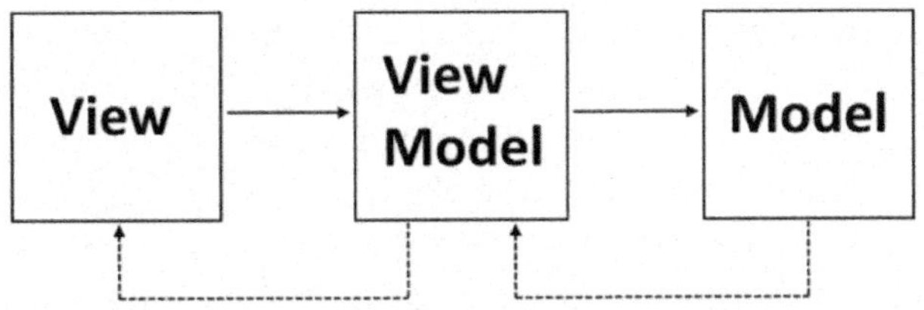

The dashed arrows demonstrate how data and information flows between the components. They go in only one direction, so the view has direct access to the view model and the view model has direct access to the model. The view doesn't have direct access to the model, though. What does it mean? It means the view can bind to properties in the view model and the view model can use classes defined in the model.

The model knows nothing about the view model and the view model knows nothing about the view. The view model separates the other two components so that the model and the view can be developed independently.

What about the solid arrows? They indicate that there is some data flow in the opposite direction as well. In case of `TwoWay` binding or commands (we're going to talk about commands soon), data flows from the view to the view model and the view model may update the model.

Let's briefly characterize the three components.

The Three Components of MVVM

The model and the view model are coded in C#. The view is usually coded in XAML, although it can also be coded in C# if this is what you prefer. Anyway, what exactly is each of the three components responsible for?

The **model** represents the app's domain model. It contains classes that represent data models and contain business logic.

The **view** is responsible for the visual representation of data. It defines the structure of a page. It also may contain some logic in the code-behind, although this should be limited to visual behaviors, not the business logic of the app.

The **view model** implements properties and commands the view can bind to. It also notifies the view if any property changes so that it can update itself. The view model prepares data it takes from the model for the view to consume. It sometimes requires data conversions.

MVVM is pretty flexible. It means you don't need a model for each and every view model and you don't need a separate view model for each view. A view model may use multiple models and each model can be used in multiple view models. If all your view needs is a string, you can just define the string in the view model - there's no need to create a model class for that. Also, if more than one view requires the same data, they can share one view model. Besides, if a view only displays static data that doesn't require any data binding, there's no need to create a view model for this view.

In our app, we're going to be using the .NET Community MVVM Toolkit framework. There are also some other MVVM frameworks. They are used to facilitate our work by, for example, simplifying the implementation of property change notification or handling commands, navigation, dependency injection, etc. But before we start using the toolkit framework, let's have a look at a basic implementation of the pattern, without any frameworks. This way you will know what is going on behind the scenes and you will be even more grateful for what the framework does for you when we start using it.

Basic MVVM

So, let's practice the basic, traditional approach on the **TestPage**. The **TestPage** is already in the **Views** folder and it's going to be our view. Let's simplify the code in the **TestPage.xaml** file like so:

```
<?xml version="1.0" encoding="utf-8" ?>
<ContentPage xmlns="http://schemas.microsoft.com/dotnet/2021/maui"
             xmlns:x="http://schemas.microsoft.com/winfx/2009/xaml"
             x:Class="Slugrace.Views.TestPage"
             Title="TestPage"
             Padding="50">

    <VerticalStackLayout>
        <Label Text="What is your favorite color?" />
        <Entry WidthRequest="100" />
        <Label Text="" />
    </VerticalStackLayout>
</ContentPage>
```

Here we have an entry and two labels. We don't actually need a model, but let's create a view model that will contain the data our **TestPage** requires. It definitely requires a string the second label will bind to. In case of the entry there's two-way binding, so the entry's **Text** property will both consume the string from the view model and update it there.

In the **ViewModels** folder create a new class and name it **TestViewModel**.

Make the class public:

```
namespace Slugrace.ViewModels;

public class TestViewModel
{
}
```

The view model is going to contain some data and also notify the view when this data changes. We can achieve that by implementing the **INotifyPropertyChanged** interface:

```
using System.ComponentModel;

namespace Slugrace.ViewModels;

public class TestViewModel : INotifyPropertyChanged
{
    public event PropertyChangedEventHandler? PropertyChanged;
}
```

As you can see, the interface provides an event. Let's create a method that will invoke the event when a property changes:

```
...
public class TestViewModel : INotifyPropertyChanged
{
    public event PropertyChangedEventHandler PropertyChanged;

    void OnPropertyChanged(string propertyName) =>
        PropertyChanged?.Invoke(this, new PropertyChangedEventArgs(propertyName));
}
```

To see how it works, let's create the **FavoriteColor** property of type **string** that the entry in the view will bind to. We'll also create a backing field for it. The getter will just return the value of the backing field. The setter will first check if the value really has changed and if so, it will set the new value and call the **OnPropertyChanged** method. The method takes the name of the property as an argument:

```
...
public class TestViewModel : INotifyPropertyChanged
{
    string favoriteColor = string.Empty;

    public string FavoriteColor
    {
        get => favoriteColor;
        set
        {
            if (favoriteColor != value)
            {
                favoriteColor = value;
                OnPropertyChanged(nameof(FavoriteColor));
            }
        }
    }

    public event PropertyChangedEventHandler? PropertyChanged;

    void OnPropertyChanged(string propertyName) =>
        PropertyChanged?.Invoke(this, new PropertyChangedEventArgs(propertyName));
}
```

We can simplify the code slightly by using the **CallerMemberName** attribute. Then we won't have to pass the name of the property to the **OnPropertyChanged** method:

```
using System.ComponentModel;
using System.Runtime.CompilerServices;

namespace Slugrace.ViewModels;

public class TestViewModel : INotifyPropertyChanged
{
    ...
    public string FavoriteColor
    {
        get => favoriteColor;
        set
        {
            ...
                OnPropertyChanged();
            }
        }
    }
    ...
    void OnPropertyChanged([CallerMemberName] string? propertyName = null) =>
        PropertyChanged?.Invoke(this, new PropertyChangedEventArgs(propertyName));
}
```

The **CallerMemberName** attribute can only be applied to parameters with default values, so we set the **propertyName** parameter to **null**. As you can see, we can now call the **OnPropertyChanged** method without the name of the property. This may be useful if there are many properties in the class.

The **OnPropertyChange** method will notify the view of the change and the entry's text will be automatically updated. And vice versa, if we set the **Text** property in the entry, it will be automatically updated in the view model due to its two-way binding mode.

But first, we must set the binding context of the view to the view model and bind the entry's **Text** property to the **FavoriteColor** property defined in the view model:

```
...
<ContentPage xmlns="http://schemas.microsoft.com/dotnet/2021/maui"
             xmlns:x="http://schemas.microsoft.com/winfx/2009/xaml"
             xmlns:viewmodels="clr-namespace:Slugrace.ViewModels"
             x:Class="Slugrace.Views.TestPage"
             Title="TestPage"
             Padding="50">

    <ContentPage.BindingContext>
        <viewmodels:TestViewModel />
    </ContentPage.BindingContext>
```

```
    <VerticalStackLayout>
        <Label Text="What is your favorite color?" />
        <Entry WidthRequest="100" Text="{Binding FavoriteColor}" />
        <Label Text="{Binding FavoriteColor}" />
    </VerticalStackLayout>
</ContentPage>
```

As you can see, I also bound the second label's **Text** property to **FavoriteColor**. If you now start entering text into the entry, the **FavoriteColor** property in the view model will be updated to the new value. The label will display the new value because it's bound to it. So, here the data goes from the entry to the view model and then from the view model to the label.

Sometimes one property in the view model depends on another property. Then, when one of them changes, the other should change too. Let's modify our view model:

```
...
public class TestViewModel : INotifyPropertyChanged
{
    string favoriteColor;

    public string FavoriteColor
    {
        get => favoriteColor;
        set
        {
            if (favoriteColor != value)
            {
                favoriteColor = value;
                OnPropertyChanged();
                OnPropertyChanged(nameof(LetterCount));
            }
        }
    }

    public int? LetterCount => FavoriteColor?.Length;

    public event PropertyChangedEventHandler PropertyChanged;
    ...
}
```

Here we have the **LetterCount** property that simply returns the length of the string that we enter in the entry. This property will change whenever the **FavoriteColor** property changes. We can achieve this by calling the **OnPropertyChange** method as many times as there are properties that should be affected. In our case it means twice. We don't have to pass the name of the property on which the method is called, but we have to provide the names of other properties, which is why we pass **LetterCount** to it.

Now let's add another label in the view and bind it to the newly created property:

```
...
<ContentPage ...>
    ...
    <VerticalStackLayout>
        ...
        <Label Text="{Binding FavoriteColor}" />
        <Label Text="{Binding LetterCount}" />
    </VerticalStackLayout>
</ContentPage>
```

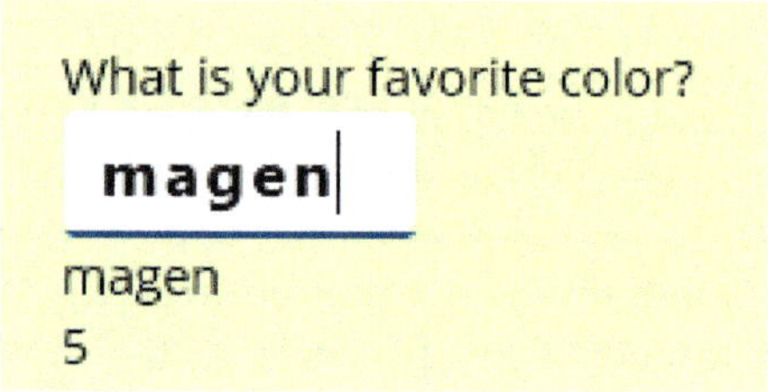

If we now enter some text in the entry, the label will display its length.

Let's say we want to add a button to our view, which, when pressed, will set the **FavoriteColor** property to a fixed value, like for instance "**red**". The problem is, we can't use events anymore. Events work in the code-behind and we now put the logic in the view model. So, there must be another way to do it. And there is - commands.

Commands

Let's start by creating a public property of type **ICommand** in the view model. This is the property we can bind to. Then, in the constructor, let's create a new **Command** instance and pass to it the method that we want to be invoked when the button is pressed. We don't have the method yet, so let's create it. The method is named **UseFixedColor** and it just sets the **FavoriteColor** property to a fixed value. Here's the code:

```
...
public class TestViewModel : INotifyPropertyChanged
{
    ...
    public int? LetterCount => FavoriteColor?.Length;

    public ICommand UseColorCommand { get; private set; }

    public event PropertyChangedEventHandler PropertyChanged;

    public TestViewModel()
    {
        UseColorCommand = new Command(UseFixedColor);
    }

    private void UseFixedColor()
    {
        FavoriteColor = "red";
    }

    void OnPropertyChanged...
}
```

Now we have to create the button in the view and bind its **Command** property to the property we just created in the view model:

```
...
<ContentPage ...>
    ...
    <VerticalStackLayout HorizontalOptions="Start">
        ...
        <Label Text="{Binding LetterCount}" />
        <Button
            Text="RED"
            Command="{Binding UseColorCommand}" />
    </VerticalStackLayout>
</ContentPage>
```

That's it. If you now run the app and press the button, the **FavoriteColor** property will change to "**red**". This change will be immediately reflected in all controls in the view that bind to **FavoriteColor**.

We can also use the command with a parameter. To this end we use the **CommandParameter** property. Let's add two more buttons that will pass a different color name to the command as an argument:

```
...
<ContentPage ...>
    ...
    <VerticalStackLayout HorizontalOptions="Start">
        ...
        <Button
            Text="RED"
            Command="{Binding UseColorCommand}"
            CommandParameter="red" />
        <Button
            Text="BLUE"
            Command="{Binding UseColorCommand}"
            CommandParameter="blue" />
        <Button
            Text="YELLOW"
            Command="{Binding UseColorCommand}"
            CommandParameter="yellow" />
    </VerticalStackLayout>
</ContentPage>
```

As now the method takes a parameter, we have to use the generic version of **Command** in the view model with the type corresponding to the type of the parameter. Let's modify the code like this:

```
...
public class TestViewModel : INotifyPropertyChanged
{
    ...
    public TestViewModel()
    {
        UseColorCommand = new Command<string>(UseFixedColor);
    }

    private void UseFixedColor(string color)
    {
        FavoriteColor = color;
    }

    ...
}
```

Now you can press the buttons to change the **`FavoriteColor`** property.

It works fine because we set the binding context to **`TestViewModel`**. Let's have a closer look at the binding context.

Binding Context

We set the binding context in XAML, but we often do it in the code-behind using dependency injection. In the **TestPage.xaml.cs** file we'll set the binding context in the constructor:

```
using Slugrace.ViewModels;

namespace Slugrace.Views;
public partial class TestPage : ContentPage
{
    public TestPage(TestViewModel testViewModel)
    {
        InitializeComponent();
        BindingContext = testViewModel;
    }
}
```

We're using here an instance of **`TestViewModel`** through dependency injection. We need to register the page and the view model with the dependency service in the **MauiProgram.cs** file:

```
using Microsoft.Extensions.Logging;
using Slugrace.Views;
using Slugrace.ViewModels;
```

```
namespace Slugrace;

public static class MauiProgram
{
	public static MauiApp CreateMauiApp()
	{
		var builder = MauiApp.CreateBuilder();
		...
#if DEBUG
		builder.Logging.AddDebug();
#endif

		builder.Services.AddSingleton<TestPage>();
		builder.Services.AddSingleton<TestViewModel>();

		return builder.Build();
	}
}
```

We're using the **AddSingleton** method here, which means the same instance will be used throughout the application. If we used **AddTransient** instead, a new instance of **TestPage** and **TestViewModel** would be delivered whenever requested. It's important to register the classes for dependency injection before the **Build** method on **builder** is called.

Finally, remove the part of the markup in the **TestPage.xaml** file where the binding context was set. I mean the following part:

```
<ContentPage.BindingContext>
    <viewmodels:TestViewModel />
</ContentPage.BindingContext>
```

We don't need it anymore because now the binding context is set in the code-behind.

The app works as before, but we have a problem with Intellisense in the XAML file. It looks like the properties defined in the view model are not listed in it. We can fix it by setting the **x:DataType** property on the page to the view model class:

```
...
<ContentPage ...
             xmlns:viewmodels="clr-namespace:Slugrace.ViewModels"
             x:DataType="viewmodels:TestViewModel"
             x:Class="Slugrace.Views.TestPage"
             ...
```

Now Intellisense works as before.

This is it as far as the basics of MVVM are concerned. We could implement our Slugrace application in the same way - just add view models and models to the already existing views. However, if you look at the **TestViewModel** class, you will see that we need quite a lot of code to implement a single property. We also have to implement the **INotifyPropertyChanged** interface for each view model.

We could simplify it a bit by creating a base view model where the interface would be implemented and then deriving the other view models from this base class. But there is even a better solution. We can use a framework that will do some of the tedious work for us. I already mentioned the .NET Community MVVM Toolkit framework that we are going to use. It relies on source generators, so it will generate optimized C# code with all the required functionality for you. We're going to implement it in the next chapter. We'll first use it for the **TestPage** so that you can see the difference and then we'll start implementing it for the actual application.

Chapter 17 – The MVVM Toolkit

code: https://github.com/prospero-apps/Slugrace/tree/chapter17

In the previous chapter we introduced the MVVM pattern in its traditional form. As you remember, there are three components, the model, the view, and the view model. The view model delivers data to the view, so whenever a property defined in the view model changes, the view is notified of this change and updates itself. With two-way bindings it works also in the opposite direction. The model, on the other hand, contains the domain classes that are used by the view model and is not required at all if only simple data is supposed to be displayed.

We used the **TestPage** as our view and we created the **TestViewModel** as the view model. We only defined two properties in the view model and we implemented the **INotifyPropertyChanged** interface. One of the properties we defined is a one-liner that depends on the other property, but even so there's quite a lot of typing. We're going to have much more properties in our app, so let's make our lives easier by using an MVVM framework that will do some of the tedious work for us. In this book, we'll be using the MVVM Toolkit, which is part of the .NET Community Toolkit. It uses source generators to generate optimized C# code that is additive to our own code. This just means that the view model class we create consists of two parts - the code we write ourselves and the code generated by the source generators. As such, the class must be marked as **partial**.

So, without further ado, let's jump right in and install the framework.

Installing the MVVM Toolkit

To install the MVVM Toolkit, right-click on the project and select Manage NuGet Packages. In the Browse tab (A) search for CommunityToolkit.Mvvm (B) and install it (C):

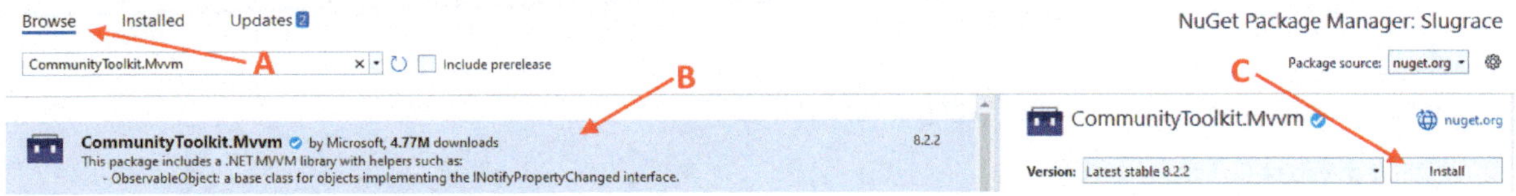

If you open the project file (by double-clicking on the project name), you will see the toolkit there:

```
<Project Sdk="Microsoft.NET.Sdk">
        ...
        <ItemGroup>
        <PackageReference Include="CommunityToolkit.Mvvm" Version="8.2.2" />
        <PackageReference Include="Microsoft.Maui.Controls" Version="$(MauiVersion)" />
        ...
</ItemGroup>
        ...
```

Naturally, depending on when you install it, you may end up with a different version of the package.

Implementing the MVVM Toolkit

Before we start implementing the MVVM Toolkit, let's have another look at the **TestViewModel** class as it looks right now:

```
using System.ComponentModel;
using System.Runtime.CompilerServices;
using System.Windows.Input;

namespace Slugrace.ViewModels;

public class TestViewModel : INotifyPropertyChanged
{
    string favoriteColor = string.Empty;

    public string FavoriteColor
    {
        get => favoriteColor;
        set
        {
            if (favoriteColor != value)
            {
                favoriteColor = value;
                OnPropertyChanged();
                OnPropertyChanged(nameof(LetterCount));
            }
        }
    }

    public int? LetterCount => FavoriteColor?.Length;
    public ICommand UseColorCommand { get; private set; }

    public event PropertyChangedEventHandler? PropertyChanged;

    public TestViewModel()
    {
        UseColorCommand = new Command<string>(UseFixedColor);
    }

    private void UseFixedColor(string color)
    {
        FavoriteColor = color;
    }

    void OnPropertyChanged([CallerMemberName]string? propertyName = null) =>
        PropertyChanged?.Invoke(this, new PropertyChangedEventArgs(propertyName));
}
```

We need 13 lines of code to implement the **FavoriteColor** property. But not if we use the MVVM Toolkit. Let's actually implement the framework and see the difference.

So, first let's mark the class as **partial** and make it inherit from **ObservableObject**. Also, we don't need to implement the **INotifyPropertyChanged** interface anymore because it will be implemented for us by the **ObservableObject**. If you right-click on it and select Go To Definition, you'll see it implements the interface:

```
public abstract class ObservableObject : INotifyPropertyChanged, INotifyPropertyChanging
```

So, here's the first part of the class:

```
using CommunityToolkit.Mvvm.ComponentModel;
using System.ComponentModel;
using System.Runtime.CompilerServices;
using System.Windows.Input;

namespace Slugrace.ViewModels;

public partial class TestViewModel : ObservableObject
{
    string favoriteColor = string.Empty;
    ...
```

Remove the **PropertyChangedEventHandler** and the **OnPropertyChanged** method. Next, remove the public **FavoriteColor** property and add the **ObservableProperty** attribute to the private backing field. This will cause the source generators to implement the public property for us. Have a look at the code:

```
...
public partial class TestViewModel : ObservableObject
{
    [ObservableProperty]
    string favoriteColor;

    public int? LetterCount => FavoriteColor?.Length;

    ...
}
```

We're not defining the **FavoriteColor** property anymore, and yet, there's no error in the code below where we define the **LetterCount** property, which in turn uses the **FavoriteColor** property. This is because the public **FavoriteColor** property is generated for us behind the scenes and its name is automatically capitalized, so we can use it as if we had defined it ourselves.

But don't take my word for it. You can see the generated code.

Go to **Dependencies**, select one of the platforms, for instance Android, and under:

Analyzers
→ CommunityToolkit.Mvvm.SourceGenerators
→ CommunityToolkit.Mvvm.SourceGenerators.ObservablePropertyGenerator

you'll find the **Slugrace.ViewModels.TestViewModel.g.cs** generated file:

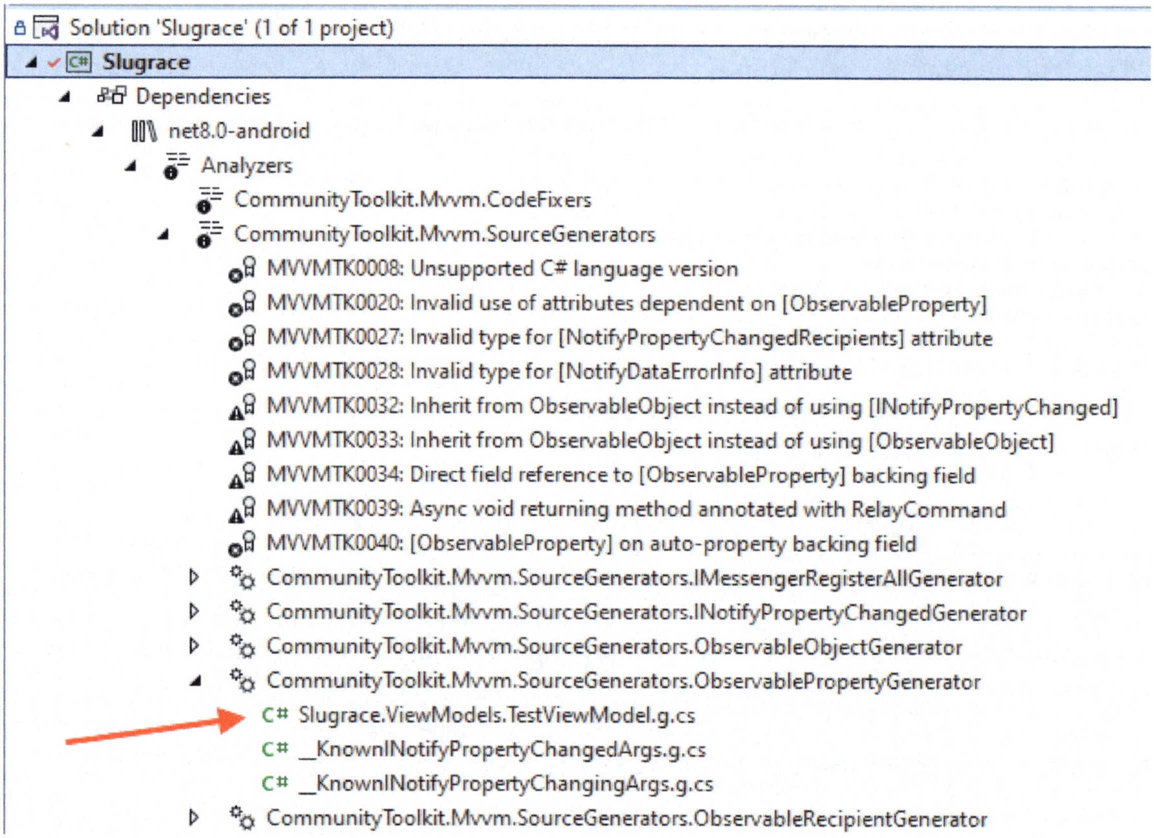

Open the file and you will see that the public property is indeed created for us:

```
// <auto-generated/>
...
namespace Slugrace.ViewModels
{
    /// <inheritdoc/>
    partial class TestViewModel
    {
        ...
        public string FavoriteColor
        {
            ...
        }
        ...
```

So, the public property exists and we can still bind to it in the view. If you run the app, it will still work.

But, as you can see, the length of the string is not displayed anymore, even though we defined the **LetterCount** property ourselves. This is because, as you may remember, the original version of the **FavoriteColor** property called the **OnPropertyChanged** method not only on itself, but also on the **LetterCount** property. This is now gone. But don't worry, we just have to tell the generator to generate this functionality for us. To this end, we have to add another attribute to the backing field, **NotifyPropertyChangedFor**, and specify the name of the property we want it to work for:

```
...
public partial class TestViewModel : ObservableObject
{
    [ObservableProperty]
    [NotifyPropertyChangedFor(nameof(LetterCount))]
    string favoriteColor = string.Empty;

    public int? LetterCount => FavoriteColor?.Length;
    ...
```

Now everything should work as before.

We're using commands to call methods defined in the view model. These are built-in .NET MAUI commands. But we're going to use MVVM Toolkit commands instead.

MVVM Toolkit Commands

By using the MVVM Toolkit commands, we can leverage source generators to further reduce our code. We don't have to create the **UseColorCommand** in the view model anymore and we don't have to instantiate it in the constructor. Instead, we just have to add the **RelayCommand** attribute to the method that is supposed to be called when the button is clicked. Now the code should look like this:

```
using CommunityToolkit.Mvvm.ComponentModel;
using CommunityToolkit.Mvvm.Input;

namespace Slugrace.ViewModels;

public partial class TestViewModel : ObservableObject
{
    [ObservableProperty]
    [NotifyPropertyChangedFor(nameof(LetterCount))]
    string favoriteColor = string.Empty;

    public int? LetterCount => FavoriteColor?.Length;

    [RelayCommand]
    void UseFixedColor(string color)
    {
        FavoriteColor = color;
    }
}
```

If you open the file with the generated code (the file ends with **RelayCommandGenerator**), you'll see the command has been generated for us:

```
// <auto-generated/>
...
namespace Slugrace.ViewModels
{
    /// <inheritdoc/>
    partial class TestViewModel
    {
        ...
        public global::CommunityToolkit.Mvvm.Input.IRelayCommand<string> UseFixedColorCommand =>
useFixedColorCommand ??= new global::CommunityToolkit.Mvvm.Input.RelayCommand<string>(new
global::System.Action<string>(UseFixedColor));
    }
}
```

As you can see, the command is named after the method. We have to use this name, **UseFixedColorCommand**, in the view:

```
...
<ContentPage ...>
    ...
        <Button
            Text="RED"
            Command="{Binding UseFixedColorCommand}"
            CommandParameter="red" />
        <Button
            Text="BLUE"
            Command="{Binding UseFixedColorCommand}"
            CommandParameter="blue" />
        <Button
            Text="YELLOW"
            Command="{Binding UseFixedColorCommand}"
            CommandParameter="yellow" />
    ...
```

The code in the view model is now much more concise. And, what's important, the app works just like before. Try it out.

Now, we've covered the most important stuff related to the MVVM Toolkit. Naturally, there's much more to it, but this is enough to start implementing it in our application. We'll be creating the models and view models progressively, adding properties and command as we proceed and as we need them. And we'll be modifying the views accordingly. Let's start by adding some models.

Models in the Slugrace Application

Our application is a 2D game. There are players who play the game and place bets on slugs. So, we're going to need three model classes: **Player**, **Slug** and **Game**.

The **Player** class will contain properties and methods related to the player, so a human being playing the game. Properties like **Name**, **InitialMoney**, **CurrentMoney**, etc. probably come to your mind. A player must also be able to place a specified amount of money on a slug, etc.

The **Slug** class will contain properties and methods related to the slug. Each slug needs a name, runs at a specified speed, can win or lose a race.

These are just some examples. In fact, our models are going to need more properties and methods as we proceed, but we'll be updating the models as we go. For now, let's create the three classes in the **Models** folder and add some basic properties to them.

So, the **Player.cs** file looks like this:

```
namespace Slugrace.Models;

public class Player
{
    public int Id { get; set; }
    public string Name { get; set; } = string.Empty
    public int InitialMoney { get; set; } = 0;
    public int CurrentMoney { get; set; }
    public int WonOrLostMoney { get; set; }
    public int BetAmount { get; set; }
    public bool IsInGame { get; set; }
}
```

For now, we just have a bunch of properties with self-explanatory names. The **Slug.cs** file looks like this:

```
namespace Slugrace.Models;

public class Slug
{
    public string Name { get; set; } = string.Empty;
}
```

Yes, I know, this isn't much, but don't worry, we'll add quite a few properties and methods in this class. All in due time. And here's the **Game.cs** file:

```
namespace Slugrace.Models;

public enum EndingCondition
{
    Money,
    Races,
    Time
}

public class Game
{
    public List<Player>? Players { get; set; }
    public List<Slug>? Slugs { get; set; }
    public EndingCondition GameEndingCondition { get; set; } = EndingCondition.Money;
    public int NumberOfRacesSet { get; set; } = 0;
    public int GameTimeSet { get; set; } = 0;
}
```

We're keeping it simple for now. I defined an enumeration here that will be used only in this class and later in the view model. By default the game is supposed to end when there's only one player with any money left or when there's none.

Let's now move on to views and view models. When we were creating the pages, we included content views in some of them. We'll create a separate view model for the **PlayerSettings** content view, but generally we'll create a separate view model for each page. Actually, some of the pages will share the same view model. Anyway, let's start with the **PlayerSettings** content view.

PlayerSettings View and View Model

There is one content view embedded in the **SettingsPage**, **PlayerSettigs**. It represents a single player. There may be between one and four players in the game. There is always at least one. In the **SettingsPage** there will always be four instances of **PlayerSettings**, but later in the game there will be as many players as we decide.

Anyway, **PlayerSettings** will be our view. Let's now create a view model for the view to bind to. In the **ViewModels** folder create a new class and name it **PlayerSettingsViewModel**. Here's the code:

```
using CommunityToolkit.Mvvm.ComponentModel;
using Slugrace.Models;

namespace Slugrace.ViewModels;

public partial class PlayerSettingsViewModel : ObservableObject
{
    const int maxNameLength = 10;
    const int minInitialMoney = 10;
    const int maxInitialMoney = 5000;

    private readonly Player player;

    public int PlayerId
    {
        get => player.Id;
        set
        {
            if (player.Id != value)
            {
                player.Id = value;
                OnPropertyChanged();
            }
        }
    }

    public string PlayerName
    {
        get => player.Name;
        set
        {
            if (player.Name != value)
            {
                player.Name = value;
                OnPropertyChanged();
```

```
                OnPropertyChanged(nameof(NameIsValid));
                OnPropertyChanged(nameof(PlayerIsValid));
            }
        }
    }

    public int PlayerInitialMoney
    {
        get => player.InitialMoney;
        set
        {
            if (player.InitialMoney != value)
            {
                player.InitialMoney = value;
                OnPropertyChanged();
                OnPropertyChanged(nameof(InitialMoneyIsValid));
                OnPropertyChanged(nameof(PlayerIsValid));
            }
        }
    }

    public bool PlayerIsInGame
    {
        get => player.IsInGame;
        set
        {
            if (player.IsInGame != value)
            {
                player.IsInGame = value;
                OnPropertyChanged();
                OnPropertyChanged(nameof(PlayerIsValid));
            }
        }
    }

    public bool NameIsValid => (PlayerName == null) || (PlayerName?.Length <= maxNameLength);

    public bool InitialMoneyIsValid => Helpers.ValueIsInRange(PlayerInitialMoney,
        minInitialMoney, maxInitialMoney);

    public bool PlayerIsValid
    {
        get
        {
            if (PlayerIsInGame)
            {
                return NameIsValid && InitialMoneyIsValid;
            }
            else
            {
                return true;
            }
        }
    }

    public PlayerSettingsViewModel()
    {
        player = new Player();
    }
}
```

This code is pretty straightforward. What do we have here?

The **Player** model is stored as a private field. We instantiate a **Player** object in the constructor and use its properties inside the view model's properties.

We don't have any methods here, just a bunch of properties. We also defined some constants that are used by the properties.

The **PlayerId** property is an integer number. It will be set to 1, 2, 3 or 4 because there are going to be up to four players.

The **PlayerName** property, if changed, will also notify of changes in other properties where it's used. This way, not only all bindings to **PlayerName** will be updated, but also bindings to **NameIsValid** and **PlayerIsValid**. Later, it will also send a message to **SettingsViewModel** (which we are going to create soon) to make sure the other view model knows about this change.

PlayerInitialMoney is very similar. If changed, it will notify of the change, as well as of the changes in two other properties, and it will sent a message (yet to be implemented) to **SettingsViewModel**.

PlayerIsInGame will be used to mark each potential player as taking or not taking part in the game. So, for example, if we decide that only two players should play in the game, the first two players will have this property set to **true**, and the other two to **false**.

There are two properties used to ensure the **PlayerName** and **PlayerInitialMoney** properties are valid. The first one is **NameIsValid**. We don't have to set the name. If we don't, the name will be later set to a generic one like Player 1 or Player 2. If we decide to set the name, it shouldn't be too long. The other one is **InitialMoneyIsValid**. In this property we're using a method defined in the **Helpers** class. It will be also used in other classes in the app. I implemented the **Helpers.ValueIsInRange** method like so:

```
...
public static class Helpers
{
    ...

    public static bool ValueIsInRange(int value, int min, int max) => value >= min && value <= max;
}
```

Finally, the **PlayerIsValid** property will be set to **true** in two cases: if the player is not in the game (like players 3 and 4 in the example above) and if they are in the game and have a valid name and initial money. This property will be used to make sure the button in the **SettingsPage** is enabled only if all players have valid data. This doesn't have to be true about players who will not take part in the game because they will not be used in the following pages in the app.

Now we can set the view model as the binding context of the view and bind to its properties. Here's the modified **PlayerSettings** content view:

```
...
<ContentView xmlns="http://schemas.microsoft.com/dotnet/2021/maui"
             xmlns:x="http://schemas.microsoft.com/winfx/2009/xaml"
             xmlns:viewmodels="clr-namespace:Slugrace.ViewModels"
             x:DataType="viewmodels:PlayerSettingsViewModel"
             IsVisible="{Binding PlayerIsInGame}"
             x:Class="Slugrace.Controls.PlayerSettings">

    <ContentView.BindingContext>
        <viewmodels:PlayerSettingsViewModel />
    </ContentView.BindingContext>

    <ContentView.Resources>
        ...
    <Grid
        RowDefinitions="*"
        Margin="0, 10">
        <Grid.ColumnDefinitions>
            <ColumnDefinition Width="{OnPlatform 150, Android=80}" />
            <ColumnDefinition Width="{OnPlatform 3*, Android=2.5*}" />
            <ColumnDefinition Width="10" />
            <ColumnDefinition Width="2*" />
        </Grid.ColumnDefinitions>

        <Label Text="{Binding PlayerId, StringFormat='Player {0}'}" />

        <Entry
            x:Name="nameEntry"
            Grid.Column="1"
            WidthRequest="{OnPlatform 300, Android=130}"
            Text="{Binding PlayerName}"
            TextChanged="OnNameTextChanged">
        </Entry>

        <Label
            Grid.Column="2"
            Text="$" />

        <Entry
            x:Name="initialMoneyEntry"
            Placeholder="1000"
            Grid.Column="3"
            WidthRequest="{OnPlatform 250, Android=100}"
            Keyboard="Numeric"
            Text="{Binding PlayerInitialMoney}"
            TextChanged="OnInitialMoneyTextChanged">
        </Entry>
    </Grid>
</ContentView>
```

Again, most of this code is pretty straightforward.

In MVVM we usually tend to leave as little code in the code-behind as possible. Ideally, we should only initialize the component and set the binding context. In our case we don't have to do the latter, because we set the binding context in XAML. All or most of the logic should go to the view model. But there's one exception to this rule, which I already mentioned before. We should keep in the code-behind all the logic that is responsible for the visual aspect of the view. Here we want to set different visual states on the entries depending on the text entered, so we'll leave the two **TextChanged** events and handle them in the **PlayerSettings.xaml.cs** file:

```
using Slugrace.ViewModels;

namespace Slugrace.Controls;

public partial class PlayerSettings : ContentView
{
    ...
    private void OnNameTextChanged(object sender, TextChangedEventArgs e)
    {
        bool nameValid = (BindingContext as PlayerSettingsViewModel)!.NameIsValid;
        GoToNameState(nameValid);
    }

    private void OnInitialMoneyTextChanged(object sender, TextChangedEventArgs e)
    {
        if (BindingContext != null)
        {
            bool initialMoneyValid = (BindingContext as PlayerSettingsViewModel)!.InitialMoneyIsValid;
            Helpers.HandleNumericEntryState(initialMoneyValid, initialMoneyEntry);
        }
    }

    void GoToNameState(bool nameValid)
    {
        string visualState = nameValid ? "Valid" : "Invalid";
        VisualStateManager.GoToState(nameEntry, visualState);
    }
}
```

Now we're using the properties defined in the view model to set the entries' visual state. We're also using a static method, **HandleNumericEntryState**, that I defined in the **Helpers** class:

```
...
public static class Helpers
{
    ...
    public static bool ValueIsInRange(...

    public static void HandleNumericEntryState(bool testedValueIsValid, Entry entry)
    {
        string visualState = testedValueIsValid ? "Valid" : "Invalid";

        if (entry != null)
        {
            bool isEmpty = entry.Text == string.Empty;

            if (isEmpty)
            {
                visualState = "Empty";
            }

            VisualStateManager.GoToState(entry, visualState);
        }
    }
}
```

The code-behind file is pretty short and it takes care just of the visual aspect of the view. But we are going to add some interesting new elements to the XAML file. We'll add a converter and a behavior. You know what converters are, but behaviors are probably not so familiar to you. Anyway, let's have a look at both.

ZeroToEmptyStringConverter

In some entries we'll be entering text, like for example in the **nameEntry**. In others, like in the **initialMoneyEntry** (but not only) we'll be entering numbers. We want the entry to be empty if the value is zero. So, if you see nothing except the placeholder text in the entry, it means the value is zero, not **null**. We'll need a converter for that. In the **Converters** folder add a new class and name it **ZeroToEmptyStringConverter**. Here's the code:

```
using System.Globalization;

namespace Slugrace.Converters;

class ZeroToEmptyStringConverter : IValueConverter
{
    public object? Convert(object? value, Type targetType, object? parameter, CultureInfo culture)
    {
        _ = int.TryParse(value?.ToString(), out int enteredNumber);

        if (enteredNumber == 0)
        {
            return string.Empty;
        }
        else
        {
            return enteredNumber.ToString();
        }
    }

    public object? ConvertBack(object? value, Type targetType, object? parameter, CultureInfo culture)
    {
        string enteredValue = value?.ToString() ?? string.Empty;

        if (string.IsNullOrEmpty(enteredValue))
        {
            return 0;
        }
        else
        {
            bool isNumber = int.TryParse(enteredValue, out int number);

            if (isNumber)
            {
                return number;
            }
            else
            {
                enteredValue = enteredValue[..^1];
                return enteredValue.Length == 0 ? 0 : int.Parse(enteredValue);
            }
        }
    }
}
```

The converter is used in a two-way binding, so we must implement both methods. And here's how the converter is used in the view:

```
...
<ContentView ...
             xmlns:viewmodels="clr-namespace:Slugrace.ViewModels"
             xmlns:converters="clr-namespace:Slugrace.Converters"
             x:DataType="viewmodels:PlayerSettingsViewModel"
             ...
    <ContentView.Resources>
        <Style TargetType="Label"...
        <converters:ZeroToEmptyStringConverter x:Key="zeroToEmptyConverter" />
    </ContentView.Resources>
    ...
        <Entry
            x:Name="initialMoneyEntry"
            ...
            Text="{Binding PlayerInitialMoney, Converter={StaticResource zeroToEmptyConverter}}"
            TextChanged="OnInitialMoneyTextChanged">
        ...
```

So, we must add the namespace first. Then we add the converter to the content view's resources and reference it in the binding.

And now it's time for something new, a behavior. What exactly is a behavior? We're about to create one on the **initialMoneyEntry**.

Behaviors

Behaviors are a nice feature in .NET MAUI that you can use to extend your control classes. Normally, to extend a class, you inherit from it and add some functionality in the derived class. With behaviors it's not necessary. When you attach a behavior to a control, the functionality defined in it acts as if it was part of the control itself.

We could implement additional functionality in the code-behind as well. But then it would be coupled with that particular view. As we want it to be reusable, we'll implement it as a behavior that we can then attach to other controls.

The functionality that we want to add is ensuring that only numeric characters can be entered in the entry. So, if you try to type any other character, like a letter or a special character, this character will not show up.

We wouldn't have to implement this functionality if our app was deployed only to Android, because we set the **Keyboard** property to **Numeric**. This will prevent you from entering other characters. But it doesn't work on Windows, where you can still enter anything.

So, let's create a new folder and name it **Behaviors**. In the folder let's create a new class and name it **NumericInputBehavior**. Here's the code:

```
namespace Slugrace.Behaviors;

public class NumericInputBehavior : Behavior<Entry>
{
    protected override void OnAttachedTo(Entry bindable)
    {
        bindable.TextChanged += Bindable_TextChanged;
        base.OnAttachedTo(bindable);
    }

    protected override void OnDetachingFrom(Entry bindable)
    {
        bindable.TextChanged -= Bindable_TextChanged;
        base.OnDetachingFrom(bindable);
    }

    private void Bindable_TextChanged(object? sender, TextChangedEventArgs e)
    {
        if (sender != null)
        {
            var entry = (Entry)sender;

            if (!string.IsNullOrEmpty(e.NewTextValue))
            {
                bool isNumeric = int.TryParse(e.NewTextValue, out int value);

                if (!isNumeric)
                {
                    entry.Text = e.OldTextValue;
                }
            }
        }
    }
}
```

As you can see, the behavior is meant to be attached to **`Entry`** controls. In particular, it's added to the **`TextChanged`** event. The implementation is simple. If the last character you entered is not a number, the **`Text`** property of the entry is set to the old text, so the text before you typed that character.

And, once again, let's have a look at how this behavior is added to the **`initialMoneyEntry`** inside the **PlayerSettings.xaml** file:

```
...
<ContentView ...
             xmlns:converters="clr-namespace:Slugrace.Converters"
             xmlns:behaviors="clr-namespace:Slugrace.Behaviors"
             x:DataType="viewmodels:PlayerSettingsViewModel"
             ...
        <Entry
            x:Name="initialMoneyEntry"
            ...
            TextChanged="OnInitialMoneyTextChanged">
            <Entry.Behaviors>
                <behaviors:NumericInputBehavior />
            </Entry.Behaviors>
        </Entry>
    ...
```

You won't be able to type non-numeric characters anymore.

The **PlayerSettings** view is embedded in the **SettingsPage**. So, let's take care of this view and create a corresponding view model.

SettingsViewModel

We'll need a view model for the **SettingsPage** (which is a view). Go to the **ViewModels** folder and create a new class. Name it **SettingsViewModel**.

Let's start by registering the page and the view model with the dependency service in the **MauiProgram** class, just like we did with the **TestPage**:

```
...
public static class MauiProgram
...
            builder.Services.AddSingleton<TestPage>();
            builder.Services.AddSingleton <TestViewModel>();

            builder.Services.AddTransient<SettingsPage>();
            builder.Services.AddTransient<SettingsViewModel>();

        return builder.Build();
       ...
```

This time we're adding them as transient. Now we can set the binding context in the code-behind using dependency injection. Here's the **SettingsPage.xaml.cs** file:

```
using Slugrace.ViewModels;

namespace Slugrace.Views;

public partial class SettingsPage : ContentPage
{
    public SettingsPage(SettingsViewModel settingsViewModel)
    {
        InitializeComponent();
        BindingContext = settingsViewModel;
    }
}
```

Now we can implement the **SettingsViewModel** class:

```
using CommunityToolkit.Mvvm.ComponentModel;
using CommunityToolkit.Mvvm.Input;
using Slugrace.Models;
using System.Collections.ObjectModel;

namespace Slugrace.ViewModels;
```

```
public partial class SettingsViewModel : ObservableObject
{
    const int minRaces = 1;
    const int maxRaces = 100;
    const int minTime = 1;
    const int maxTime = 120;

    private readonly Game game;

    [ObservableProperty]
    [NotifyPropertyChangedFor(nameof(AllSettingsAreValid))]
    private ObservableCollection<PlayerSettingsViewModel> players;

    public EndingCondition GameEndingCondition
    {
        get => game.GameEndingCondition;
        set
        {
            if (game.GameEndingCondition != value)
            {
                game.GameEndingCondition = value;
                OnPropertyChanged();
                OnPropertyChanged(nameof(AllSettingsAreValid));
            }
        }
    }

    public int NumberOfRacesSet
    {
        get => game.NumberOfRacesSet;
        set
        {
            if (game.NumberOfRacesSet != value)
            {
                game.NumberOfRacesSet = value;
                OnPropertyChanged();
                OnPropertyChanged(nameof(AllSettingsAreValid));
            }
        }
    }

    public int GameTimeSet
    {
        get => game.GameTimeSet;
        set
        {
            if (game.GameTimeSet != value)
            {
                game.GameTimeSet = value;
                OnPropertyChanged();
                OnPropertyChanged(nameof(AllSettingsAreValid));
            }
        }
    }

    public bool MaxRacesIsValid => Helpers.ValueIsInRange(NumberOfRacesSet,
        minRaces, maxRaces);

    public bool MaxTimeIsValid => Helpers.ValueIsInRange(GameTimeSet,
        minTime, maxTime);

    [ObservableProperty]
    [NotifyPropertyChangedFor(nameof(AllSettingsAreValid))]
    [NotifyPropertyChangedFor(nameof(OnlyOnePlayer))]
    [NotifyPropertyChangedFor(nameof(RacesEndingConditionSet))]
    private int currentNumberOfPlayers = 2;

    public bool OnlyOnePlayer => CurrentNumberOfPlayers == 1;
```

```
public bool RacesEndingConditionSet
    => (CurrentNumberOfPlayers == 1 && GameEndingCondition != EndingCondition.Time)
    || GameEndingCondition == EndingCondition.Races;

[ObservableProperty]
[NotifyPropertyChangedFor(nameof(AllSettingsAreValid))]
private string? changedPlayerName;

[ObservableProperty]
[NotifyPropertyChangedFor(nameof(AllSettingsAreValid))]
private int? changedPlayerInitialMoney;

public bool AllSettingsAreValid
{
    get
    {
        bool conditionPlayers = Players.All(p => p.PlayerIsValid);
        bool conditionMoney = GameEndingCondition == EndingCondition.Money;
        bool conditionRaces = GameEndingCondition == EndingCondition.Races && MaxRacesIsValid;
        bool conditionTime = GameEndingCondition == EndingCondition.Time && MaxTimeIsValid;

        return conditionPlayers && (conditionMoney || conditionRaces || conditionTime);
    }
}

public SettingsViewModel()
{
    game = new Game();

    Players =
    [
        new() { PlayerId = 1, PlayerIsInGame = true },
        new() { PlayerId = 2, PlayerIsInGame = true },
        new() { PlayerId = 3, PlayerIsInGame = false },
        new() { PlayerId = 4, PlayerIsInGame = false }
    ];
}

private void OnPlayerNameChangedMessageReceived(string value)
{
    ChangedPlayerName = value;
}

private void OnPlayerInitialMoneyChangedMessageReceived(int? value)
{
    ChangedPlayerInitialMoney = value;
}

[RelayCommand]
void CreatePlayerList(int numberOfPlayers)
{
    for (int i = 0; i < Players.Count; i++)
    {
        Players[i].PlayerIsInGame = i < numberOfPlayers;
    }

    CurrentNumberOfPlayers = numberOfPlayers;

    if (OnlyOnePlayer)
    {
        GameEndingCondition = EndingCondition.Races;
    }
}

[RelayCommand]
void SetEndingCondition(string condition)
{
    GameEndingCondition = condition switch
    {
        "money" => EndingCondition.Money,
```

```
            "races" => EndingCondition.Races,
            "time" => EndingCondition.Time,
            _ => EndingCondition.Money
        };
    }
}
```

There are a couple constants, a couple observable properties and a couple regular properties. There are a couple methods, too.

At the beginning of the file, we define a private **game** variable that we set to a new instance of **Game** in the constructor. We also define the observable collection called **players**, which we populate in the constructor, too. There are going to be up to four players in the game, so we need four instances of **PlayerSettingsViewModel** to allow the user to set the names and initial money of the players. Here, in the constructor, we set the **PlayerId** property of each player, which will be used to display the player's generic name (**Player 1**, **Player 2**, etc.). We also set the **PlayerIsInGame** property of the first two players to **true**, and of the other two players to **false**. This is because we assume the game is by default for two players, which can be naturally changed in the **SettingsPage**.

As we're at the constructor, we're going to register two messages here. We'll be talking about the messaging system in a moment.

And now let's have a look at the properties that we have in the view model.

The **GameEndingCondition**, **NumberOfRacesSet** and **GameTimeSet** are properties related to the game itself, so we use the **game** object in them.

The **MaxRacesIsValid** and **MaxTimeIsValid** are responsible for ensuring that the user of the app sets the number of races or the time of the game, depending on which ending condition is chosen, to a value within a certain range.

The **currentNumberOfPlayers** observable property is an important one. Look how many change notifications are involved with it. Its value will be set by the radio buttons in the upper part of the **SettingsPage**.

The **RacesEndingConditionSet** property will be used to ensure that if there is only one player selected and the first ending condition (**Money**) is unavailable (because it wouldn't make sense to end the game when there's only one player with any money left in this situation), the default ending condition will be set to **Races**.

The last property is **AllSettingsAreValid**. There are a couple conditions defined in it to ensure that that everything is set to a valid value in the **SettingsPage**. Only if this property is **true**, will the Ready button be enabled.

Next, we have the **CreatePlayerList** method that will handle the players when we check one of the radio buttons. It will set the players' **PlayerIsInGame** property and the

CurrentNumberOfPlayers property. If the one-player game mode is selected and the current ending condition is **Money**, it will be changed to **Races**, because **Money** is unavailable in this mode.

Finally, the **SetEndingCondition** method will do exactly what its name suggests.

We have the view model, so let's take care of the view. The **SettingsPage.xaml** file is pretty lengthy, but we're going to discuss it piece by piece.

SettingsPage View

So, beware! Here comes the **SettingsPage**:

```
<?xml version="1.0" encoding="utf-8" ?>
<ContentPage xmlns="http://schemas.microsoft.com/dotnet/2021/maui"
             xmlns:x="http://schemas.microsoft.com/winfx/2009/xaml"
             xmlns:toolkit="http://schemas.microsoft.com/dotnet/2022/maui/toolkit"
             xmlns:controls="clr-namespace:Slugrace.Controls"
             xmlns:viewmodels="clr-namespace:Slugrace.ViewModels"
             xmlns:behaviors="clr-namespace:Slugrace.Behaviors"
             xmlns:converters="clr-namespace:Slugrace.Converters"
             x:DataType="viewmodels:SettingsViewModel"
             x:Class="Slugrace.Views.SettingsPage">

    <ContentPage.Resources>
        <x:Double x:Key="entryWidth">300</x:Double>
        <x:Double x:Key="invisible">0</x:Double>
        <converters:ZeroToEmptyStringConverter x:Key="zeroToEmptyConverter" />
        <toolkit:InvertedBoolConverter x:Key="invertedBoolConverter" />
    </ContentPage.Resources>
    ...
        <!--the Players panel-->
        ...
                    <HorizontalStackLayout>
                        <RadioButton
                            ...
                                        <On Platform="Android" Value="1" />
                                ...
                            </RadioButton.Content>
                            <RadioButton.Behaviors>
                                <toolkit:EventToCommandBehavior
                                    EventName="CheckedChanged"
                                    Command="{Binding CreatePlayerListCommand}">
                                    <toolkit:EventToCommandBehavior.CommandParameter>
                                        <x:Int32>1</x:Int32>
                                    </toolkit:EventToCommandBehavior.CommandParameter>
                                </toolkit:EventToCommandBehavior>
                            </RadioButton.Behaviors>
                        </RadioButton>

                        <RadioButton
                            x:Name="players2"
                            IsChecked="True"
                            GroupName="players">
                            ...
                            </RadioButton.Content>
                            <RadioButton.Behaviors>
                                <toolkit:EventToCommandBehavior
                                    EventName="CheckedChanged"
                                    Command="{Binding CreatePlayerListCommand}">
                                    <toolkit:EventToCommandBehavior.CommandParameter>
                                        <x:Int32>2</x:Int32>
                                    </toolkit:EventToCommandBehavior.CommandParameter>
                                </toolkit:EventToCommandBehavior>
                            </RadioButton.Behaviors>
                        </RadioButton>

                        <RadioButton
                            x:Name="players3"
                            GroupName="players">
                            ...
                            </RadioButton.Content>
                            <RadioButton.Behaviors>
                                <toolkit:EventToCommandBehavior
                                    EventName="CheckedChanged"
                                    Command="{Binding CreatePlayerListCommand}">
                                    <toolkit:EventToCommandBehavior.CommandParameter>
                                        <x:Int32>3</x:Int32>
                                    </toolkit:EventToCommandBehavior.CommandParameter>
                                </toolkit:EventToCommandBehavior>
                            </RadioButton.Behaviors>
                        </RadioButton>
```

```
                <RadioButton
                    x:Name="players4"
                    GroupName="players">
                    ...
                    </RadioButton.Content>
                    <RadioButton.Behaviors>
                        <toolkit:EventToCommandBehavior
                            EventName="CheckedChanged"
                            Command="{Binding CreatePlayerListCommand}">
                            <toolkit:EventToCommandBehavior.CommandParameter>
                                <x:Int32>4</x:Int32>
                            </toolkit:EventToCommandBehavior.CommandParameter>
                        </toolkit:EventToCommandBehavior>
                    </RadioButton.Behaviors>
                </RadioButton>
            </HorizontalStackLayout>

            <Grid
                ...
            <VerticalStackLayout>
                <controls:PlayerSettings>
                    <controls:PlayerSettings.BindingContext>
                        <Binding Path="Players[0]" />
                    </controls:PlayerSettings.BindingContext>
                </controls:PlayerSettings>

                <controls:PlayerSettings>
                    <controls:PlayerSettings.BindingContext>
                        <Binding Path="Players[1]" />
                    </controls:PlayerSettings.BindingContext>
                </controls:PlayerSettings>

                <controls:PlayerSettings>
                    <controls:PlayerSettings.BindingContext>
                        <Binding Path="Players[2]" />
                    </controls:PlayerSettings.BindingContext>
                </controls:PlayerSettings>

                <controls:PlayerSettings>
                    <controls:PlayerSettings.BindingContext>
                        <Binding Path="Players[3]" />
                    </controls:PlayerSettings.BindingContext>
                </controls:PlayerSettings>
            </VerticalStackLayout>
        ...
<!--the Ending Conditions panel-->
...
        <Grid
            RowDefinitions="*, *, *"
            ColumnDefinitions="4*, 2*">
            <RadioButton
                IsChecked="True"
                IsVisible="{Binding OnlyOnePlayer, Converter={StaticResource invertedBoolConverter}}"
                GroupName="endingConditions">
                ...
                                <On Platform="Android" Value="last player left" />
                    ...
                </RadioButton.Content>
                <RadioButton.Behaviors>
                    <toolkit:EventToCommandBehavior
                            EventName="CheckedChanged"
                            Command="{Binding SetEndingConditionCommand}"
                            CommandParameter="money">
                    </toolkit:EventToCommandBehavior>
                </RadioButton.Behaviors>
            </RadioButton>

            <RadioButton
                Grid.Row="1"
                IsChecked="{Binding RacesEndingConditionSet}"
                GroupName="endingConditions">
                ...
                </RadioButton.Content>
                <RadioButton.Behaviors>
                    <toolkit:EventToCommandBehavior
                            EventName="CheckedChanged"
                            Command="{Binding SetEndingConditionCommand}"
                            CommandParameter="races">
                    </toolkit:EventToCommandBehavior>
                </RadioButton.Behaviors>
                <VisualStateManager.VisualStateGroups>
                    ...
            </RadioButton>

            <Entry
                x:Name="maxRacesEntry"
                ...
                IsEnabled="False"
                Text="{Binding NumberOfRacesSet, Converter={StaticResource zeroToEmptyConverter}}"
                TextChanged="OnMaxRacesTextChanged">
                ...
                </Entry.Placeholder>
                <Entry.Behaviors>
                    <behaviors:NumericInputBehavior />
                </Entry.Behaviors>
            </Entry>
```

```
                <RadioButton
                    Grid.Row="2"
                    ...
                    </RadioButton.Content>
                    <RadioButton.Behaviors>
                        <toolkit:EventToCommandBehavior
                            EventName="CheckedChanged"
                            Command="{Binding SetEndingConditionCommand}"
                            CommandParameter="time">
                        </toolkit:EventToCommandBehavior>
                    </RadioButton.Behaviors>
                    <VisualStateManager.VisualStateGroups>
                        ...
                </RadioButton>

                <Entry
                    x:Name="maxTimeEntry"
                    ...
                    IsEnabled="False"
                    Text="{Binding GameTimeSet, Converter={StaticResource zeroToEmptyConverter}}"
                    TextChanged="OnMaxTimeTextChanged">
                    ...
                    </Entry.Placeholder>
                    <Entry.Behaviors>
                        <behaviors:NumericInputBehavior />
                    </Entry.Behaviors>
                </Entry>
            </Grid>
        </VerticalStackLayout>
    </Border>

    <!--the Ready button-->
    <Button
        Grid.Row="3"
        Text="Ready"
        IsEnabled="{Binding AllSettingsAreValid}">
    </Button>
</Grid>
</ContentPage>
```

And now let's have a closer look at it.

Let's start with the **PlayerSettings** controls. Look how they're bound to the particular players defined in **ObservableCollection** in the view model. Here's the first player as an example:

```
<controls:PlayerSettings>
    <controls:PlayerSettings.BindingContext>
        <Binding Path="Players[0]" />
    </controls:PlayerSettings.BindingContext>
</controls:PlayerSettings>
```

This is where the binding context is set, so let's remove the following code from **PlayerSettings.xaml**:

```
<ContentView.BindingContext>
    <viewmodels:PlayerSettingsViewModel />
</ContentView.BindingContext>
```

Next, have a look at the first radio button in the Ending Conditions section. Its **IsVisible** property is bound to the **OnlyOnePlayer** property defined in the view model:

```
IsVisible="{Binding OnlyOnePlayer, Converter={StaticResource invertedBoolConverter}}"
```

We're using the **InvertedBoolConverter** that we get from the Community Toolkit. We added it to the page's resources:

```
<ContentPage.Resources>
    ...
    <toolkit:InvertedBoolConverter x:Key="invertedBoolConverter" />
</ContentPage.Resources>
```

We want the first radio button to be visible only when there are at least two players.

The two entries in the Ending Conditions section should behave like the entries in the **PlayerSettings** controls. The input must be valid in order to proceed. That's why we added the **TextChanged** events. In the code-behind, the **SettingsPage.xaml.cs** file, they're implemented like so:

```
...
public partial class SettingsPage : ContentPage
{
    public SettingsPage(SettingsViewModel settingsViewModel)
    {
        InitializeComponent();
        BindingContext = settingsViewModel;
    }

    private void OnMaxRacesTextChanged(object sender, TextChangedEventArgs e)
    {
        if (BindingContext != null && maxRacesEntry != null)
        {
            bool maxRacesValid = (BindingContext as SettingsViewModel)!.MaxRacesIsValid;

            Helpers.HandleNumericEntryState(maxRacesValid, maxRacesEntry);
        }
    }

    private void OnMaxTimeTextChanged(object sender, TextChangedEventArgs e)
    {
        if (BindingContext != null && maxTimeEntry != null)
        {
            bool maxTimeValid = (BindingContext as SettingsViewModel)!.MaxTimeIsValid;

            Helpers.HandleNumericEntryState(maxTimeValid, maxTimeEntry);
        }
    }
}
```

There's also an interesting behavior that requires some more explanation.

EventToCommandBehavior

Let's start with the player radio buttons, so the four radio buttons used to select the number of players in the game. They all look similar. The second button has the **IsChecked** property set to **True**, because the default number of players is two. Here's the first button:

```
<RadioButton
    GroupName="players">
    ...
    </RadioButton.Content>
    <RadioButton.Behaviors>
        <toolkit:EventToCommandBehavior
            EventName="CheckedChanged"
            Command="{Binding CreatePlayerListCommand}">
            <toolkit:EventToCommandBehavior.CommandParameter>
                <x:Int32>1</x:Int32>
            </toolkit:EventToCommandBehavior.CommandParameter>
        </toolkit:EventToCommandBehavior>
    </RadioButton.Behaviors>
</RadioButton>
```

We want to implement the method that we'll use to add and remove players from the **`Players`** observable collection. As you remember, the **`CreatePlayerList`** method has the **`RelayCommand`** attribute, which means it can be used in commanding. In the **`TestPage`** we bound the button's **`Command`** property to a method, but now we have to bind the radio buttons. The problem is that, unlike buttons, radio buttons don't support commands. This means we have to stick with events… unless we use the .NET MAUI Community Toolkit and its **`EventToCommandBehavior`**.

Remember the **`NumericInputBehavior`** in the **`PlayerSettings`** view? We defined that behavior ourselves. Here we're using a behavior defined in the Community Toolkit.

First, we have to install a NuGet package. Right-click the project and select Manage NuGet Packages… Search for the CommunityToolkit.Maui package (A) and install it (B):

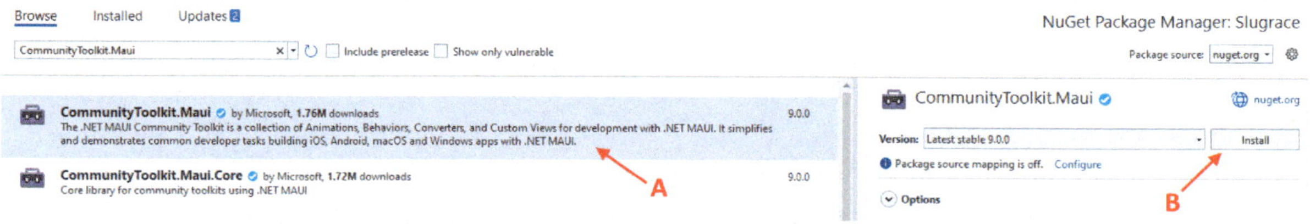

When the package is installed, you will see some instructions to follow. We have to initialize the package. Go to the **MauiProgram.cs** file, add the appropriate using statement at the top of the file and call the **`UseMauiCommunityToolkit`** extension method on the builder object:

```
using Microsoft.Extensions.Logging;
using Slugrace.Views;
using Slugrace.ViewModels;
using CommunityToolkit.Maui;

namespace Slugrace;

public static class MauiProgram
{
        public static MauiApp CreateMauiApp()
        {
                var builder = MauiApp.CreateBuilder();
                builder
                        .UseMauiApp<App>()
                        .UseMauiCommunityToolkit()
                        .ConfigureFonts(fonts =>
                        ...
```

Also in the instructions, you can see how to use the toolkit in XAML. You have to add the following namespace:

```
xmlns:toolkit="http://schemas.microsoft.com/dotnet/2022/maui/toolkit"
```

After adding this namespace in the **SettingsPage**, we can make use of the **EventToCommandBehavior**. It allows us to invoke a command through an event.

We're passing a parameter to the command, which is the number of players this button is supposed to set.

We also added the **EventToCommandBehavior** to the ending condition radio buttons below where the **Command** property is set to the **SetEndingCondition** method in the view model.

There's one more piece of the puzzle we have to talk about, the messaging system. We're sending and receiving messages between view models.

The Messaging System

Views bind their properties to properties in view models, but sometimes two view models have to communicate with each other. It's possible to implement a messaging system that sends messages from one part of the application to any other part, even if the two parts are completely decoupled.

In our app, the button in the **SettingsPage** must respond to what happens in each particular **PlayerSettings** control. More precisely, it has to be disabled if the player's name or initial money gets invalid. Let's take the player's name as an example. In this property's setter a couple notifications are sent so that other properties can be updated if necessary. Here's the **PlayerSettingsViewModel.cs** file:

```
...
public partial class PlayerSettingsViewModel : ObservableObject
{
    ...
    public string PlayerName
    {
        get => player.Name;
        set
        {
            if (player.Name != value)
            {
                player.Name = value;
                OnPropertyChanged();
                OnPropertyChanged(nameof(NameIsValid));
                OnPropertyChanged(nameof(PlayerIsValid));
                ...
```

But the button in the **SettingsPage** also needs to be notified in order to adjust its **IsEnabled** property. We can bind this property to a property in the **SettingsViewModel**, but not to a property in the **PlayerSettingsViewModel**. Fortunately, a property in one view model can send a message that will be received by another view model and a property in the other view model, to which the button can bind, will be set appropriately. Looks a bit complicated, so let's analyze it step by step.

The first step is to create the message. We're going to need two messages: one will be sent by the **PlayerName** property when it changes, the other by the **PlayerInitialMoney** when it changes, so let's create a folder in the root of our app and name it **Messages**. In the folder let's create two classes and name them **PlayerNameChangedMessage** and **PlayerInitialMoneyChangedMessage**. Here's how the former is implemented:

```
using CommunityToolkit.Mvvm.Messaging.Messages;

namespace Slugrace.Messages;

public class PlayerNameChangedMessage(string value) : ValueChangedMessage<string>(value)
{
}
```

The other one looks almost the same:

```
using CommunityToolkit.Mvvm.Messaging.Messages;

namespace Slugrace.Messages;

public class PlayerInitialMoneyChangedMessage(int? value) : ValueChangedMessage<int?>(value)
{
}
```

The MVVM Toolkit supports two types of messengers. The one we're interested in is **WeakReferenceMessenger**. As the name suggests, it uses weak references internally. It offers automatic memory management for the recipients, so you don't have to remember to unsubscribe the recipients.

Now, with our messages created, the two properties of the **PlayerSettingsViewModel** class can send them:

```
using CommunityToolkit.Mvvm.ComponentModel;
using CommunityToolkit.Mvvm.Messaging;
using Slugrace.Messages;
using Slugrace.Models;

namespace Slugrace.ViewModels;

public partial class PlayerSettingsViewModel : ObservableObject
{
    ...
    public string PlayerName
    {
        get => player.Name;
        set
        {
            if (player.Name != value)
            {
                ...
                OnPropertyChanged(nameof(PlayerIsValid));

                WeakReferenceMessenger.Default.Send(new PlayerNameChangedMessage(value));
            }
        }
    }
```

```
    public int PlayerInitialMoney
    {
        get => player.InitialMoney;
        set
        {
            if (player.InitialMoney != value)
            {
                ...
                OnPropertyChanged(nameof(PlayerIsValid));

                WeakReferenceMessenger.Default.Send(new PlayerInitialMoneyChangedMessage(value));
            }
        }
    }
    ...
```

Sending is one thing. Another thing is receiving. Which object is supposed to receive the messages? Well, definitely the **SettingsViewModel**. The message must be registered there and, naturally, handled. So, let's open the **SettingsViewModel.cs** file and register the messages in the constructor:

```
using CommunityToolkit.Mvvm.ComponentModel;
using CommunityToolkit.Mvvm.Input;
using CommunityToolkit.Mvvm.Messaging;
using Slugrace.Messages;
using Slugrace.Models;
using System.Collections.ObjectModel;
...
public partial class SettingsViewModel : ObservableObject
...
    public SettingsViewModel()
    {
        ...
        Players =
        ...

        WeakReferenceMessenger.Default.Register<PlayerNameChangedMessage>(this, (r, m) =>
            OnPlayerNameChangedMessageReceived(m.Value));

        WeakReferenceMessenger.Default.Register<PlayerInitialMoneyChangedMessage>(this, (r, m) =>
            OnPlayerInitialMoneyChangedMessageReceived(m.Value));
    }
    ...
```

As you can see, there are two methods that will handle the messages with pretty long names: **OnPlayerNameChangedMessageReceived** and **OnPlayerInitialMoneyChangedMessageReceived**. Before we implement them, let's add two observable properties they will make use of, **changedPlayerName** and **changedPlayerInitialMoney**:

```
...
public partial class SettingsViewModel : ObservableObject
...
    public bool RacesEndingConditionSet
        ...
    [ObservableProperty]
    [NotifyPropertyChangedFor(nameof(AllSettingsAreValid))]
    private string changedPlayerName;
```

```
    [ObservableProperty]
    [NotifyPropertyChangedFor(nameof(AllSettingsAreValid))]
    private int? changedPlayerInitialMoney;

    public bool AllSettingsAreValid
    ...
```

And here's how the methods are implemented:

```
...
public partial class SettingsViewModel : ObservableObject
...
    public SettingsViewModel()
    ...
    private void OnPlayerNameChangedMessageReceived(string value)
    {
        ChangedPlayerName = value;
    }

    private void OnPlayerInitialMoneyChangedMessageReceived(int? value)
    {
        ChangedPlayerInitialMoney = value;
    }

    [RelayCommand]
    void CreatePlayerList(int numberOfPlayers)
    ...
```

These two methods set the **ChangedPlayerName** and **ChangedPlayerInitialMoney** properties respectively to the value passed by the message.

As you can see, whenever one of these properties changes, the **AllSettingsAreValid** property is notified and this is the property the button's **IsEnabled** property binds to. The button can now react to any changes in the properties that sent the messages from a different object.

Now the app works as expected. For example, the button gets disabled when the initial money of one of the players is invalid.

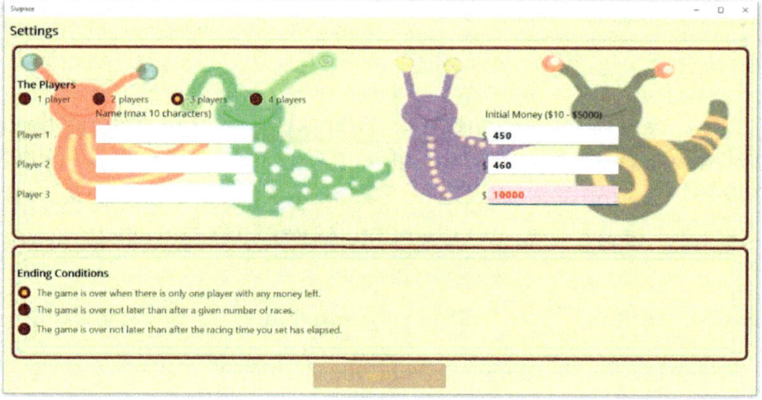

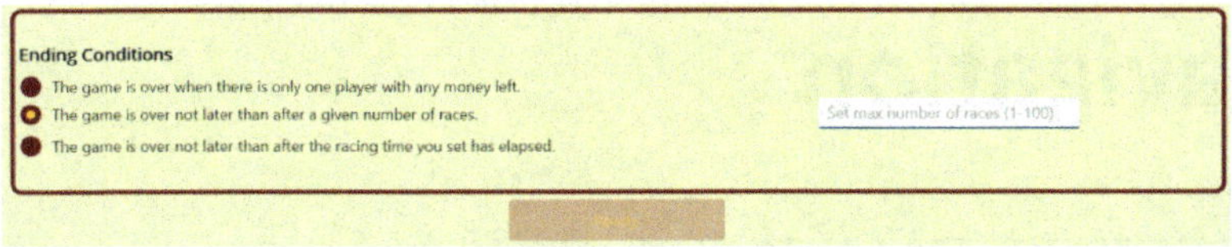

It's also disabled if you choose the Races ending condition but don't specify the number of races.

OK, we've spent so much time trying to enable or disable the button, depending on the data delivered in the entries, that we didn't even have time to think about what this button is for in the first place…

And the button is for navigation. If you click it, it will navigate to the **RacePage** where the actual game begins. Navigation is going to be the subject of the next chapter.

Chapter 18 - Navigation

code: https://github.com/prospero-apps/Slugrace/tree/chapter18

In the previous chapter we were implementing the **SettingsPage** view, its corresponding view model and the **PlayerSettings** view and view model. This is where we set the number of players, their names and initial money, as well as the ending condition. When this is all done correctly, the Ready button is enabled and if we hit it, we navigate to the **RacePage**. Well, this is what we want the button to do. For now it does nothing.

So, in this chapter we'll implement the navigation to the **RacePage**, and navigation in general. There are going to be several places in our app, where navigation between pages will be required, in particular:

- from **SettingsPage** to **RacePage** when the Ready button is pressed,

- from **RacePage** to **InstructionsPage** when the Instructions button is pressed, and back when a Back button in the **InstructionsPage** is pressed (we haven't created this page yet),

- from **RacePage** to **GameOverPage** when the game is over,

- from **GameOverPage** to **SettingsPage** when the Play Again button in the former is pressed.

We'll implement all this functionality in this chapter. We'll also create the missing view models and a basic **InstructionsPage** as we proceed.

To implement navigation to the **GameOverPage**, we'll create a basic game simulation.

To practice navigation, we'll start by implementing a navigation system between the **SettingsPage** and **TestPage**. For now, when the Ready button is clicked, we'll navigate to the **TestPage** and we'll be able to navigate back to the **SettingsPage** from there. So, let's begin.

Navigation to Another Page

Let's simplify the **TestPage.xaml** file like so:

```
<?xml version="1.0" encoding="utf-8" ?>
<ContentPage xmlns="http://schemas.microsoft.com/dotnet/2021/maui"
             xmlns:x="http://schemas.microsoft.com/winfx/2009/xaml"
             xmlns:viewmodels="clr-namespace:Slugrace.ViewModels"
             x:DataType="viewmodels:TestViewModel"
             x:Class="Slugrace.Views.TestPage"
             Title="TestPage"
             Padding="50">
```

```
    <VerticalStackLayout WidthRequest="{OnPlatform 600, Android=200}">
        <Label Text="Test Page"
               FontSize="40" />
    </VerticalStackLayout>
</ContentPage>
```

Also, we don't need the properties we defined before in the **TestViewModel**. Make sure this class looks for now like so:

```
using CommunityToolkit.Mvvm.ComponentModel;

namespace Slugrace.ViewModels;

public partial class TestViewModel : ObservableObject
{
}
```

There are different ways navigation can be implemented in .NET MAUI. We're going to use URI Shell-based navigation, which looks like navigation to a website. The .NET MAUI Shell gives a structure to the application. We used it to set a starting page that is displayed when the app runs.

In order to be able to navigate to the **TestPage**, we have to register this page with the routing system of .NET Shell. Open the **AppShell.xaml.cs** file and add the following code:

```
using Slugrace.Views;

namespace Slugrace;

public partial class AppShell : Shell
{
    public AppShell()
    {
        InitializeComponent();
        Routing.RegisterRoute(nameof(TestPage), typeof(TestPage));
    }
}
```

The **RegisterRoute** method takes two parameters. The first one is the route itself, the second one is the type that should be associated with this route. We're using here the name of the page as the route, but you can use any name you like.

Now, we want to navigate to from **SettingsPage** to **TestPage** when the Ready button is pressed. Let's create a method in the **SettingsViewModel** and add a **RelayCommand** attribute to it:

```
...
public partial class SettingsViewModel : ObservableObject
{
    ...
    [RelayCommand]
    void SetEndingCondition(string condition)
```

```
    ...
    [RelayCommand]
    async Task StartGame()
    {
        await Shell.Current.GoToAsync("TestPage");
    }
}
```

This is an asynchronous method used for Shell navigation. Here we passed the route as a string literal, but we could also do it using **nameof**:

```
...
using Slugrace.Views;
...
public partial class SettingsViewModel : ObservableObject
{
    ...
        await Shell.Current.GoToAsync(nameof(TestPage));
    ...
```

Now go to the **SettingsPage** and bind the button's **Command** property to the method:

```
...
<ContentPage ...>
    ...
        <!--the Ready button-->
        <Button
            Grid.Row="3"
            Text="Ready"
            IsEnabled="{Binding AllSettingsAreValid}"
            Command="{Binding StartGameCommand}">
        </Button>
    ...
```

Now run the app, fill in some valid data and hit the Ready button. This will take you to the **TestPage**. Here's what it looks like on Windows.

You can see a little arrow in the upper left corner. If you click it, you will navigate back to the **SettingsPage**.

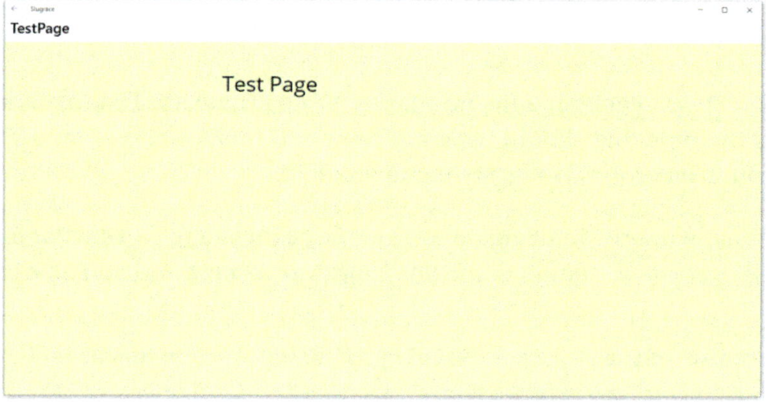

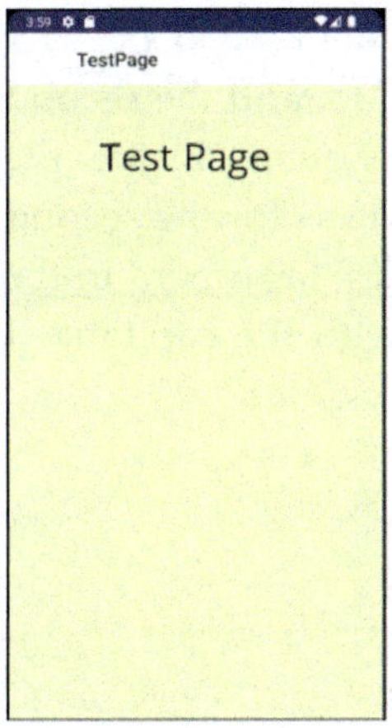

Here's what it looks like on Android.

Here the arrow is practically invisible because it's white, just like the background. But if you click it, it works.

In the actual game we shouldn't be able to navigate from the **RacePage** back to the **SettingsPage**, so we have to take care of it. But first let's see how to pass data from page to page.

Passing Data Between Pages

We can pass information from page to page. To do that, we can define query parameters or a dictionary. Let's have a look at the first approach. It's used for simple data types, like strings, ints, etc.

If you want to pass any query parameters in your web browser, they're separated by a question mark. We also use a question mark in .NET MAUI.

So, suppose we want to pass the value of **maxRaces** to the **TestPage**. This is how we do it:

```
...
public partial class SettingsViewModel : ObservableObject
{
    ...
    [RelayCommand]
    async Task StartGame()
    {
        await Shell.Current.GoToAsync($"{nameof(TestPage)}?Limit={maxRaces}");
    }
}
```

So, we're using an interpolated string where the route is followed by **?**, then the query identifier (**Limit**) and the value that we want to pass (**maxRaces**).

Next, we have to receive the data in the page we navigate to. As we're using the MVVM pattern, we'll do it in the **TestViewModel**:

```
using CommunityToolkit.Mvvm.ComponentModel;

namespace Slugrace.ViewModels;

[QueryProperty("MaxLimit", "Limit")]

public partial class TestViewModel : ObservableObject
{
}
```

We're using the **QueryProperty** attribute with two arguments. The first argument (**MaxLimit**) is the name of the property defined in the view model that we will be able to bind to, and the second argument (**Limit**) is the name of the query identifier that we used in the query inside the **GoToAsync** method. We could use any name for the first parameter, also the same as for the second one. Anyway, then we have to define the property with the same name as the first argument in the class. In our case we're using an observable property, so the actual property with the capitalized name will be generated for us. Here's the code:

```
...
[QueryProperty("MaxLimit", "Limit")]
public partial class TestViewModel : ObservableObject
{
    [ObservableProperty]
    int maxLimit;
}
```

We can use **nameof** for the first argument as well:

```
...
[QueryProperty(nameof(MaxLimit), "Limit")]
...
```

Let's now bind to this property. We'll create a new label in the **TestPage** view and bind its **Text** property to **MaxLimit**:

```
...
<ContentPage ...>

    <VerticalStackLayout WidthRequest="{OnPlatform 600, Android=200}">
        <Label Text="Test Page"
               FontSize="40" />
        <Label Text="{Binding MaxLimit, StringFormat='maximum number of races: {0}'}"
               FontSize="30" />
    </VerticalStackLayout>
</ContentPage>
```

Now you can see the value displayed correctly:

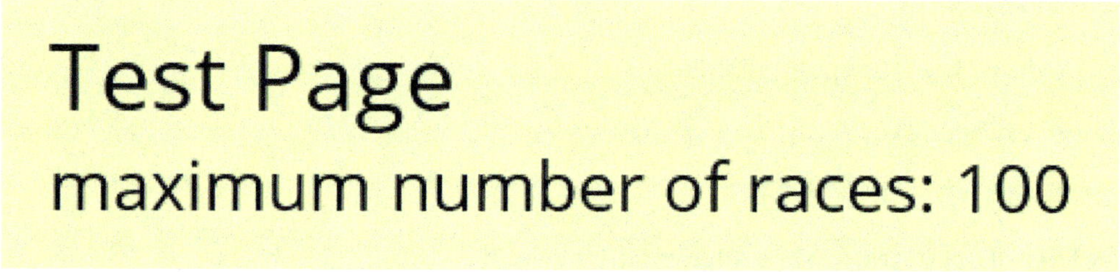

You can also pass multiple query parameters. Let's modify the **StartGame** method:

```
...
public partial class SettingsViewModel : ObservableObject
{
    ...
    [RelayCommand]
    async Task StartGame()
    {
        await Shell.Current.GoToAsync(
            $"{nameof(TestPage)}?Limit={maxRaces}&Word={GameEndingCondition}");
    }
}
```

Here we added a second parameter. Now, let's receive both parameters in the **TestViewModel**:

```
...
[QueryProperty(nameof(MaxLimit), "Limit")]
[QueryProperty(nameof(Word), "Word")]
public partial class TestViewModel : ObservableObject
{
    [ObservableProperty]
    int maxLimit;

    [ObservableProperty]
    string? word;
}
```

Let's bind to this property in the **TestPage**, too:

```
...
<ContentPage ...>
    ...
        <Label Text="{Binding MaxLimit... />
        <Label Text="{Binding Word, StringFormat='favorite word: {0}'}"
               FontSize="20" />
    ...
```

Run the app and you'll see this:

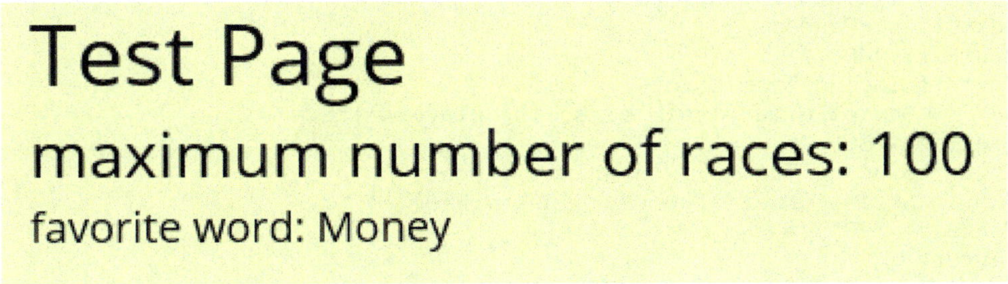

If you want to pass complex objects, you should add another argument to the **GoToAsync** method, which is a **Dictionary<string, object>**, like for example:

```
...
public partial class SettingsViewModel : ObservableObject
{
    ...
    [RelayCommand]
    async Task StartGame()
    {
        await Shell.Current.GoToAsync($"{nameof(TestPage)}",
            new Dictionary<string, object>
            {
                {"Team", Players }
            });
    }
}
```

How do we receive navigation data in the **TestViewModel** now? Exactly the same as before:

```
using CommunityToolkit.Mvvm.ComponentModel;
using System.Collections.ObjectModel;

namespace Slugrace.ViewModels;

[QueryProperty(nameof(Team), "Team")]
public partial class TestViewModel : ObservableObject
{
    [ObservableProperty]
    ObservableCollection<PlayerSettingsViewModel>? team;
}
```

Let's bind to it:

```
...
<ContentPage ...>

    <VerticalStackLayout WidthRequest="600">
        <Label Text="Test Page"
               FontSize="40" />
        <Label Text="{Binding Team.Count,
                      StringFormat='team size: {0} players'}"
               FontSize="30" />
        <Label Text="{Binding Team[0].PlayerInitialMoney,
                      StringFormat='The captain has ${0}.'}"
               FontSize="20" />
</VerticalStackLayout>
</ContentPage>
```

If we set the first player's initial money to 2000 and hit the Ready button, this is what we'll see.

Fine. But what if we want to navigate back?

Navigating Back

Suppose we don't want the user to navigate back. Then we have to remove the back button. The back button can be manipulated by setting the **BackButtonBehavior** attached property to a **BackButtonBehavior** object in the page you navigate to. There are a couple properties in the **BackButtonBehavior** class, but the two that are of interest to us now are **IsEnabled** and **IsVisible**. We just have to set them to **False**. Add the following code to the **TestPage.xaml** file:

```
...
<ContentPage ...>

    <Shell.BackButtonBehavior>
        <BackButtonBehavior IsEnabled="False" IsVisible="False" />
    </Shell.BackButtonBehavior>

    <VerticalStackLayout WidthRequest="{OnPlatform 600, Android=200}">
        ...
```

If you now run the app, you won't see the back button anymore.

As we're at it, let's add these same three lines of XAML code to the pages we'll be navigating to. This way we won't be able to navigate back by hitting the arrow. In particular, let's add them to the **RacePage**:

```
...
<ContentPage ...
             x:Class="Slugrace.Views.RacePage"
             Padding="5">

    <Shell.BackButtonBehavior>
        <BackButtonBehavior IsEnabled="False" IsVisible="False" />
    </Shell.BackButtonBehavior>

    <Grid>
        ...
```

and to the **GameOverPage**:

```
...
<ContentPage ...
             x:Class="Slugrace.Views.GameOverPage">

    <Shell.BackButtonBehavior>
        <BackButtonBehavior IsEnabled="False" IsVisible="False" />
    </Shell.BackButtonBehavior>

    <ContentPage.Resources>
        ...
```

Let's get back to the **TestPage** and implement backward navigation programmatically, though. First let's add a button in the **TestPage** to navigate back to the **SettingsPage** and bind its **Command** property to a method that we have to create in the view model. Actually, let's start with the method:

```
...
[QueryProperty(nameof(Team), "Team")]
public partial class TestViewModel : ObservableObject
{
    [ObservableProperty]
    ObservableCollection<PlayerSettingsViewModel> team;

    [RelayCommand]
    async Task NavigateBack()
    {
        await Shell.Current.GoToAsync("..");
    }
}
```

We don't have to specify the page we want to navigate to by its name. If we use the two dots, it just means we want to move one level up the stack, so to the page we navigated from.

And here's the button in the **TestPage** view:

```
...
<ContentPage ...>
    ...
        <Label Text="{Binding Team[0].PlayerInitialMoney, ...
        <Button Text="Back to settings"
                Command="{Binding NavigateBackCommand}"
                HorizontalOptions="Start" />
    </VerticalStackLayout>
</ContentPage>
```

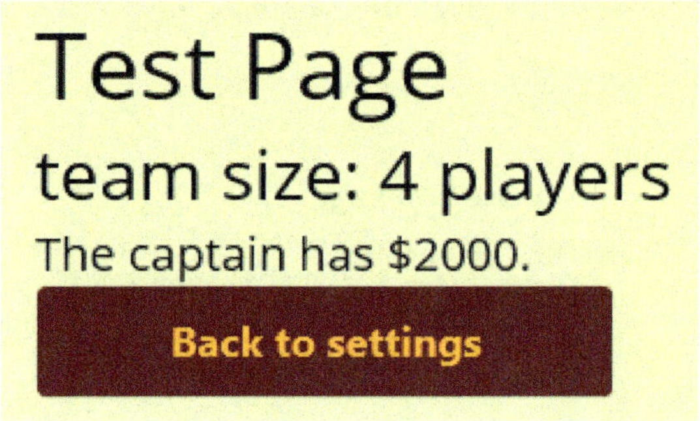

If you run the app, you'll see the button. If you hit it, you'll go back to where you came from.

It's time to implement navigation in our app. But first let's create the view model for the **RacePage**.

GameViewModel

We'll create a view model that will be used by the **RacePage** and later also by the **InstructionsPage**. This view model will end up pretty complex because it will include information about the entire game.

We'll need a **RaceStatus** enumeration to keep track of whether we're waiting for a race to begin, or whether a race is currently going on, or whether it just finished. So, add a **RaceStatus** enum to the root of the app and implement it like so:

```
namespace Slugrace;

public enum RaceStatus
{
    NotYetStarted,
    Started,
    Finished
}
```

And now add a **GameViewModel** class to the **ViewModels** folder and implement it like so:

```
using CommunityToolkit.Mvvm.ComponentModel;

namespace Slugrace.ViewModels;

public partial class GameViewModel : ObservableObject
{
    [ObservableProperty]
    RaceStatus raceStatus;
}
```

Let's register the page and the view model with the dependency service in **MauiProgram.cs**:

```
...
public static class MauiProgram
{
        ...
        builder.Services.AddTransient<SettingsViewModel>();

        builder.Services.AddTransient<RacePage>();
        builder.Services.AddTransient<GameViewModel>();

        return builder.Build();
    }
}
```

Next, in **RacePage.xaml.cs**, let's inject the view model in the constructor and set the binding context of the view to the view model:

```
using Slugrace.ViewModels;
...
public partial class RacePage : ContentPage
{
    public RacePage(GameViewModel gameViewModel)
    {
        InitializeComponent();
        BindingContext = gameViewModel;
    }
}
```

We want to be able to navigate to **RacePage**, so let's register the route in **AppShell.xaml.cs**:

```
...
public partial class AppShell : Shell
{
    public AppShell()
    {
        InitializeComponent();
        Routing.RegisterRoute(nameof(RacePage), typeof(RacePage));
    }
}
```

We removed the route to the **TestPage** because we don't need it anymore.

The navigation should start when the Ready button is pressed. We'll create a **StartGame** method in the **SettingsViewModel** and use it as a command.

In the method we'll populate the **Game** object with the slugs and players. To do that, let's add some more properties to the **Slug** model class. It now should look like this:

```
...
public class Slug
{
    public string Name { get; set; } = string.Empty;
    public double Odds { get; set; }
    public double PreviousOdds { get; set; }
    public int WinNumber { get; set; }
    public string ImageUrl { get; set; } = string.Empty;
    public string EyeImageUrl { get; set; } = string.Empty;
    public string BodyImageUrl { get; set; } = string.Empty;
    public double BaseOdds { get; set; }
    public bool IsRaceWinner { get; set; }
}
```

The properties we want to set in the **SettingsPage** are: **Name**, **BaseOdds**, **ImageUrl**, **EyeImageUrl** and **BodyImageUrl**. Each slug will have a fixed name and **BaseOdds**. Speedster will have the lowest **BaseOdds**, because this slug will be the most probable to win. Similarly, as the least probable to win, Slowpoke will have the highest **BaseOdds**.

The **ImageUrl** refers to the silhouette image of the slug. The **EyeImageUrl** and **BodyImageUrl** properties will be used for the images in top view.

Before we move on, let's also add some properties to the other model classes. We're going to need them soon. So, here's the **Player** class:

```
...
public class Player
{
    ...
    public bool IsInGame { get; set; }
    public int PreviousMoney { get; set; }
    public bool IsBankrupt { get; set; }
}
```

And here's the **Game** class:

```
...
public class Game
{
    ...
    public int GameTimeSet { get; set; } = 0;
    public string GameOverReason { get; set; } = string.Empty;
    public List<Player> Winners { get; set; } = [];
    public int RaceNumber { get; set; }
    public int TimeElapsed { get; set; }
}
```

We'll discuss all the new properties when we need them. With that in place, let's create the real **StartGame** method (rather that the one we created before to test navigation using the **TestPage**) in the **SettingsViewModel**:

```
...
public partial class SettingsViewModel : ObservableObject
{
    ...
    void SetEndingCondition(string condition)
    ...
    [RelayCommand]
    async Task StartGame()
    {
        // Populate the Game object
        game.Slugs =
        [
            new Slug
            {
                Name = "Speedster",
                BaseOdds = 1.33,
                ImageUrl = "speedster.png",
                EyeImageUrl = "speedster_eye.png",
                BodyImageUrl = "speedster_body.png"
            },
```

```
            new Slug
            {
                Name = "Trusty",
                BaseOdds = 1.59,
                ImageUrl = "trusty.png",
                EyeImageUrl = "trusty_eye.png",
                BodyImageUrl = "trusty_body.png"
            },
            new Slug
            {
                Name = "Iffy",
                BaseOdds = 2.5,
                ImageUrl = "iffy.png",
                EyeImageUrl = "iffy_eye.png",
                BodyImageUrl = "iffy_body.png"
            },
            new Slug
            {
                Name = "Slowpoke",
                BaseOdds = 2.89,
                ImageUrl = "slowpoke.png",
                EyeImageUrl = "slowpoke_eye.png",
                BodyImageUrl = "slowpoke_body.png"
            }
        ];

        var playersInGame = Players.Where(p => p.PlayerIsInGame).ToList();

        game.Players = [];

        foreach (var player in playersInGame)
        {
            game.Players.Add(new Player
            {
                Id = player.PlayerId,
                Name = string.IsNullOrEmpty(player.PlayerName)
                    ? "Player " + player.PlayerId
                    : player.PlayerName,
                IsInGame = true,
                InitialMoney = player.PlayerInitialMoney,
                CurrentMoney = player.PlayerInitialMoney
            });
        }

        // Navigate to RacePage
        await Shell.Current.GoToAsync($"{nameof(RacePage)}",
            new Dictionary<string, object>
            {
                {"Game", game }
            });
    }
}
```

Here we're populating the **Game** object with the data collected from the **SettingsPage**. This object is then passed to the **RacePage**.

We already bound the method to the **Command** property of the Ready button in the **SettingsPage**:

```
...
<ContentPage ...>
    ...
        <!--the Ready button-->
        <Button
            Grid.Row="3"
            Text="Ready"
            IsEnabled="{Binding AllSettingsAreValid}"
            Command="{Binding StartGameCommand}">
        </Button>
    ...
```

Next, in the **GameViewModel**, we have to add the **QueryProperty** attribute and create a property to store the data passed from the **SettingsPage**:

```
using CommunityToolkit.Mvvm.ComponentModel;
using Slugrace.Models;
...
[QueryProperty(nameof(Game), "Game")]
public partial class GameViewModel : ObservableObject
{
    [ObservableProperty]
    private Game? game;

    [ObservableProperty]
    RaceStatus raceStatus;
...
```

If we now run the app, set the players (their names and initial money) and the ending condition, and then hit the Ready button, we'll navigate to the **RacePage**. We'll take all the game information with us. Now we can consume it in the **RacePage**.

There are several content views nested in the **RacePage** that need information about the **Game** object, the **Player** objects and the **Slug** objects. All this information will be contained in the **GameViewModel**.

GameInfo

Let's start with the **GameInfo** view. As a child of the **RacePage**, it will bind to the **GameViewModel**, just like its parent. We have to add some properties to the view model that this content view will bind to. Here's the **GameViewModel** class:

```
...
[QueryProperty(nameof(Game), "Game")]
public partial class GameViewModel : ObservableObject
{
    ...
    RaceStatus raceStatus;

    [ObservableProperty]
    [NotifyPropertyChangedFor(nameof(EndingConditionIsRaces))]
    [NotifyPropertyChangedFor(nameof(EndingConditionIsTime))]
    private EndingCondition gameEndingCondition;
    public bool EndingConditionIsRaces => GameEndingCondition == EndingCondition.Races;

    public bool EndingConditionIsTime => GameEndingCondition == EndingCondition.Time;

    private int raceNumber;
    public int RaceNumber
    {
        get => raceNumber;
        set
        {
            if (raceNumber != value)
            {
                raceNumber = value;
                OnPropertyChanged();
                OnPropertyChanged(nameof(RacesFinished));
                OnPropertyChanged(nameof(RacesToGo));
            }
        }
    }

    [ObservableProperty]
    [NotifyPropertyChangedFor(nameof(RacesToGo))]
    private int numberOfRacesSet;

    public int RacesFinished => RaceNumber - 1;

    public int RacesToGo => NumberOfRacesSet - RacesFinished;

    [ObservableProperty]
    [NotifyPropertyChangedFor(nameof(TimeRemaining))]
    private TimeSpan gameTimeSet;

    [ObservableProperty]
    [NotifyPropertyChangedFor(nameof(TimeRemaining))]
    private TimeSpan timeElapsed;

    public TimeSpan TimeRemaining => GameTimeSet - TimeElapsed;
}
```

Here we have all the properties that our view needs. Now we can bind to them. The race number will be visible independent of the ending condition, but other information will be displayed depending on which ending condition is set. Here's the **GameInfo.xaml** file:

```
...
<ContentView xmlns="http://schemas.microsoft.com/dotnet/2021/maui"
             xmlns:x="http://schemas.microsoft.com/winfx/2009/xaml"
             xmlns:viewmodels="clr-namespace:Slugrace.ViewModels"
             x:DataType="viewmodels:GameViewModel"
             x:Class="Slugrace.Controls.GameInfo">
```

```
<Grid
    ...
    <Label
        Grid.Row="1"
        Grid.Column="1"
        Text="{Binding RaceNumber}" />

    <!--displayed if Races ending condition-->
    <Label
        IsVisible="{Binding EndingConditionIsRaces}"
        Grid.Row="2">
        <Label.Text>
            <OnPlatform x:TypeArguments="x:String">
                <On Platform="WinUI" Value="Number of races set:" />
                <On Platform="Android" Value="Total races:" />
            </OnPlatform>
        </Label.Text>
    </Label>
    <Label
        IsVisible="{Binding EndingConditionIsRaces}"
        Grid.Row="2"
        Grid.Column="1"
        Text="{Binding NumberOfRacesSet}" />
    <Label
        IsVisible="{Binding EndingConditionIsRaces}"
        Grid.Row="3"
        Text="Races finished:" />
    <Label
        IsVisible="{Binding EndingConditionIsRaces}"
        Grid.Row="3"
        Grid.Column="1"
        Text="{Binding RacesFinished}" />
    <Label
        IsVisible="{Binding EndingConditionIsRaces}"
        Grid.Row="4"
        Text="Races to go:" />
    <Label
        IsVisible="{Binding EndingConditionIsRaces}"
        Grid.Row="4"
        Grid.Column="1"
        Text="{Binding RacesToGo}" />

    <!--displayed if Time ending condition-->
    <Label
        IsVisible="{Binding EndingConditionIsTime}"
        Grid.Row="2">
        <Label.Text>
            <OnPlatform x:TypeArguments="x:String">
                <On Platform="WinUI" Value="Game time set:" />
                <On Platform="Android" Value="Total time:" />
            </OnPlatform>
        </Label.Text>
    </Label>
    <Label
        IsVisible="{Binding EndingConditionIsTime}"
        Grid.Row="2"
        Grid.Column="1"
        Text="{Binding GameTimeSet}" />
```

```
        <Label
            IsVisible="{Binding EndingConditionIsTime}"
            Grid.Row="3"
            Text="Time elapsed:" />
        <Label
            IsVisible="{Binding EndingConditionIsTime}"
            Grid.Row="3"
            Grid.Column="1"
            Text="{Binding TimeElapsed}" />
        <Label
            IsVisible="{Binding EndingConditionIsTime}"
            Grid.Row="4"
            Text="Time remaining:" />
        <Label
            IsVisible="{Binding EndingConditionIsTime}"
            Grid.Row="4"
            Grid.Column="1"
            Text="{Binding TimeRemaining}" />
    </Grid>
</ContentView>
```

We have to modify the **GameViewModel** now because we need information from the **Game** object passed from the **SettingsPage**. However, we can't do it in the constructor because there the **Game** object isn't available. That's why we have to add a partial method **OnGameChanged** and do it there:

```
...
public partial class GameViewModel : ObservableObject
{
    ...
    public TimeSpan TimeRemaining => GameTimeSet - TimeElapsed;

    partial void OnGameChanged(Game? value)
    {
        GameEndingCondition = value!.GameEndingCondition;

        RaceStatus = RaceStatus.NotYetStarted;

        RaceNumber = 1;

        NumberOfRacesSet = value.NumberOfRacesSet;

        GameTimeSet = TimeSpan.FromMinutes(value.GameTimeSet);
    }
    ...
}
```

We're done. If you now run the app, select the **Money** ending condition and press the Ready button, you will only see the race number in the Game Info panel.

If you select the **Races** ending condition and set the number of races to 20, you will see only races-related data.

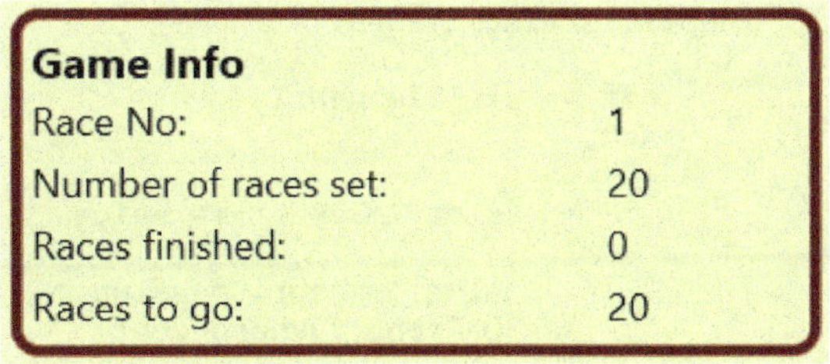

Finally, if you select the **Time** ending condition and set the time to 45 minutes, you will see only time-related data:

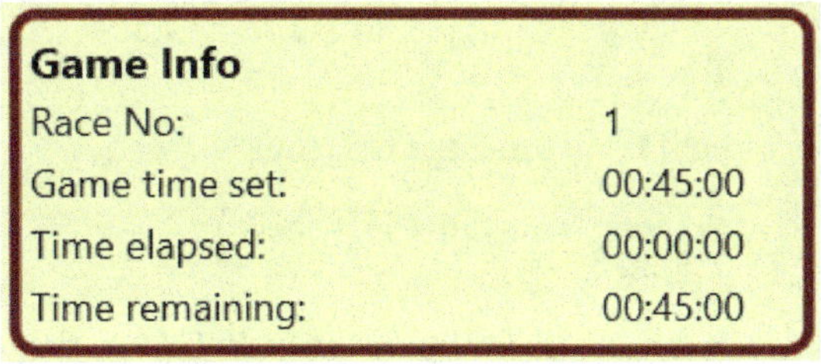

With this in place, let's move on to the Slugs' Stats and Players' Stats panels. These panels need information about the slugs and players. There are more content views in the app that need information about the slugs and players, so let's create separate view models to serve them all.

SlugViewModel

Let's start with the slugs. So, add a new class to the **ViewModels** folder and name it **SlugViewModel**. Here's the code:

```
using CommunityToolkit.Mvvm.ComponentModel;
using CommunityToolkit.Mvvm.Messaging;
using Slugrace.Messages;
using Slugrace.Models;

namespace Slugrace.ViewModels;

public partial class SlugViewModel : ObservableObject
{
    private readonly Slug slug;

    public string Name
    {
        get => slug.Name;
        set
        {
            if (slug.Name != value)
            {
                slug.Name = value;
                OnPropertyChanged();
            }
        }
    }
```

```
public string ImageUrl
{
    get => slug.ImageUrl;
    set
    {
        if (slug.ImageUrl != value)
        {
            slug.ImageUrl = value;
            OnPropertyChanged();
        }
    }
}

public string EyeImageUrl
{
    get => slug.EyeImageUrl;
    set
    {
        if (slug.EyeImageUrl != value)
        {
            slug.EyeImageUrl = value;
            OnPropertyChanged();
        }
    }
}

public string BodyImageUrl
{
    get => slug.BodyImageUrl;
    set
    {
        if (slug.BodyImageUrl != value)
        {
            slug.BodyImageUrl = value;
            OnPropertyChanged();
        }
    }
}

[ObservableProperty]
[NotifyPropertyChangedFor(nameof(WinPercentage))]
private int currentRaceNumber;

public int WinNumber
{
    get => slug.WinNumber;
    set
    {
        if (slug.WinNumber != value)
        {
            slug.WinNumber = value;
            OnPropertyChanged();
            OnPropertyChanged(nameof(WinPercentage));
            OnPropertyChanged(nameof(WinNumberText));
        }
    }
}

public string WinNumberText => WinNumber == 1 ? $"{WinNumber} win" : $"{WinNumber} wins";
```

```
[ObservableProperty]
private int winPercentage;

public bool IsRaceWinner
{
    get => slug.IsRaceWinner;
    set
    {
        if (slug.IsRaceWinner != value)
        {
            slug.IsRaceWinner = value;
            OnPropertyChanged();
            OnPropertyChanged(nameof(Odds));
        }
    }
}

public double Odds
{
    get => slug.Odds;
    set
    {
        if (slug.Odds != value)
        {
            slug.Odds = value;
            OnPropertyChanged();
        }
    }
}

public double PreviousOdds
{
    get => slug.PreviousOdds;
    set
    {
        if (slug.PreviousOdds != value)
        {
            slug.PreviousOdds = value;
            OnPropertyChanged();
        }
    }
}

public SlugViewModel()
{
    slug = new Slug();

    CurrentRaceNumber = 1;

    WeakReferenceMessenger.Default.Register<RaceFinishedMessage>(this, (r, m) =>
        OnRaceFinishedMessageReceived(m.Value));
}

private void OnRaceFinishedMessageReceived(RaceStatus value)
{
    if (value == RaceStatus.Finished)
    {
        WinPercentage = (int)((double)WinNumber / CurrentRaceNumber * 100);

        PreviousOdds = Odds;
```

```
            Odds = IsRaceWinner
            ? Math.Round(Math.Max(1.01, Math.Min(Odds * .96, 20)), 2)
            : Math.Round(Math.Max(1.01, Math.Min(Odds * 1.03, 20)), 2);
        }
    }

    public void RecalculateStats(int raceNumber)
    {
        CurrentRaceNumber = raceNumber;

        if (IsRaceWinner)
        {
            WinNumber++;
        }
    }
}
```

This is the complete code that is required by all the views where slug information is required. Let's break it down.

So, we have the **Name** property, followed by three properties related to the slug images. We also have a **WinNumber** property that will increase by 1 every time the slug wins a race.

There are some more properties that are related to the winning position of the slug after each race. The **IsRaceWinner** property will be set to **true** if the slug wins. The **WinNumberText** property will be used to display the number of wins correctly.

Another property is **WinPercentage**. This property will tell us what part (expressed as a percentage) of the total number of races the slug has won. To calculate this property, we have to know how many races have already finished, hence the **CurrentRaceNumber** property. We'll use a message to notify the **WinPercentage** property each time a race finishes. Let's create the message first.

In the **Messages** folder add a new class and name it **RaceFinishedMessage**. Here's the code:

```
using CommunityToolkit.Mvvm.Messaging.Messages;

namespace Slugrace.Messages;

public class RaceFinishedMessage(RaceStatus value) : ValueChangedMessage<RaceStatus>(value)
{
}
```

This message will be sent each time the race status changes to **Finished**. Let's modify the **RaceStatus** property in the **GameViewModel**:

```
...
public partial class GameViewModel : ObservableObject
{
    ...
    private RaceStatus raceStatus;

    public RaceStatus RaceStatus
    {
        get => raceStatus;
        set
        {
            if (raceStatus != value)
            {
                raceStatus = value;
                OnPropertyChanged();

                if (raceStatus == RaceStatus.Finished)
                {
                    WeakReferenceMessenger.Default.Send(new RaceFinishedMessage(value));
                }
            }
        }
    }

    [ObservableProperty]
    [NotifyPropertyChangedFor(nameof(EndingConditionIsRaces))]
    ...
```

The message is registered in the **SlugViewModel** class's constructor. In the **OnRaceFinishedMessageReceived** method **WinPercentage** is calculated after each race. Also the **Odds** and **PreviousOdds** are recalculated depending on whether the slug won the race or not. The odds decrease if the slug wins and increase otherwise.

We also have the **RecalculateStats** method that we will call later from inside the **GameViewModel** for each slug.

This is all about slugs. What about the players?

PlayerViewModel

Add a **PlayerViewModel** class. It will contain all player-related data:

```
using CommunityToolkit.Mvvm.ComponentModel;
using CommunityToolkit.Mvvm.Input;
using CommunityToolkit.Mvvm.Messaging;
using Slugrace.Messages;
using Slugrace.Models;

namespace Slugrace.ViewModels;
```

```
public partial class PlayerViewModel : ObservableObject
{
    private readonly Player player;

    public string Name
    {
        get => player.Name;
        set
        {
            if (player.Name != value)
            {
                player.Name = value;
                OnPropertyChanged();
            }
        }
    }

    public int InitialMoney
    {
        get => player.InitialMoney;
        set
        {
            if (player.InitialMoney != value)
            {
                player.InitialMoney = value;
                OnPropertyChanged();
            }
        }
    }

    public int CurrentMoney
    {
        get => player.CurrentMoney;
        set
        {
            if (player.CurrentMoney != value)
            {
                player.CurrentMoney = value;
                OnPropertyChanged();
            }
        }
    }

    public int BetAmount
    {
        get => player.BetAmount;
        set
        {
            if (player.BetAmount != value)
            {
                player.BetAmount = value;
                OnPropertyChanged();
                OnPropertyChanged(nameof(BetAmountIsValid));
                OnPropertyChanged(nameof(PlayerIsValid));

                WeakReferenceMessenger.Default.Send(
                    new PlayerBetAmountChangedMessage(value));
            }
        }
    }
```

```
public int PreviousMoney
{
    get => player.PreviousMoney;
    set
    {
        if (player.PreviousMoney != value)
        {
            player.PreviousMoney = value;
            OnPropertyChanged();
        }
    }
}

public int WonOrLostMoney
{
    get => player.WonOrLostMoney;
    set
    {
        if (player.WonOrLostMoney != value)
        {
            player.WonOrLostMoney = value;
            OnPropertyChanged();
        }
    }
}

public bool IsInGame
{
    get => player.IsInGame;
    set
    {
        if (player.IsInGame != value)
        {
            player.IsInGame = value;
            OnPropertyChanged();
        }
    }
}

public bool IsBankrupt
{
    get => player.IsBankrupt;
    set
    {
        if (player.IsBankrupt != value)
        {
            player.IsBankrupt = value;
            OnPropertyChanged();
        }
    }
}

[ObservableProperty]
private List<SlugViewModel> slugs = [];

private SlugViewModel? selectedSlug;

public SlugViewModel? SelectedSlug
{
    get => selectedSlug;
```

```
            set
            {
                if (selectedSlug != value)
                {
                    selectedSlug = value;
                    OnPropertyChanged();
                    OnPropertyChanged(nameof(SelectedSlugIsValid));
                    OnPropertyChanged(nameof(PlayerIsValid));

                    WeakReferenceMessenger.Default.Send(
                        new PlayerSelectedSlugChangedMessage(value!));
                }
            }
        }

        public bool BetAmountIsValid => Helpers.ValueIsInRange(BetAmount,
            1, CurrentMoney);

        public bool SelectedSlugIsValid => SelectedSlug != null;

        public bool PlayerIsValid =>
            IsBankrupt || (BetAmountIsValid && SelectedSlugIsValid);

        [ObservableProperty]
        private string resultMessage = string.Empty;

        public PlayerViewModel()
        {
            player = new Player();
        }

        [RelayCommand]
        void SelectSlug(string name)
        {
            var slug = Slugs.Find(s => s.Name == name);

            if (slug != null)
            {
                SelectedSlug = slug;
            }
        }

        public void CalculateMoney(SlugViewModel raceWinnerSlug)
        {
            PreviousMoney = CurrentMoney;

            bool wonRace = SelectedSlug == raceWinnerSlug;

            WonOrLostMoney = (int)(wonRace
                ? BetAmount * (SelectedSlug!.Odds - 1)
                : -BetAmount);

            CurrentMoney += WonOrLostMoney;

            ResultMessage = wonRace
                ? (WonOrLostMoney == 0
                    ? $"- won less than $1"
                    : $"- won ${WonOrLostMoney}")
                : $"- lost ${Math.Abs(WonOrLostMoney)}";
        }
    }
```

Again, this is the complete code. Here we have some basic properties like **Name**, **InitialMoney** or **CurrentMoney**. We have the **BetAmount** property to store the amount of money a player bets on a slug. We store the current money in the **PreviousMoney** property so that we can see how much money the player had before the race. After the race the **CurrentMoney** property changes depending on the value of **WonOrLostMoney**, which, in turn, depends on whether the player won or lost.

The player also holds a reference to the slugs and before each race a slug is selected and stored in the **SelectedSlug** property.

When the **BetAmount** and **SelectedSlug** properties change, messages are sent. Let's implement them. In the **Messages** folder add the **PlayerBetAmountChangedMessage** and **PlayerSelectedSlugChangedMessage**. The former should be implemented like this:

```
using CommunityToolkit.Mvvm.Messaging.Messages;

namespace Slugrace.Messages;

public class PlayerBetAmountChangedMessage(int value) : ValueChangedMessage<int>(value)
{
}
```

The latter should be implemented like this:

```
using CommunityToolkit.Mvvm.Messaging.Messages;
using Slugrace.ViewModels;

namespace Slugrace.Messages;

public class PlayerSelectedSlugChangedMessage(SlugViewModel value)
    : ValueChangedMessage<SlugViewModel>(value)
{
}
```

These messages must be registered in the **GameViewModel**'s constructor, but we'll see to it in a moment. For now, let's stay in the **PlayerViewModel** class.

The player must be valid in order for the Go button in the Bets panel to be enabled. To check the validity, we have three properties: **BetAmountIsValid**, **SelectedSlugIsValid** and **PlayerIsValid**.

We also have the **SelectSlug** method that will be called when a radio button representing a slug is checked. Finally, after each race, the money properties are recalculated and a result message is created. For this we need the **CalculateMoney** method and the **ResultMessage** property.

And now let's go to the **GameViewModel**, add the slugs and players, and register the messages:

```
...
public partial class GameViewModel : ObservableObject
{
    ...
    public TimeSpan TimeRemaining => GameTimeSet - TimeElapsed;

    [ObservableProperty]
    private List<SlugViewModel> slugs = [];

    [ObservableProperty]
    private List<PlayerViewModel> players = [];

    [ObservableProperty]
    private ObservableCollection<PlayerViewModel> playersStillInGame = [];

    [ObservableProperty]
    private List<PlayerViewModel> winners = [];

    [ObservableProperty]
    private SlugViewModel? raceWinnerSlug;

    private int changedBetAmount;
    public int ChangedBetAmount
    {
        get => changedBetAmount;
        set
        {
            OnPropertyChanged();
            OnPropertyChanged(nameof(AllPlayersAreValid));

            if (changedBetAmount != value)
            {
                changedBetAmount = value;
            }
        }
    }

    private SlugViewModel? changedSelectedSlug;
    public SlugViewModel ChangedSelectedSlug
    {
        get => changedSelectedSlug!;
        set
        {
            OnPropertyChanged();
            OnPropertyChanged(nameof(AllPlayersAreValid));

            if (changedSelectedSlug != value)
            {
                changedSelectedSlug = value;
            }
        }
    }

    public bool? AllPlayersAreValid => Players?.All(p => p.PlayerIsValid);

    public GameViewModel()
    {
        WeakReferenceMessenger.Default.Register<PlayerBetAmountChangedMessage>(
            this, (r, m) => OnBetAmountChangedMessageReceived(m.Value));
```

```
        WeakReferenceMessenger.Default.Register<PlayerSelectedSlugChangedMessage>(
            this, (r, m) => OnSelectedSlugChangedMessageReceived(m.Value));
    }

    private void OnBetAmountChangedMessageReceived(int value)
    {
        ChangedBetAmount = value;
    }

    private void OnSelectedSlugChangedMessageReceived(SlugViewModel value)
    {
        ChangedSelectedSlug = value;
    }

    partial void OnGameChanged(Game? value)
    {
        ...
        GameTimeSet = TimeSpan.FromMinutes(value.GameTimeSet);

        Winners = [];

        Slugs =
        [
            new()
            {
                Name = value.Slugs![0].Name,
                ImageUrl = value.Slugs[0].ImageUrl,
                EyeImageUrl = value.Slugs[0].EyeImageUrl,
                BodyImageUrl = value.Slugs[0].BodyImageUrl,
                WinNumber = 0,
                Odds = Math.Round(value.Slugs[0].BaseOdds
                    + new Random().Next(0, 10) / 100, 2),
                PreviousOdds = value.Slugs[0].BaseOdds
            },
            new()
            {
                Name = value.Slugs[1].Name,
                ImageUrl = value.Slugs[1].ImageUrl,
                EyeImageUrl = value.Slugs[1].EyeImageUrl,
                BodyImageUrl = value.Slugs[1].BodyImageUrl,
                WinNumber = 0,
                Odds = Math.Round(value.Slugs[1].BaseOdds
                    + new Random().Next(0, 10) / 100, 2),
                PreviousOdds = value.Slugs[1].BaseOdds
            },
            new()
            {
                Name = value.Slugs[2].Name,
                ImageUrl = value.Slugs[2].ImageUrl,
                EyeImageUrl = value.Slugs[2].EyeImageUrl,
                BodyImageUrl = value.Slugs[2].BodyImageUrl,
                WinNumber = 0,
                Odds = Math.Round(value.Slugs[2].BaseOdds
                    + new Random().Next(0, 10) / 100, 2),
                PreviousOdds = value.Slugs[2].BaseOdds
            },
            new()
            {
                Name = value.Slugs[3].Name,
                ImageUrl = value.Slugs[3].ImageUrl,
                EyeImageUrl = value.Slugs[3].EyeImageUrl,
```

```
            BodyImageUrl = value.Slugs[3].BodyImageUrl,
            WinNumber = 0,
            Odds = Math.Round(value.Slugs[3].BaseOdds
                + new Random().Next(0, 10) / 100, 2),
            PreviousOdds = value.Slugs[3].BaseOdds
        },
    ];

    List<PlayerViewModel> players = [];

    foreach (var player in value.Players!)
    {
        players.Add
        (
            new()
            {
                Name = player.Name,
                InitialMoney = player.InitialMoney,
                CurrentMoney = player.CurrentMoney,
                BetAmount = 0,
                IsInGame = player.IsInGame,
                PreviousMoney = player.CurrentMoney,
                WonOrLostMoney = 0,
                Slugs = Slugs,
                SelectedSlug = null
            }
        );
    }

    Players = players;

    PlayersStillInGame = Players.ToObservableCollection();
  }
}
```

In the **OnGameChanged** method we create the slugs and players. We'll be talking about the **PlayersStillInGame**, **Winners** and **RaceWinnerSlug** properties a bit later. In the constructor we register the two messages we just created. We also define the **AllPlayersAreValid** property to check whether we can start the next race.

Now that we have the **SlugViewModel** and **PlayerViewModel** classes, let's bind to them. Let's start with the Slugs' Stats content view.

Slugs' Stats and Slug Stats

In the Slugs' Stats panel we can view the achievements of all the slugs. The binding context for this content view is **GameViewModel**. There we use the **SlugStats** content views for each slug. Each **SlugStats** control binds to one slug:

```
...
<ContentView xmlns="http://schemas.microsoft.com/dotnet/2021/maui"
             xmlns:x="http://schemas.microsoft.com/winfx/2009/xaml"
             xmlns:controls="clr-namespace:Slugrace.Controls"
             xmlns:viewmodels="clr-namespace:Slugrace.ViewModels"
```

```
             x:DataType="viewmodels:GameViewModel"
             x:Class="Slugrace.Controls.SlugsStats">

    <ContentView.Resources>
        <Style TargetType="Label" BasedOn="{StaticResource labelBaseStyle}" />
    </ContentView.Resources>

    <Grid
        RowDefinitions="*, *, *, *, *"
        ColumnDefinitions="*">
        <Label
            Text="Slugs' Stats"
            Style="{OnPlatform {StaticResource labelSectionTitleStyle},
                Android={StaticResource androidLabelSectionTitleStyle}}" />
        <controls:SlugStats
            BindingContext="{Binding Slugs[0]}"
            Grid.Row="1" />
        <controls:SlugStats
            BindingContext="{Binding Slugs[1]}"
            Grid.Row="2" />
        <controls:SlugStats
            BindingContext="{Binding Slugs[2]}"
            Grid.Row="3" />
        <controls:SlugStats
            BindingContext="{Binding Slugs[3]}"
            Grid.Row="4" />
    </Grid>
</ContentView>
```

So, let's have a look at a single slug now. The binding context for the **SlugStats** view is **SlugViewModel**. We bind to the properties we defined there:

```
...
<ContentView xmlns="http://schemas.microsoft.com/dotnet/2021/maui"
             xmlns:x="http://schemas.microsoft.com/winfx/2009/xaml"
             xmlns:viewmodels="clr-namespace:Slugrace.ViewModels"
             x:DataType="viewmodels:SlugViewModel"
             x:Class="Slugrace.Controls.SlugStats">

    <ContentView.BindingContext>
        <viewmodels:SlugViewModel />
    </ContentView.BindingContext>

    <ContentView.Resources>
        ...
    <Grid
        RowDefinitions="*">
        <Grid.ColumnDefinitions>
            ...
        <Label
            Text="{Binding Name}" />
```

```
        <Label
            Grid.Column="1"
            Text="{Binding WinNumberText}" />
        <Label
            Grid.Column="2"
            Text="{Binding WinPercentage, StringFormat='{0}%'}" />
    </Grid>
</ContentView>
```

If we now run the app and navigate to the **RacePage**, we'll see the actual slug-related data instead of the placeholder text we had before.

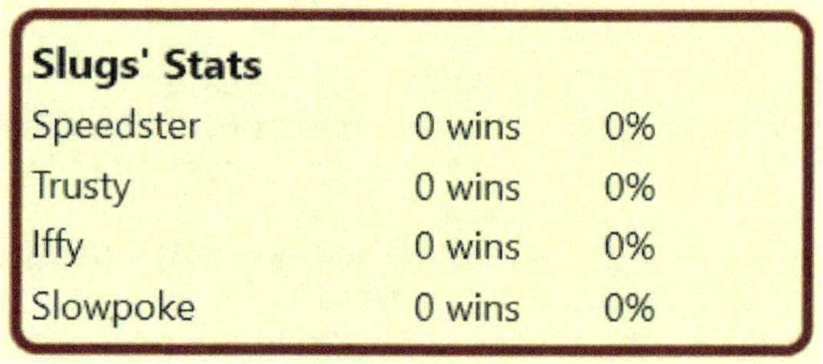

The stats will be recalculated after each race. We'll implement this in a moment when we create a game simulation. For now, though, let's move on to the Players' Stats panel.

Players' Stats and Player Stats

The binding context for the **PlayersStats** content view is **GameViewModel**. For the slugs we added four **SlugStats** controls to the **SlugsStats** view because there are always four slugs. But the number of players may vary between one and four, so we'll add a **CollectionView** and set the **Players** as its source. We'll use the **PlayerStats** control as the item template:

```
...
<ContentView xmlns="http://schemas.microsoft.com/dotnet/2021/maui"
             xmlns:x="http://schemas.microsoft.com/winfx/2009/xaml"
             xmlns:controls="clr-namespace:Slugrace.Controls"
             xmlns:viewmodels="clr-namespace:Slugrace.ViewModels"
             x:DataType="viewmodels:GameViewModel"
             x:Class="Slugrace.Controls.PlayersStats">

    <ContentView.Resources>
        <Style TargetType="Label" BasedOn="{StaticResource labelBaseStyle}" />
    </ContentView.Resources>

    <Grid
        RowDefinitions="*, *, *, *, *"
        ColumnDefinitions="*">
        <Label
            Text="Players' Stats"
            Style="{OnPlatform {StaticResource labelSectionTitleStyle},
                Android={StaticResource androidLabelSectionTitleStyle}}" />

        <CollectionView
            Grid.Row="1"
            Grid.RowSpan="4"
            ItemsSource="{Binding Players}">
```

```
            <CollectionView.ItemTemplate>
                <DataTemplate>
                    <controls:PlayerStats Margin="0, 2.5"/>
                </DataTemplate>
            </CollectionView.ItemTemplate>
        </CollectionView>
    </Grid>
</ContentView>
```

And now let's have a look at a single player. The binding context of the **PlayerStats** control is **PlayerViewModel**:

```
...
<ContentView xmlns="http://schemas.microsoft.com/dotnet/2021/maui"
             xmlns:x="http://schemas.microsoft.com/winfx/2009/xaml"
             xmlns:toolkit="http://schemas.microsoft.com/dotnet/2022/maui/toolkit"
             xmlns:viewmodels="clr-namespace:Slugrace.ViewModels"
             x:DataType="viewmodels:PlayerViewModel"
             x:Class="Slugrace.Controls.PlayerStats">

    <ContentView.BindingContext>
        <viewmodels:PlayerViewModel />
    </ContentView.BindingContext>

    <ContentView.Resources>
        <Style TargetType="Label"
                  BasedOn="{OnPlatform {StaticResource labelBaseStyle},
                     Android={StaticResource androidLabelBaseStyle}}" />
        <toolkit:InvertedBoolConverter x:Key="invertedBoolConverter" />
    </ContentView.Resources>

    <Grid
        RowDefinitions="*">
        <Grid.ColumnDefinitions>
            <ColumnDefinition Width="{OnPlatform 2.5*, Android=*}" />
            <ColumnDefinition Width="{OnPlatform 1.5*, Android=*}" />
        </Grid.ColumnDefinitions>

        <Label
            IsVisible="{Binding IsBankrupt, Converter={StaticResource invertedBoolConverter}}"
            Text="{Binding Name}"
            Margin="0, 3" />
        <Label
            IsVisible="{Binding IsBankrupt}"
            Text="{Binding Name}"
            TextColor="Red"
            Opacity=".4"
            Margin="0, 3" />
        <Label
            IsVisible="{Binding IsBankrupt, Converter={StaticResource invertedBoolConverter}}"
            Grid.Column="1"
            Text="{Binding CurrentMoney, StringFormat='has ${0}'}"
            Margin="0, 3" />
        <Label
            IsVisible="{Binding IsBankrupt}"
            Grid.Column="1"
            Text="is bankrupt"
            TextColor="Red"
            Opacity=".4"
            Margin="0, 3" />
    </Grid>
</ContentView>
```

Here we use the **InvertedBoolConverter** from the Toolkit. If a player is not bankrupt, their data will be displayed in black. Otherwise, it will be displayed in red. We'll handle going bankrupt soon.

Up until now, we always saw dummy data representing four players in the Player's Stats panel. From now on, though, we'll only see as many players as there really are in the game, along with their names and money amounts. For example, if we decide to start a game with three players, this is what we can expect.

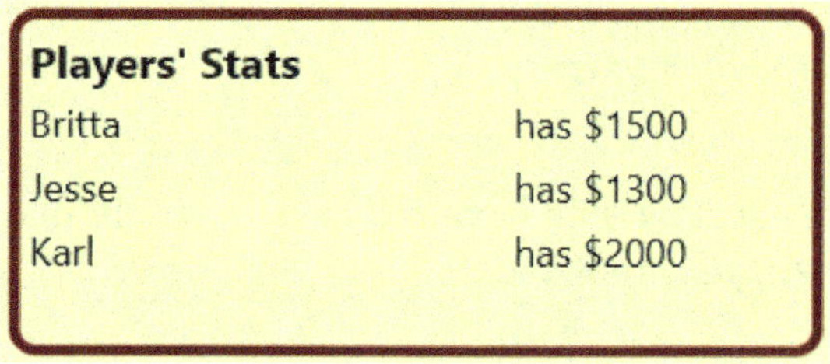

Let's move on to the racetrack now. There we have the slug images and some slug info.

Slug Image, Slug Info and TrackImage

The binding context for the **SlugImage** and **SlugInfo** content views is **SlugViewModel**. In the **SlugImage** control we bind to the top-view image properties:

```
...
<ContentView xmlns="http://schemas.microsoft.com/dotnet/2021/maui"
             xmlns:x="http://schemas.microsoft.com/winfx/2009/xaml"
             xmlns:viewmodels="clr-namespace:Slugrace.ViewModels"
             x:DataType="viewmodels:SlugViewModel"
             x:Class="Slugrace.Controls.SlugImage">

    <AbsoluteLayout>
        <Image
            Source="{Binding EyeImageUrl}"
            ...
        <Image
            Source="{Binding EyeImageUrl}"
            ...
        <Image
            Source="{Binding BodyImageUrl}"
            ...
    </AbsoluteLayout>
</ContentView>
```

The **SlugInfo** content view is used to display the slugs' names, wins and odds:

```
...
<ContentView xmlns="http://schemas.microsoft.com/dotnet/2021/maui"
             xmlns:x="http://schemas.microsoft.com/winfx/2009/xaml"
             xmlns:viewmodels="clr-namespace:Slugrace.ViewModels"
             x:DataType="viewmodels:SlugViewModel"
             x:Class="Slugrace.Controls.SlugInfo">
```

```
<ContentView.Resources>
    ...
<Grid
    Padding="5, 2, 0, 2"
    RowDefinitions="*, *"
    ColumnDefinitions="6.8*, 2.2*">
    <Label
        Text="{Binding Name}"
        ...
    <Label
        Grid.Row="1"
        Text="{Binding WinNumberText}"
        ...
    <Label
        Grid.Column="1"
        Grid.RowSpan="2"
        VerticalOptions="{StaticResource defaultLayoutOptions}"
        Text="{Binding Odds, StringFormat='{0:F2}'}"
        ...
```

Now we have to bind to the individual slugs in the **TrackImage** view:

```
...
<ContentView ...
             xmlns:controls="clr-namespace:Slugrace.Controls"
             xmlns:viewmodels="clr-namespace:Slugrace.ViewModels"
             x:DataType="viewmodels:GameViewModel"
             x:Class="Slugrace.Controls.TrackImage">

    <AbsoluteLayout>
        <!--Racetrack-->
        <Image
            Source="racetrack.png"
            ...
        <!--Speedster-->
        <controls:SlugImage
            BindingContext="{Binding Slugs[0]}"
            AbsoluteLayout.LayoutBounds=".1, .05, .15, .15"
            AbsoluteLayout.LayoutFlags="All"/>
        <controls:SlugInfo
            BindingContext="{Binding Slugs[0]}"
            AbsoluteLayout.LayoutBounds="0, 0, 1, .25"
            AbsoluteLayout.LayoutFlags="All"/>

        <!--Trusty-->
        <controls:SlugImage
            BindingContext="{Binding Slugs[1]}"
            AbsoluteLayout.LayoutBounds=".1, .35, .15, .15"
            AbsoluteLayout.LayoutFlags="All"/>
        <controls:SlugInfo
            BindingContext="{Binding Slugs[1]}"
            AbsoluteLayout.LayoutBounds="0, .35, 1, .25"
            AbsoluteLayout.LayoutFlags="All"/>
```

```
        <!--Iffy-->
        <controls:SlugImage
            BindingContext="{Binding Slugs[2]}"
            AbsoluteLayout.LayoutBounds=".1, .65, .15, .15"
            AbsoluteLayout.LayoutFlags="All"/>
        <controls:SlugInfo
            BindingContext="{Binding Slugs[2]}"
            AbsoluteLayout.LayoutBounds="0, .68, 1, .25"
            AbsoluteLayout.LayoutFlags="All"/>

        <!--Slowpoke-->
        <controls:SlugImage
            BindingContext="{Binding Slugs[3]}"
            AbsoluteLayout.LayoutBounds=".1, .95, .15, .15"
            AbsoluteLayout.LayoutFlags="All"/>
        <controls:SlugInfo
            BindingContext="{Binding Slugs[3]}"
            AbsoluteLayout.LayoutBounds="0, 1.02, 1, .25"
            AbsoluteLayout.LayoutFlags="All"/>
    </AbsoluteLayout>
</ContentView>
```

If we now run the app and navigate to the **RacePage**, we'll see all four slugs on the racetrack:

Next, let's move on to the Bets and Results panels.

Bets and Results

We'll use **GameViewModel** as the binding context for the Bets and Results views. For the **PlayerBet** and **PlayerResult** controls we'll use **PlayerViewModel**.

In the **Bets** content view we'll use a **CollectionView** for the individual players:

```
...
<ContentView xmlns="http://schemas.microsoft.com/dotnet/2021/maui"
             xmlns:x="http://schemas.microsoft.com/winfx/2009/xaml"
             xmlns:controls="clr-namespace:Slugrace.Controls"
             xmlns:viewmodels="clr-namespace:Slugrace.ViewModels"
             x:DataType="viewmodels:GameViewModel"
             x:Class="Slugrace.Controls.Bets">
```

```
    <ContentView.Resources>
        ...
    <Grid>
        <Grid.RowDefinitions>
            ...
        <Label
            ...
        <VerticalStackLayout
            x:Name="betControls"
            Grid.Row="1">

            <CollectionView ItemsSource="{Binding Players}">
                <CollectionView.ItemTemplate>
                    <DataTemplate>
                        <controls:PlayerBet />
                    </DataTemplate>
                </CollectionView.ItemTemplate>
            </CollectionView>
        </VerticalStackLayout>

        <Button
            Grid.Row="2"
            Text="Go"
            Margin="0, 0, 0, 5"
            IsEnabled="{Binding AllPlayersAreValid}" />
    </Grid>
</ContentView>
```

The **PlayerBet** control looks a bit complex:

```
...
<ContentView xmlns="http://schemas.microsoft.com/dotnet/2021/maui"
             xmlns:x="http://schemas.microsoft.com/winfx/2009/xaml"
             xmlns:toolkit="http://schemas.microsoft.com/dotnet/2022/maui/toolkit"
             xmlns:viewmodels="clr-namespace:Slugrace.ViewModels"
             xmlns:behaviors="clr-namespace:Slugrace.Behaviors"
             xmlns:converters="clr-namespace:Slugrace.Converters"
             x:DataType="viewmodels:PlayerViewModel"
             IsVisible="{Binding IsInGame}"
             x:Class="Slugrace.Controls.PlayerBet">

    <ContentView.Resources>
        ...
                  Android={StaticResource androidLabelBaseStyle}}" />
        <converters:ZeroToEmptyStringConverter x:Key="zeroToEmptyConverter" />
        <converters:SelectedSlugToBoolConverter x:Key="slugToBoolConverter" />
        <toolkit:InvertedBoolConverter x:Key="invertedBoolConverter" />
    </ContentView.Resources>

    <Grid>

        <Grid
            IsVisible="{Binding IsBankrupt,
                                Converter={StaticResource invertedBoolConverter}}"
            BackgroundColor="{OnPlatform
                Android={AppThemeBinding
```

```
        Light={StaticResource backgroundColorLight},
        Dark={StaticResource backgroundColorDark}}}"
Margin="0, 0, 0, 2">

<Grid.RowDefinitions>
    ...
<Label
    Text="{Binding Name}" />
...
<Entry
    x:Name="betAmountEntry"
    Grid.Column="3"
    WidthRequest="{OnPlatform 200, Android=80}"
    Placeholder="{Binding CurrentMoney, StringFormat='1 - {0}'}"
    BackgroundColor="{OnPlatform Android=Transparent}"
    TextColor="{AppThemeBinding Dark=White}"
    Keyboard="Numeric"
    Text="{Binding BetAmount, Converter={StaticResource zeroToEmptyConverter}}"
    TextChanged="OnBetAmountTextChanged">
    <Entry.Behaviors>
        <behaviors:NumericInputBehavior />
    </Entry.Behaviors>
</Entry>

<Slider
    Grid.Column="4"
    Margin="0, 0, 30, 0"
    Value="{Binding BetAmount}"
    Minimum="0"
    Maximum="{Binding CurrentMoney}" />
...
<Grid
    ...
    <RadioButton
        IsChecked="{Binding SelectedSlug, Mode=OneWay,
                    Converter={StaticResource slugToBoolConverter},
                    ConverterParameter=Speedster}"
        GroupName="{Binding Name}">
        <RadioButton.Content>
            ...
        </RadioButton.Content>

        <RadioButton.GestureRecognizers>
            <TapGestureRecognizer Command="{Binding SelectSlugCommand}"
                                  CommandParameter="Speedster" />
        </RadioButton.GestureRecognizers>
    </RadioButton>

    <RadioButton
        Grid.Column="1"
        IsChecked="{Binding SelectedSlug, Mode=OneWay,
                            Converter={StaticResource slugToBoolConverter},
                            ConverterParameter=Trusty}"
        GroupName="{Binding Name}">
        <RadioButton.Content>
            ...
        </RadioButton.Content>
```

```
                <RadioButton.GestureRecognizers>
                    <TapGestureRecognizer Command="{Binding SelectSlugCommand}"
                          CommandParameter="Trusty" />
                </RadioButton.GestureRecognizers>
            </RadioButton>

            <RadioButton
                Grid.Column="2"
                IsChecked="{Binding SelectedSlug, Mode=OneWay,
                                    Converter={StaticResource slugToBoolConverter},
                                    ConverterParameter=Iffy}"
                GroupName="{Binding Name}">
                <RadioButton.Content>
                    ...
                </RadioButton.Content>

                <RadioButton.GestureRecognizers>
                    <TapGestureRecognizer Command="{Binding SelectSlugCommand}"
                          CommandParameter="Iffy" />
                </RadioButton.GestureRecognizers>
            </RadioButton>

            <RadioButton
                Grid.Column="3"
                IsChecked="{Binding SelectedSlug, Mode=OneWay,
                                    Converter={StaticResource slugToBoolConverter},
                                    ConverterParameter=Slowpoke}"
                GroupName="{Binding Name}">
                <RadioButton.Content>
                    ...
                </RadioButton.Content>

                <RadioButton.GestureRecognizers>
                    <TapGestureRecognizer Command="{Binding SelectSlugCommand}"
                          CommandParameter="Slowpoke" />
                </RadioButton.GestureRecognizers>
            </RadioButton>
        </Grid>
    </Grid>

    <Grid
        IsVisible="{Binding IsBankrupt}"
        RowDefinitions="*">
        <Grid.ColumnDefinitions>
            <ColumnDefinition Width="{OnPlatform 150, Android=80}" />
            <ColumnDefinition Width="*" />
        </Grid.ColumnDefinitions>

        <Label
            Text="{Binding Name}"
            TextColor="Red"
            TextDecorations="Strikethrough"
            Opacity=".4" />
    </Grid>

  </Grid>
</ContentView>
```

It's lengthy, but pretty straightforward. The entries where the bet amount is to be typed are empty at the beginning. We ensure this in the code-behind. Also in the code-behind we take care of the **TextChanged** event that gets fired every time something is typed in the entries:

```
using Slugrace.ViewModels;

namespace Slugrace.Controls;

public partial class PlayerBet : ContentView
{
    public PlayerBet()
    {
        InitializeComponent();
        VisualStateManager.GoToState(betAmountEntry, "Empty");
    }

    private void OnBetAmountTextChanged(object sender, TextChangedEventArgs e)
    {
        if (BindingContext != null)
        {
            bool betAmountValid = (BindingContext as PlayerViewModel)!.BetAmountIsValid;
            Helpers.HandleNumericEntryState(betAmountValid, betAmountEntry);
        }
    }
}
```

Now, back to the XAML file. We bind the radio buttons to the **SelectedSlug** property of **PlayerViewModel** using a converter that we haven't created yet.

So, add the **SelectedSlugToBoolConverter** to the **Converters** folder and implement it like so:

```
using Slugrace.ViewModels;
using System.Globalization;

namespace Slugrace.Converters;

public class SelectedSlugToBoolConverter : IValueConverter
{
    public object? Convert(object? value, Type targetType, object? parameter,
        CultureInfo culture)
    {
        if ((value as SlugViewModel) == null)
        {
            return false;
        }
        else
        {
            return (value as SlugViewModel)!.Name == parameter!.ToString();
        }
    }

    public object? ConvertBack(object? value, Type targetType, object? parameter,
        CultureInfo culture)
    {
        throw new NotImplementedException();
    }
}
```

Now we can pass the names of the slugs as converter parameters.

As I mentioned before, the **SelectSlug** method in the **PlayerViewModel** is called when a radio button is checked. In order to avoid calling this method twice, the first time when a radio button is unchecked and the second time a radio button is checked, we use the **TapGestureRecognizer**. This way the method is called only once, when the radio button is checked.

Let's use the Bets panel in the **RacePage** to test it:

```
...
<ContentPage ...
             x:Class="Slugrace.Views.RacePage"
             Padding="5">
    ...
        <!--Bets/Results panel-->
        <Border
            ...
            HorizontalOptions="{OnPlatform Android=Fill}">
            <controls:Bets />
        </Border>
    ...
```

Now we can run the app and navigate to the **RacePage**:

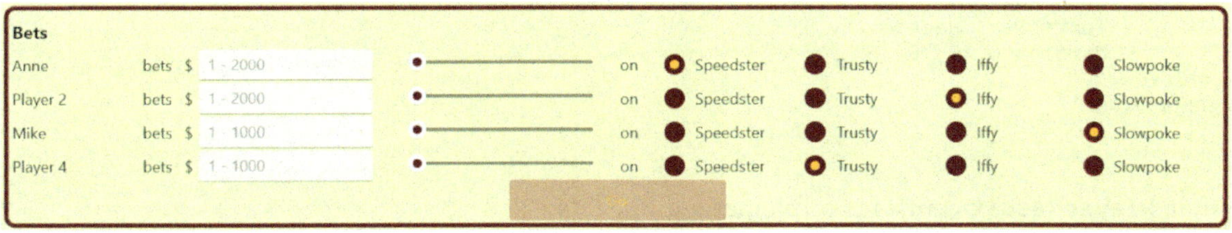

In the **SettingsPage** I set the names of two players. The other two names are generic ones. I set the initial money of the first two players to 2000 and of the other two to 1000. These values are bound to in the Bets panel. We can now only select one slug in each group. The Go button is disabled because the players haven't placed their bets yet. As soon as they do, it will be enabled:

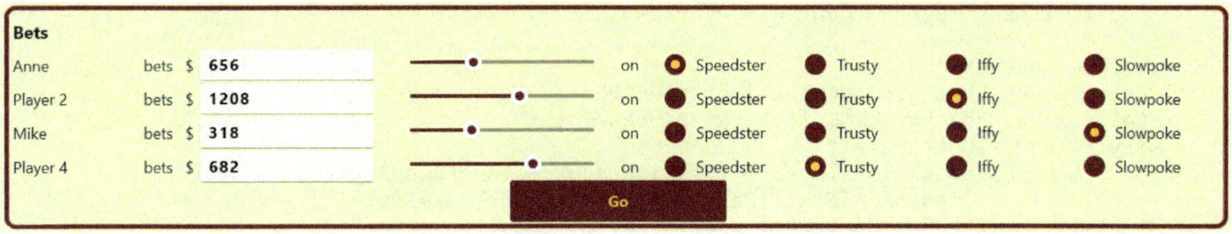

Next, let's have a look at the **Results** content view. It's implemented in the same way as the **Bets** view:

```
...
<ContentView xmlns="http://schemas.microsoft.com/dotnet/2021/maui"
             xmlns:x="http://schemas.microsoft.com/winfx/2009/xaml"
             xmlns:controls="clr-namespace:Slugrace.Controls"
             xmlns:toolkit="http://schemas.microsoft.com/dotnet/2022/maui/toolkit"
             xmlns:viewmodels="clr-namespace:Slugrace.ViewModels"
             x:DataType="viewmodels:GameViewModel"
             x:Class="Slugrace.Controls.Results">

    <ContentView.Resources>
        <Style TargetType="Label" BasedOn="{StaticResource labelBaseStyle}" />
        <toolkit:InvertedBoolConverter x:Key="invertedBoolConverter" />
    </ContentView.Resources>

    <Grid>
        ...
        <VerticalStackLayout
            Grid.Row="1"
            Spacing="{OnPlatform 0, Android=15}">

            <CollectionView ItemsSource="{Binding Players}">
                <CollectionView.ItemTemplate>
                    <DataTemplate>
                        <controls:PlayerResult />
                    </DataTemplate>
                </CollectionView.ItemTemplate>
            </CollectionView>
        </VerticalStackLayout>

        <Button
            Grid.Row="2"
            Text="Next Race"
            Margin="0, 0, 0, 5" />
    </Grid>
</ContentView>
```

A single **PlayerResult** control is implemented like this:

```
...
<ContentView xmlns="http://schemas.microsoft.com/dotnet/2021/maui"
             xmlns:x="http://schemas.microsoft.com/winfx/2009/xaml"
             xmlns:toolkit="http://schemas.microsoft.com/dotnet/2022/maui/toolkit"
             xmlns:viewmodels="clr-namespace:Slugrace.ViewModels"
             x:DataType="viewmodels:PlayerViewModel"
             IsVisible="{Binding IsInGame}"
             x:Class="Slugrace.Controls.PlayerResult">

    <ContentView.Resources>
        <Color x:Key="backgroundColorLight">#FFF4E5</Color>
        <Color x:Key="backgroundColorDark">Black</Color>
        <Style TargetType="Label"
               BasedOn="{OnPlatform {StaticResource labelBaseStyle},
                   Android={StaticResource androidLabelBaseStyle}}" />
        <toolkit:InvertedBoolConverter x:Key="invertedBoolConverter" />
    </ContentView.Resources>
```

```
    <Grid>
        <Grid
            IsVisible="{Binding IsBankrupt, Converter={StaticResource invertedBoolConverter}}"
            BackgroundColor="{OnPlatform
                Android={AppThemeBinding
                    Light={StaticResource backgroundColorLight},
                    Dark={StaticResource backgroundColorDark}}}"
            RowSpacing="{OnPlatform 0, Android=10}"
            Margin="0, 0, 0, 5">

            <Grid.RowDefinitions>
                ...
            <Label
                Text="{Binding Name}" />
            <Label
                Grid.Column="1"
                Text="{Binding PreviousMoney, StringFormat='had ${0},'}" />
            <Label
                Grid.Column="2"
                Text="{Binding BetAmount, StringFormat='bet ${0}'}" />
            <Label
                Grid.Column="3"
                Text="{Binding SelectedSlug.Name, StringFormat='on {0},'}" />
            <Label
                Grid.Row="{OnPlatform 0, Android=1}"
                Grid.Column="{OnPlatform 4, Android=0}"
                Text="{Binding ResultMessage, StringFormat='{0},'}" />
            <Label
                Grid.Row="{OnPlatform 0, Android=1}"
                Grid.Column="{OnPlatform 5, Android=1}"
                Text="{OnPlatform {Binding CurrentMoney, StringFormat='now has ${0}.'},
                    Android={Binding CurrentMoney, StringFormat='has ${0}.'}}" />
            <Label
                Grid.Row="{OnPlatform 0, Android=2}"
                Grid.Column="{OnPlatform 6, Android=2}"
                Grid.ColumnSpan="{OnPlatform 1, Android=2}"
                Text="{Binding SelectedSlug.PreviousOdds,
                               StringFormat='The odds were {0:F2}'}" />
        </Grid>

        <Grid
            IsVisible="{Binding IsBankrupt}"
            RowDefinitions="*">
            <Grid.ColumnDefinitions>
                <ColumnDefinition Width="{OnPlatform *, Android=1.2*}" />
                <ColumnDefinition Width="*" />
            </Grid.ColumnDefinitions>

            <Label
                Text="{Binding Name}"
                TextColor="Red"
                TextDecorations="Strikethrough"
                Opacity=".4" />
        </Grid>
    </Grid>
</ContentView>
```

Let's now use the Results panel in the **RacePage** to test it:

```
...
<ContentPage ...
             x:Class="Slugrace.Views.RacePage"
             Padding="5">
    ...
        <!--Bets/Results panel-->
        <Border
            ...
            HorizontalOptions="{OnPlatform Android=Fill}">
            <controls:Results />
        </Border>
    ...
```

I think this code is pretty straightforward. Now that we have most of the pieces of the puzzle, let's start a game simulation.

Game Simulation

Before we discuss animation, we can only simulate the races. So, for now, the winners will be picked randomly right after a race begins. In the final version each race will be animated and it will take some time to complete.

The game begins when all players have placed valid bets on the slugs and the Go button is pressed. This is when the first race begins. Depending on which ending condition was chosen, there may be a different number of races. Anyway, we have to bind the Go button in the **Bets** content view to a **StartRace** command and implement the command in the **GameViewModel**. Here's the Bets panel:

```
...
<ContentView ...
             x:Class="Slugrace.Controls.Bets">
    ...
        <Button
            ...
            IsEnabled="{Binding AllPlayersAreValid}"
            Command="{Binding StartRaceCommand}" />
    </Grid>
</ContentView>
```

Let's add this method to **GameViewModel**:

```
...
public partial class GameViewModel : ObservableObject
{
    ...
    partial void OnGameChanged(Game? value)
    ...
    [RelayCommand]
    void StartRace()
    {
        // Start race
        RaceStatus = RaceStatus.Started;

        if (RaceNumber == 1 && GameEndingCondition == EndingCondition.Time)
        {
            gameTimer.Start();
        }

        RunRace();
    }
}
```

This method just sets the **RaceStatus** to **Started** and calls the **RunRace** method (yet to be implemented). Additionally, if we chose the **Time** ending condition, it starts the **gameTimer** before the first race. Speaking of which…

Yes, we need a timer to count down the time of the game. When the time is up, the game will be over. We'll add a timer of type **IDispatcherTimer** like so:

```
...
public partial class GameViewModel : ObservableObject
{
    readonly IDispatcherTimer gameTimer;
    ...

    public GameViewModel()
    {
        gameTimer = Application.Current!.Dispatcher.CreateTimer();
        gameTimer.Interval = TimeSpan.FromSeconds(1);
        gameTimer.Tick += (sender, e) =>
        {
            if (TimeRemaining > TimeSpan.Zero)
            {
                TimeElapsed += TimeSpan.FromSeconds(1);
            }

            if (TimeRemaining == TimeSpan.Zero
                && RaceStatus == RaceStatus.Finished)
            {
                CheckForGameOver();
            }
        };
```

```
        ...
        WeakReferenceMessenger.Default.Register<PlayerBetAmountChangedMessage>(this, (r, m) =>
            OnBetAmountChangedMessageReceived(m.Value));

        ...
    }

    ...

    [RelayCommand]
    void StartRace()
    ...
}
```

The timer object is created in the constructor. The **Tick** event will fire every second (we set the **Interval** property to this amount of time) and will increase the **TimeElapsed** property, which will automatically decrease the **TimeRemaining** property.

When the time is up, so when the **TimeRemaining** property equals zero and the **RaceStatus** is **Finished**, the **CheckForGameOver** method is called. We'll implement this method in a moment. For now, let's see what happens next.

Next, the **RunRace** method is called. Here it is:

```
...
public partial class GameViewModel : ObservableObject
{
    ...
    void StartRace()
    ...

    void RunRace()
    {
        // random winner slug
        var random = new Random();
        RaceWinnerSlug = Slugs[random.Next(Slugs.Count)];
        RaceWinnerSlug.IsRaceWinner = true;

        HandleSlugsAfterRace();

        HandlePlayersAfterRace();

        FinishRace();
    }
}
```

In this method, naturally only for now, a random slug is selected to be the winner. The **IsRaceWinner** property of the **RaceWinnerSlug** property is set to **true**. Then three methods are called to handle the slugs and the players after the race and to finish the race. Let's have a look at how they are implemented:

```
...
public partial class GameViewModel : ObservableObject
{
    ...
    void RunRace()
    ...

    void HandleSlugsAfterRace()
    {
        foreach (var slug in Slugs)
        {
            if (slug != RaceWinnerSlug)
            {
                slug.IsRaceWinner = false;
            }

            slug.RecalculateStats(RaceNumber);
        }
    }

    void HandlePlayersAfterRace()
    {
        foreach (var player in Players)
        {
            player.CalculateMoney(RaceWinnerSlug!);

            if (player.CurrentMoney == 0)
            {
                player.IsBankrupt = true;
            }

            PlayersStillInGame = PlayersStillInGame
                                 .Where(p => !p.IsBankrupt).ToObservableCollection();
        }
    }

    void FinishRace()
    {
        RaceStatus = RaceStatus.Finished;

        CheckForGameOver();
    }
}
```

The slug stats are recalculated. The players' money is calculated and if all money is lost, the **IsBankrupt** property is set to **true**. The **ObservableCollection** of **PlayersStillInGame** is populated with just the players who did not go bankrupt.

In the **FinishRace** method, the **RaceStatus** is set to **Finished**. When this happens, the **WinnerInfo** content view is displayed. Here's the **WinnerInfo** view:

```
...
<ContentView xmlns="http://schemas.microsoft.com/dotnet/2021/maui"
             xmlns:x="http://schemas.microsoft.com/winfx/2009/xaml"
             xmlns:local="clr-namespace:Slugrace"
             xmlns:toolkit="http://schemas.microsoft.com/dotnet/2022/maui/toolkit"
             xmlns:viewmodels="clr-namespace:Slugrace.ViewModels"
             x:DataType="viewmodels:GameViewModel"
             x:Class="Slugrace.Controls.WinnerInfo">
```

```
<ContentView.Resources>
        ...
        <toolkit:EnumToBoolConverter x:Key="raceStatusConverter" />
    </ContentView.Resources>

    <Grid
        IsVisible="{Binding RaceStatus,
           Converter={StaticResource raceStatusConverter},
           ConverterParameter={x:Static local:RaceStatus.Finished}}"
        RowDefinitions=".6*, *, 3*">

        <Label
            Text="The winner is"
            FontSize="{OnPlatform 28, Android=10}" />
        <Label
            Grid.Row="1"
            Text="{Binding RaceWinnerSlug.Name}"
            FontSize="{OnPlatform 36, Android=12}" />
        <Image
            Grid.Row="2"
            Source="{Binding RaceWinnerSlug.ImageUrl}" />
    </Grid>
</ContentView>
```

From now on, the real winner slug will be shown, not just Speedster like up to now.

Then a method is called to check whether, by any chance, the conditions are met to end the game. And these conditions will be different for each ending condition. Here's how the **CheckForGameOver** method is implemented:

```
...
public partial class GameViewModel : ObservableObject
{
    ...
    void FinishRace()
    ...
    void CheckForGameOver(bool endedManually = false)
    {
        // This is for the case when the game is ended manually
        if (endedManually)
        {
            GetWinners();
            GameOverReason = "You ended the game manually.";
            EndGame();
        }

        // This works the same for each ending condition.
        // scenario 1: there's only 1 player with money
        // (except one-player mode) - it's the winner
        else if (Players.Count > 1 && PlayersStillInGame.Count == 1)
        {
            Winners.Add(PlayersStillInGame[0]);
            GameOverReason = "There's only one player with any money left.";
            EndGame();
        }
```

```
        // scenario 2: all players go bankrupt simultaneously
        // - no winner
        else if (PlayersStillInGame.Count == 0)
        {
            GameOverReason = Players.Count == 1
                ? "You are bankrupt."
                : "All players are bankrupt.";
            EndGame();
        }

        // This works for the Races ending condition
        else if (GameEndingCondition == EndingCondition.Races
            && RaceNumber == NumberOfRacesSet)
        {
            GetWinners();

            GameOverReason = "The number of races you set has been reached.";
            EndGame();
        }
        // This works for the Time ending condition
        else if (GameEndingCondition == EndingCondition.Time
            && TimeRemaining == TimeSpan.Zero)
        {
            GetWinners();

            GameOverReason = "The game time you set is up.";
            EndGame();
        }
    }
}
```

Here we have a **GameOverReason** property that will store the text that will be displayed in the **GameOverPage**. This text will tell us why the game is over. Naturally, there may be different reasons.

The **endedManually** parameter is for the case when we end the game manually by clicking the End Game button in the race screen. We'll see to this soon.

We also have two methods, **GetWinners** and **EndGame**. Let's implement the **GameOverReason** property and the two methods:

```
...
public partial class GameViewModel : ObservableObject
{
    ...
    public bool? AllPlayersAreValid => Players?.All(p => p.PlayerIsValid);

    [ObservableProperty]
    private string gameOverReason = string.Empty;

    ...

    private async Task CheckForGameOver(bool endedManually = false)
    ...
```

```
    void GetWinners()
    {
        int maxMoney = PlayersStillInGame.Max(p => p.CurrentMoney);

        foreach (var player in PlayersStillInGame)
        {
            if (player.CurrentMoney == maxMoney)
            {
                Winners.Add(player);
            }
        }
    }

    void EndGame()
    {
        gameTimer.Stop();

        IsShowingFinalResults = true;

        gameOverPageDelayTimer.Start();

        gameOverPageDelayTimer.Tick += async (sender, e) =>
        {
            gameOverPageDelayTimer.Stop();

            IsShowingFinalResults = false;

            // Navigate to GameOverPage
            await Shell.Current.GoToAsync($"{nameof(GameOverPage)}",
                new Dictionary<string, object>
                {
                    {"Game", this }
                });
        };
    }
}
```

The **GetWinners** method just picks the player or players who won the most money and adds them to the **Winners** list.

The **EndGame** method seems more interesting. Here the **gameTimer** is stopped and the **IsShowingFinalResults** property is set to **true**. Let's add this property now:

```
...
public partial class GameViewModel : ObservableObject
{
    ...
    private string gameOverReason = string.Empty;

    [ObservableProperty]
    private bool isShowingFinalResults;

    public GameViewModel()
    ...
```

Then another timer is started (we'll implement it in a minute) and stopped after a couple seconds. Finally, we navigate to the **GameOverPage**.

In order for the navigation to work, let's register the route in the **AppShell.xaml.cs** file:

```
...
public partial class AppShell : Shell
{
        public AppShell()
        {
         InitializeComponent();
         Routing.RegisterRoute(nameof(RacePage), typeof(RacePage));
         Routing.RegisterRoute(nameof(GameOverPage), typeof(GameOverPage));
    }
}
```

For the **GameOverPage** we'll create a **GameOverViewModel** in the ViewModels folder. Here's the code:

```
using CommunityToolkit.Mvvm.ComponentModel;
using CommunityToolkit.Mvvm.Input;
using Slugrace.Views;
using System.Text;

namespace Slugrace.ViewModels;

[QueryProperty(nameof(Game), "Game")]
public partial class GameOverViewModel : ObservableObject
{
    [ObservableProperty]
    private GameViewModel? game;

    [ObservableProperty]
    private string gameOverReason = string.Empty;

    [ObservableProperty]
    private int originalNumberOfPlayers;

    [ObservableProperty]
    private List<PlayerViewModel> winners = [];

    [ObservableProperty]
    public string winnerInfo = string.Empty;

    partial void OnGameChanged(GameViewModel? value)
    {
        OriginalNumberOfPlayers = value!.Players.Count;
        GameOverReason = value.GameOverReason;
        Winners = value.Winners;
```

```
        WinnerInfo = Winners.Count switch
        {
            0 => OriginalNumberOfPlayers == 1
                 ? "There are no winners in 1-player mode."
                 : "There is no winner!",
            1 => OriginalNumberOfPlayers == 1
                 ? $"You were playing in 1-player mode.\n"
                    + $"You started with ${Winners[0].InitialMoney}, "
                    + $"and you're leaving with ${Winners[0].CurrentMoney}."
                 : $"The winner is {Winners[0].Name}, "
                    + $"having started with ${Winners[0].InitialMoney}, "
                    + $"leaving with ${Winners[0].CurrentMoney}.",
            _ => $"There's a tie. The joint winners are:\n\n"
                  + $"{DisplayWinners()}"
        };
    }

    private string DisplayWinners()
    {
        StringBuilder displayMessage = new StringBuilder();

        foreach (var winner in Winners)
        {
            displayMessage.Append($"{winner.Name}, "
                + $"having started with ${winner.InitialMoney}, "
                + $"leaving with ${winner.CurrentMoney}.\n");
        }

        return displayMessage.ToString();
    }

    [RelayCommand]
    async Task RestartGame()
    {
        // Navigate to SettingsPage
        await Shell.Current.GoToAsync($"//{nameof(SettingsPage)}");
    }
}
```

This is the page we're navigating to from the **RacePage**. We pass the **GameViewModel** object, so we need to add the **QueryProperty** attribute, just like before. As the **GameViewModel** object is not available in the constructor, we're using it in the **OnGameChanged** method. We also define the **DisplayWinners** method and the **RestartGame** method that will be bound to from the Play Again button.

We set the binding context in the code-behind file of the **GameOverPage**:

```
using Slugrace.ViewModels;
...
public partial class GameOverPage : ContentPage
{
    public GameOverPage(GameOverViewModel gameOverViewModel)
    {
        InitializeComponent();
        BindingContext = gameOverViewModel;
    }
}
```

The **GameOverPage** should look like so:

```
<?xml version="1.0" encoding="utf-8" ?>
<ContentPage xmlns="http://schemas.microsoft.com/dotnet/2021/maui"
             xmlns:x="http://schemas.microsoft.com/winfx/2009/xaml"
             xmlns:viewmodels="clr-namespace:Slugrace.ViewModels"
             x:DataType="viewmodels:GameOverViewModel"
             x:Class="Slugrace.Views.GameOverPage">
    ...
    <ContentPage.Resources>
        ...
    <Grid
        ...
        <Label
            Grid.Row="1"
            Text="{Binding GameOverReason}" />
        <Label
            Grid.Row="2"
            Text="{Binding WinnerInfo}"
            HorizontalTextAlignment="Center"
            FontSize="30" />
        <FlexLayout
            ...
            <Button
                Text="Play Again"
                Command="{Binding RestartGameCommand}" />
            <Button
                Text="Quit" />
        </FlexLayout>
    </Grid>
</ContentPage>
```

Let's not forget to register the the **GameOverPage** and the **GameOverViewModel** with the dependency service in the **MauiProgram.cs** file:

```
...
public static class MauiProgram
{
        ...
        builder.Services.AddTransient<GameViewModel>();

        builder.Services.AddTransient<GameOverPage>();
        builder.Services.AddTransient<GameOverViewModel>();

        return builder.Build();
    }
}
```

About the other timer. It's used to delay the navigation to the **GameOverPage** so that you can view the results of the last race. Without it, you wouldn't be able to see the results because the **GameOverPage** would be navigated to immediately.

Fine, let's implement the timer then:

```
...
public partial class GameViewModel : ObservableObject
{
    ...
    readonly IDispatcherTimer gameTimer;
    readonly IDispatcherTimer gameOverPageDelayTimer;

    ...

    public GameViewModel()
    {
        ...

        gameOverPageDelayTimer = Application.Current!.Dispatcher.CreateTimer();
        gameOverPageDelayTimer.Interval = TimeSpan.FromSeconds(3);

        WeakReferenceMessenger.Default.Register<PlayerBetAmountChangedMessage>(this, (r, m) =>
            OnBetAmountChangedMessageReceived(m.Value));

        ...
```

OK, we know what happens if the ending conditions are met. But if they're not, we can click the Next Race button in the **Results** view to call a **NextRace** method in **GameViewModel**. Here it is:

```
...
public partial class GameViewModel : ObservableObject
{
    ...
    void EndGame()
    ...
    [RelayCommand]
    void NextRace()
    {
        RaceStatus = RaceStatus.NotYetStarted;
        RaceNumber++;

        foreach (var player in Players)
        {
            player.BetAmount = 0;
            player.SelectedSlug = null;
        }
    }
}
```

Here the race number is increased, the race status is reset to **NotYetStarted** and each player is reset.

And here's how we bind to it in the Results panel:

```
...
<ContentView ...
             x:Class="Slugrace.Controls.Results">
    ...
        <Button
            Grid.Row="2"
            Text="Next Race"
            Margin="0, 0, 0, 5"
            IsEnabled="{Binding IsShowingFinalResults,
                                Converter={StaticResource invertedBoolConverter}}"
            Command="{Binding NextRaceCommand}" />
    </Grid>
</ContentView>
```

The button is disabled after the last race and before the **GameOverPage** appears. This is to avoid clicking on the Next Race button when there shouldn't be a next race anymore.

Before we start the simulation, let's take care of a couple minor issues in the **RacePage**. First of all, let's make sure the Bets and Results panels are swapped correctly. Actually, there are going to be three panels, of which only one can be displayed at any given time. Besides the Bets and Results panels, there will also be the Race Started panel. It will be visible while the race is going on. At this moment the race won't take any time and we'll see the results immediately, but later it will take a few seconds while the slugs are animated. This is when this panel will be visible.

Anyway, let's implement all the three panels in the RacePage now:

```
...
<ContentPage ...
             x:Class="Slugrace.Views.RacePage"
             Padding="5">
    ...
        <!--Racetrack-->
        ...
        <!--Bets panel-->
        <Border
            IsVisible="{Binding RaceStatus,
                                Converter={StaticResource raceStatusConverter},
                                ConverterParameter={x:Static local:RaceStatus.NotYetStarted}}"
            Grid.Row="{OnPlatform 2, Android=0}"
            Grid.ColumnSpan="4"
            HorizontalOptions="{OnPlatform Android=Fill}">
            <controls:Bets />
        </Border>

        <!--Race Started panel -->
        <Border
            IsVisible="{Binding RaceStatus,
                      Converter={StaticResource raceStatusConverter},
                      ConverterParameter={x:Static local:RaceStatus.Started}}"
            Grid.Row="{OnPlatform 2, Android=0}"
            Grid.ColumnSpan="4"
```

```
            HorizontalOptions="{OnPlatform Android=Fill}">
            <Label
                Text="RACE STARTED"
                VerticalOptions="Center"
                HorizontalOptions="Center"
                FontSize="50"
                CharacterSpacing="2" />
        </Border>

        <!--Results panel-->
        <Border
            IsVisible="{Binding RaceStatus,
                    Converter={StaticResource raceStatusConverter},
                    ConverterParameter={x:Static local:RaceStatus.Finished}}"
            Grid.Row="{OnPlatform 2, Android=0}"
            Grid.ColumnSpan="4"
            HorizontalOptions="{OnPlatform Android=Fill}">
            <controls:Results />
        </Border>
    </Grid>
</ContentPage>
```

Secondly, the End Game and Instructions buttons should be disabled unless the **RaceStatus** is **Finished**. Here's how it's implemented:

```
...
<ContentPage xmlns="http://schemas.microsoft.com/dotnet/2021/maui"
             xmlns:x="http://schemas.microsoft.com/winfx/2009/xaml"
             xmlns:toolkit="http://schemas.microsoft.com/dotnet/2022/maui/toolkit"
             xmlns:local="clr-namespace:Slugrace"
             xmlns:controls="clr-namespace:Slugrace.Controls"
             xmlns:viewmodels="clr-namespace:Slugrace.ViewModels"
             x:DataType="viewmodels:GameViewModel"
             x:Class="Slugrace.Views.RacePage"
             Padding="5">
    ...
        <!--the buttons-->
        ...
            <Button
                Text="End Game"
                IsEnabled="{Binding RaceStatus,
                    Converter={StaticResource raceStatusConverter},
                    ConverterParameter={x:Static local:RaceStatus.Finished}}" />
            <Button
                Text="Instructions"
                IsEnabled="{Binding RaceStatus,
                    Converter={StaticResource raceStatusConverter},
                    ConverterParameter={x:Static local:RaceStatus.Finished}}" />
            <Button
                ...
```

Let's now run the app and see if everything works as expected. First on Windows, then on Android. Let's say we'll have three players and the game should end not later than after 1 minute. Here's the **SettingsPage**:

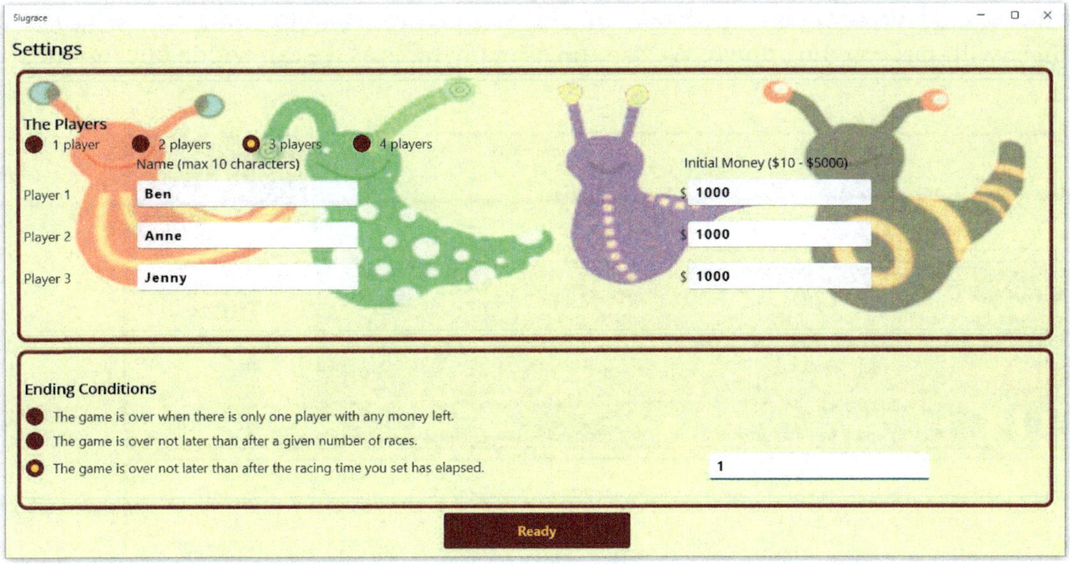

If you now hit the Ready button, you'll navigate to the **RacePage**:

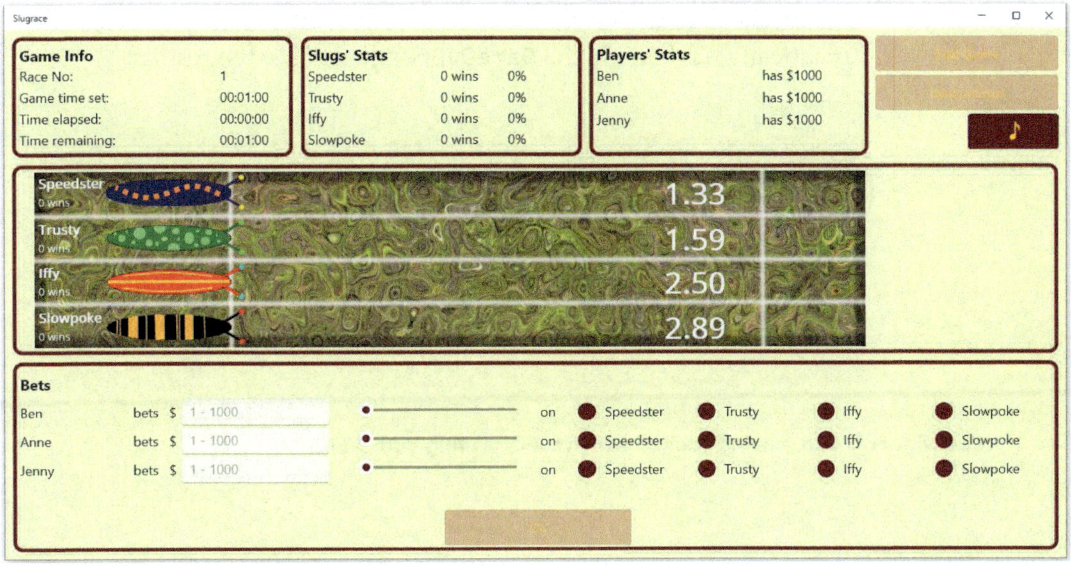

The Go button is disabled because we have to set the bet amount for each player and select the slugs, for example like this:

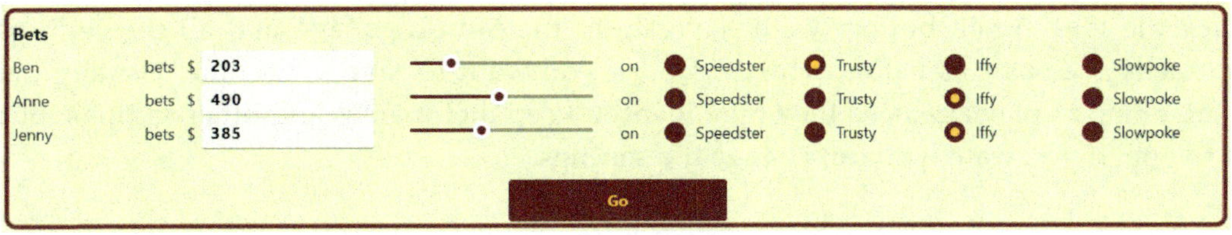

If we now hit the Go button, we'll immediately see the slug that won and the stats will be updated. Also, the timer will start counting down. We can run as many races as we can within one minute:

When the time is up, we automatically navigate to the **GameOverPage** and see the results:

If we now click the Play Again button, we'll navigate to the **SettingsPage** and all the settings there will be exactly the same as before. This is good if you want to save some time. Usually the same people are going to play again, so they may want to keep their names and other settings. But it's totally up to you. If you want, you can change the settings.

Try it out with other numbers of players and ending conditions. It should work fine.

And now let's run the app on Android. Here's the **SettingsPage** with the same settings as before.

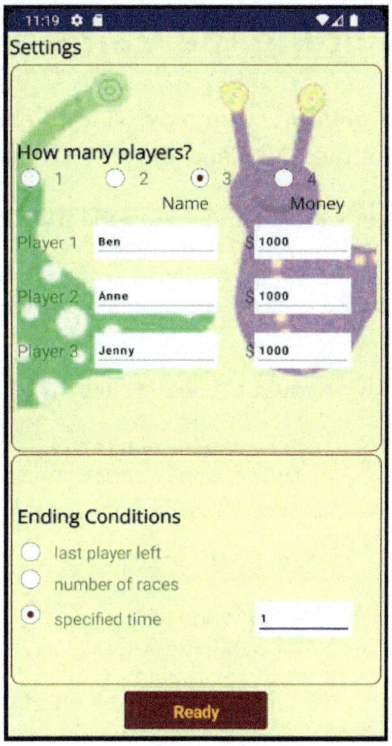

Let's hit the Ready button and place some bets:

Let's press the Go button. Now we have one minute to play. Here's what we can expect to see during the game:

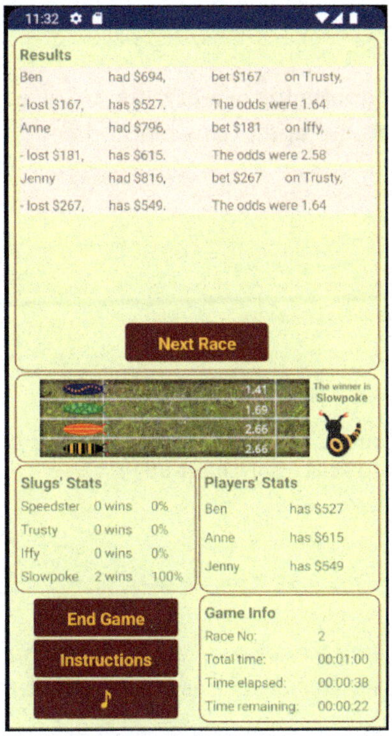

The **GameOverPage** looks like here on the right.

Our game simulation works fine. Before we implement the actual game flow, though, let's take care of the End Game and Instructions buttons in **RacePage**.

Ending the Game Manually

Sometimes you may want to end the game earlier than set at the beginning. All you have to do is hit the End Game button in the **RacePage**.

Let's create an **EndGameManually** method in the **GameViewModel**:

```
...
public partial class GameViewModel : ObservableObject
{
    ...
    private bool isShowingFinalResults;

    [ObservableProperty]
    private bool gameEndedManually;

    ...
    void NextRace()
    ...
    [RelayCommand]
    void EndGameManually()
    {
        CheckForGameOver(true);
    }

    ...
}
```

This method just calls the **CheckForGameOver** method with the **endedManually** argument set to **true**. Now we have to bind the **Command** parameter of the button in **RacePage** to this method:

```
...
<ContentPage ...>
    ...
        <!--the buttons-->
        <VerticalStackLayout
            ...
            <Button
                Text="End Game"
                IsEnabled="{Binding RaceStatus,
                    Converter={StaticResource raceStatusConverter},
                    ConverterParameter={x:Static local:RaceStatus.Finished}}"
                Command="{Binding EndGameManuallyCommand}" />
            <Button
                ...
```

The button will be enabled after each race, so there must be at least one race. Now if we run the app and press the button, the game will end before the ending condition we decided on is actually met.

Finally, let's handle the Instructions button.

InstructionsPage

We haven't created the **InstructionsPage** yet. Let's create a very basic one for now so that we can navigate to it. Add a new **ContentPage** to the **Views** folder, name it **InstructionsPage**, and implement it like so:

```
<?xml version="1.0" encoding="utf-8" ?>
<ContentPage xmlns="http://schemas.microsoft.com/dotnet/2021/maui"
             xmlns:x="http://schemas.microsoft.com/winfx/2009/xaml"
             x:Class="Slugrace.Views.InstructionsPage"
             xmlns:viewmodels="clr-namespace:Slugrace.ViewModels"
             x:DataType="viewmodels:GameViewModel">

    <Shell.BackButtonBehavior>
        <BackButtonBehavior IsEnabled="False" IsVisible="False" />
    </Shell.BackButtonBehavior>

    <VerticalStackLayout>
        <Label
            Text="INSTRUCTIONS"
            VerticalOptions="Center"
            HorizontalOptions="Center" />
        <Button
            Text="Back"
            Command="{Binding NavigateBackCommand}" />
    </VerticalStackLayout>
</ContentPage>
```

In the code-behind let's set the binding context to the **GameViewModel**:

```
using Slugrace.ViewModels;

namespace Slugrace.Views;

public partial class InstructionsPage : ContentPage
{
        public InstructionsPage(GameViewModel gameViewModel)
        {
                InitializeComponent();
                BindingContext = gameViewModel;
        }
}
```

Let's also register the page with the dependency service in **MauiProgram.cs**:

```
...
public static class MauiProgram
{
        ...
        builder.Services.AddTransient<GameOverViewModel>();

        builder.Services.AddTransient<InstructionsPage>();

        return builder.Build();
    ...
```

In the **GameViewModel**, let's define two methods, one for navigating to the **InstructionsPage** and one for navigating back:

```
...
public partial class GameViewModel : ObservableObject
{
    ...
    void EndGameManually()
    ...
    [RelayCommand]
    async Task SeeInstructions()
    {
        // Navigate to InstructionsPage
        await Shell.Current.GoToAsync($"{nameof(InstructionsPage)}");
    }

    [RelayCommand]
    async Task NavigateBack()
    {
        await Shell.Current.GoToAsync("..");
    }
}
```

We mustn't forget to add the route in the **AppShell.xaml.cs** file:

```
using Slugrace.Views;

namespace Slugrace;

public partial class AppShell : Shell
{
    public AppShell()
    {
        InitializeComponent();
        Routing.RegisterRoute(nameof(RacePage), typeof(RacePage));
        Routing.RegisterRoute(nameof(GameOverPage), typeof(GameOverPage));
        Routing.RegisterRoute(nameof(InstructionsPage), typeof(InstructionsPage));
    }
}
```

The last piece of the puzzle is to bind the Instructions button in **RacePage** to the **SeeInstructions** method:

```
<?xml version="1.0" encoding="utf-8" ?>
<ContentPage ...>
    ...
        <!--the buttons-->
        ...
            <Button
                Text="Instructions"
                IsEnabled="{Binding RaceStatus,
                    Converter={StaticResource raceStatusConverter},
                    ConverterParameter={x:Static local:RaceStatus.Finished}}"
                Command="{Binding SeeInstructionsCommand}" />
            <Button
                ...
```

The button will be enabled after each race. Let's run the app and hit the Instructions button. This will take us to the new page:

If we click the Back button, we'll go back to **RacePage**.

So, our game simulation works. But it's just a simulation. In the real game the slugs will be animated. In order to implement this, we need to learn about animations in .NET MAUI. This is the topic of the next chapter.

Chapter 19 – Animation

code: https://github.com/prospero-apps/Slugrace/tree/chapter19

In the previous chapter we created a simple game simulation where the slugs win randomly without moving at all. But in real races, slugs (or, more commonly, horses or greyhounds) do have to move to win, or even to finish the race. Our slugs are no exception to this rule. In this chapter we'll implement animations and make the slugs run.

We're going to create a couple animations. Not only are the slugs going to move from one end of the racetrack to the other, but they're also going to have some moving parts, like the tentacles with the eyes.

But before we implement any of that, let's have a look at some theory. Let's see how animation works in .NET MAUI and what we can do with it. We'll make use of the **TestPage** at first, so that we can practice the new stuff. Then we'll implement the animations in our app.

Basic Animations

Animations consist in a gradual change of a property between two values over a period of time. The four basic animations supported by .NET MAUI are:

- **FadeTo**

- **TranslateTo**

- **RotateTo**

- **ScaleTo**

But there are more, like **RelScaleTo**, **RotateXTo** or **ScaleYTo**, to mention just a few. They can be used with **VisualElement** objects. The animations listed above are extension methods of the **ViewExtensions** class. The methods are asynchronous and return a **Task<bool>** object. If an animation completes, the return value is **false**. If it's canceled, the return value is **true**.

We can use the **await** keyword to combine animations sequentially. These are so-called **compound animations**. If we don't use the **await** keyword, we can combine the animations to run simultaneously. These are so-called **composite animations**.

We have to keep in mind, too, that on Android animations can be disabled to save power. If this is the case, the animations immediately jump to their finished state.

Let's modify the **TestPage** to contain just a **Label**, a **BoxView** and a **Button**:

```
<?xml version="1.0" encoding="utf-8" ?>
<ContentPage xmlns="http://schemas.microsoft.com/dotnet/2021/maui"
             xmlns:x="http://schemas.microsoft.com/winfx/2009/xaml"
             xmlns:viewmodels="clr-namespace:Slugrace.ViewModels"
             x:DataType="viewmodels:TestViewModel"
             x:Class="Slugrace.Views.TestPage"
             Title="TestPage"
             Padding="50">

    <VerticalStackLayout>
        <Label x:Name="label"
               Text="Test Page"
               HorizontalOptions="Center"
               Margin="0, 0, 0, 100"
               FontSize="40" />
        <BoxView x:Name="box"
                 Color="Red"
                 WidthRequest="150"
                 HeightRequest="100" />
        <Button
            x:Name="button"
            Text="Start Animation"
            Margin="0, 100, 0, 0"
            Clicked="Button_Clicked" />
    </VerticalStackLayout>
</ContentPage>
```

We'll use the button to start our animations. We can now simplify the **TestViewModel** class like so:

```
using CommunityToolkit.Mvvm.ComponentModel;

namespace Slugrace.ViewModels;

public partial class TestViewModel : ObservableObject
{
}
```

We're going to use the code-behind file to implement the animations. And now let's have a look at some of the basic animations one by one.

Fading

Most animation methods take two parameters. The first parameter is the target value and the second parameter is the duration of the animation in milliseconds.

Let's make the box fade out in three seconds. The method takes the current value of the **Opacity** property (which is 1) for the start of the animation and fades out from this value to 0:

```
using Slugrace.ViewModels;

namespace Slugrace.Views;

public partial class TestPage : ContentPage
{
    public TestPage(TestViewModel testViewModel)
    {
        InitializeComponent();
        BindingContext = testViewModel;
    }

    private async void Button_Clicked(object sender, EventArgs e)
    {
        await box.FadeTo(0, 3000);
    }
}
```

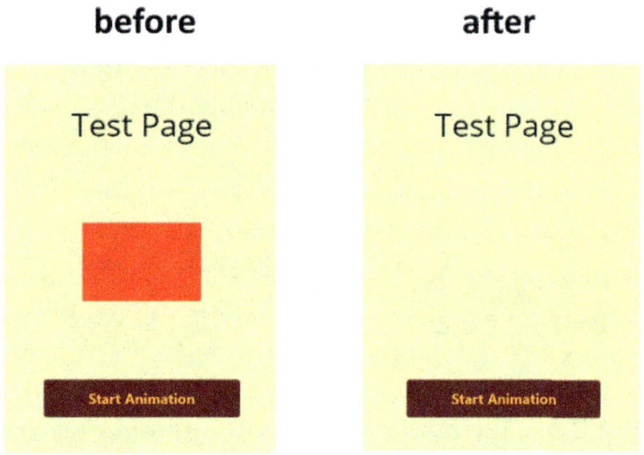

If you now run the app and press the button, the box will start fading out.

Let's move on to the next basic animation.

Translation

To move an element from one location to another we use the **TranslateTo** method. It takes three parameters. The first two are for the **TranslationX** and **TranslationY** properties, and the last one is the duration of the animation.

Let's translate the box 200 device-independent units to the right and 50 units down over a period of 4 seconds:

```
...
public partial class TestPage : ContentPage
{
    ...
    private async void Button_Clicked(object sender, EventArgs e)
    {
        await box.TranslateTo(200, 50, 4000);
    }
}
```

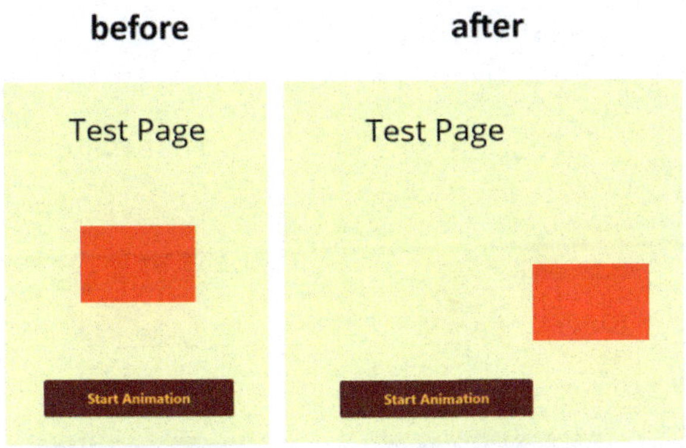

Press the button and the box's journey will begin.

Next, let's see how rotation works.

Rotation and Relative Rotation

We can rotate around any of the three axes: X, Y or Z. The Z axis is the one that goes through the screen, so, if we rotate around it, the element will rotate in the plane of the screen. This is the most common scenario. We use the **Rotate** method for this rotation. We pass the target angle and duration as parameters.

So, let's rotate the label 15 degrees in clockwise direction over a period of 2 seconds:

```
...
public partial class TestPage : ContentPage
{
    ...
    private async void Button_Clicked(object sender, EventArgs e)
    {
        await label.RotateTo(15, 2000);
    }
}
```

Here's what it looks like:

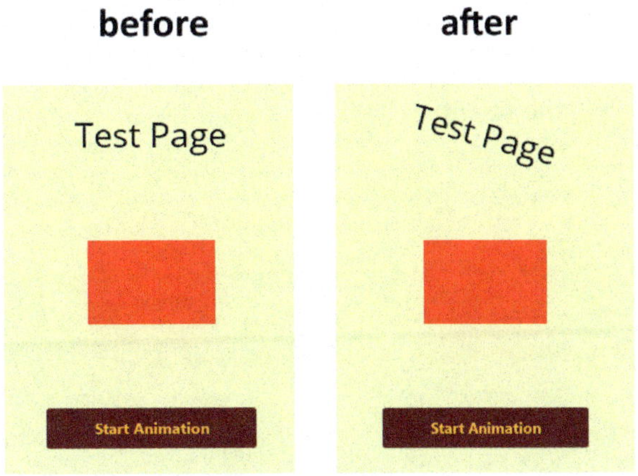

In order to rotate around the X and Y axes, we respectively use the **RotateXTo** and **RotateYTo** methods. Let's rotate around the X axis first:

```
...
public partial class TestPage : ContentPage
{
    ...
    private async void Button_Clicked(object sender, EventArgs e)
    {
        await label.RotateXTo(45, 2000);
    }
}
```

Here's the result:

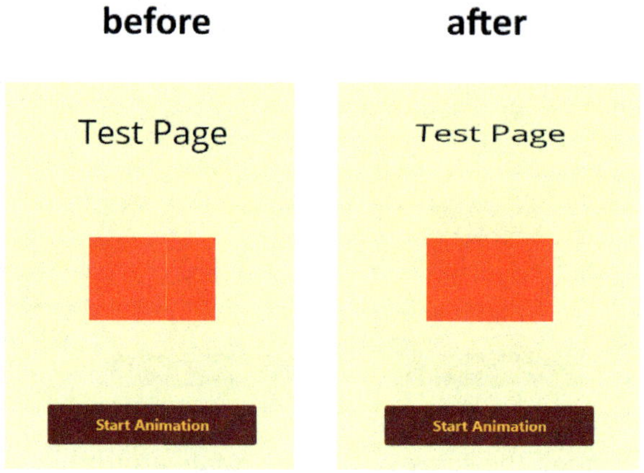

And now around the Y axis:

```
...
public partial class TestPage : ContentPage
{
    ...
    private async void Button_Clicked(object sender, EventArgs e)
    {
        await label.RotateYTo(45, 2000);
    }
}
```

Here's the result:

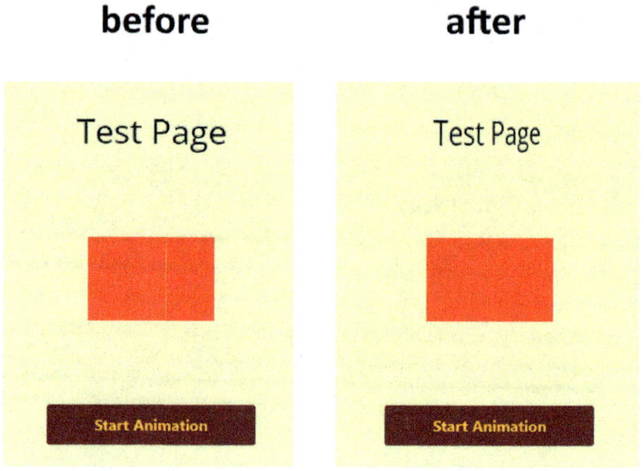

The methods above rotate from the current value of **Rotation**, **RotationX** or **RotationY** to the target values. Let's set the **Rotation** property in the XAML file to 45:

```
...
<ContentPage ...>
    <VerticalStackLayout>
        <Label ...
               Rotation="45" />
        ...
```

Let's use the **RotateTo** method and pass the angle of 90 degrees as the first argument:

```
...
public partial class TestPage : ContentPage
{
    ...
    private async void Button_Clicked(object sender, EventArgs e)
    {
        await label.RotateTo(90, 2000);
    }
}
```

The label will now be rotated from the angle of 45 degrees to the angle of 90 degrees.

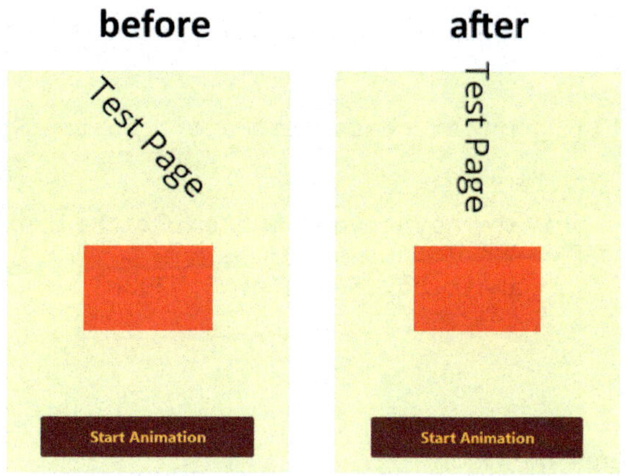

If we want to to rotate it by an angle of 90 degrees, so from 45 to 135 degrees, we should use relative rotation. This can be accomplished by using the **RelRotateTo** method:

```
...
public partial class TestPage : ContentPage
{
    ...
    private async void Button_Clicked(object sender, EventArgs e)
    {
        await label.RelRotateTo(90, 2000);
    }
}
```

Here's the result (look right).

We're done experimenting with rotation. Let's now remove the **Rotation** property from the XAML code.

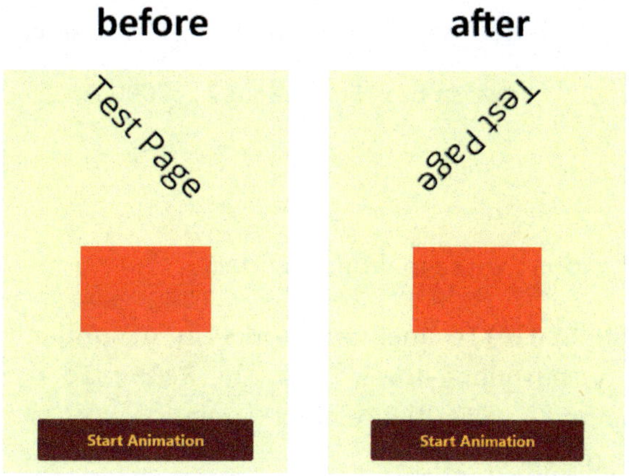

Scaling and Relative Scaling

The scaling methods work pretty much the same as the rotating ones. We have the **ScaleTo** method to scale the element uniformly in both directions, the **ScaleXTo** and **ScaleYTo** methods to scale it along just one axis, and **RelScaleTo** for relative scaling.

All these methods take the scaling factor as the first parameter and duration as the second.

So, let's scale down the box over a period of 2 seconds:

```
...
public partial class TestPage : ContentPage
{
    ...
    private async void Button_Clicked(object sender, EventArgs e)
    {
        await box.ScaleTo(.5, 2000);
    }
}
```

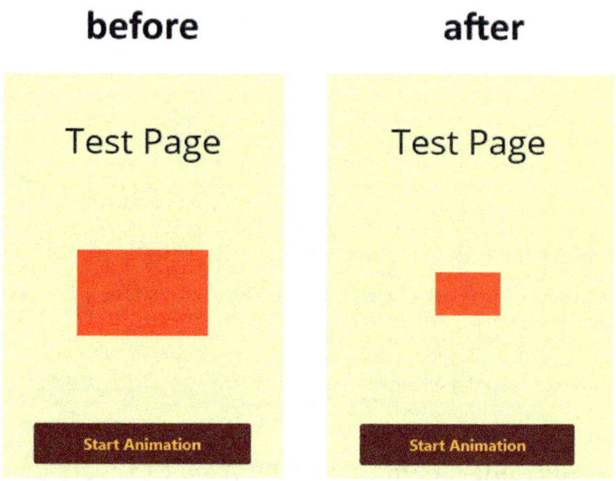

Here's the result:

Now let's scale it only along the X axis:

```
...
public partial class TestPage : ContentPage
{
    ...
    private async void Button_Clicked(object sender, EventArgs e)
    {
        await box.ScaleXTo(2, 2000);
    }
}
```

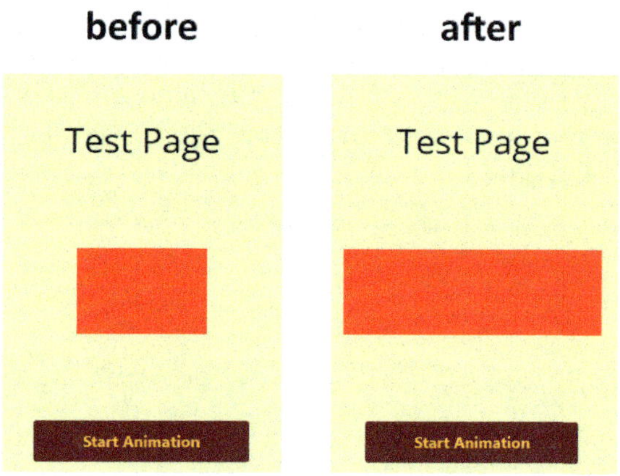

This time, we're making it wider.

The **ScaleYTo** method works in a similar way, but along the Y axis. The **RelScaleTo** method scales the element relative to its current value.

In the rotating and scaling animations above, the transformation is always performed relative to the center of an element. But it doesn't have to be the case.

Anchors

We can set the center of rotation or scaling by using the **AnchorX** and **AnchorY** properties. The values should be between 0 (left for **AnchorX** and top for **AnchorY**) to 1 (right for **AnchorX** and bottom for **AnchorY**). The default value of either property is 0.5, which corresponds to the center of the visual element.

Let's rotate the box 45 degrees around its top-left corner:

```
...
public partial class TestPage : ContentPage
{
    ...
    private async void Button_Clicked(object sender, EventArgs e)
    {
        box.AnchorX = 0;
        box.AnchorY = 0;
        await box.RotateTo(45, 2000);
    }
}
```

Here's the result:

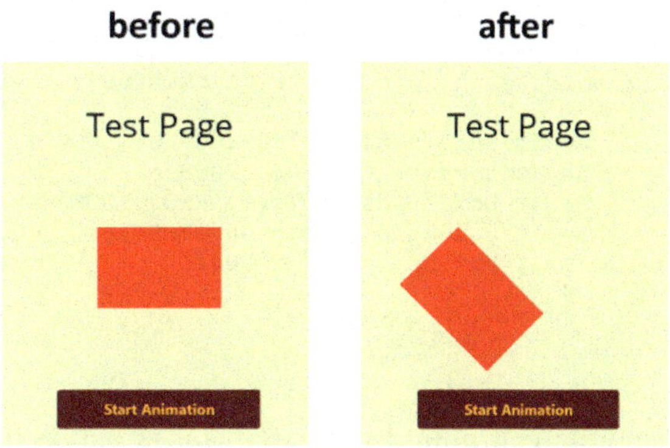

Next, let's scale the button relative to its bottom-right corner:

```
...
public partial class TestPage : ContentPage
{
    ...
    private async void Button_Clicked(object sender, EventArgs e)
    {
        button.AnchorX = 1;
        button.AnchorY = 1;
        await button.ScaleTo(2, 2000);
    }
}
```

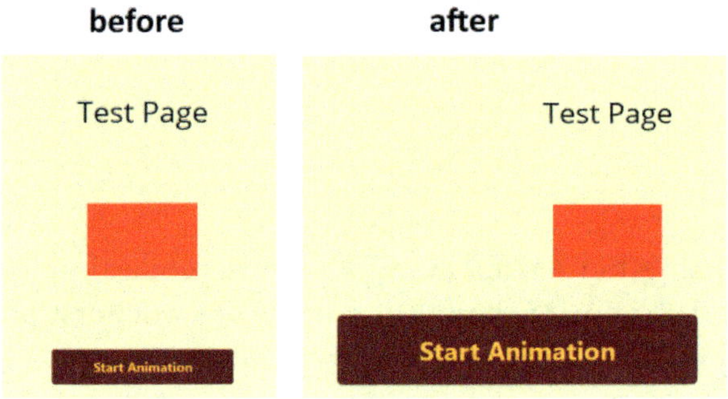

Here's what we should see when the animation completes.

We know how to create single animations. But we can combine multiple animations to achieve all sorts of effects.

Compound Animations

Multiple animations can be combined sequentially. We just have to use the **`await`** keyword. Let's create a compound animation on the box:

```
...
public partial class TestPage : ContentPage
{
    ...
    private async void Button_Clicked(object sender, EventArgs e)
    {
        await box.TranslateTo(-100, 0, 1000);
        await box.RotateTo(45, 2000);
        await box.TranslateTo(0, -50, 1000);
        await box.RelRotateTo(45, 2000);
        await box.ScaleTo(2, 500);
    }
}
```

The whole compound animation takes 6.5 seconds to complete. First the box moves to the left. When this movement is complete, the rotation starts, and so on.

Composite Animations

Animations can also run simultaneously. This will happen if we omit the **`await`** keyword. Let's translate, rotate and scale the box all at the same time:

```
...
public partial class TestPage : ContentPage
{
    ...
    private void Button_Clicked(object sender, EventArgs e)
    {
        box.TranslateTo(-100, 0, 3000);
        box.RotateTo(45, 3000);
        box.ScaleTo(2, 3000);
    }
}
```

If you run the app now and press the button, all three animations will start simultaneously. The whole composite animation will take 3 seconds to complete.

We can also mix and match. Let's create a composite animation where some single animations are awaited and others are not:

```
...
public partial class TestPage : ContentPage
{
    ...
    private async void Button_Clicked(object sender, EventArgs e)
    {
        label.ScaleXTo(3, 4000);
        await label.RotateTo(15, 2000);
        await label.RotateTo(0, 2000);
    }
}
```

Here the label will be scaled and rotated simultaneously. The two rotation animations will be run sequentially at the same time as the scaling animation.

We can also create composite animations where multiple asynchronous methods run concurrently. Let's have a look at it next.

WhenAll and WhenAny

We can create composite animations using two methods, **`Task.WhenAny`** and **`Task.WhenAll`**. They return a **`Task`** object. We pass to them a collection of methods that also return a **`Task`** object.

The **`Task.WhenAny`** method completes when any of the methods in its collection completes. Have a look:

```
...
public partial class TestPage : ContentPage
{
    ...
    private async void Button_Clicked(object sender, EventArgs e)
    {
        await Task.WhenAny
        (
            label.TranslateTo(400, 0, 5000),
            label.ScaleTo(2, 2000)
        );

        await label.ScaleTo(1, 3000);
    }
}
```

Here we have a **Task.WhenAny** method with two tasks. The first task starts translating the label to the right, the second task starts scaling it. The second task needs two seconds to complete. When it completes, the **Task.WhenAny** method also completes. While the translation is still running (it needs three more seconds to complete), the second **ScaleTo** method can start running. The second scaling and the translation will complete at the same time.

Whereas the **Task.WhenAny** method completes when any of its tasks completes, the **Task.WhenAll** method completes when all the tasks it contains complete. Have a look:

```
...
public partial class TestPage : ContentPage
{
    ...
    private async void Button_Clicked(object sender, EventArgs e)
    {
        await Task.WhenAll
        (
            box.ScaleXTo(3, 3000),
            box.RotateTo(360, 500),
            box.TranslateTo(100, 0, 7000)
        );

        await box.ScaleTo(0, 100);
    }
}
```

Here we have three tasks with different durations. The box first completes the rotation, then the scaling on the X axis, and then the translation. Only when the last task completes, the **Task.WhenAll** method completes. As last runs the scaling to zero.

Canceling Animations

We can easily cancel animations by calling the **CancelAnimations** method. Let's add another button to the **TestPage**:

```
<?xml version="1.0" encoding="utf-8" ?>
<ContentPage ...>
    <VerticalStackLayout>
        ...
        <Button
            x:Name="button"
            ...
        <Button
            x:Name="cancel"
            Text="Cancel Animations"
            Margin="0, 100, 0, 0"
            Clicked="Cancel_Clicked" />
    </VerticalStackLayout>
</ContentPage>
```

And here's the code-behind:

```
...
public partial class TestPage : ContentPage
{
    ...
    private void Button_Clicked(object sender, EventArgs e)
    {
        box.TranslateTo(100, 0, 5000);
        box.RotateTo(90, 4000);
        box.ScaleTo(2, 4000);
    }

    private void Cancel_Clicked(object sender, EventArgs e)
    {
        box.CancelAnimations();
    }
}
```

When you press the first button, all three animations start running simultaneously. When you press the second button, they are immediately canceled.

Easing Functions

Animations can run with constant speed or with different speed and acceleration as they proceed. They can start slow and then accelerate. They can start fast and then decelerate. You can create your own patterns or use the ones we get out of the box.

There's a class that contains easing functions that enable just that. The class is called **Easing** and it contains the following easing functions: **BounceIn**, **BounceOut**, **CubicIn**, **CubicInOut**, **CubicOut**, **Linear**, **SinIn**, **SinInOut**, **SinOut**, **SpringIn** and **SpringOut**. The **-In** suffix is used if the effect should be visible at the beginning of the animation. The suffix **-Out** - if at the end. If both suffixes are used, the effect is visible at both the beginning and the end.

To use an easing function, we just add it as the last argument to the animation method. Let's check it out.

We'll create a simple translation for our box. By default the **Linear** easing function is used. All the animations we've created so far use this default value. Let's bounce the box at the beginning of the animation. To this end, we can use the **BounceIn** easing function:

```
...
public partial class TestPage : ContentPage
{
    ...
    private void Button_Clicked(object sender, EventArgs e)
    {
        box.TranslateTo(300, 0, 3000, Easing.BounceIn);
    }
    ...
```

Run the animation to see how it works.

Or let's smoothly accelerate the box at the beginning and decelerate it at the end of the animation:

```
...
public partial class TestPage : ContentPage
{
    ...
    private void Button_Clicked(object sender, EventArgs e)
    {
        box.TranslateTo(300, 0, 3000, Easing.SinInOut);
    }
    ...
```

This effect is often used.

Feel free to check out the other easing functions. They also work with rotation or scaling.

Custom Animations

We can use the **Animation** class to create custom animations. We use the **Commit** method to run an animation. Let's create and run an animation in the **TestPage**. Let's first remove the second button and the related code in the code-behind. The code should now look like so:

```
...
public partial class TestPage : ContentPage
{
    ...
    private void Button_Clicked(object sender, EventArgs e)
    {
        var animation = new Animation(v => box.Rotation = v, 0, 45);

        animation.Commit(
            this,
            "RotationAnimation",
            16,
            3000,
            Easing.SinInOut,
            (v, c) => box.Rotation = 0,
            () => true);
    }
}
```

We pass a callback, the start value and the end value as arguments to the **Animation** class's constructor. As the callback we use a lambda expression that sets the box's **Rotation** property to values between the start value (0 degrees) and the end value (45 degrees).

Then we run the animation. The **Commit** method takes a few parameters. The first parameter is the owner of the animation. This is the visual element the animation is set on or another visual element, such as the page. In our case we pass **this** for the page.

The second parameter is the name of the animation. The name and the owner are used jointly to uniquely identify the animation.

The third parameter is the rate of the animation. It's expressed in milliseconds. In our case the rate is 16, so 16 milliseconds must elapse between calls to the callback method we passed to the **Animation** object's constructor.

The fourth parameter is the duration of the animation. In our case it's 3000 milliseconds, so 3 seconds.

The fifth parameter is the easing function we want to use for the animation.

The sixth parameter is a callback that will be executed when the animation completes. It takes two arguments, **v** and **c**. The **v** argument is the final value. The **c** argument, of type bool, is set to **true** if the animation is canceled.

Finally, the last parameter is a callback that we use to repeat the animation. In our case it returns **true**, so the animation will be repeated.

Now run the app and hit the button. You'll see the box rotate, then go to the state with **Rotation** equal to zero. And this pattern will repeat.

Child Animations

We can combine and synchronize multiple animations in a parent-child relationship. To do that, we create a parent animation and add child animations to it. For the child animations we specify the time frame in which they are supposed to run relative to the duration of the parent animation. Let's create an example to demonstrate how it works.

We'll create a parent animation using the parameterless constructor. Next, we'll create three child animations using the constructor with parameters. By the way, this time we'll define the easing functions in the constructor, which is an alternative way of doing it. Finally, we'll add the child animations to the parent animation. Here's the code:

```
...
public partial class TestPage : ContentPage
{
    ...
    private void Button_Clicked(object sender, EventArgs e)
    {
        var parentAnimation = new Animation();

        var childAnimation1 = new Animation(
            v => label.ScaleY = v, 1, 2, Easing.CubicIn);

        var childAnimation2 = new Animation(
            v => label.Rotation = v, 0, 30, Easing.SpringIn);

        var childAnimation3 = new Animation(
            v => label.Rotation = v, 30, 0, Easing.SpringOut);

        parentAnimation.Add(0, 1, childAnimation1);
        parentAnimation.Add(0, .5, childAnimation2);
        parentAnimation.Add(.5, 1, childAnimation3);

        parentAnimation.Commit(
            this,
            "LabelAnimation",
            16,
            5000,
            null,
            (v, c) => label.Text += " |",
            () => true);
    }
}
```

The first two arguments passed to the **Add** method are the time frames for the child animations. They must be between 0 and 1. So, the first animation will run for the entire duration of the parent animation. The second child animation will run during the first half of the parent animation, and the third child animation will run during the second half.

If you now run the app, you'll see the label scale up for 5 seconds. During the first 2.5 seconds it will rotate in clockwise direction, during the next 2.5 seconds it will rotate back. Additionally, we change the **Text** property of the label after the animation is finished (before the next repetition).

The code above can be simplified:

```
...
public partial class TestPage : ContentPage
{
    ...
    private void Button_Clicked(object sender, EventArgs e)
    {
        new Animation
        {
            { 0, 1, new Animation(
                v => label.ScaleY = v, 1, 2, Easing.CubicIn) },
            { 0, .5, new Animation(
                v => label.Rotation = v, 0, 30, Easing.SpringIn) },
            { .5, 1, new Animation(
                v => label.Rotation = v, 30, 0, Easing.SpringOut) }
        }.Commit(
            this,
            "LabelAnimation",
            16,
            5000,
            null,
            (v, c) => label.Text += " |",
            () => true);
    }
}
```

Naturally, it works the same.

Animating Properties

Visual elements implement the **IAnimatable** interface, which contains the **Animate** method. We can use this method to create and start an animation.

For example, we can animate the label's **FontSize** property like so:

```
...
public partial class TestPage : ContentPage
{
    ...
    private void Button_Clicked(object sender, EventArgs e)
    {
        label.Animate(
            "Move",
            new Animation(x => label.FontSize = x, 5, 50),
            16,
            5000);
    }
}
```

The **Animate** method takes a couple arguments. The first argument is the name, which is used as a unique key. The second argument is the animation that we want to run. Here we're animating the **FontSize** property of the label from 5 to 50. The two remaining arguments are the rate and the duration of the animation. There are also other overloaded versions of the **Animate** method.

We can even animate the whole **ContentPage**. Let's rotate it:

```
...
public partial class TestPage : ContentPage
{
    ...
    private void Button_Clicked(object sender, EventArgs e)
    {
        this.Animate(
            "Rotate",
            new Animation(x => Rotation = x, 0, 360),
            16,
            3000);
    }
}
```

This animation looks like this:

Animations in MVVM

Our project uses the MVVM pattern. Let's have a look at how to create animations in an app that uses that pattern. First, make sure your **TestViewModel** class looks like so:

```
using CommunityToolkit.Mvvm.ComponentModel;
using CommunityToolkit.Mvvm.Input;

namespace Slugrace.ViewModels;

public partial class TestViewModel : ObservableObject
{
    [ObservableProperty]
    private bool isHidden;

    [ObservableProperty]
    private bool isRunning;

    [RelayCommand]
    async Task Animate()
    {
        IsRunning = true;
        await Task.Delay(5000);
        IsRunning = false;
    }
}
```

Here we have two properties and a method. The first property will indicate whether an element (like the box in our case) should be visible or hidden. The second property will be used to indicate whether a simulated task is running.

The method will just set the **IsRunning** property to **true**, wait for 5 seconds and then set it to **false**. It will be used as a command.

Let's now have a look at the **TestPage.xaml** file, slightly modified:

```
...
<ContentPage ...>
    <VerticalStackLayout>
        <Label x:Name="label"
           Text="0"
           ...
        <BoxView x:Name="box"
                 ...
        <Button
            x:Name="button"
            Text="Start Animation"
            Margin="0, 100, 0, 0"
            Command="{Binding AnimateCommand}" />
    </VerticalStackLayout>
</ContentPage>
```

It hasn't changed much. The label's **Text** is now initially set to "**0**" and we don't have the **Clicked** event anymore. The button's **Command** property now binds to the method we created in the view model.

Finally, let's modify the code-behind:

```
using Slugrace.ViewModels;

namespace Slugrace.Views;

public partial class TestPage : ContentPage
{
    TestViewModel vm;

    readonly Animation rotation;

    public TestPage(TestViewModel testViewModel)
    {
        InitializeComponent();

        rotation = new Animation(HandleTransformations, 0, 360);

        BindingContext = testViewModel;
        vm = (TestViewModel)BindingContext;

        vm.PropertyChanged += Vm_PropertyChanged;
    }

    void HandleTransformations(double value)
    {
        box.Rotation = value;

        label.Text = ((int)value).ToString();

        if ((int)value % 20 == 0)
        {
            if (vm.IsHidden)
            {
                ShowBox();
            }
            else
            {
                HideBox();
            }
        }
    }

    void HideBox()
    {
        box.Opacity = 0;
        vm.IsHidden = true;
    }

    void ShowBox()
    {
        box.Opacity = 1;
        vm.IsHidden = false;
    }
```

```
    private void Vm_PropertyChanged(object? sender,
        System.ComponentModel.PropertyChangedEventArgs e)
    {
        if (e.PropertyName == nameof(vm.IsRunning))
        {
            if (vm.IsRunning)
            {
                rotation.Commit(
                    this,
                    "rotate",
                    16,
                    5000,
                    Easing.Linear,
                    (v, c) => box.Rotation = 0,
                    () => false);
            }
            else
            {
                this.AbortAnimation("rotate");
            }
        }
    }
}
```

Here we have an instance of our view model. In the constructor we create an animation. We define a callback and the start and end values.

We create a method, **HandleTransformations**, and pass it as the callback. In the method we change the rotation of the box, modify the text on the label and hide or show the box.

We also have the **PropertyChanged** event handler in the constructor. In the **Vm_PropertyChanged** method we start the animation when the value of **IsRunning** in the view model changes to **true**. We cancel the animation when it changes to **false**.

If we now run the app and press the button, we'll see the box rotate and the label text change. Every 20 degrees the box will disappear or reappear.

Fine. We know enough about animations to implement them in our project.

Animations in the Slugrace App

We're going to create several custom animations in our project. The most important one is the translation of the slug images from left to right. This is a racing game after all, so the slugs must be able to run.

We're also going to animate the slugs' tentacles. Rotating them will definitely bring some life to the slugs.

Finally, we're going to implement some animations related to accidents that may happen to the slugs.

The Running Animation

So, let's start with the running animation. The racetrack image and the slug images are inside the **TrackImage** control. Let's give them names so that we can reference them later:

```
...
<ContentView ...>
    <AbsoluteLayout>
        <!--Racetrack-->
        <Image
            x:Name="track"
            ...
        <!--Speedster-->
        <controls:SlugImage
            x:Name="speedster"
            ...
        <!--Trusty-->
        <controls:SlugImage
            x:Name="trusty"
            ...
        <!--Iffy-->
        <controls:SlugImage
            x:Name="iffy"
            ...
        <!--Slowpoke-->
        <controls:SlugImage
            x:Name="slowpoke"
            ...
```

The slug running animations will be implemented in the code behind because they transform the graphics. But we'll need a link to the **GameViewModel** in order to correlate the states of the slugs and of the game with the animated graphics. Let's create that link by adding an instance of **GameViewModel** in the code-behind:

```
using Slugrace.ViewModels;

namespace Slugrace.Controls;

public partial class TrackImage : ContentView
{
    GameViewModel? vm;

    public TrackImage()
    {
        InitializeComponent();
    }
}
```

We'll create four animations, one for each slug. The slugs will run along the racetrack. This is why we need to know the length of the racetrack. However, the **Width** property of the track is unavailable in the constructor because at the time when the constructor is run, the children are not yet laid out.

To make sure that the **Width** property is set, we have to override the **LayoutChildren** method. We create a **trackLength** variable to hold the distance the slugs should cover.

Also in the **LayoutChildren** method we instantiate the four animations. As the first argument, we pass methods to them that we define below. These methods just take care of translating the **SlugImage** objects. As the start and end values we pass 0 and **trackLength** respectively:

```
...
namespace Slugrace.Controls;

public partial class TrackImage : ContentView
{
    GameViewModel? vm;
    double trackLength;

    Animation? speedsterMovement;
    Animation? trustyMovement;
    Animation? iffyMovement;
    Animation? slowpokeMovement;

    public TrackImage()
    {
        InitializeComponent();
    }

    protected override void LayoutChildren(double x, double y, double width, double height)
    {
        base.LayoutChildren(x, y, width, height);
        trackLength = track.Width * .79;

        speedsterMovement = new Animation(SpeedsterMoveForward, 0, trackLength);
        trustyMovement = new Animation(TrustyMoveForward, 0, trackLength);
        iffyMovement = new Animation(IffyMoveForward, 0, trackLength);
        slowpokeMovement = new Animation(SlowpokeMoveForward, 0, trackLength);
    }

    private void SpeedsterMoveForward(double value)
    {
        speedster.TranslationX = value;
    }

    private void TrustyMoveForward(double value)
    {
        trusty.TranslationX = value;
    }

    private void IffyMoveForward(double value)
    {
        iffy.TranslationX = value;
    }
```

```
    private void SlowpokeMoveForward(double value)
    {
        slowpoke.TranslationX = value;
    }
}
```

We have the animations, but we haven't run them yet. When do we want them to run? Well, they should start when the race begins. And this happens when the race status changes to **Started**.

So, we need a way to tell when the status changes. To this end, we'll use the **PropertyChanged** event handler. Let's add a **BindingContextChanged** event handler to the **TrackImage** class:

```
...
<ContentView ...
             x:DataType="viewmodels:GameViewModel"
             BindingContextChanged="ContentView_BindingContextChanged"
             x:Class="Slugrace.Controls.TrackImage">
    ...
```

In the code-behind, let's assign the binding context to the view model instance and let's assign a **Vm_PropertyChanged** method to the event handler:

```
...
namespace Slugrace.Controls;

public partial class TrackImage : ContentView
{
    ...
    protected override void LayoutChildren(double x, double y, double width, double height)
    ...
    private void ContentView_BindingContextChanged(object sender, EventArgs e)
    {
        vm = (GameViewModel)BindingContext;
        vm.PropertyChanged += Vm_PropertyChanged;
    }

    private void SpeedsterMoveForward(double value)
    ...
}
```

Before we proceed, let's add a **RunningTime** property to the **SlugViewModel** class:

```
...
public partial class SlugViewModel : ObservableObject
{
    ...
    public double PreviousOdds
    ...

    [ObservableProperty]
    private uint runningTime;

    public SlugViewModel()
    ...
}
```

We'll also need three time-related properties in the **GameViewModel**:

```
...
public partial class GameViewModel : ObservableObject
{
    ...
    private bool gameEndedManually;

    [ObservableProperty]
    private uint raceTime;

    [ObservableProperty]
    private uint minTime;

    [ObservableProperty]
    private uint finishTime;

    public GameViewModel()
    ...
```

What do they refer to?

The first property, **RaceTime**, is the time of the entire race, so until the last slug finishes the race.

The second property, **MinTime**, is the time the fastest slug needs to finish the race.

The **FinishTime** property is the time when the race should be considered resolved because the winner is already known, but the slugs are still running.

And now let's take care of all the different scenarios as far as the change of the race status is concerned.

So, if the status changes to **Started**, we first define the running times of all the slugs. The shorter the time, the faster the slug will run. The first slug, for example, will have a random running time between 3000 and 7000 milliseconds. This is going to be the statistically fastest slug. No other slug will be able to cover the distance in 3 seconds.

Then we create an array of the running times. Next, we set the three time properties we just added to the **GameViewModel**.

The **RaceTime** is set to the running time of the slowest slug.

The **MinTime** is set to the running time of the fastest slug.

The **FinishTime** is set to 79% of **MinTime**.

We're going to use these properties in the **RunRace** method in the view model. With this in place, we start the animations.

If the race status changes to **NotYetStarted**, which happens after each race when we hit the Next Race button, the slugs' **TranslationX** property is reset and the images move to where they started off.

If the status changes to **Finished**, the animations are canceled and the slugs stop running. Here you can see all three cases:

```
using Slugrace.ViewModels;
using System.ComponentModel;

namespace Slugrace.Controls;

public partial class TrackImage : ContentView
{
    ...
    private void SlowpokeMoveForward(double value)
    ...
    private void Vm_PropertyChanged(object? sender, PropertyChangedEventArgs e)
    {
        if (e.PropertyName == nameof(vm.RaceStatus))
        {
            if (vm!.RaceStatus == RaceStatus.Started)
            {
                vm.Slugs[0].RunningTime = (uint)new Random().Next(3000, 7000);
                vm.Slugs[1].RunningTime = (uint)new Random().Next(4000, 7000);
                vm.Slugs[2].RunningTime = (uint)new Random().Next(4000, 6000);
                vm.Slugs[3].RunningTime = (uint)new Random().Next(5000, 8000);

                uint[] runningTimes = [
                    vm.Slugs[0].RunningTime,
                    vm.Slugs[1].RunningTime,
                    vm.Slugs[2].RunningTime,
                    vm.Slugs[3].RunningTime
                ];

                vm.RaceTime = runningTimes.Max();
                vm.MinTime = runningTimes.Min();
                vm.FinishTime = (uint)(.79 * vm.MinTime);

                speedsterMovement?.Commit(
                    this,
                    "moveSpeedster",
                    16,
                    vm.Slugs[0].RunningTime,
                    Easing.Linear,
                    null,
                    () => false);

                trustyMovement?.Commit(
                    this,
                    "moveTrusty",
                    16,
                    vm.Slugs[1].RunningTime,
                    Easing.Linear,
                    null,
                    () => false);
```

```
                iffyMovement?.Commit(
                    this,
                    "moveIffy",
                    16,
                    vm.Slugs[2].RunningTime,
                    Easing.Linear,
                    null,
                    () => false);

                slowpokeMovement?.Commit(
                    this,
                    "moveSlowpoke",
                    16,
                    vm.Slugs[3].RunningTime,
                    Easing.Linear,
                    null,
                    () => false);
            }
            else if (vm.RaceStatus == RaceStatus.NotYetStarted)
            {
                speedster.TranslationX = 0;
                trusty.TranslationX = 0;
                iffy.TranslationX = 0;
                slowpoke.TranslationX = 0;
            }
            else
            {
                this.AbortAnimation("moveSpeedster");
                this.AbortAnimation("moveTrusty");
                this.AbortAnimation("moveIffy");
                this.AbortAnimation("moveSlowpoke");
            }
        }
    }
}
```

Now, let's modify the **RunRace** method in the **GameViewModel**:

```
...
public partial class GameViewModel : ObservableObject
{
    ...
    async Task RunRace()
    {
        await Task.Delay((int)FinishTime);

        RaceWinnerSlug = Slugs.Where(s => s.RunningTime == MinTime).FirstOrDefault();

        await Task.Delay((int)(RaceTime - FinishTime));

        if (RaceWinnerSlug != null)
        {
            RaceWinnerSlug.IsRaceWinner = true;
        }

        HandleSlugsAfterRace();

        HandlePlayersAfterRace();

        FinishRace();
    }
```

```
    private void HandleSlugsAfterRace()
    ...
```

The method is now asynchronous. Its return type is no longer **void**, but **async Task**. This means the method must be awaited everywhere in the code where it's called. So, the **StartRace** method, in which it's called, must be asynchronous, too:

```
...
public partial class GameViewModel : ObservableObject
{
    ...

    partial void OnGameChanged(Game? value)
    ...
    [RelayCommand]
    async Task StartRace()
    {
        // Start race
        RaceStatus = RaceStatus.Started;

        if (RaceNumber == 1 && GameEndingCondition == EndingCondition.Time)
        {
            gameTimer.Start();
        }

        await RunRace();
    }

    async Task RunRace()
    ...
```

In the **RunRace** method, we introduce a delay of a couple seconds. During this time, the race status is **Started** and the slugs are running. The **RaceWinnerSlug** is now set to the fastest slug. We have the winner, but the slugs are still running until the slowest one finishes. Then we continue like before.

There is also one change in the **WinnerInfo** class. We want the winner info to be visible not when all slugs finish the race, but rather when the winner is known, so after the fastest slug crosses the finish line.

So, we bind the **IsVisible** property to **RaceWinnerSlug**. We also use the **IsNotNullConverter** from the Community Toolkit, so that the **WinnerInfo** view should be visible only when there is a **RaceWinnerSlug**:

```
...
<ContentView ...>

    <ContentView.Resources>
        ...
        <toolkit:IsNotNullConverter x:Key="raceResolvedConverter" />
    </ContentView.Resources>
```

```
<Grid
    IsVisible="{Binding RaceWinnerSlug,
        Converter={StaticResource raceResolvedConverter}}"
    ...
```

As you can see, we don't need the **EnumToBoolConverter** anymore.

We also must make sure that the **RaceWinnerSlug** is set to **null** in the **NextRace** method in **GameViewModel**:

```
...
public partial class GameViewModel : ObservableObject
{
    ...
    void NextRace()
    {
        RaceStatus = RaceStatus.NotYetStarted;
        RaceNumber++;

        RaceWinnerSlug = null;

        foreach (var player in Players)
        ...
    }
    ...
```

This way the **WinnerInfo** view will be invisible when the next race begins.

If we now run the app and then start the first race, the slugs start running:

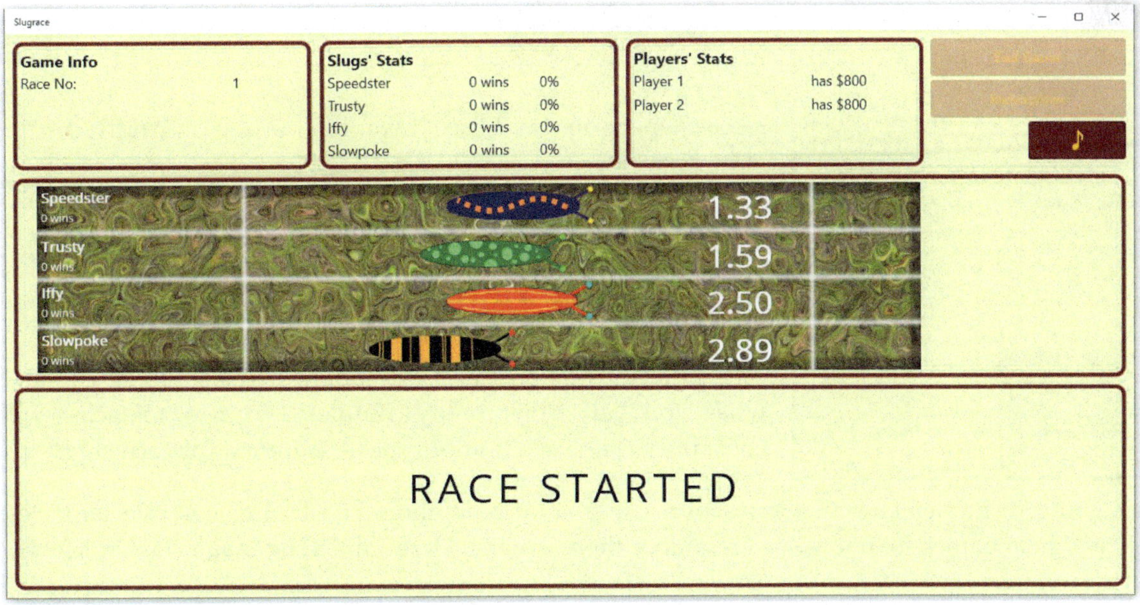

The moment the first slug crosses the finish line, the **WinnerInfo** is displayed:

The slugs continue running until all of them have completed the race:

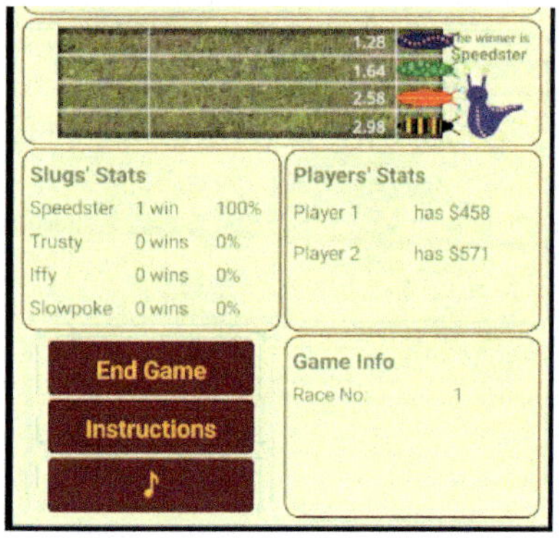

Here's what you should see if you ran the app on Android.

Now the race is finished and we can hit the Next Race button. This will move the slugs to the beginning of the track.

Rotating the Tentacles

The tentacle rotation (or eye rotation, it really doesn't matter what you call it) is pretty simple. The two tentacles will constantly rotate at a random speed, different for each slug.

We're going to implemenet this animation using child animations. Each slug has two tentacles. Let's give them names so that we can reference them in code. Here's the **SlugImage** class in XAML:

```
...
<ContentView ...>

    <AbsoluteLayout>
        <Image
            x:Name="leftEye"
            Source="{Binding EyeImageUrl}"
            ...
        <Image
            x:Name="rightEye"
            Source="{Binding EyeImageUrl}"
            ...
        <Image
            Source="{Binding BodyImageUrl}"
            ...
```

And now let's implement the rotation in the code-behind:

```
namespace Slugrace.Controls;

public partial class SlugImage : ContentView
{
    public SlugImage()
    {
        InitializeComponent();

        uint rotationSpeed = (uint)new Random().Next(2000, 4000);

        new Animation()
        {
            {0, .5, new Animation(v => leftEye.Rotation = v, 0, -30) },
            {0, .5, new Animation(v => rightEye.Rotation = v, 0, 30) },
            {.5, 1, new Animation(v => leftEye.Rotation = v, -30, 0) },
            {.5, 1, new Animation(v => rightEye.Rotation = v, 30, 0) }
        }.Commit(this, "eyeRotation", 16, rotationSpeed, null, null, () => true);
    }
}
```

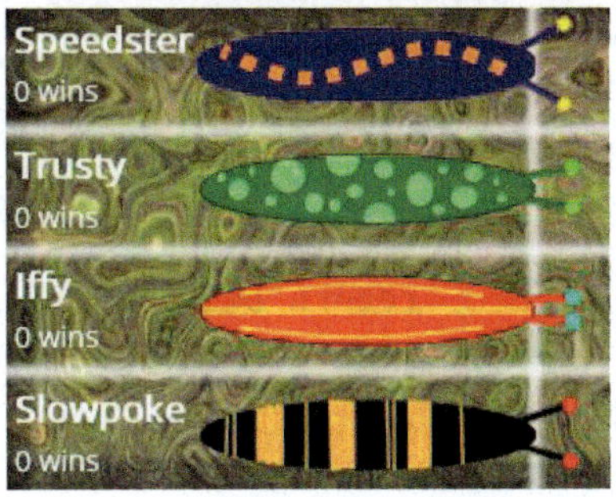

Here we have four child animations, two for the left eye and two for the right eye. Each eye rotates in one direction during the first half of the animation and then back. This animation is repeated.

Now, as soon as the slugs appear on the screen, they rotate their tentacles.

Great, we have animations in our app now. But how cool would it be if we had some background music and sound effects as well? Well, this is what we're going to see to in the next chapter.

Chapter 20 – Sound

code: https://github.com/prospero-apps/Slugrace/tree/chapter20

A game without audio seems incomplete. We're going to implement background music and sound effects in our app. To do that, we need a plugin.

Plugin.Maui.Audio

The plugin is called **`Plugin.Maui.Audio`**. Let's install the NuGet package:

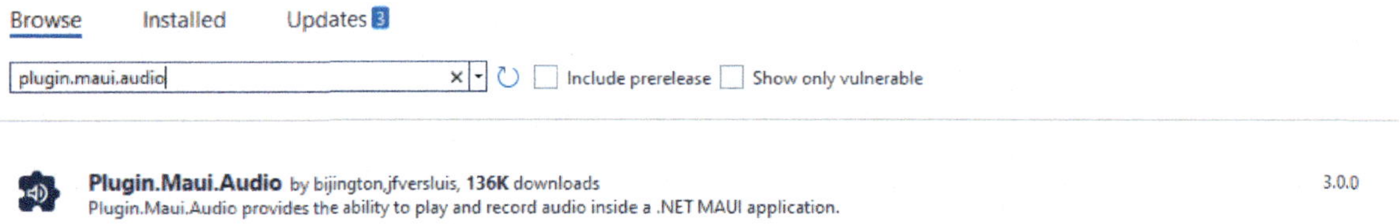

We have to register it in the dependency injection container, so go to the **MauiProgram.cs** file and add the following code:

```
...
using Plugin.Maui.Audio;

namespace Slugrace;

public static class MauiProgram
{
    public static MauiApp CreateMauiApp()
    {
        ...
        builder.Services.AddTransient<InstructionsPage>();

        builder.Services.AddSingleton(AudioManager.Current);

        return builder.Build();
    }
}
```

Let's create a view model that will handle sound in our app.

SoundViewModel

Create a new class in the **ViewModels** folder and name it **SoundViewModel**. We inject the **AudioManager** in the constructor:

```
using CommunityToolkit.Mvvm.ComponentModel;
using Plugin.Maui.Audio;

namespace Slugrace.ViewModels;

public partial class SoundViewModel : ObservableObject
{
    private readonly IAudioManager audioManager;

    public SoundViewModel(IAudioManager audioManager)
    {
        this.audioManager = audioManager;
    }
}
```

Let's also register the view model with the dependency service in the **MauiProgram** class:

```
...
public static class MauiProgram
{
    public static MauiApp CreateMauiApp()
    {
        ...
        builder.Services.AddTransient<InstructionsPage>();

        builder.Services.AddTransient<SoundViewModel>();

        builder.Services.AddSingleton(AudioManager.Current);

        return builder.Build();
      }
}
```

To play sounds, we need... Well, sounds.

Sound Files

Before we move on, we have to add the sound files we need to the **Raw** folder inside the **Resources** folder. You will find these files on Github.

The sound files are contained in three folders:

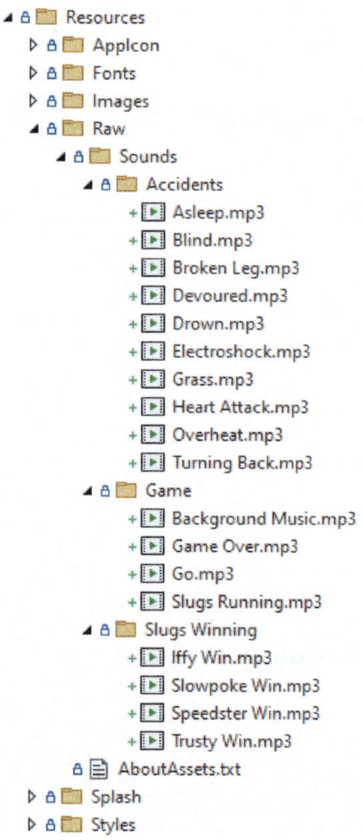

In the **Accidents** folder we have sounds that will be associated with the accidents that may happen to the slugs. We're going to implement them in the next chapter.

In the **Game** folder there are sounds that will be used when a race begins, while the slugs are running and when the game is over. There's also a file that will be used as background music.

In the **Slugs Winning** folder there are files that will be played when the slugs win a race. Each slug will use a different sound to express his joy after winning a race.

All sounds that I'm using for the project were downloaded from Zapsplat. I renamed them so that you can easily see what each file is going to be used for.

In the table below you can see both the names that we are going to use in the project and the original ones.

So, in the **Game** folder we have the following sounds:

File Name in Slugrace	Original Zapsplat File Name
Background Music.mp3	music_zapsplat_game_music_kids_warm_soft_slow_chilled_piano_bass_warm_pads_vocal_ahs_022.mp3
Slugs Running.mp3	zapsplat_animals_leach_or_worm_slimy_movement_squelch_003_10795.mp3
Game Over.mp3	cartoon_success_fanfair.mp3
Go.mp3	esm_8bit_explosion_medium_with_voice_bomb_boom_blast_cannon_retro_old_school_classic_cartoon.mp3

The **Background Music.mp3** file is going to be used for the background music.

The **Slugs Running.mp3** file will start playing when a race begins and loop until all slugs have finished the race.

The **Game Over.mp3** file will play just once when the Game Over screen appears.

The **Go.mp3** file will be played just once the moment a race starts.

In the **Slugs Winning** folder we have the following files:

File Name in Slugrace	Original Zapsplat File Name
Speedster Win.mp3	**human-toddler-18-months-boy-single-laugh.mp3**
Trusty Win.mp3	**human_baby_3_months_short_laugh.mp3**
Iffy Win.mp3	**jessey_drake_vox_10month_baby_SMOOCH_really_excited_laugh_build_HEX_JD.mp3**
Slowpoke Win.mp3	**zapsplat_human_boy_3_years_old_british_laugh_001.mp3**

Each of these sounds will be played just once when the corresponding slug wins a race, so you will hear just one of them in each race.

Finally, in the **Accidents** folder we have the following files:

File Name in Slugrace	Original Zapsplat File Name
Asleep.mp3	**zapsplat_human_man_elderly_snore_20087.mp3**
Blind.mp3	**horror_eyes_gouged_out_001.mp3**
Broken Leg.mp3	**zapsplat_horror_gore_bone_arm_leg_break_crunch_57125.mp3**
Devoured.mp3	**fork_media_horror_monster_roar_growl_reverberant.mp3**
Drown.mp3	**zapsplat_nature_water_bubble_rise_underwater_002_20093.mp3**
Electroshock.mp3	**sound_design_effect_electricity_electric_arc.mp3**
Grass.mp3	**zapsplat_animals_slug_eat_designed_001_42438.mp3**
Heart Attack.mp3	**zapsplat_human_child_heartbeat_fast_26491.mp3**
Overheat.mp3	**Blastwave_FX_AcidBurnSizzle_S011SF.3.mp3**
Turning Back.mp3	**zapsplat_cartoon_voice_funny_gibberish_worried_scared_19920.mp3**

Each of these sounds will be associated with one of the accidents. The names of the files are pretty self-explanatory. But, as mentioned above, we're not going to use these sounds for now.

Playing Sounds

We have one audio manager, but we can have as many audio players as we need. We can create a separate audio player for each sound.

An audio player is an object that implements the **IAudioPlayer** interface. We use it to play the sound, stop it, check if it's playing, set its volume, make it loop, and so on.

Audio players are disposable objects. We should dispose of them after they're done playing their sound. This way we'll avoid memory leaks.

In our app we'll create an audio player to handle the background music. We'll name it just **audioPlayer**. We'll also create a list of audio players for the sound effects. We'll name the list **effectPlayers**. Each time a sound should be played, a new audio player will be created and added to that list. It will be disposed of when it's done its job.

So, let's add the audio players to the **SoundViewModel**. Let's also create the methods to play the sounds:

```
...
public partial class SoundViewModel : ObservableObject
{
    private readonly IAudioManager audioManager;
    private IAudioPlayer? audioPlayer;
    private List<IAudioPlayer> effectPlayers;

    public SoundViewModel(IAudioManager audioManager)
    {
        this.audioManager = audioManager;
        effectPlayers = [];
    }

    public async Task PlayBackgroundMusic(string folderName, string fileName)
    {
        string path = Path.Combine("Sounds", folderName, fileName);

        audioPlayer = audioManager.CreatePlayer(
            await FileSystem.OpenAppPackageFileAsync(path));
        audioPlayer.Loop = true;
        audioPlayer.Volume = .3;
        audioPlayer.Play();
    }

    public async Task PlaySound(string folderName, string fileName,
        double volume = 1, bool loop = false)
    {
        Clean();

        string path = Path.Combine("Sounds", folderName, fileName);

        var player = audioManager.CreatePlayer(
            await FileSystem.OpenAppPackageFileAsync(path));

        effectPlayers.Add(player);
```

```
        player.Volume = volume;
        player.Loop = loop;
        player.Play();
    }

    public void Stop()
    {
        if (audioPlayer != null && audioPlayer.IsPlaying)
        {
            audioPlayer.Stop();
            audioPlayer.Dispose();
        }
    }

    public void Clean()
    {
        foreach (var player in effectPlayers)
        {
            if (player.IsPlaying)
            {
                player.Stop();
            }

            player.Dispose();
        }

        effectPlayers.Clear();
    }
}
```

We create an audio player for each sound. We pass a stream to the **CreatePlayer** method. To create a stream from a file we use the **FileSystem.OpenAppPackageFileAsync** method. We also set the **Loop** property of the player.

The **Stop** and **Clean** methods, among other things, dispose of the audio players. We'll use the former in a minute. We use the **Clean** method inside the **PlaySound** method to dispose of any audio players that might still be there and clear the list.

The volume should be set to a value between 0 (silent) to 1 (full volume).

Background Music

Let's create an instance of the **SoundViewModel** in the **GameViewModel**:

```
...
public partial class GameViewModel : ObservableObject
{
    SoundViewModel soundViewModel;

    readonly IDispatcherTimer gameTimer;
```

```
...
public GameViewModel(SoundViewModel soundViewModel)
{
    ...
    gameOverPageDelayTimer.Interval = TimeSpan.FromSeconds(3);

    this.soundViewModel = soundViewModel;

    WeakReferenceMessenger.Default.Register<PlayerBetAmountChangedMessage>(this, (r, m) =>
        OnBetAmountChangedMessageReceived(m.Value));
    ...
```

The background music should start playing in a loop the moment the game starts, so after we click the Ready button in the **SettingsPage**. So, let's call the **PlayBackgroundMusic** method in the **OnGameChanged** method:

```
...
public partial class GameViewModel : ObservableObject
{
    ...
    partial void OnGameChanged(Game value)
    {
        ...
        PlayersStillInGame = Players.ToObservableCollection();

        _ = soundViewModel.PlayBackgroundMusic("Game", "Background Music.mp3");
    }

    [RelayCommand]
    async Task StartRace()
    ...
```

The background music will now play throughout the entire game. It will stop playing only when the game is over. During the short period of time after the last race and before the **GameOverPage** is shown, the sound should attenuate. Let's create the **Attenuate** method in the **SoundViewModel**:

```
...
public partial class SoundViewModel : ObservableObject
{
    ...
    public void Clean()
    ...

    public async Task Attenuate()
    {
        if (audioPlayer != null) {
            while (audioPlayer.Volume > 0.01)
            {
                await Task.Delay(10);
                audioPlayer.Volume -= .001;
            }
        }
    }
}
```

This method will gradually decrease the volume until we can't hear anything.

Now, let's call this method in the **EndGame** method in the **GameViewModel**. We'll also call the **Stop** method we defined in the **SoundViewModel** to stop the background music if it is still playing for some reason and to dispose of the audio player:

```
...
public partial class GameViewModel : ObservableObject
{
    ...

    async Task EndGame()
    {
        ...
        gameOverPageDelayTimer.Start();

        await soundViewModel.Attenuate();

        gameOverPageDelayTimer.Tick += async (sender, e) =>
        ...

        soundViewModel.Stop();
    }

    [RelayCommand]
    void NextRace()
    ...
}
```

We've introduced some asynchrony to the code, so, consequently, we have to make some of the methods we defined before asynchronous:

```
...
public partial class GameViewModel : ObservableObject
{
    ...
    public GameViewModel(SoundViewModel soundViewModel)
    {
        ...
        gameTimer.Tick += async (sender, e) =>
        {
            ...
            if (TimeRemaining == TimeSpan.Zero
                && RaceStatus == RaceStatus.Finished)
            {
                await CheckForGameOver();
            }
        };
        ...
    async Task FinishRace()
    {
        RaceStatus = RaceStatus.Finished;
```

```
    await CheckForGameOver();
}

async Task CheckForGameOver(bool endedManually = false)
{
    // This is for the case when the game is ended manually
    if (endedManually)
    {
        ...
        await EndGame();
    }
    ...
    else if (Players.Count > 1 && PlayersStillInGame.Count == 1)
    {
        ...
        await EndGame();
    }
    ...
    else if (PlayersStillInGame.Count == 0)
    {
        ...
        await EndGame();
    }
    ...
    else if (GameEndingCondition == EndingCondition.Races
        && RaceNumber == NumberOfRacesSet)
    {
        ...
        await EndGame();
    }
    ...
    else if (GameEndingCondition == EndingCondition.Time
        && TimeRemaining == TimeSpan.Zero)
    {
        ...
        await EndGame();
    }
}
...
private async Task RunRace()
{
    ...
    await FinishRace();
}
...
[RelayCommand]
async Task EndGameManually()
{
    await CheckForGameOver(true);
}
...
```

If you now run the app and hit the Ready button, you'll be able to hear the background music.

Sound Effects

We're going to implement some sound effects in the game. There are going to be sounds associated with accidents that happen to the slugs, but we'll take care of them in the next chapter. For now, let's add the other sound effects.

The first effect we want to implement is the sound that we hear when the game is over. Let's play the sound in the **EndGame** method:

```
...
public partial class GameViewModel : ObservableObject
{
    ...

    async Task EndGame()
    {
        ...
        gameOverPageDelayTimer.Tick += async (sender, e) =>
        {
            ...
            IsShowingFinalResults = false;

            await soundViewModel.PlaySound("Game", "Game Over.mp3", .5);

            // Navigate to GameOverPage
            await Shell.Current.GoToAsync($"{nameof(GameOverPage)}",
                ...
        };

        soundViewModel.Stop();
    }

    [RelayCommand]
    void NextRace()
    ...
}
```

We'll still hear the sound when the **GameOverPage** shows up.

The next two sound effects are the shot that should be heard when a race begins and the sound that can be heard while the slugs are running. The latter sound should be looped. We'll implement them in the **StartRace** and **RunRace** methods:

```
...
public partial class GameViewModel : ObservableObject
{
    ...
    async Task StartRace()
    {
        ...
        if (RaceNumber == 1 && GameEndingCondition == EndingCondition.Time)
```

```
        ...
        _ = soundViewModel.PlaySound("Game", "Go.mp3", .2);

        await RunRace();
    }

    private async Task RunRace()
    {
        _ = soundViewModel.PlaySound("Game", "Slugs Running.mp3", .5, true);

        await Task.Delay((int)FinishTime);

        ...
        soundViewModel.Clean();

        HandleSlugsAfterRace();
        ...
    }

    private void HandleSlugsAfterRace()
    ...
}
```

We also call the **Clean** method in the **RunRace** method because we don't want the running sound to continue in the next race.

Finally, we'll add a victory sound for each slug. Each slug will rejoice in a different way when they win.

Let's start by adding a **WinSound** property to the **Slug** model class:

```
namespace Slugrace.Models;

public class Slug
{
    ...
    public bool IsRaceWinner { get; set; }
    public string WinSound {  get; set; } = string.Empty;
}
```

Next, in the **SettingsViewModel**, where the slugs are created in the **StartGame** method, let's assign the sound file names to this new property:

```
...
public partial class SettingsViewModel : ObservableObject
{
    ...
    async Task StartGame()
    {
        // Populate the Game object
```

```
        game.Slugs =
        [
            new Slug
            {
                ...
                BodyImageUrl = "speedster_body.png",
                WinSound = "Speedster Win.mp3"
            },
            new Slug
            {
                ...
                BodyImageUrl = "trusty_body.png",
                WinSound = "Trusty Win.mp3"
            },
            new Slug
            {
                ...
                BodyImageUrl = "iffy_body.png",
                WinSound = "Iffy Win.mp3"
            },
            new Slug
            {
                ...
                BodyImageUrl = "slowpoke_body.png",
                WinSound = "Slowpoke Win.mp3"
            }
        ];

        ...
```

Let's also add a **WinSound** property to the **SlugViewModel**:

```
...
public partial class SlugViewModel : ObservableObject
{
    ...
    public double PreviousOdds
    ...

    public string WinSound
    {
        get => slug.WinSound;
        set
        {
            if (slug.WinSound != value)
            {
                slug.WinSound = value;
                OnPropertyChanged();
            }
        }
    }
```

```
    [ObservableProperty]
    private uint runningTime;
    ...
```

Now, back in the **GameViewModel**, let's revisit the **OnGameChanged** method and assign the sounds:

```
...
public partial class GameViewModel : ObservableObject
{
    ...
    partial void OnGameChanged(Game value)
    {
        ...
        Slugs =
        [
            new()
            {
                ...
                PreviousOdds = value.Slugs[0].BaseOdds,
                WinSound = value.Slugs[0].WinSound
            },
            new()
            {
                ...
                PreviousOdds = value.Slugs[1].BaseOdds,
                WinSound = value.Slugs[1].WinSound
            },
            new()
            {
                ...
                PreviousOdds = value.Slugs[2].BaseOdds,
                WinSound = value.Slugs[2].WinSound
            },
            new()
            {
                ...
                PreviousOdds = value.Slugs[3].BaseOdds,
                WinSound = value.Slugs[3].WinSound
            },
        ];

        ...
    }
    ...
```

This victory joy sound should be played when we have a slug winner, so in the **RunRace** method:

```
...
public partial class GameViewModel : ObservableObject
{
    ...
```

```
    private async Task RunRace()
    {
        ...
        RaceWinnerSlug = Slugs.Where(
            s => s.RunningTime == MinTime).FirstOrDefault();

        if (RaceWinnerSlug != null)
        {
            _ = soundViewModel.PlaySound("Slugs Winning", RaceWinnerSlug.WinSound);
        }

        await Task.Delay((int)(RaceTime - FinishTime));
        ...
```

Now play the game and wait until each of the slugs wins at least once so that you can hear all the different sounds.

If you like the sound effects, that's great. These effects will be always turned on. If you really can't stand them, just mute your device.

But you will be able to turn the background music on and off. There's one button in the **RacePage** we haven't talked about so far. Let's have a look at it now.

The Sound Button

The Sound button in the **RacePage**, which is the one with a note image on it, has one simple job to do. It should toggle the background music on and off. Also, when clicked, the image on it should change.

We'll create a command for this button in the **GameViewModel**. However, as we want to keep all the sound-related code in one place, which is the **SoundViewModel**, let's start by adding some properties and a method there.

So, we'll make some modifications in the **SoundViewModel**:

```
...
public partial class SoundViewModel : ObservableObject
{
    ...
    private List<IAudioPlayer> effectPlayers;

    [ObservableProperty]
    private double volume;

    [ObservableProperty]
    private bool muted;
```

```
    public SoundViewModel(IAudioManager audioManager)
    {
        this.audioManager = audioManager;
        effectPlayers = [];
        Volume = .3;
    }

    public async Task PlayBackgroundMusic(string folderName, string fileName)
    {
        ...
        audioPlayer.Volume = Volume;
        audioPlayer.Play();
    }

    ...
    public async Task Attenuate()
    ...
    public void MuteUnmute()
    {
        double defaultVolume = Volume > 0 ? Volume : .3;

        Muted = !Muted;

        Volume = Muted ? 0 : defaultVolume;

        if (audioPlayer != null)
        {
            audioPlayer.Volume = Volume;
        }
    }
}
```

So, here we can see two new properties: **Volume** and **Muted**. The former is used for the background music. We also have a new method, **MuteUnmute**. As the name suggests, it will mute the background music if it's on and turn it back on if it's off.

As we have access to an instance of **SoundViewModel** in the **GameViewModel**, we can create properties and methods there that we'll use for data binding. In particular, we'll add a **Muted** property and a **MuteUnmute** method:

```
...
public partial class GameViewModel : ObservableObject
{
    ...
    private uint finishTime;

    [ObservableProperty]
    private bool muted;

    public GameViewModel(SoundViewModel soundViewModel)
    ...
    async Task NavigateBack()
```

```
    ...

    [RelayCommand]
    public void MuteUnmute()
    {
        soundViewModel.MuteUnmute();
        Muted = soundViewModel.Muted;
    }
}
```

Now we can bind them in the **RacePage** XAML file. For simplicity's sake, we'll move most of the Sound button's properties to a style. We'll duplicate the Sound button. One will be visible when the background music is on, the other when it's off. The image on either button will be different.

So, here's the code:

```
...
<ContentPage ...>
    <ContentPage.Resources>
        <toolkit:EnumToBoolConverter x:Key="raceStatusConverter" />
        <toolkit:InvertedBoolConverter x:Key="invertedBoolConverter" />
        <Style x:Key="soundStyle" TargetType="Button">
            <Setter Property="WidthRequest"
                    Value="{OnPlatform 125, Android=150}" />
            <Setter Property="HorizontalOptions"
                    Value="{OnPlatform Default=End, Android=Center}" />
            <Setter Property="Command"
                    Value="{Binding MuteUnmuteCommand}" />
        </Style>
    </ContentPage.Resources>
    ...
        <!--the buttons-->
        <VerticalStackLayout
            ...
            <Button
                Text="Instructions"
                ...
            <Button
                Style="{StaticResource soundStyle}"
                ImageSource="{AppThemeBinding Light=sound_on.png,
                                              Dark=sound_on_dark.png}"
                IsVisible="{Binding Muted,
                                Converter={StaticResource invertedBoolConverter}}" />
            <Button
                Style="{StaticResource soundStyle}"
                ImageSource="{AppThemeBinding Light=sound_off.png,
                                              Dark=sound_off_dark.png}"
                IsVisible="{Binding Muted}" />
        </VerticalStackLayout>
        ...
```

Let's run the app. When we leave the **SettingsPage** and enter the **RacePage**, the background music is on. The Sound button looks like before (the image on the left).

When you press the button, the music will be off and the other Sound button will be visible (the image on the right).

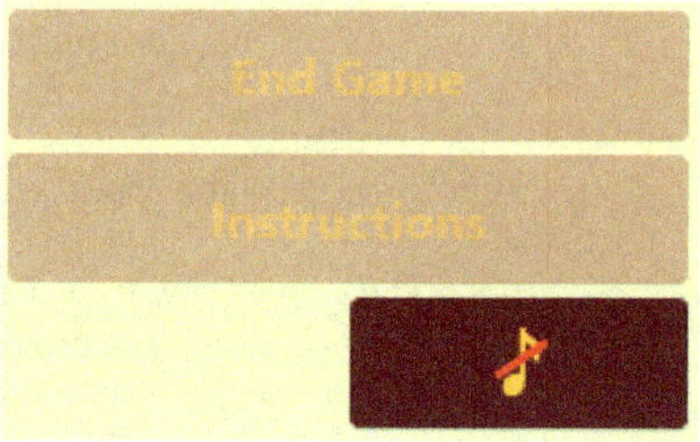

If you now decide the music wasn't that bad, you can always unmute it.

In the next chapter we'll implement even more sound effects. They will be associated with accidents that can happen to the slugs. We'll also see how to use popups to deliver a short message and offer some options to the user.

Chapter 21 - Popups

code: https://github.com/prospero-apps/Slugrace/tree/chapter21

You may sometimes want to show a popup message to the user. This can be just a simple message, or you can add a button or two to let the user do something, like confirm, cancel, etc.

In our app a popup will be displayed when the user clicks the Quit button in the **GameOverPage**. It will ask the user if they are sure they want to quit the game. There will be two buttons. One of them will be used to cancel and close the popup. The other will actually quit the app.

We're also going to show a popup when an accident happens. We haven't implemented accidents yet, so we'll take care of it first. Then we'll implement the popups.

There are a couple ways to create a popup. We'll be using the Community Toolkit **Popup** class. As our popups are going to be rather simple, we won't create view models for them. Instead we'll implement the logic in the code-behind.

So, let's start with the first popup.

Quit Popup

We're going to create a couple popups in our app, so let's put them in a folder. Create a new folder in the app root and name it **Popups**. In it, create a new **ContentView** and name it **QuitPopup**. Here's the code:

```
<?xml version="1.0" encoding="utf-8" ?>
<toolkit:Popup xmlns="http://schemas.microsoft.com/dotnet/2021/maui"
             xmlns:x="http://schemas.microsoft.com/winfx/2009/xaml"
             xmlns:toolkit="http://schemas.microsoft.com/dotnet/2022/maui/toolkit"
             x:Class="Slugrace.Popups.QuitPopup"
             CanBeDismissedByTappingOutsideOfPopup="False"
             Color="Coral">
    <VerticalStackLayout
        HorizontalOptions="Center"
        VerticalOptions="Center">
        <Label
            Text="Are you sure you want to quit?"
            Margin="5, 20, 5, 40"
            FontSize="30"
            VerticalOptions="Center"
            HorizontalOptions="Center" />
        <FlexLayout
            Direction="Column"
            JustifyContent="Center"
            AlignItems="Center">
            <Button
                Text="No, I was wrong. Cancel."
```

```
                WidthRequest="300"
                Margin="20"
                Clicked="CancelButtonClicked"/>
            <Button
                Text="Yes, I'm sure. Quit."
                WidthRequest="300"
                Margin="20"
                Clicked="QuitButtonClicked"/>
        </FlexLayout>
    </VerticalStackLayout>
</toolkit:Popup>
```

So, first of all, we changed the type from **ContentView** to **toolkit:Popup**.

We also set the **CanBeDismissedByTappingOutsideOfPopup** property to **False**. For this and the **Color** property to work, the class must inherit from the **CommunityToolkit.Maui.Views.Popup** class, which we're going to implement in a moment.

This way we won't be able to close the popup by clicking anywhere outside it. We want to close it only when a button is clicked.

Speaking of which... There are two buttons. We define the **Clicked** event for each of them. Let's now have a look at the code-behind to see what should happen when the buttons are clicked:

```
using CommunityToolkit.Maui.Views;

namespace Slugrace.Popups;

public partial class QuitPopup : Popup
{
    public QuitPopup()
    {
        InitializeComponent();
    }

    private async void CancelButtonClicked(object sender, EventArgs e)
    {
        await CloseAsync();
    }

    private void QuitButtonClicked(object sender, EventArgs e)
    {
        Application.Current!.Quit();
    }
}
```

So, as I just mentioned, the class now inherits from **Popup**. The first button just closes the popup. The second button quits the app.

Our popup is ready to use. We now have to make the Quit button in the **GameOverPage** open it:

```
...
<ContentPage ...
             x:Class="Slugrace.Views.GameOverPage">
    ...
            <Button
                Text="Play Again"
                ...
            <Button
                Text="Quit"
                Clicked="QuitButtonClicked" />
        </FlexLayout>
    ...
```

And here's the code-behind:

```
using CommunityToolkit.Maui.Views;
using Slugrace.Popups;
using Slugrace.ViewModels;

namespace Slugrace.Views;

public partial class GameOverPage : ContentPage
{
    public GameOverPage(GameOverViewModel gameOverViewModel)
    ...
    private void QuitButtonClicked(object sender, EventArgs e)
    {
        this.ShowPopup(new QuitPopup());
    }
}
```

This is how we display a popup. Let's run the app, finish one race and hit the End Game button to navigate to the **GameOverPage**. Now let's click the Quit button. We should see the popup:

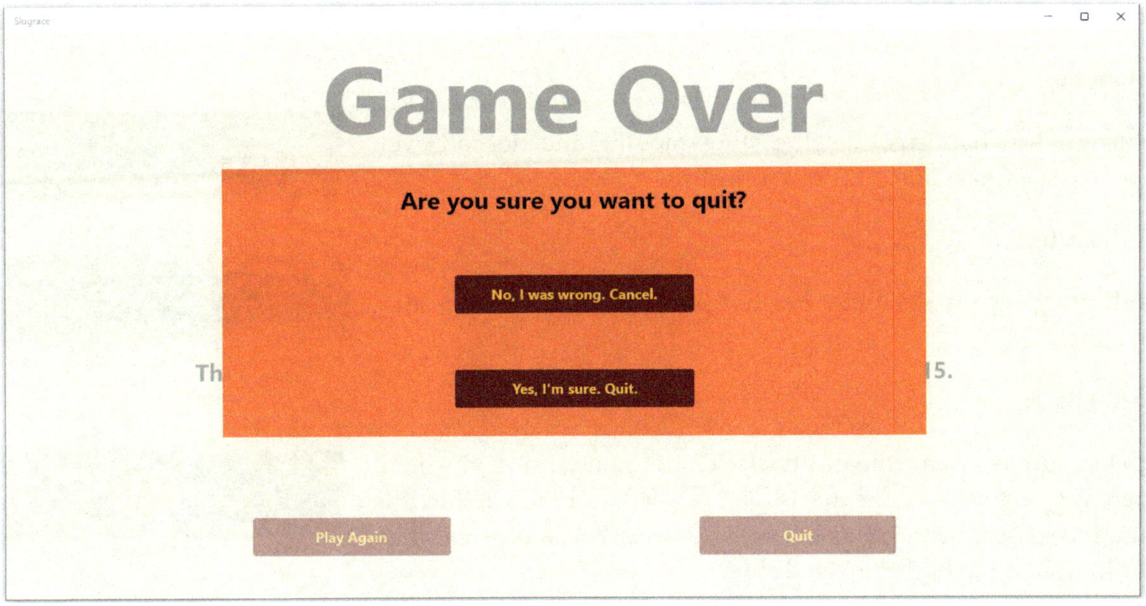

This is a modal popup. If you now click the first button, it will close the popup and you'll see the **GameOverPage** again. If you click the second button, you will actually quit the app.

Let's now run the app on Android. Here it looks like so (look left).

We're done with this one. Now let's move on to implementing accidents.

Accidents

Accidents happen. Also to slugs. During a race an accident may happen to one of the slugs. It's not going to be very frequent, but still, it may influence the result of the race when it happens. I'm using the name 'accident' here to keep things simple, but some of them may be convenient for the slugs and even help them win.

Anyway, whatever happens, it will only have consequences in the race in which it happens. In the following race the affected slug will be up and running again.

Each accident will have a graphical representation, which you can see below. Later, we'll also add sound effects to the accidents.

So, here are the accidents that may happen to the slugs:

Broken Leg

If this accident happens, the slug stops moving and doesn't even make it to the finish line. This race is lost.

Overheating

Overheating means stopping and not being able to continue the race either.

Heart Attack

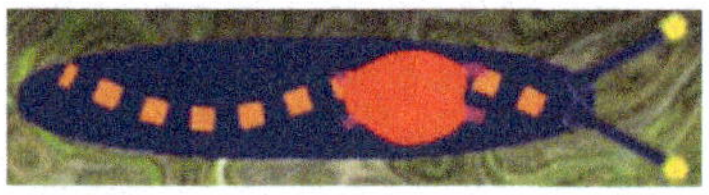

If a slug suffers from a heart attack, it's definitely not convenient either. The race is over for that slug. He needs a rest. His heart is beating like crazy, which you can see and hear. You will see a small heart image on top of the affected slug.

Power Grass

This is the first accident that may be convenient actually. First, some magic grass appears on the racetrack, just in front of the slug, and he stops to eat it, which takes a while. But the grass powers him up and then he starts racing much faster than before.

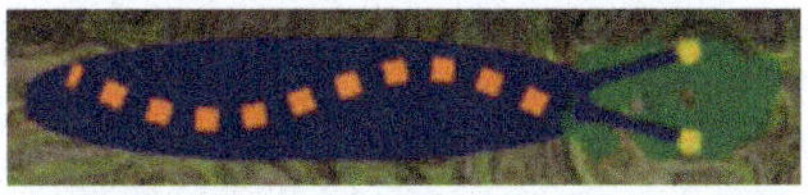

Falling Asleep

Falling asleep during a race is never a good idea. The slug stops and starts breathing slowly. You can hear him snore and see some changes in his size when the sleeping animation is played.

Going Blind

If a slug goes blind, he doesn't stop running, but without his eyes he starts staggering, so winning the race becomes pretty difficult.

Drowning in a Puddle

Drowning sucks. When this accident happens, a puddle of water appears on the racetrack and when the slug enters it, he drown. The slug becomes less and less visible under the water until he disappears completely.

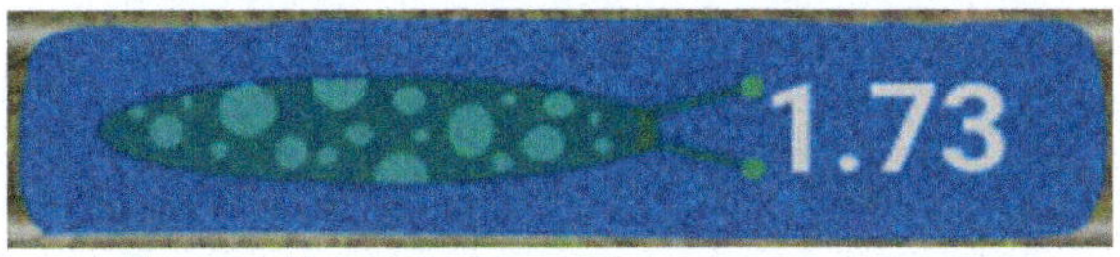

Electroshock

An electroshock is good, at least for a slug in our game. Not only doesn't it kill him, but it even speeds him up considerably, which often results in a vistory. You'll see a pulsating bolt on the slug's back.

Turning Back

Sometimes a slug forgets something and turns back. By doing so he looses his chances of winning.

Slug Monster

In the worst scenario, a slug may be devoured by the horrifying slug monster.

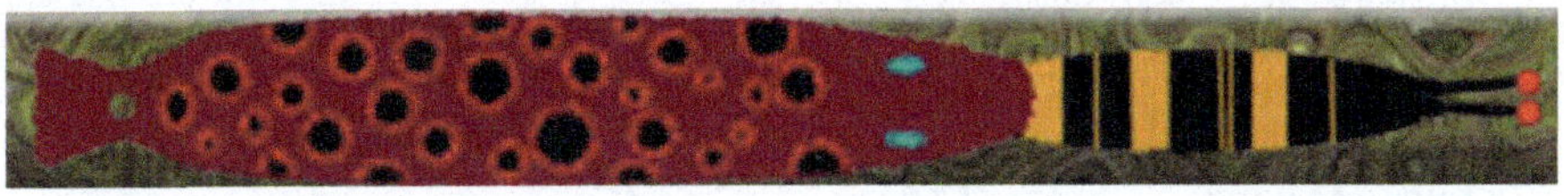

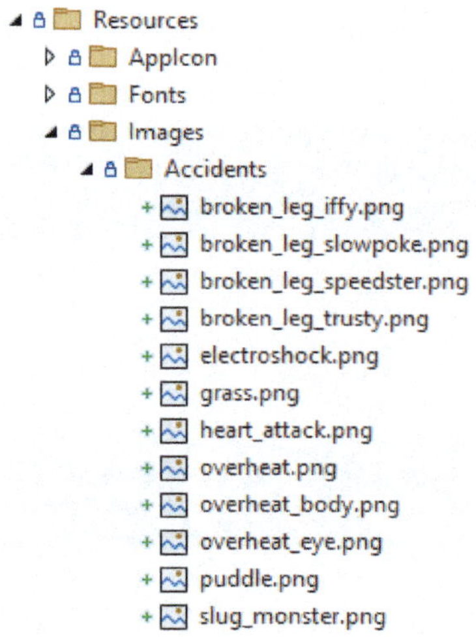

So, these are all the accidents that may happen in the game. Now we'll have a look at the graphical assets we need for the accidents and then we'll implement the classes that we need to handle the accidents.

Assets

As you can see, we'll need some graphical assets for the accidents. You can grab them from the Github repository. Create an **Accidents** folder inside the **Images** folder and add them there.

Most of the images will be shared by all the slugs. The broken leg images, however, will be different for each slug.

To use the images, just like we did before, we have to select them all and set their Build Action property to **`MauiImage`**.

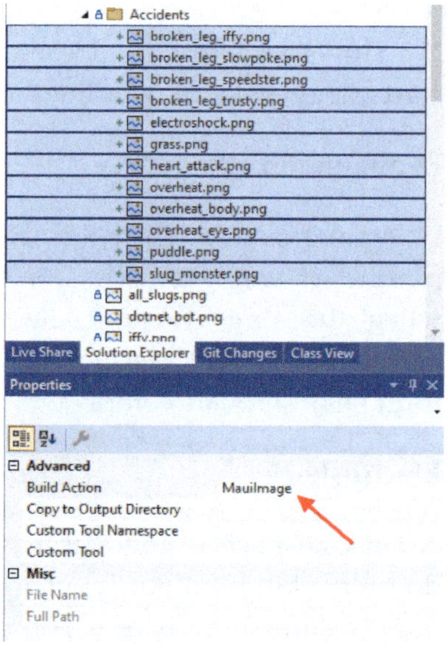

And now let's start implementing the accidents in code.

Accident Model Class

Let's start by adding a new class to the **Models** folder and naming it **`Accident`**. Here's the code:

```
namespace Slugrace.Models;

public enum AccidentType
{
    BrokenLeg,
    Overheat,
    HeartAttack,
    Grass,
    Asleep,
    Blind,
    Puddle,
    Electroshock,
    TurningBack,
    Devoured
}

public class Accident
{
    public AccidentType Type { get; set; }
    public string Name { get; set; } = string.Empty;
    public string Headline { get; set; } = string.Empty;
    public string Sound { get; set; } = string.Empty;
    public uint TimePosition { get; set; }
}
```

We also defined an enumaration that will be used by this class. There are ten accident types that may happen. The **Name** property will be used to set a name for each accident. The **Headline** property will be set to a succinct description of the accident. The **Sound** property will be set to the path to the sound file associated with a particular accident. The **TimePosition** property will store information about the time when the accident is supposed to happen, counting from the race start. Next, let's create a view model.

AccidentViewModel

Let's create a new class in the **ViewModels** folder and name it **AccidentViewModel**. Here's the code:

```
using CommunityToolkit.Mvvm.ComponentModel;
using Slugrace.Models;

namespace Slugrace.ViewModels;

public partial class AccidentViewModel : ObservableObject
{
    private readonly Accident accident;

    private readonly Dictionary<AccidentType, string> AccidentNames = new()
    {
        { AccidentType.BrokenLeg, "Broken Leg" },
        { AccidentType.Overheat, "Overheat" },
        { AccidentType.HeartAttack, "Heart Attack" },
        { AccidentType.Grass, "Grass" },
        { AccidentType.Asleep, "Asleep" },
        { AccidentType.Blind, "Blind" },
        { AccidentType.Puddle, "Puddle" },
        { AccidentType.Electroshock, "Electroshock" },
        { AccidentType.TurningBack, "Turning Back" },
        { AccidentType.Devoured, "Devoured" }
    };

    private readonly Dictionary<AccidentType, string[]> Headlines = new()
    {
        { AccidentType.BrokenLeg, [
            "just broke his leg and is grounded!",
            "broke his leg, which is practically all he consists of!",
            "suffered from an open fracture. All he can do now is watch the others win!",
            "broke his only leg and now looks pretty helpless!",
            "tripped over a root and broke his leg!"
        ] },
        { AccidentType.Overheat, [
            "has been running faster than he should have. He burned of overheat!",
            "burned by friction. Needs to cool down a bit before the next race!",
            "roasted on the track from overheat. He's been running way too fast!",
            "looks like he has been running faster than his body cooling system can handle!",
            "shouldn't have been speeding like that. Overheating can be dangerous!"
        ] },
        { AccidentType.HeartAttack, [
            "had a heart attack. Definitely needs a rest!",
            "has a poor heart condition. Hadn't he stopped now, it could have killed him!",
            "beaten by cardiac infarction. He'd better go to hospital asap!",
            "almost killed by heart attack. He had a really narrow escape!",
            "beaten by his weak heart. He'd better get some rest!"
        ] },
```

```
        { AccidentType.Grass, [
            "just found magic grass. It's famous for powering slugs up!",
            "just about to speed up after eating magic grass!",
            "powered up by magic grass found unexpectedly on the track!",
            "seems to be full of beans after having eaten the magic grass on his way!",
            "heading perhaps even for victory after his magic grass meal!"
        ] },
        { AccidentType.Asleep, [
            "just fell asleep for a while after the long and wearisome running!",
            "having a nap. He again has chosen just the perfect time for that!",
            "sleeping instead of running. It's getting one of his bad habits!",
            "always takes a short nap at this time of the day, no matter what he's doing!",
            "knows how important sleep is. Even if it's not the best time for that!"
        ] },
        { AccidentType.Blind, [
            "gone blind. Now staggering to find his way!",
            "shouldn't have been reading in dark. Now it's hard to find the way!",
            "temporarily lost his eyesight. Now it's difficult for him to follow the track!",
            "trying hard to find his way after going blind on track!",
            "staggering to finish the race after going blind because of an infection!"
        ] },
        { AccidentType.Puddle, [
            "drowning in a puddle of water!",
            "beaten by yesterday's heavy rainfalls. Just drowning in a puddle!",
            "shouldn't have skipped his swimming lessons. Drowning in a puddle now!",
            "has always neglected his swimming lessons. How wrong he’s been!",
            "disappearing in a puddle of water formed afted heavy rainfall!"
        ] },
        { AccidentType.Electroshock, [
            "speeding up after being struck by lightning!",
            "powered up by lightning. Now running really fast!",
            "hit by electric discharge. Seems to have been powered up by it!",
            "accelerated by a book of electric discharges!",
            "now running much faster after being struck by lightning!"
        ] },
        { AccidentType.TurningBack, [
            "has forgotten to turn off the gas. Must hurry home before it's too late!",
            "just received a phone call. His house is on fire. No time to lose!",
            "seems to have more interesting stuff to do than racing.",
            "seems to have lost orientation. Well, how these little brains work!",
            "has left his snack in the kitchen. He won't race when he's hungry!"
        ] },
        { AccidentType.Devoured, [
            "devoured by the infamous slug monster. Bad luck!",
            "just swallowed by the terrible slug monster!",
            "next on the long list of the slug monster's victims!",
            "has never suspected he's gonna end up as a snack!",
            "devoured by the legendary slug monster from the nearby swamps!"
        ] }
    };

    private readonly Dictionary<AccidentType, string> Sounds = new()
    {
        { AccidentType.BrokenLeg, "Broken Leg.mp3" },
        { AccidentType.Overheat, "Overheat.mp3" },
        { AccidentType.HeartAttack, "Heart Attack.mp3" },
        { AccidentType.Grass, "Grass.mp3" },
        { AccidentType.Asleep, "Asleep.mp3" },
        { AccidentType.Blind, "Blind.mp3" },
        { AccidentType.Puddle, "Drown.mp3" },
        { AccidentType.Electroshock, "Electroshock.mp3" },
```

```
        { AccidentType.TurningBack, "Turning Back.mp3" },
        { AccidentType.Devoured, "Devoured.mp3" }
    };

    private readonly Dictionary<AccidentType, uint> AccidentDurations = new()
    {
        { AccidentType.BrokenLeg, 0 },
        { AccidentType.Overheat, 0 },
        { AccidentType.HeartAttack, 0 },
        { AccidentType.Grass, 2000 },
        { AccidentType.Asleep, 0 },
        { AccidentType.Blind, 10000 },
        { AccidentType.Puddle, 0 },
        { AccidentType.Electroshock, 2000 },
        { AccidentType.TurningBack, 0 },
        { AccidentType.Devoured, 0 }
    };

    [ObservableProperty]
    [NotifyPropertyChangedFor(nameof(Name))]
    [NotifyPropertyChangedFor(nameof(Headline))]
    [NotifyPropertyChangedFor(nameof(Sound))]
    private AccidentType accidentType;

    public string Name => AccidentNames[AccidentType];

    public string Headline
    {
        get
        {
            var availableHeadlines = Headlines[AccidentType];
            return availableHeadlines[new Random().Next(0, availableHeadlines.Length)];
        }
    }

    public string Sound => Sounds[AccidentType];

    public uint TimePosition
    {
        get => accident.TimePosition;
        set
        {
            if (accident.TimePosition != value)
            {
                accident.TimePosition = value;
                OnPropertyChanged();
            }
        }
    }

    public uint Duration => AccidentDurations[AccidentType];

    [ObservableProperty]
    private SlugViewModel? affectedSlug;

    public AccidentViewModel(AccidentType accidentType)
    {
        accident = new Accident();
        AccidentType = accidentType;
    }
}
```

In the constructor we create a new instance of **Accident** of a specified type. We use a couple dictionaries with the accident type as the key. They contain accident names, headlines, sounds and accident durations. Then we can easily define the properties. These are readonly properties where a value from a dictionary is returned by key. The **Headline** property is set to a random string from the **Headlines** dictionary, so that we don't see the same message over and over again.

We also define a couple properties that are not readonly. One of them is **TimePosition**. Another is **AffectedSlug**. The latter will store a **SlugViewModel** instance representing the slug to which the accident is going to happen.

We're going to use the **AccidentViewModel** in the **GameViewModel** to control accidents. Let's do it next.

Controlling Accidents

We'll need access to **AccidentViewModel** and some other stuff in the **GameViewModel**, so let's modify it:

```
...
public partial class GameViewModel : ObservableObject
{
    SoundViewModel soundViewModel;
    private readonly IPopupService? popupService;
    public AccidentViewModel? AccidentViewModel;

    readonly IDispatcherTimer gameTimer;
    ...
    private uint finishTime;

    [ObservableProperty]
    private uint secondTime;

    [ObservableProperty]
    private bool muted;

    [ObservableProperty]
    private bool accidentShouldHappen;

    [ObservableProperty]
    private IAudioPlayer? accidentSoundPlayer;

    [ObservableProperty]
    private uint afterAccidentTime = 0;

public GameViewModel(SoundViewModel soundViewModel, IPopupService popupService)
    {
        ...
        this.soundViewModel = soundViewModel;
        this.popupService = popupService;
        ...
    }

    ...
}
```

Here we added a couple properties we're going to need. Some of them are related to different times associated with accidents. We also have properties that will be used for accident sounds and popups. We'll create a special popup to be used with accidents in a moment.

We'll discuss all these properties in more detail when we need them.

Let's have a look at the **StartRace** method first. At this moment the slugs run pretty fast. This is good for testing purposes, but they shouldn't be that fast in the actual game, so I doubled the slugs' running times to make them run slower. Now it's time to implement the accident logic:

```
...
public partial class GameViewModel : ObservableObject
{
    ...
    async Task StartRace()
    {
        Slugs[0].RunningTime = (uint)new Random().Next(6000, 14000);
        Slugs[1].RunningTime = (uint)new Random().Next(8000, 14000);
        Slugs[2].RunningTime = (uint)new Random().Next(8000, 14000);
        Slugs[3].RunningTime = (uint)new Random().Next(10000, 16000);

        // Check for accident.
        bool thereIsAnAccident;
        bool accidentExpected = new Random().Next(0, 4) == 0;

        // Should there be an accident?
        if (RaceNumber > 5 && accidentExpected)
        {
            // If so, then...
            thereIsAnAccident = true;

            // Which one?
            AccidentType[] accidentTypes = (AccidentType[])Enum.GetValues(
                typeof(AccidentType));

            var type = accidentTypes[new Random().Next(0, accidentTypes.Length)];

            AccidentViewModel = new AccidentViewModel(type);

            // Which slug should be affected?
            AccidentViewModel.AffectedSlug = Slugs[new Random().Next(0, Slugs.Count)];

            // When should it happen?
            AccidentViewModel.TimePosition = (uint)new Random().Next(
                (int)(AccidentViewModel.AffectedSlug.RunningTime * .2),
                (int)(AccidentViewModel.AffectedSlug.RunningTime * .4));
            // Modify affected slug's running time
            if (AccidentViewModel.Duration > 0)
            {
                if (AccidentViewModel.AccidentType == AccidentType.Grass)
                {
                    AfterAccidentTime = AccidentViewModel.AffectedSlug.RunningTime / 4;

                    AccidentViewModel.AffectedSlug.RunningTime =
                        AccidentViewModel.TimePosition
                        + AccidentViewModel.Duration
                        + AfterAccidentTime;
                }
```

```
            if (AccidentViewModel.AccidentType == AccidentType.Electroshock)
            {
                AfterAccidentTime = AccidentViewModel.AffectedSlug.RunningTime / 4;

                AccidentViewModel.AffectedSlug.RunningTime =
                    AccidentViewModel.TimePosition
                    + AccidentViewModel.Duration
                    + AfterAccidentTime;
            }
        }
    }
    else
    {
        thereIsAnAccident = false;
    }

    // Set race-related times
    uint[] runningTimes = [
        Slugs[0].RunningTime,
        Slugs[1].RunningTime,
        Slugs[2].RunningTime,
        Slugs[3].RunningTime
    ];

    RaceTime = runningTimes.Max();
    MinTime = runningTimes.Min();
    FinishTime = (uint)(.79 * MinTime);
    SecondTime = runningTimes.Order().ToArray()[1];

    AccidentShouldHappen = thereIsAnAccident;

    // Start race
    RaceStatus = RaceStatus.Started;
    ...
```

The particular parts of the code above are commented in a clear way, so that you know what they're for.

So, first of all, we must decide whether there should be an accident at all. We don't want any accidents to happen in the first couple races so that the user can get used to the game. After the fifth race, an accident will happen if the **accidentExpected** variable is set to **true**. This variable is set randomly by comparing a random integer between 0 and 3 to 0. If it's true, an accident is expected to happen. Otherwise, no accident will happen in a given race.

If an accident is to happen, we must decide which one. This is also set randomly. And then the **AccidentViewModel** object of the specified type is created.

Next, a random slug is picked to be affected by the accident.

The time when the accident should happen is also set randomly, within a certain range.

For some accidents, the running time of the affected slug is adjusted.

Then we gather all the running times of the slugs and set the **RaceTime** property to the max running time. We also set the **MinTime** property, the **FinishTime** property and the **SecondTime** property. The **SecondTime** property will be needed when the fastest slug is stopped by an accident and can't continue the race.

After all these properties are set, the **RunRace** method is called. Let's have a look at it next:

```
...
public partial class GameViewModel : ObservableObject
{
    ...
    private async Task RunRace()
    {
        _ = soundViewModel.PlaySound("Game", "Slugs Running.mp3", .5, true);

        // Modify finish time if the fastest slug has an accident.
        if (AccidentViewModel != null
            && AccidentViewModel.AffectedSlug != null
            && AccidentViewModel.AffectedSlug.RunningTime == MinTime)
        {
            if (AccidentViewModel.Duration == 0)
            {
                FinishTime = (uint)(.79 * SecondTime);
            }
            else
            {
                uint secondFinishTime = (uint)(SecondTime * .79);

                if (secondFinishTime < FinishTime)
                {
                    FinishTime = secondFinishTime;
                    MinTime = SecondTime;
                }
            }
        }

        await Task.Delay((int)FinishTime);

        RaceWinnerSlug = Slugs.Where(
            s => s.RunningTime == MinTime).FirstOrDefault();

        if (AccidentShouldHappen
            && AccidentViewModel != null
            && RaceWinnerSlug == AccidentViewModel.AffectedSlug
            && AccidentViewModel.Duration == 0)
        {
            RaceWinnerSlug = Slugs.Where(
                s => s.RunningTime == SecondTime).FirstOrDefault();
        }

        if (RaceWinnerSlug != null)
        {
            _ = soundViewModel.PlaySound("Slugs Winning", RaceWinnerSlug.WinSound);
        ...
```

First, we modify the finish time if the fastest slug has an accident, and in particular, if it's an accident where the **Duration** property is set to zero. These are accidents in which the slug stops running and never reaches the finish line, so the winner is the slug with the second time.

Fine, but where are the accidents handled actually? Well, let's see.

Handling the Accidents

The accidents will be implemented as animations, so we'll write the code in the code-behind. Let's start by opening the **TrackImage.xaml** file and making sure the layout is given a name so that we can reference it in code:

```
...
<ContentView ...>

    <AbsoluteLayout x:Name="layout">
        <!--Racetrack-->
        <Image
            ...
```

And now let's open the code-behind. This is where the actual accident animations will be handled.

We'll need some variables for accident handling. Let's define and initialize them now:

```
...
public partial class TrackImage : ContentView
{
    ...
    Animation? slowpokeMovement;

    // accident handling
    SlugImage? slugImage;
    string? runningAnimationName;

    string? brokenLegImage;
    string overheatBodyImage;
    string overheatEyeImage;
    string heartImage;
    string grassImage;
    string puddleImage;
    string boltImage;
    string monsterImage;

    Image? accidentImage;
    Animation? accidentAnimation;

    public TrackImage()
    {
        InitializeComponent();

        overheatBodyImage = "overheat_body.png";
        overheatEyeImage = "overheat_eye.png";
```

```
        heartImage = "heart_attack.png";
        grassImage = "grass.png";
        puddleImage = "puddle.png";
        boltImage = "electroshock.png";
        monsterImage = "slug_monster.png";
    }

    protected override void LayoutChildren(...)
    ...
```

In the constructor we assign images to the particular variables.

Next, let's modify the **Vm_PropertyChanged** method to also take accidents into account. We'll do it by defining a method, **HandleAccident**, and calling it inside **Vm_PropertyChanged** whenever the **AccidentShouldHappen** property in the **GameViewModel** changes. Besides, we'll add another method, **HandleRunning** that will hold most of the current functionality, plus it will reset before each race the properties modified by an accident, like **ZIndex**, **Opacity** or **ScaleX** and also remove the accident image. It will also restart the affected slug's eye rotation because in some accidents the eyes stop moving.

Let's start with the eye rotation actually. To make things easier, let's add a **StartEyeRotation** method to the **SlugImage** class:

```
namespace Slugrace.Controls;

public partial class SlugImage : ContentView
{
    Animation eyeAnimation;
    uint rotationSpeed;

    public Image LeftEye { get; set; }
    public Image RightEye { get; set; }

    public SlugImage()
    {
        InitializeComponent();

        eyeAnimation = new Animation()
        {
            {0, .5, new Animation(v => leftEye.Rotation = v, 0, -30) },
            {0, .5, new Animation(v => rightEye.Rotation = v, 0, 30) },
            {.5, 1, new Animation(v => leftEye.Rotation = v, -30, 0) },
            {.5, 1, new Animation(v => rightEye.Rotation = v, 30, 0) }
        };

        LeftEye = leftEye;
        RightEye = rightEye;

        StartEyeRotation();
    }
```

```
    public void StartEyeRotation()
    {
        rotationSpeed = (uint)new Random().Next(2000, 4000);
        eyeAnimation.Commit(
            this,
            "eyeRotation",
            16,
            rotationSpeed,
            null,
            null,
            () => true);
    }
}
```

And now we can modify the **TrackImage** class:

```
...
public partial class TrackImage : ContentView
{
    ...
    private void Vm_PropertyChanged(object sender, PropertyChangedEventArgs e)
    {
        if (e.PropertyName == nameof(vm.RaceStatus))
        {
            HandleRunning();
        }
        else if (e.PropertyName == nameof(vm.AccidentShouldHappen))
        {
            _ = HandleAccident();
        }
    }

    private void HandleRunning()
    {
        if (vm.RaceStatus == RaceStatus.Started)
        {
            speedsterMovement?.Commit(
                ...
            trustyMovement?.Commit(
                ...
            iffyMovement?.Commit(
                ...
            slowpokeMovement?.Commit(
                ...
        }
        else if (vm.RaceStatus == RaceStatus.NotYetStarted)
        {
            ...
            slowpoke.TranslationX = 0;

            if (layout.Contains(accidentImage))
            {
                if (accidentImage != null && accidentImage.ZIndex != 0)
                {
                    accidentImage.ZIndex = 0;
                }
```

```
                layout.Remove(accidentImage);
            }

            if (accidentAnimation != null)
            {
                this.AbortAnimation("accidentAnimation");
            }

            if (slugImage != null)
            {
                slugImage.StartEyeRotation();

                if (slugImage.ZIndex != 0)
                {
                    slugImage.ZIndex = 0;
                }

                if (slugImage.Opacity != 1)
                {
                    slugImage.Opacity = 1;
                }

                if (slugImage.ScaleX != 1)
                {
                    slugImage.ScaleX = 1;
                }
            }
        }
        else
        {
            this.AbortAnimation("moveSpeedster");
            this.AbortAnimation("moveTrusty");
            this.AbortAnimation("moveIffy");
            this.AbortAnimation("moveSlowpoke");
        }
    }

    private async Task HandleAccident()
    {
        if (vm != null
            && vm.AccidentViewModel != null
            && vm.AccidentShouldHappen)
        {
            // slug data
            if (vm.AccidentViewModel != null
                && vm.AccidentViewModel.AffectedSlug == vm.Slugs[0])
            {
                slugImage = speedster;
                runningAnimationName = "moveSpeedster";
                brokenLegImage = "broken_leg_speedster.png";
            }
            else if (vm.AccidentViewModel.AffectedSlug == vm.Slugs[1])
            {
                slugImage = trusty;
                runningAnimationName = "moveTrusty";
                brokenLegImage = "broken_leg_trusty.png";
            }
```

```
            else if (vm.AccidentViewModel.AffectedSlug == vm.Slugs[2])
            {
                slugImage = iffy;
                runningAnimationName = "moveIffy";
                brokenLegImage = "broken_leg_iffy.png";
            }
            else if (vm.AccidentViewModel.AffectedSlug == vm.Slugs[3])
            {
                slugImage = slowpoke;
                runningAnimationName = "moveSlowpoke";
                brokenLegImage = "broken_leg_slowpoke.png";
            }

            // accident type
            switch (vm.AccidentViewModel.AccidentType)
            {
                case AccidentType.BrokenLeg:
                    await HandleBrokenLeg();
                    break;
                case AccidentType.Overheat:
                    await HandleOverheat();
                    break;
                case AccidentType.HeartAttack:
                    await HandleHeartAttack();
                    break;
                case AccidentType.Grass:
                    await HandleGrass();
                    break;
                case AccidentType.Asleep:
                    await HandleAsleep();
                    break;
                case AccidentType.Blind:
                    await HandleBlind();
                    break;
                case AccidentType.Puddle:
                    await HandlePuddle();
                    break;
                case AccidentType.Electroshock:
                    await HandleElectroshock();
                    break;
                case AccidentType.TurningBack:
                    await HandleTurningBack();
                    break;
                case AccidentType.Devoured:
                    await HandleDevoured();
                    break;
                default:
                    break;
            }
        }
    }
}
```

As you can see, in the **HandleAccident** method we assign images and animations and call a method to handle the accident, depending on which accident type is to happen.

Before we implement the particular methods to handle the accidents, we'll have to create a popup that will show up whenever an accident happens.

Accident Popup

We'll create a small popup that will appear if an accident happens. It will contain the image of the slug affected by the accident and a headline. We'll also create a separate view model for the popup. Actually, let's start with that. In the **ViewModels** folder add a new class and name it **AccidentPopupViewModel**. Here's the code:

```
using CommunityToolkit.Mvvm.ComponentModel;

namespace Slugrace.ViewModels;

public partial class AccidentPopupViewModel : ObservableObject
{
    [ObservableProperty]
    private string affectedSlugImageUrl = string.Empty;

    [ObservableProperty]
    [NotifyPropertyChangedFor(nameof(HeadlineMessage))]
    private string affectedSlugName = string.Empty;

    [ObservableProperty]
    [NotifyPropertyChangedFor(nameof(HeadlineMessage))]
    private string accidentHeadline = string.Empty;

    public string HeadlineMessage => $"{AffectedSlugName} {AccidentHeadline}";

    public void ShowAccidentInfo(AccidentViewModel accidentViewModel)
    {
        if (accidentViewModel.AffectedSlug != null)
        {
            AffectedSlugImageUrl = accidentViewModel.AffectedSlug.ImageUrl;
            AffectedSlugName = accidentViewModel.AffectedSlug.Name;
            AccidentHeadline = accidentViewModel.Headline;
        }
    }
}
```

Here we define a couple properties that will be required by the popup. The **HeadlineMessage** property combines the name of the affected slug with the actual headline.

Next, let's create the popup itself. Add a new class to the **Popups** folder and name it **AccidentPopup**. Here's the XAML file:

```
<?xml version="1.0" encoding="utf-8" ?>
<toolkit:Popup xmlns="http://schemas.microsoft.com/dotnet/2021/maui"
             xmlns:x="http://schemas.microsoft.com/winfx/2009/xaml"
             xmlns:toolkit="http://schemas.microsoft.com/dotnet/2022/maui/toolkit"
             x:Class="Slugrace.Popups.AccidentPopup"
```

```
            HorizontalOptions="Center"
            VerticalOptions="Start"
            Color="Black">
    <VerticalStackLayout
        Padding="10"
        WidthRequest="500"
        HeightRequest="240">
        <Label
            Text="BREAKING NEWS"
            FontSize="30"
            TextColor="Red" />
        <Line
            Stroke="CadetBlue"
            StrokeThickness="1"
            X1="10"
            Y1="10"
            X2="460"
            Y2="10" />
        <Grid
            Margin="10"
            ColumnDefinitions="1.5*, 3.5*">
            <Image
                Source="{Binding AffectedSlugImageUrl}" />
            <Label
                Grid.Column="1"
                HorizontalTextAlignment="Start"
                VerticalTextAlignment="Center"
                Text="{Binding HeadlineMessage}"
                FontSize="25"
                FontAttributes="Bold,Italic"
                TextColor="Red" />
        </Grid>
    </VerticalStackLayout>
</toolkit:Popup>
```

The popup will be centered horizontally and it will appear at the top of the window. There are a couple elements: a label, a horizontal line and a grid with the image of the slug and the headline message.

Here's the code-behind:

```
using CommunityToolkit.Maui.Views;
using Slugrace.ViewModels;

namespace Slugrace.Popups;

public partial class AccidentPopup : Popup
{
    public AccidentPopup(AccidentPopupViewModel accidentPopupViewModel)
    {
        InitializeComponent();
        BindingContext = accidentPopupViewModel;
    }
}
```

All we do here is set the binding context. Let's also register the popup and the view model with the dependency service in **MauiProgram.cs**:

```
...
public static class MauiProgram
{
    ...
        builder.Services.AddSingleton(AudioManager.Current);
        builder.Services.AddTransientPopup<AccidentPopup, AccidentPopupViewModel>();

        return builder.Build();
        }
}
```

We need a way to display the popup. To this end, we'll add a **DisplayAccidentPopup** method to the **GaveViewModel**:

```
...
public partial class GameViewModel : ObservableObject
{
    ...
    public void MuteUnmute()
    ...
    public void DisplayAccidentPopup()
    {
        if (popupService != null && AccidentViewModel != null)
        {
            popupService.ShowPopup<AccidentPopupViewModel>(
            onPresenting: viewModel => viewModel.ShowAccidentInfo(AccidentViewModel));
        }
    }
}
```

We're using an **IPopupService** here, which has the **ShowPopup** method that we can use. We have to specify the view model we want to use. As we also want to pass data to the popup view model, we have to use the **onPresenting** parameter, which is of the **Action<TViewModel>** delegate type. Here the **ShowAccidentInfo** method is called that we defined in the view model.

If you click anywhere outside the popup, it will be dismissed.

Besides displaying the accident popup when an accident happens, we also should hear a sound associated with the accident. Let's take care of it next.

Accident Sound

As far as sound is concerned in our app, it's the responsibility of the **SoundViewModel**, so let's start right there. We'll modify the code slightly:

```
...
public partial class SoundViewModel : ObservableObject
{
    ...
    private List<IAudioPlayer> effectPlayers;
    private List<IAudioPlayer> loopingAccidentPlayers;

    [ObservableProperty]
    private double volume;
    ...
    public SoundViewModel(IAudioManager audioManager)
    {
        this.audioManager = audioManager;
        effectPlayers = [];
        loopingAccidentPlayers = [];
        Volume = .3;
    }
    ...
    public async Task PlaySound(
        string folderName,
        string fileName,
        double volume = 1,
        bool loop = false,
        bool loopingAccidentSound = false)
    {
        ...
        var player = audioManager.CreatePlayer(
            await FileSystem.OpenAppPackageFileAsync(path));

        if (!loopingAccidentSound)
        {
            effectPlayers.Add(player);
        }
        else
        {
            loopingAccidentPlayers.Add(player);
        }

        player.Volume = volume;
        ...
    }
    ...
    public void Clean(bool loopingAccidentSound = false)
    {
        if (!loopingAccidentSound)
        {
            foreach (var player in effectPlayers)
            {
                if (player.IsPlaying)
                {
                    player.Stop();
                }

                player.Dispose();
            }

            effectPlayers.Clear();
        }
        else
        {
            foreach (var player in loopingAccidentPlayers)
```

```
            {
                if (player.IsPlaying)
                {
                    player.Stop();
                }

                player.Dispose();
            }

            loopingAccidentPlayers.Clear();
        }
    }

    public async Task Attenuate()
    ...
}
```

First, we add a list of **IAudioPlayer**s called **loopingAccidentPlayers** to store sounds that should be played continuously in a loop when an accident happens. This will be the case, for example, with the HeartAttack accident when we will hear the heart beating until we hit the Next Race button. The list is instantiated in the constructor.

Next, we modify the **PlaySound** method. It now takes an additional **loopingAccidentSound** parameter of type bool. If it's set to **false**, the **IAudioPlayer** is added to the **effectPlayers** list. Otherwise, it's added to the **loopingAccidentPlayers** list.

We also modify the **Clean** method. It now also takes a **loopingAccidentSound** parameter. Depending on its value, either the **effectPlayers** or the **loopingAccidentPlayers** list is cleared.

With that in place, let's add two methods to the **GameViewModel**: one to play and the other to stop the accident sound:

```
...
public partial class GameViewModel : ObservableObject
{
    ...
    void NextRace()
    {
        soundViewModel.Clean();
        soundViewModel.Clean(true);

        RaceStatus = RaceStatus.NotYetStarted;
        ...
    }
    ...
    public void DisplayAccidentPopup()
    ...
    public void PlayAccidentSound(bool loop = false, bool loopingAccidentSound = false)
    {
        if (AccidentViewModel != null)
        {
            _ = soundViewModel.PlaySound(
                "Accidents",
                AccidentViewModel.Sound,
```

```
                loop: loop,
                loopingAccidentSound: loopingAccidentSound);
        }
    }

    public void StopAccidentSound()
    {
        soundViewModel.Clean(true);
    }
}
```

We also call the **Clean** method in the **NextRace** method twice to clear both **IAudioPlayer** lists.

And now we're ready to implement the particular accidents. However, accidents are supposed to happen randomly and rather not too frequently, which makes it difficult and time-consuming to test them. This is why we have to temporarily modify the accident-related code in the **GameViewModel**.

Testing Accidents

We want to ensure two things to make testing accidents easier. First, the accident should happen in each race. Secondly, we should be able to decide which accident happens.

To do the former, let's comment out the line of code where the condition is checked whether an accident should happen and use a condition that is always true, like 2 + 2 == 4.

To do the latter, let's manually pass the index from the **accidentTypes** list. Let's start with index 0, which corresponds the Broken Leg accident:

```
...
public partial class GameViewModel : ObservableObject
{
    ...
    async Task StartRace()
    {
        ...
        // Should there be an accident?
        //if (RaceNumber > 5 && AccidentViewModel.Expected)
        if (2 + 2 == 4)
        {
            // If so, then...
            thereIsAnAccident = true;

            // Which one?
            AccidentType[] accidentTypes = (
                AccidentType[])Enum.GetValues(typeof(AccidentType));

            //var type = accidentTypes[new Random().Next(0, accidentTypes.Length)];
            var type = accidentTypes[0];

            AccidentViewModel = new AccidentViewModel(type);

            // Which slug should be affected?
            ...
```

And now let's implement the accidents one by one. Each accident will be implemented in a separate asynchronous method in the **TrackImage** class. In order for the code to compile, let's add some temporary implementations of the methods (we'll make them asynchronous later):

```
...
public partial class TrackImage : ContentView
{
    ...
    private async Task HandleAccident()
    {
        ...
            // accident type
            switch (vm.AccidentViewModel.AccidentType)
            ...
        }
    }

    private Task HandleBrokenLeg()
    {
        throw new NotImplementedException();
    }

    private Task HandleOverheat()
    {
        throw new NotImplementedException();
    }

    private Task HandleHeartAttack()
    {
        throw new NotImplementedException();
    }

    private Task HandleGrass()
    {
        throw new NotImplementedException();
    }

    private Task HandleAsleep()
    {
        throw new NotImplementedException();
    }

    private Task HandleBlind()
    {
        throw new NotImplementedException();
    }

    private Task HandlePuddle()
    {
        throw new NotImplementedException();
    }

    private Task HandleElectroshock()
    {
        throw new NotImplementedException();
    }
```

```
    private Task HandleTurningBack()
    {
        throw new NotImplementedException();
    }

    private Task HandleDevoured()
    {
        throw new NotImplementedException();
    }
}
```

Let's start with the Broken Leg accident.

Broken Leg Accident

This accident will be implemented inside the **HandleBrokenLeg** method. When the race begins, nothing happens until the accident's **TimePosition** is reached, which is a randomized value and may differ from race to race within a certain range.

When this time has elapsed, the running animation is canceled and the slug stops moving.

The **BodyImageUrl** property is set to **brokenLegImage**, which is different for each slug.

We also hear the accident sound and see the accident popup.

Here's the code:

```
...
public partial class TrackImage : ContentView
{
    ...
    private async Task HandleAccident()
    ...
    private async Task HandleBrokenLeg()
    {
        if (vm != null
            && vm.AccidentViewModel != null
            && vm.AccidentViewModel.AffectedSlug != null
            && brokenLegImage != null)
        {
            await Task.Delay((int)vm.AccidentViewModel.TimePosition);
            this.AbortAnimation(runningAnimationName);
            vm.AccidentViewModel.AffectedSlug.BodyImageUrl = brokenLegImage;
            vm.PlayAccidentSound();
            vm.DisplayAccidentPopup();
        }
    }
    ...
}
```

Let's now run the app and start a race. After a while, one of the slugs will break his leg. Here's what it looks like with the popup on Windows and Android:

WINDOWS

ANDROID

And here's what it looks like when you dismiss the popup on Windows:

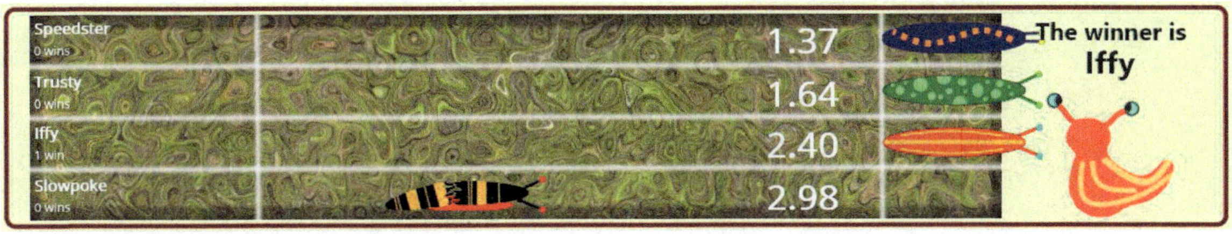

With the other accidents, I'll show you what it looks like without the popup on Windows. On Android it looks pretty much the same.

If we now hit the Next Race button, Iffy will start the next race with a broken leg, which isn't what we want. Remember: Whatever happens to the slugs in a race, they don't suffer and they always start the next race fully healed.

So, let's take care of the healing process.

As the body image and the eye images of the slugs will be replaced in some accidents, like the body image here, let's add two properties to the **`Slug`** model to store the default values, so the ones the slugs should always start with.

Here's the **`Slug`** class:

```
namespace Slugrace.Models;

public class Slug
{
    ...
    public string EyeImageUrl { get; set; } = string.Empty;
    public string BodyImageUrl { get; set; } = string.Empty;
    public string DefaultEyeImageUrl { get; set; } = string.Empty;
    public string DefaultBodyImageUrl { get; set; } = string.Empty;
    public double BaseOdds { get; set; }
    ...
}
```

We also need to implement the default image properties in the **`SlugViewModel`**:

```
...
public partial class SlugViewModel : ObservableObject
{
    ...
    public string BodyImageUrl
    ...
    public string DefaultEyeImageUrl
    {
        get => slug.DefaultEyeImageUrl;
```

```
        set
        {
            if (slug.DefaultEyeImageUrl != value)
            {
                slug.DefaultEyeImageUrl = value;
                OnPropertyChanged();
            }
        }
    }

    public string DefaultBodyImageUrl
    {
        get => slug.DefaultBodyImageUrl;
        set
        {
            if (slug.DefaultBodyImageUrl != value)
            {
                slug.DefaultBodyImageUrl = value;
                OnPropertyChanged();
            }
        }
    }

    [ObservableProperty]
    [NotifyPropertyChangedFor(nameof(WinPercentage))]
    private int currentRaceNumber;
    ...
```

Next, let's go to the **`SettingsViewModel`** and set the properties for each slug there:

```
...
public partial class SettingsViewModel : ObservableObject
{
    ...
    async Task StartGame()
    {
        // Populate the Game object
        game.Slugs =
        [
            new Slug
            {
                ...
                EyeImageUrl = "speedster_eye.png",
                BodyImageUrl = "speedster_body.png",
                DefaultEyeImageUrl = "speedster_eye.png",
                DefaultBodyImageUrl = "speedster_body.png",
                WinSound = "Speedster Win.mp3"
            },
            new Slug
            {
                ...
                EyeImageUrl = "trusty_eye.png",
                BodyImageUrl = "trusty_body.png",
                DefaultEyeImageUrl = "trusty_eye.png",
                DefaultBodyImageUrl = "trusty_body.png",
                WinSound = "Trusty Win.mp3"
            },
            new Slug
            {
                ...
                EyeImageUrl = "iffy_eye.png",
                BodyImageUrl = "iffy_body.png",
                DefaultEyeImageUrl = "iffy_eye.png",
                DefaultBodyImageUrl = "iffy_body.png",
                WinSound = "Iffy Win.mp3"
            },
            new Slug
            {
                ...
                EyeImageUrl = "slowpoke_eye.png",
                BodyImageUrl = "slowpoke_body.png",
                DefaultEyeImageUrl = "slowpoke_eye.png",
                DefaultBodyImageUrl = "slowpoke_body.png",
                WinSound = "Slowpoke Win.mp3"
            }
        ];

        var playersInGame = Players.Where(p => p.PlayerIsInGame).ToList();
        ...
```

We also have to set the appropriate properties in the **OnGameChanged** method of the **GameViewModel**:

```
...
public partial class GameViewModel : ObservableObject
...
    partial void OnGameChanged(Game? value)
    {
        ...
        Slugs =
        [
            new()
            {
                ...
                EyeImageUrl = value.Slugs[0].EyeImageUrl,
                BodyImageUrl = value.Slugs[0].BodyImageUrl,
                DefaultEyeImageUrl = value.Slugs[0].DefaultEyeImageUrl,
                DefaultBodyImageUrl = value.Slugs[0].DefaultBodyImageUrl,
                WinNumber = 0,
                ...
            },
            new()
            {
                ...
                EyeImageUrl = value.Slugs[1].EyeImageUrl,
                BodyImageUrl = value.Slugs[1].BodyImageUrl,
                DefaultEyeImageUrl = value.Slugs[1].DefaultEyeImageUrl,
                DefaultBodyImageUrl = value.Slugs[1].DefaultBodyImageUrl,
                WinNumber = 0,
                ...
            },
            new()
            {
                ...
                EyeImageUrl = value.Slugs[2].EyeImageUrl,
                BodyImageUrl = value.Slugs[2].BodyImageUrl,
                DefaultEyeImageUrl = value.Slugs[2].DefaultEyeImageUrl,
                DefaultBodyImageUrl = value.Slugs[2].DefaultBodyImageUrl,
                WinNumber = 0,
                ...
            },
            new()
            {
                ...
                EyeImageUrl = value.Slugs[3].EyeImageUrl,
                BodyImageUrl = value.Slugs[3].BodyImageUrl,
                DefaultEyeImageUrl = value.Slugs[3].DefaultEyeImageUrl,
                DefaultBodyImageUrl = value.Slugs[3].DefaultBodyImageUrl,
                WinNumber = 0,
                ...
            },
        ];

        List<PlayerViewModel> players = [];
        ...
```

Finally, let's restore the images in the **NextRace** method in the **GameViewModel** to the default values so that the default images are used in the next race. In case of the Broken Leg accident, we didn't replace the eye images, but in some other accidents they will be replaced, that's why we reset both images here. We also set **AccidentViewModel** to **null** because if there should be an accident in the next race, a new instance will be created anyway. By default there is no accident in a race, so we set **AccidentShouldHappen** to **false**:

```
...
public partial class GameViewModel : ObservableObject
{
    ...
    void NextRace()
    {
        ...
        RaceWinnerSlug = null;

        AccidentViewModel = null;

        AccidentShouldHappen = false;

        foreach (var player in Players)
        ...
        foreach (var slug in Slugs)
        {
            if (slug.BodyImageUrl != slug.DefaultBodyImageUrl)
            {
                slug.BodyImageUrl = slug.DefaultBodyImageUrl;
            }

            if (slug.EyeImageUrl != slug.DefaultEyeImageUrl)
            {
                slug.EyeImageUrl = slug.DefaultEyeImageUrl;
            }
        }
    }
    ...
}
```

Now we're done. The slug is healed. We can now move on to the next accident.

Overheat Accident

First of all, remember to change the accident type index in **GameViewModel**, so that the Overheat accident is selected:

```
...
public partial class GameViewModel : ObservableObject
{
    ...
    async Task StartRace()
    {
        ...
            var type = accidentTypes[1];
            ...
```

This is how we'll be changing the accidents to test them one by one. Just remember to change the index as we discuss each of the remaining accidents.

Then, in the **TrackImage** class add the **HandleOverheat** method:

```
...
public partial class TrackImage : ContentView
{
    ...
    private async Task HandleBrokenLeg()
    ...
    private async Task HandleOverheat()
    {
        if (vm != null
            && vm.AccidentViewModel != null
            && vm.AccidentViewModel.AffectedSlug != null
            && slugImage != null)
        {
            await Task.Delay((int)vm.AccidentViewModel.TimePosition);
            this.AbortAnimation(runningAnimationName);
            slugImage.StopEyeRotation();
            vm.AccidentViewModel.AffectedSlug.BodyImageUrl = overheatBodyImage;
            vm.AccidentViewModel.AffectedSlug.EyeImageUrl = overheatEyeImage;
            vm.PlayAccidentSound();
            vm.DisplayAccidentPopup();
        }
    }
    ...
}
```

Just like before, when the time position is reached, the running animation is canceled. But this time, we also want the eye rotation animation to stop. To this end, we define a **StopEyeRotation** method in the **SlugImage** class:

```
...
public partial class SlugImage : ContentView
{
    ...
    public void StartEyeRotation()
    ...
    public void StopEyeRotation()
    {
        this.AbortAnimation("eyeRotation");
    }
}
```

Then the body and eye images are replaced so that the slug really looks as if he was burned. We also hear the sound and see the popup.

If we now run the app and start a race, we should see the accident in action:

Naturally, the images will be reset in the following race. And now let's move on to a more complicated accident.

Heart Attack Accident

In this accident we'll use an accident image. It will be set differently for the Windows and Android platforms so that it looks similar on both of them. Here's the code:

```
...
public partial class TrackImage : ContentView
{
    ...
    private async Task HandleOverheat()
    ...
    private async Task HandleHeartAttack()
    {
        if (vm != null
            && vm.AccidentViewModel != null
            && slugImage != null)
        {
            await Task.Delay((int)vm.AccidentViewModel.TimePosition);
            this.AbortAnimation(runningAnimationName);

            accidentImage = new Image { Source = heartImage };
            layout.Add(accidentImage);

#if ANDROID
            layout.SetLayoutBounds(accidentImage, new Rect(
                slugImage.X + slugImage.TranslationX - .2 * slugImage.Width,
                slugImage.Y - slugImage.Height,
                accidentImage.Width,
                accidentImage.Height));

            accidentAnimation = new Animation()
            {
                {0, .24, new Animation(v => accidentImage.Scale = v, .4, .3) },
                {.24, 1, new Animation(v => accidentImage.Scale = v, .3, .4) }
            };
#endif

#if WINDOWS
            layout.SetLayoutBounds(accidentImage, new Rect(
                slugImage.X + slugImage.TranslationX + .4 * slugImage.Width,
                slugImage.Y,
                accidentImage.Width,
                accidentImage.Height));
```

```
            accidentAnimation = new Animation()
            {
                {0, .24, new Animation(v => accidentImage.Scale = v, .8, .6) },
                {.24, 1, new Animation(v => accidentImage.Scale = v, .6, .8) }
            };
#endif
            accidentAnimation?.Commit(
                this,
                "accidentAnimation",
                16,
                820,
                Easing.CubicInOut,
                null,
                () => true);

            vm.PlayAccidentSound(true, true);
            vm.DisplayAccidentPopup();
        }
    }
    ...
}
```

So, again, when the time position is reached, the running animation is canceled. Then the accident image representing a heart is added and positioned. Also, a heart beating animation is created. The positioning of the image and the animation are different for each platform. But then the animation is started the same way for both platforms. As always, there's a sound (a looping one this time) and we can see the popup.

If the accident happens, we should see something like this:

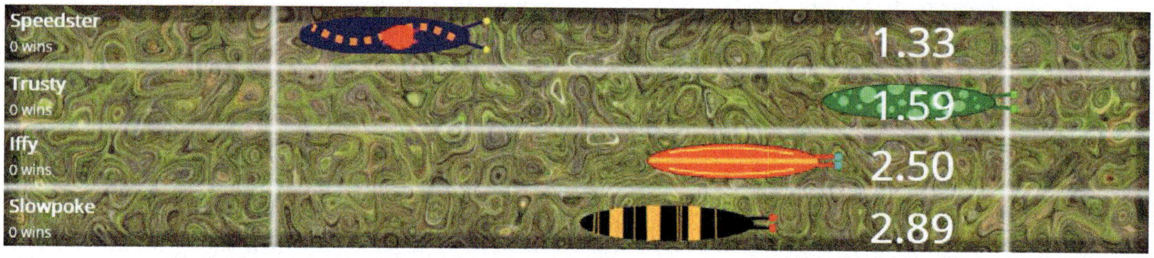

Fine, we're done with this accident. The next one is going to be even more complicated.

Grass Accident

The Grass accident consists of a couple parts. First the slug notices some grass and stops to eat. He spends some time eating. The grass gives him more strength, so after the meal he starts running faster than before. Here we have the grass image, which will be scaled and positioned differently for each platform:

```
...
public partial class TrackImage : ContentView
{
    ...
    private async Task HandleHeartAttack()
```

```
    ...
    private async Task HandleGrass()
    {
        if (vm != null
            && vm.AccidentViewModel != null
            && vm.AccidentViewModel.AffectedSlug != null
            && slugImage != null)
        {
            await Task.Delay((int)vm.AccidentViewModel.TimePosition);
            this.AbortAnimation(runningAnimationName);

            accidentImage = new Image { Source = grassImage };
            layout.Add(accidentImage);

#if ANDROID
            accidentImage.ScaleX = .5;
            accidentImage.ScaleY = .25;

            layout.SetLayoutBounds(accidentImage, new Rect(
                slugImage.X + slugImage.TranslationX + .5 * slugImage.Width,
                slugImage.Y - 2 * slugImage.Height,

                accidentImage.Width,
                accidentImage.Height));
#endif

#if WINDOWS
            layout.SetLayoutBounds(accidentImage, new Rect(
                slugImage.X + slugImage.TranslationX + slugImage.Width,
                .9 * slugImage.Y,
                accidentImage.Width,
                accidentImage.Height));
#endif

            accidentAnimation = new Animation()
            {
                {0, .24, new Animation(v => slugImage.ScaleX = v, 1, .9) },
                {.24, 1, new Animation(v => slugImage.ScaleX = v, .9, 1) }
            };

            accidentAnimation.Commit(
                this,
                "accidentAnimation",
                16,
                500,
                Easing.CubicInOut,
                null,
                () => true);

            vm.PlayAccidentSound(true, true);
            vm.DisplayAccidentPopup();

            await Task.Delay((int)vm.AccidentViewModel.Duration);

            this.AbortAnimation("accidentAnimation");

            if (layout.Contains(accidentImage))
            {
                layout.Remove(accidentImage);
            }
```

```
            vm.StopAccidentSound();

            accidentAnimation = new Animation(
                v => slugImage.TranslationX = v,
                slugImage.X + slugImage.TranslationX,
                trackLength);

            accidentAnimation.Commit(
                this,
                "accidentAnimation",
                16,
                vm.AccidentViewModel.AffectedSlug.RunningTime / 4,
                Easing.Linear, null, () => false);
        }
    }
    ...
}
```

So, after the running animation is canceled, the grass image appears, the eating sound starts playing, the popup appears, and a new animation is started. This animation scales the slug image horizontally up and down so that it looks like the slug is eating.

Next, the grass image is removed and the eating sound is stopped. A running animation is started so that the slug can finish the race. He now runs faster, but still isn't sure (although more probable) to win.

Here's what the accident looks like halfway, when the grass image is visible:

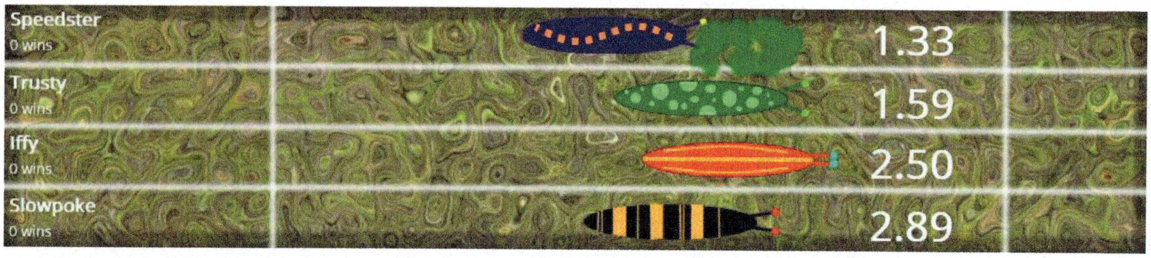

Here the slug speeds up after a nice meal. But sometimes he just falls asleep...

Asleep Accident

Here's the Asleep accident implementation:

```
...
public partial class TrackImage : ContentView
{
    ...
    private async Task HandleGrass()
    ...
    private async Task HandleAsleep()
    {
        if (vm != null
            && vm.AccidentViewModel != null
```

```
            && slugImage != null)
        {
            await Task.Delay((int)vm.AccidentViewModel.TimePosition);
            this.AbortAnimation(runningAnimationName);

            slugImage.StopEyeRotation();

            accidentAnimation = new Animation()
            {
                {0, .46, new Animation(v => slugImage.Scale = v, 1, 1.05) },
                {.46, 1, new Animation(v => slugImage.Scale = v, 1.05, 1) }
            };

            accidentAnimation.Commit(
                this,
                "accidentAnimation",
                16,
                5600,
                Easing.CubicInOut,
                null,
                () => true);


            vm.PlayAccidentSound(true, true);
            vm.DisplayAccidentPopup();
        }
    }
    ...
}
```

When this accident happens, the slug stops running and stops moving his tentacles. A new animation is started in which the slug is scaled up and down, which looks like he's breathing steadily in his sleep. We can also hear a looping snoring sound.

This accident isn't very spectacular. Here you can see the affected slug (Iffy) is slightly bigger than the other slugs, but it's hard to notice in a static image like below:

In the next accident, the slug will go blind.

Blind Accident

From time to time, a slug may lose his tentacles and go blind. Here's how this accident is implemented:

```
...
public partial class TrackImage : ContentView
{
    ...
    private async Task HandleAsleep()
    ...
    private async Task HandleBlind()
    {
        if (vm != null
            && vm.AccidentViewModel != null
            && vm.AccidentViewModel.AffectedSlug != null
            && slugImage != null)
        {
            await Task.Delay((int)vm.AccidentViewModel.TimePosition);

            vm.AccidentViewModel.AffectedSlug.EyeImageUrl = string.Empty;

            accidentAnimation = new Animation()
            {
                {0, .25, new Animation(v => slugImage.Rotation = v, 0, 15) },
                {.25, .5, new Animation(v => slugImage.Rotation = v, 15, 0) },
                {.5, .75, new Animation(v => slugImage.Rotation = v, 0, -15) },
                {.75, 1, new Animation(v => slugImage.Rotation = v, -15, 0) }
            };
            accidentAnimation.Commit(
                this,
                "accidentAnimation",
                16,
                1000,
                Easing.Linear,
                null,
                () => true);

            vm.PlayAccidentSound();
            vm.DisplayAccidentPopup();

            await Task.Delay((int)vm.AccidentViewModel.Duration);

            slugImage.Rotation = 0;

            this.AbortAnimation("accidentAnimation");
        }
    }
    ...
}
```

The slug doesn't stop running when the accident happens. He just loses his eyes (the eye image is set to an empty string) and starts moving in a seemingly chaotic way, just like Slowpoke in the image below:

Unfortunately, a slug may also fall into a puddle and drown. Let's have a look at this accident next.

Puddle Accident

Let's now implement the next accident. In this accident the slug drowns in a puddle of water:

```
...
public partial class TrackImage : ContentView
{
    ...
    private async Task HandleBlind()
    ...
    private async Task HandlePuddle()
    {
        if (vm != null
            && vm.AccidentViewModel != null
            && slugImage != null)
        {
            await Task.Delay((int)vm.AccidentViewModel.TimePosition);
            this.AbortAnimation(runningAnimationName);
            accidentImage = new Image
            {
                Source = puddleImage,
                ZIndex = 1
            };

            slugImage.ZIndex = 2;

            layout.Add(accidentImage);

#if ANDROID
            accidentImage.ScaleX = .25;
            accidentImage.ScaleY = .25;

            layout.SetLayoutBounds(accidentImage, new Rect(
            slugImage.X + slugImage.TranslationX - 3 * slugImage.Width,
            slugImage.Y - 2 * slugImage.Height,
            accidentImage.Width,
            accidentImage.Height));
#endif

#if WINDOWS
            layout.SetLayoutBounds(accidentImage, new Rect(
            slugImage.X + slugImage.TranslationX - slugImage.Width / 3,
            slugImage.Y - .3 * slugImage.Height,
            accidentImage.Width,
            accidentImage.Height));
#endif

            accidentAnimation = new Animation()
            {
                {0, .1, new Animation(v => slugImage.Opacity = v, .6, 0) },
                {.1, .8, new Animation(v => slugImage.Opacity = v, 0, .3) },
                {.8, 1, new Animation(v => slugImage.Opacity = v, .3, .6) }
            };

            accidentAnimation.Commit(
                this,
                "accidentAnimation",
```

```
                16,
                vm.RaceTime,
                Easing.CubicInOut,
                null,
                () => true);

            vm.PlayAccidentSound(true, true);
            vm.DisplayAccidentPopup();
        }
    }
    ...
}
```

The image is scaled and positioned per platform. We set the **ZIndex** property so that the puddle image appears under the slug image instead of on top of it. We then animate the **Opacity** property so that the slug disappears in the water, then reappears, and so on.

Here's what it looks like:

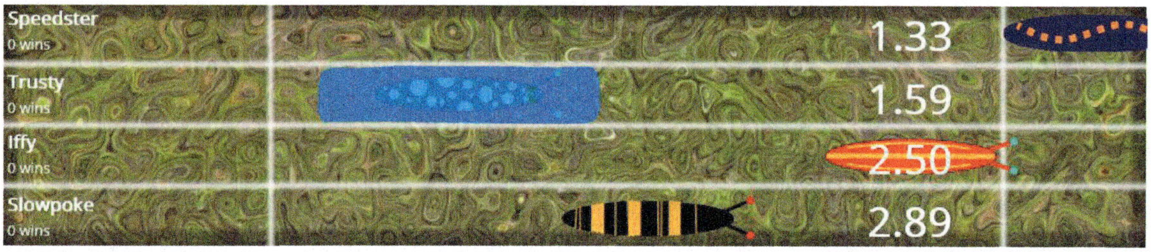

Let's move on to the next accident.

Electroshock Accident

The next accident, Electroshock, is implemented like so:

```
...
public partial class TrackImage : ContentView
{
    ...
    private async Task HandlePuddle()
    ...
    private async Task HandleElectroshock()
    {
        if (vm != null
            && vm.AccidentViewModel != null
            && vm.AccidentViewModel.AffectedSlug != null
            && slugImage != null)
        {
            await Task.Delay((int)vm.AccidentViewModel.TimePosition);
            this.AbortAnimation(runningAnimationName);

            accidentImage = new Image { Source = boltImage };
            layout.Add(accidentImage);

            accidentImage.Rotation = -15;
```

```
#if ANDROID
            accidentImage.Scale = .2;

            layout.SetLayoutBounds(accidentImage, new Rect(
                    slugImage.X + slugImage.TranslationX - slugImage.Width,
                    slugImage.Y - 2 * slugImage.Height,
                    accidentImage.Width,
                    accidentImage.Height));
#endif

#if WINDOWS
            accidentImage.Scale = .7;

            layout.SetLayoutBounds(accidentImage, new Rect(
                    slugImage.X + slugImage.TranslationX,
                    .9 * slugImage.Y,
                    accidentImage.Width,
                    accidentImage.Height));
#endif
            accidentAnimation = new Animation()
            {
                {0, .5, new Animation(v => accidentImage.Opacity = v, 0, 1) },
                {.5, 1, new Animation(v => accidentImage.Opacity = v, 1, 0) }
            };

            accidentAnimation.Commit(
                this,
                "accidentAnimation",
                16,
                500,
                Easing.Linear,
                null,
                () => true);

            vm.PlayAccidentSound(true, true);
            vm.DisplayAccidentPopup();

            await Task.Delay((int)vm.AccidentViewModel.Duration);

            this.AbortAnimation("accidentAnimation");

            if (layout.Contains(accidentImage))
            {
                layout.Remove(accidentImage);
            }

            vm.StopAccidentSound();

            accidentAnimation = new Animation(
                v => slugImage.TranslationX = v,
                slugImage.TranslationX,
                trackLength);

            accidentAnimation.Commit(
                this,
                "accidentAnimation",
                16,
                vm.AccidentViewModel.AffectedSlug.RunningTime / 4,
                Easing.Linear,
                null,
                () => false);
        }
    }
    ...
}
```

The running animation is canceled and a bolt image appears. We animate its **Opacity** to imitate lightning. After that, there's another running animation, but this time the slug runs faster.

Here's a slug just being struck by lightning:

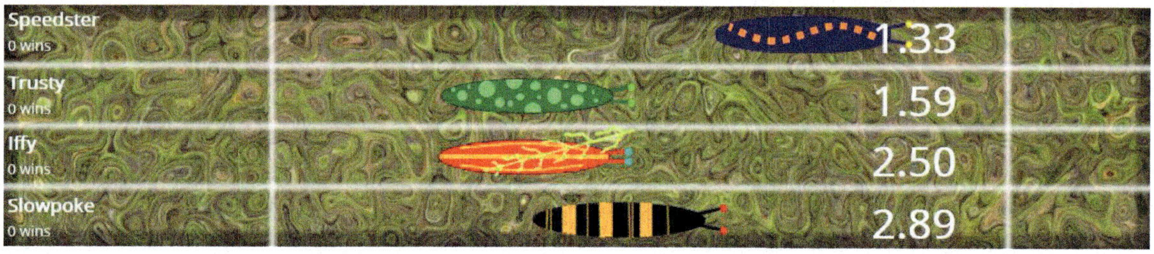

Sometimes nothing special happens to a slug, but they just turn back. Let's implement this.

Turning Back Accident

Here's the Turning Back accident:

```
...
public partial class TrackImage : ContentView
{
    ...
    private async Task HandleElectroshock()
    ...
    private async Task HandleTurningBack()
    {
        if (vm != null
            && vm.AccidentViewModel != null
            && slugImage != null)
        {
            await Task.Delay((int)vm.AccidentViewModel.TimePosition);
            this.AbortAnimation(runningAnimationName);

            accidentAnimation = new Animation()
            {
                {0, .2, new Animation(
                    v => slugImage.ScaleX = v, 1, -1) },

                {.2, 1, new Animation(
                    v => slugImage.TranslationX = v,
                    slugImage.TranslationX, -400) }
            };

            accidentAnimation.Commit(
                this,
                "accidentAnimation",
                16,
                5000,
                Easing.Linear,
                null,
                () => false);
```

```
                vm.PlayAccidentSound();
                vm.DisplayAccidentPopup();
            }
        }
        ...
}
```

The running animation is stopped and a new animation is started that consists of two simple animations: one where the **ScaleX** property changes from 1 to -1, which flips the slug horizontally, and one where the slug runs from his current position to the left.

Here's the effect:

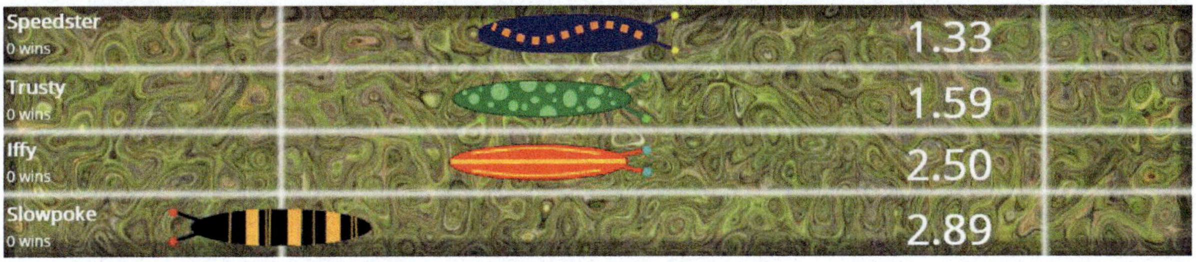

And there is one more accident, the most terrible one…

Devoured Accident

The worst thing, at least theoretically, that may happen to a slug, is being devoured by the terrible slug monster that occasionally haunts the area where the races take place. The slug monster catches the slug and eats it. Here's how this is implemented in our app:

```
...
public partial class TrackImage : ContentView
{
    ...
    private async Task HandleTurningBack()
    ...
    private async Task HandleDevoured()
    {
        if (vm != null
            && vm.AccidentViewModel != null
            && slugImage != null)
        {
            await Task.Delay((int)vm.AccidentViewModel.TimePosition);
            this.AbortAnimation(runningAnimationName);

            accidentImage = new Image { Source = monsterImage };
            layout.Add(accidentImage);

#if ANDROID
            accidentImage.ScaleX = .25;
            accidentImage.ScaleY = .25;
```

```
            layout.SetLayoutBounds(accidentImage, new Rect(
                -100,
                slugImage.Y - 2 * slugImage.Height,
                accidentImage.Width,
                accidentImage.Height));
            accidentAnimation = new Animation(
                v => accidentImage.TranslationX = v,
                0,
                slugImage.TranslationX);
#endif

#if WINDOWS
            layout.SetLayoutBounds(accidentImage, new Rect(
                -accidentImage.Width,
                slugImage.Y - .3 * slugImage.Height,
                accidentImage.Width,
                accidentImage.Height));
            accidentAnimation = new Animation(
                v => accidentImage.TranslationX = v,
                0,
                slugImage.X + slugImage.TranslationX + accidentImage.Width);
#endif

            accidentAnimation?.Commit(
                this,
                "accidentAnimation",
                16,
                1000,
                Easing.CubicInOut,
                null,
                () => false);

            vm.PlayAccidentSound();
            vm.DisplayAccidentPopup();
        }
    }
}
```

The slug monster comes from the left-hand side of the window. Here's what it looks like:

Poor Trusty. But don't worry, he'll be up and running in the next race.

And that's it. We've covered all the accidents that may happen to a slug. But we don't want them to happen too frequently, and for sure not in every race, so restore the original code in **GameViewModel** that is responsible for deciding whether an accident should happen and picking its type.

Great, looks like our app is almost finished. There are just a couple final touches I'd like to take care of before we deploy our app. They are the topic of the next chapter.

Chapter 22 - Final Touches

code: https://github.com/prospero-apps/Slugrace/tree/chapter22

We're almost done with our app. In this chapter we'll add some final touches to it so that it is complete. In particular, we'll disable app window resizing and implement the InstructionsPage.

Fixed Window Size on Windows

The next thing I'd like to fix is the app window size on Windows. If we run the app now, we can drag the borders of the window to resize it. It doesn't always look good, like for example here:

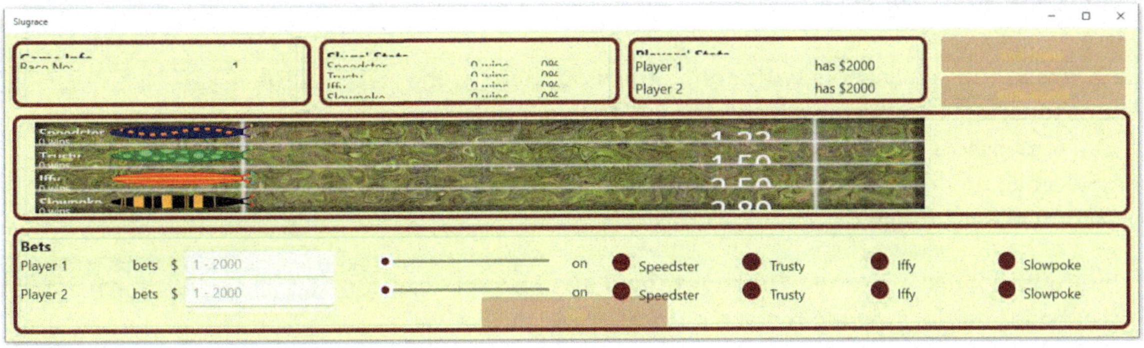

We can set the size of the window programmatically. To do that, we have to override the **CreateWindow** method in the **App** class and set the size there. The **Width** and **Height** properties are used for the size when the window first appears after launching the app. We can also set the minimum and maximum dimensions. In our case, we'll set all dimensions, inluding the maximum and minimum ones, to the same values so that it's no longer possible to resize the window.

Here's the code:

```
namespace Slugrace;

public partial class App : Application
{
    public App()
    {
        InitializeComponent();

        MainPage = new AppShell();
    }
```

```
#if WINDOWS
    protected override Window CreateWindow(IActivationState? activationState)
    {
        var window = base.CreateWindow(activationState);

        window.Width = window.MinimumWidth = window.MaximumWidth = 1440;
        window.Height = window.MinimumHeight = window.MaximumHeight = 800;

        return window;
    }
#endif
}
```

If you now run the app, you won't be able to resize the window.

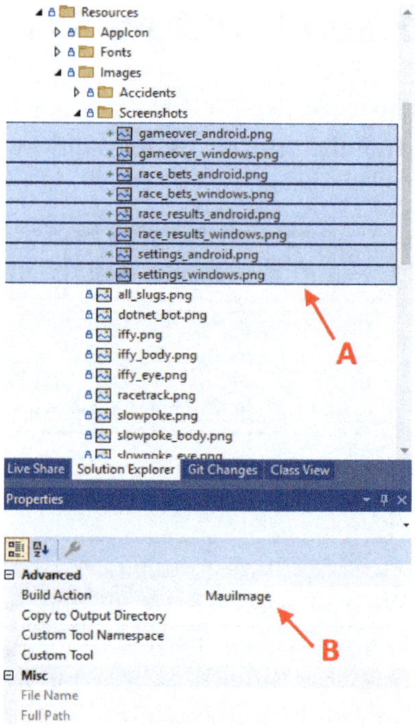

InstructionsPage

We're going to use screenshots with annotations on them in the **InstructionsPage**. You can grab the images from Github. Put them in a **Screenshots** folder inside the **Images** folder in **Resources** folder. Select all the images (A) and in the Properties window set Build Action to **MauiImage** (B).

The binding context of the **InstructionsPage** is set to **GameViewModel**, so let's define the screenshots there so that we can bind to them.

In the **GameViewModel** class add a **Screenshots** property of type **List<string>**. Initialize the list in the constructor, using different images for each platform:

```
...
public partial class GameViewModel : ObservableObject
{
    ...
    private uint afterAccidentTime = 0;

    // Game screenshots used for the InstructionsPage
    [ObservableProperty]
    private List<string> screenshots;

    public GameViewModel(SoundViewModel soundViewModel, IPopupService popupService)
    {
        ...
        WeakReferenceMessenger.Default.Register<PlayerSelectedSlugChangedMessage>(...);

#if WINDOWS
        Screenshots =
        [
            "settings_windows.png",
```

```
            "race_bets_windows.png",
            "race_results_windows.png",
            "gameover_windows.png"
        ];
#endif

#if ANDROID
        Screenshots =
        [
            "settings_android.png",
            "race_bets_android.png",
            "race_results_android.png",
            "gameover_android.png"
        ];
#endif
    }

    private void OnBetAmountChangedMessageReceived(int value)
    ...
```

Next, let's implement the **InstructionsPage**. We'll use a **CarouselView** in it, so we will be able to use the arrow keys (on Windows) or swipe (on Android) to loop through the screenshots:

```
...
<ContentPage ...>
    ...
    </Shell.BackButtonBehavior>

    <Grid RowDefinitions=".5*, 10*, 1*, .5*, *, .5*">
        <Border
            Grid.Row="1"
            Padding="20">
            <CarouselView
                ItemsSource="{Binding Screenshots}"
                IndicatorView="indicatorView">
                <CarouselView.ItemTemplate>
                    <DataTemplate>
                        <Image
                            Source="{Binding}" />
                    </DataTemplate>
                </CarouselView.ItemTemplate>
            </CarouselView>
        </Border>

        <IndicatorView
            x:Name="indicatorView"
            Grid.Row="2"
            IndicatorColor="LightBlue"
            SelectedIndicatorColor="DarkBlue"
            VerticalOptions="Center"
            HorizontalOptions="Center" />

        <Label
            Grid.Row="3"
            HorizontalOptions="Center"
            FontSize="15"
            Text="{OnPlatform 'Use arrows to navigate between slides.',
                Android='Swipe to navigate between pages.'}"/>
```

```
        <Button
            Grid.Row="4"
            Text="Back"
            Command="{Binding NavigateBackCommand}" />
    </Grid>
</ContentPage>
```

The **ItemsSource** property is bound to the list of screenshots that we just defined in the **GameViewModel**. We also use an **IndicatorView** to see our position in the collection of images.

If we now hit the Instructions button in the **RacePage**, we'll navigate to the **InstructionsPage**. Here's what it looks like on Windows:

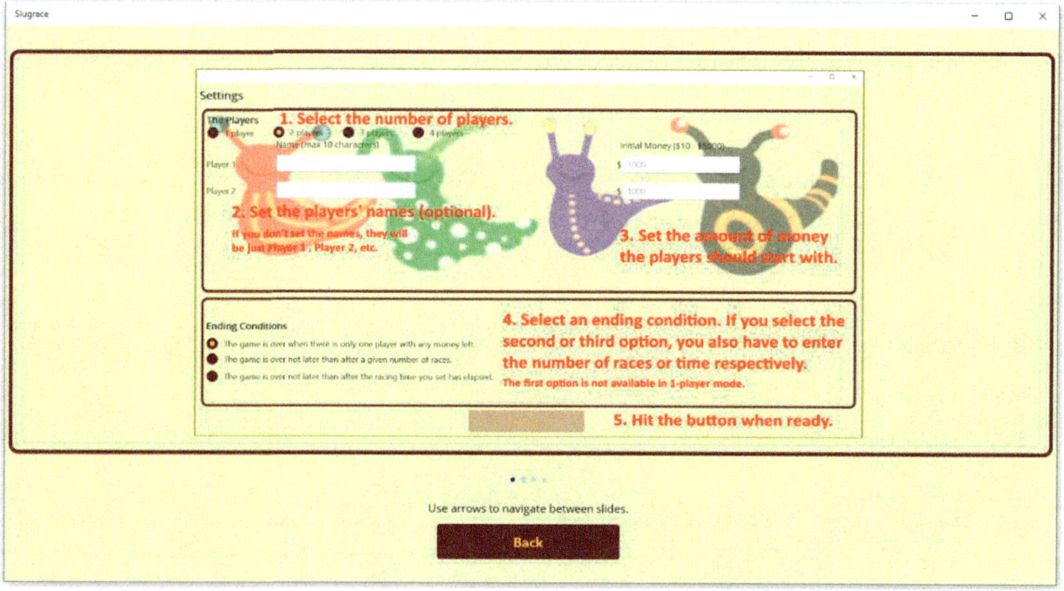

Here we can see the first screenshot out of four. We can use the arrow keys or the scroll wheel on our mouse to loop through all of them. Here's the second screenshot, for example:

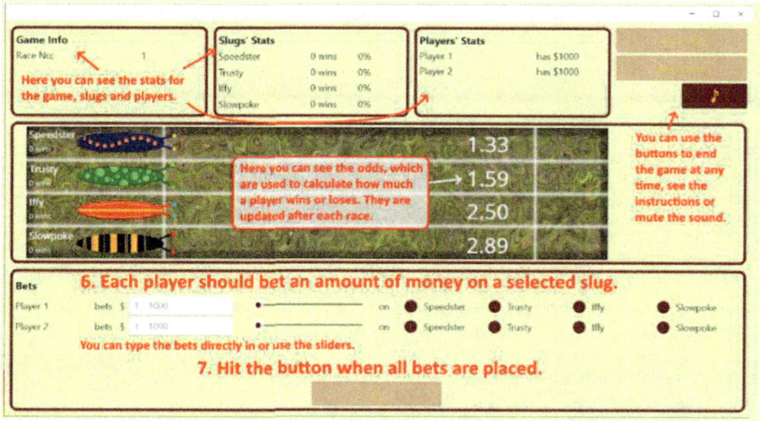

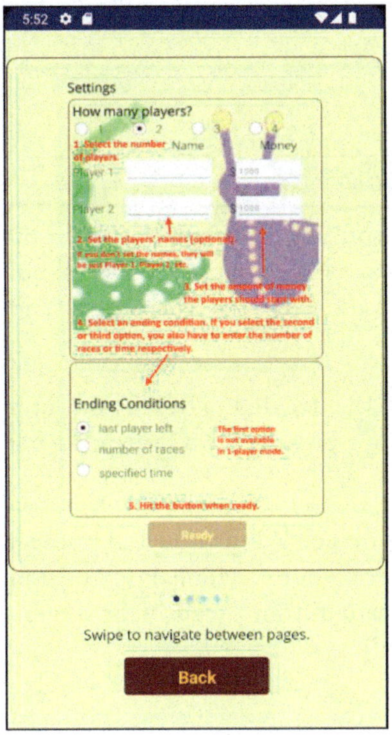

On Android it looks similar.

As soon as we navigate to the **InstructionsPage**, we'll also see the appropriate screenshot of the **SettingsPage** with the same annotations on it.

Again, you can swipe to see the other screenshots, like for example the screenshot of the **GameOverPage** (look right).

Now our app is finished. In the next (and last) chapter we'll deploy it to Windows and Android.

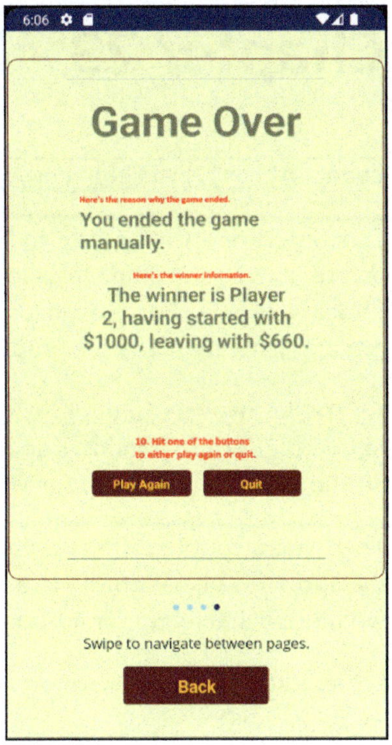

Chapter 23 - Deployment

code: https://github.com/prospero-apps/Slugrace/tree/chapter23

Our Slugrace app is ready to be published. Well, to be exact, it wouldn't hurt to polish it a bit before, maybe run some tests to see if everything works and if there aren't any dangerous bugs, but I'll leave it as is. For our purposes, let's say we've already made all the necessary corrections and our app is really ready for production.

As you know, we can deploy .NET MAUI apps to a lot of platforms. We decided to deploy our app to two platforms, Windows and Android. As we can only build for one platform at a time in Visual Studio, let's build the app for Windows first and then for Android.

There are a couple different ways to publish an app for each platform. For Windows we'll publish the app with Visual Studio to a folder, from which it can be installed on your machine. For Android we'll publish the app for ad-hoc distribution so that it can be downloaded from a website or server.

So, let's start with the Windows deployment.

Publishing for Windows to a Folder

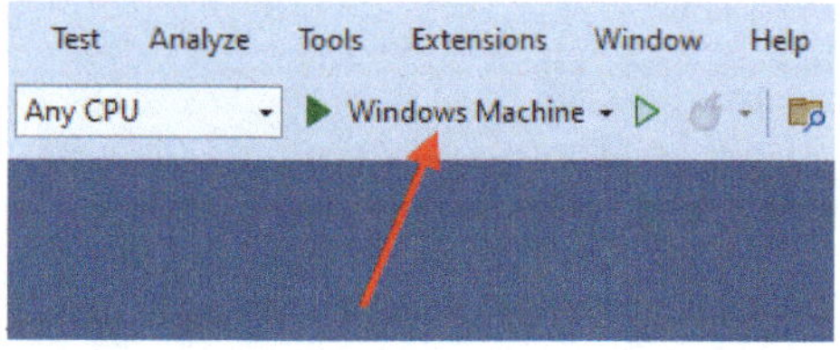

We're going to use Visual Studio to publish the app for Windows. We'll package it into an MSIX package, which we can use to install the app on a machine.

First, let's make sure the target platform is set to Windows Machine.

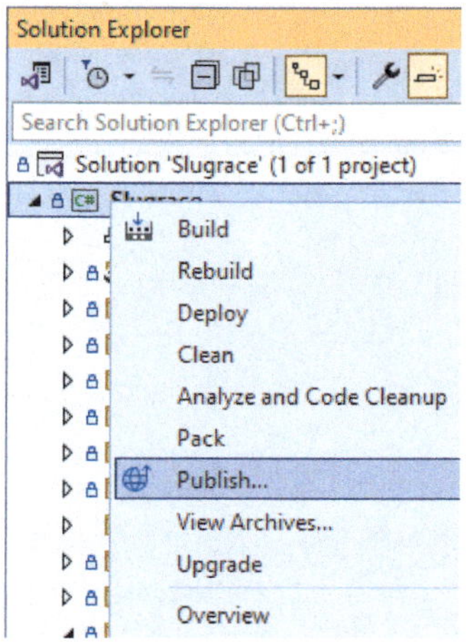

Right-click the project in the Solution Explorer and select Publish…

In the Create App Packages window select Sideloading and hit Next.

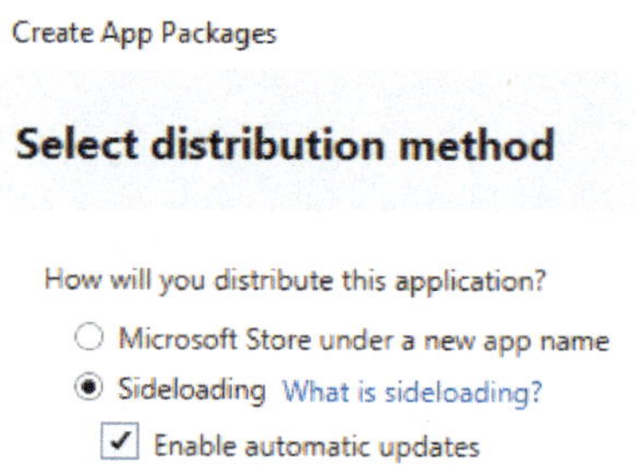

We need a certificate to publish the app. Select the second option (A) and hit Create (B):

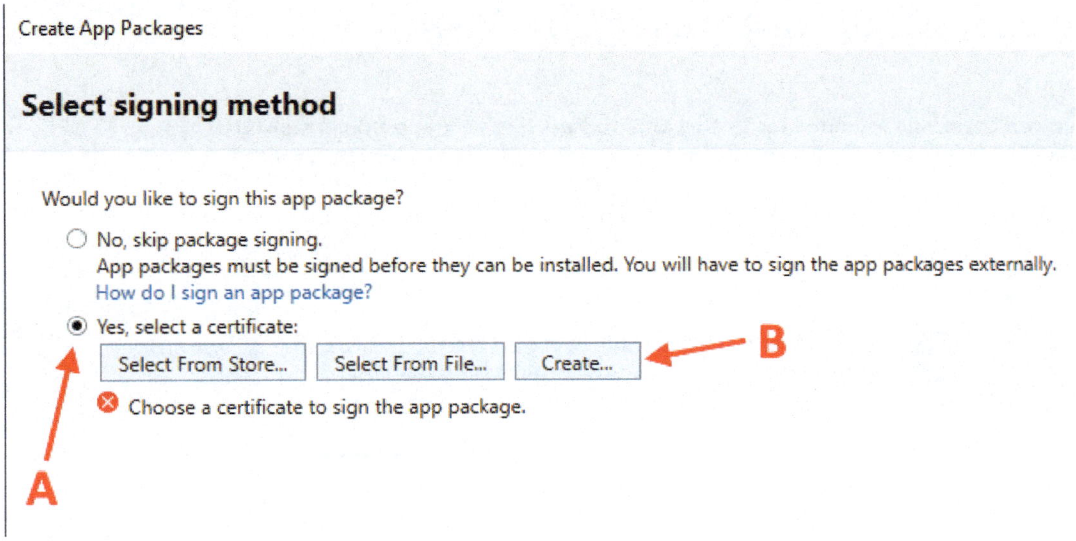

We're going to create a temporary self-signed certificate that can be used for testing. We shouldn't use it to distribute the package, though. For our purposes this will do.

Provide a company name and a password, then hit OK:

You will see a box with some information about the certificate. Hit OK:

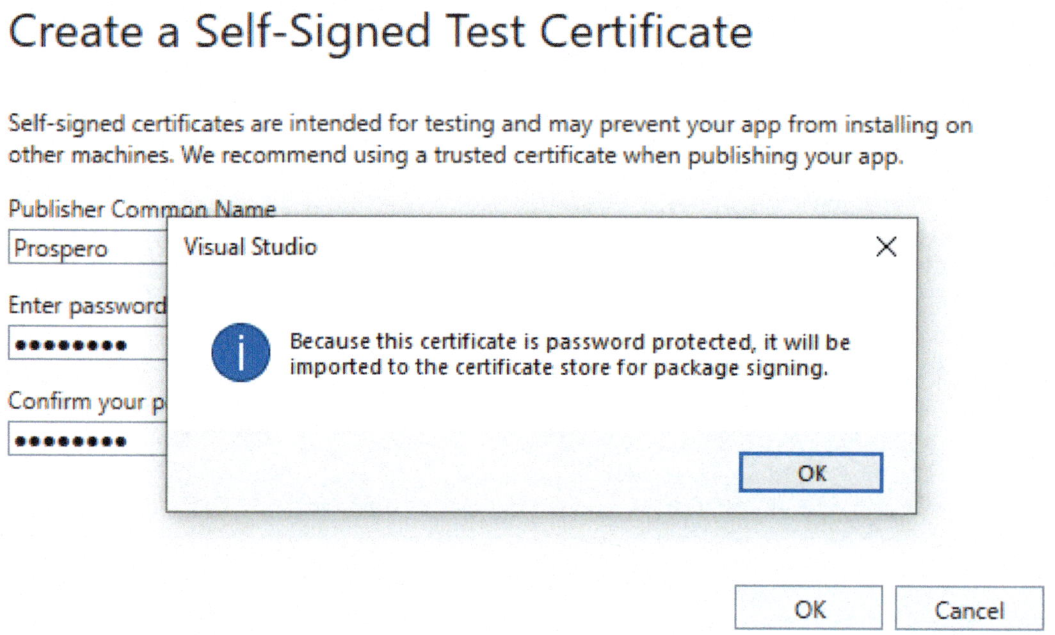

You want to use this certificate, so check the **Yes, us the current certificate** option and hit Next:

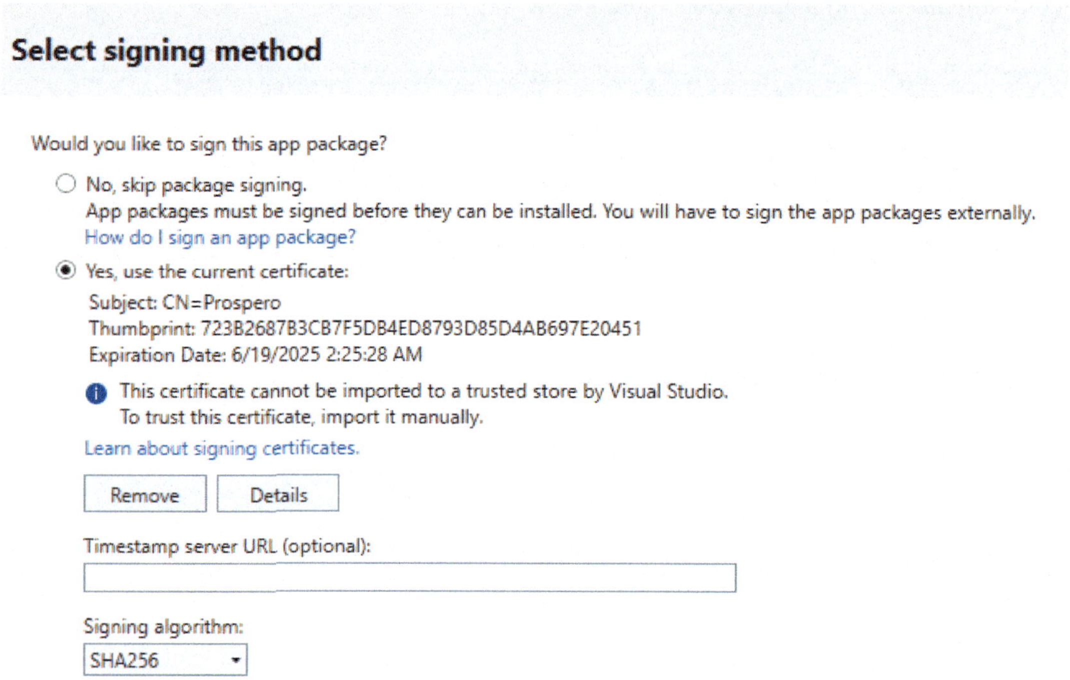

You can leave the package version as is (A). By checking the **Automatically increment** box (B), you make sure the version will be incremented each time the package is published. In the Publishing profile drop-down select <New…> (C):

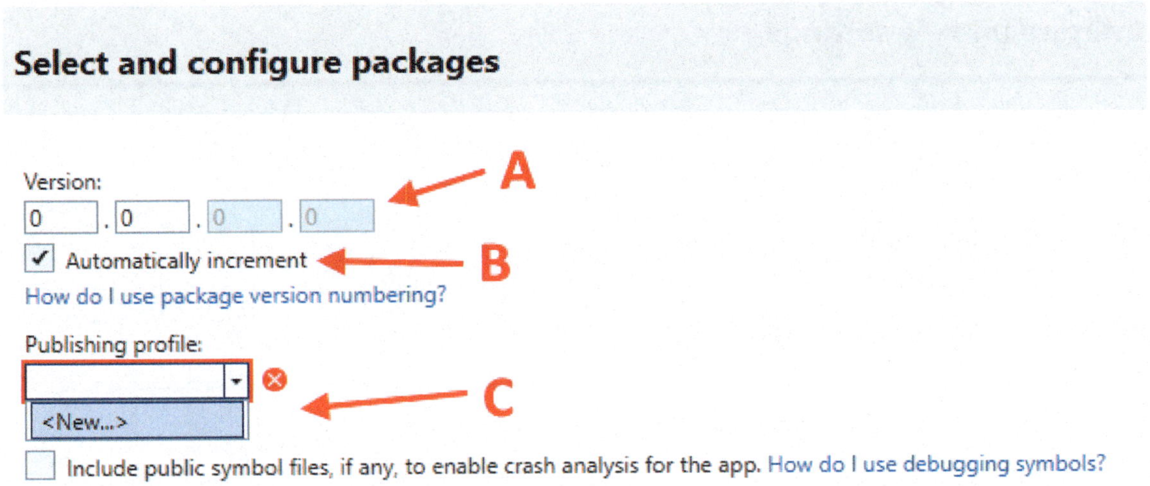

In the window that appears, set Configuration to Release I Any CPU and Target Runtime depending on which version of Windows you want to publish for. Then hit OK:

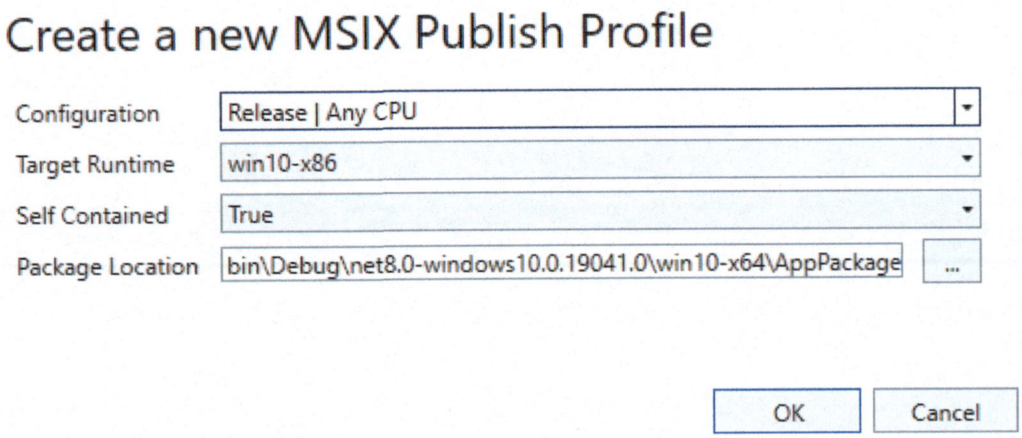

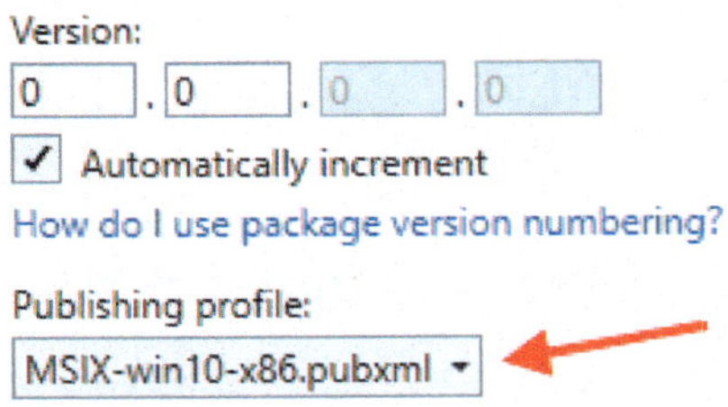

Now you can see the publishing profile in the drop-down. Hit the Next button.

In the next dialog enter the path to the folder in which you want to keep the installer (A). Also check one of the radio buttons to specify how often the app should look for updates (B). In our case, we'll check for updates every time the app runs. Whenever a new version of the app is published, it will overwrite the old version. When done, hit the Create button:

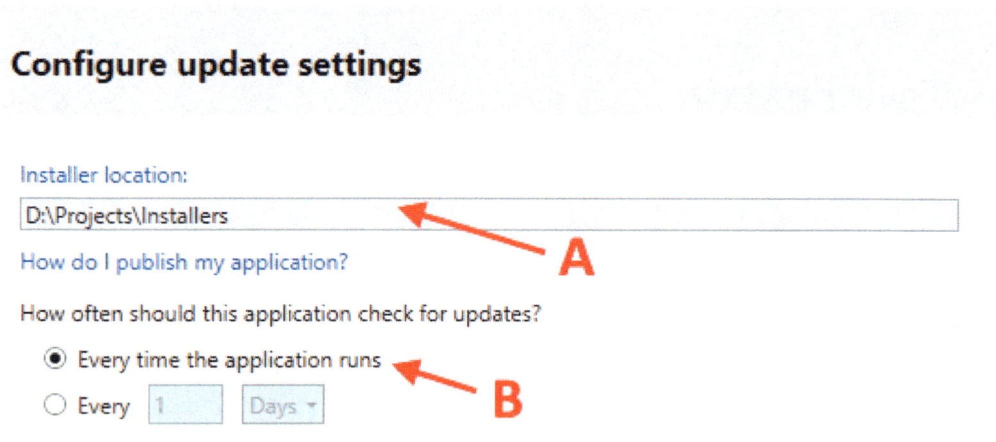

Now the installer is being created. It may take some time. You can see it proceed in the Output window in Visual Studio. After that, you'll see the following dialog with a package summary:

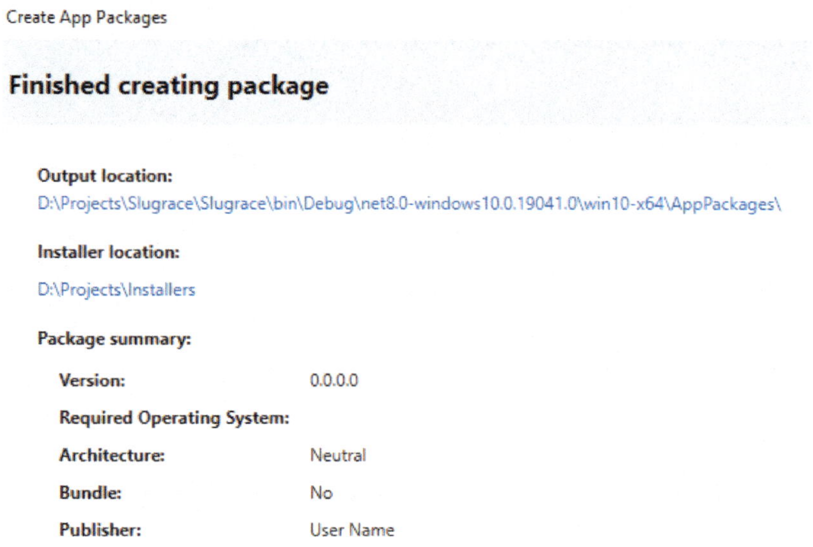

Hit the Copy and Close button to copy the package to the installer location you selected before.

The package is ready to be installed. Go to the folder where the installer was copied. In my case there's the Slugrace_1.0.0.1_Test folder. It contains the MSIX file.

Let's install the app. If you double-click the MSIX file, you'll see the following dialog:

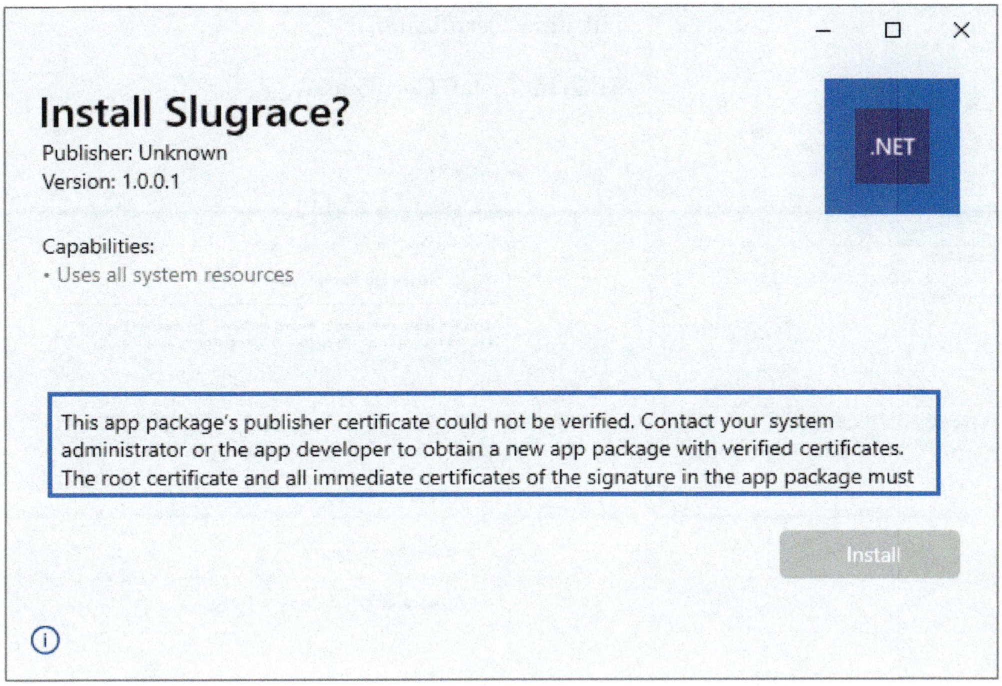

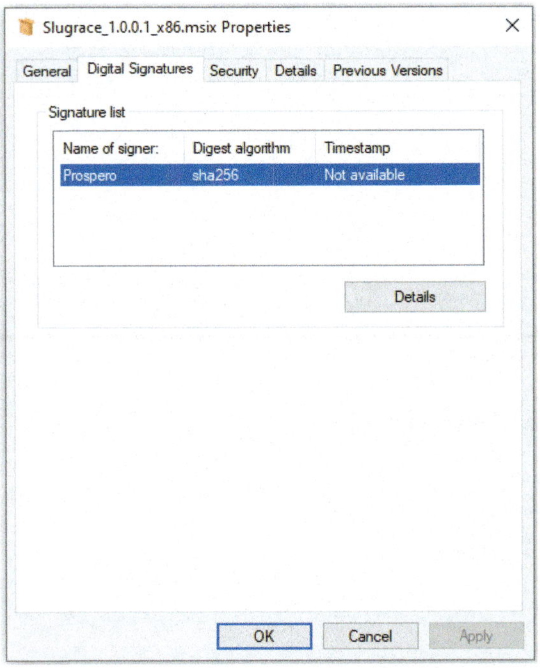

The Install button is disabled. This is because of the certificate. We first have to install the certificate. Close the dialog, right-click the MSIX file, select Properties and then the Digital Signatures tab. Select the certificate in the list and hit Details.

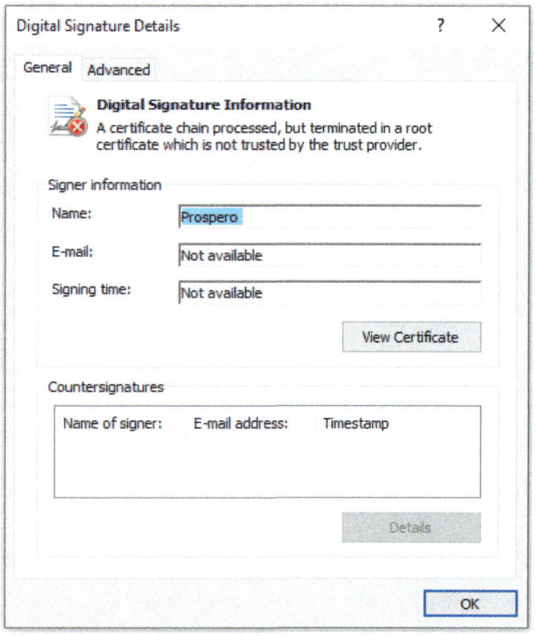

Hit View Certificate.

Then hit Install Certificate…

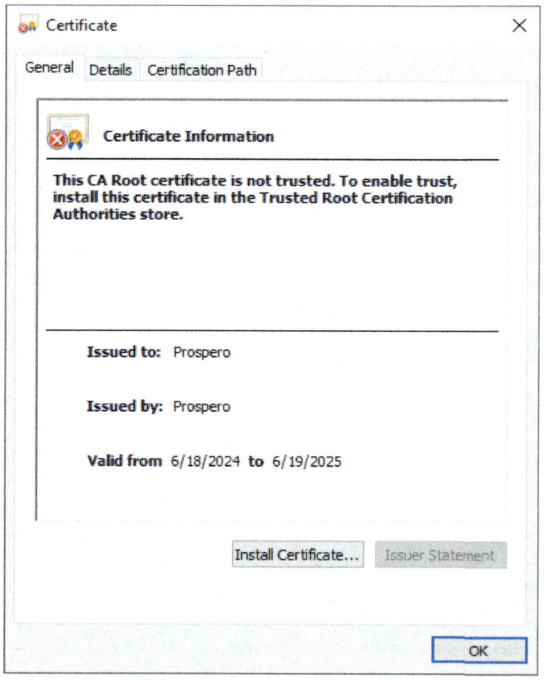

Select Local Machine and hit Next:

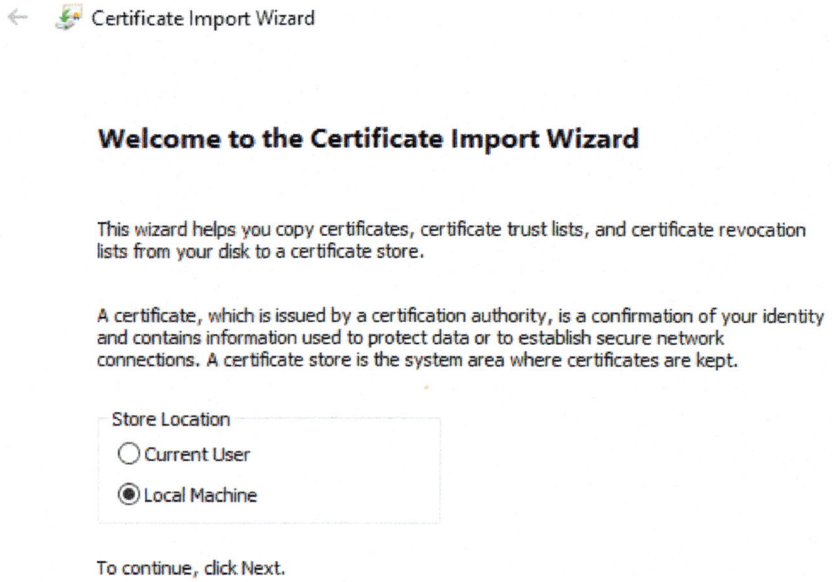

Allow the changes on your device if you're prompted to do so. In the next dialog check the **Place all certificates in the following store** radio button (A), click the Browse… button (B), select Trusted People from the list (C) and hit OK (D):

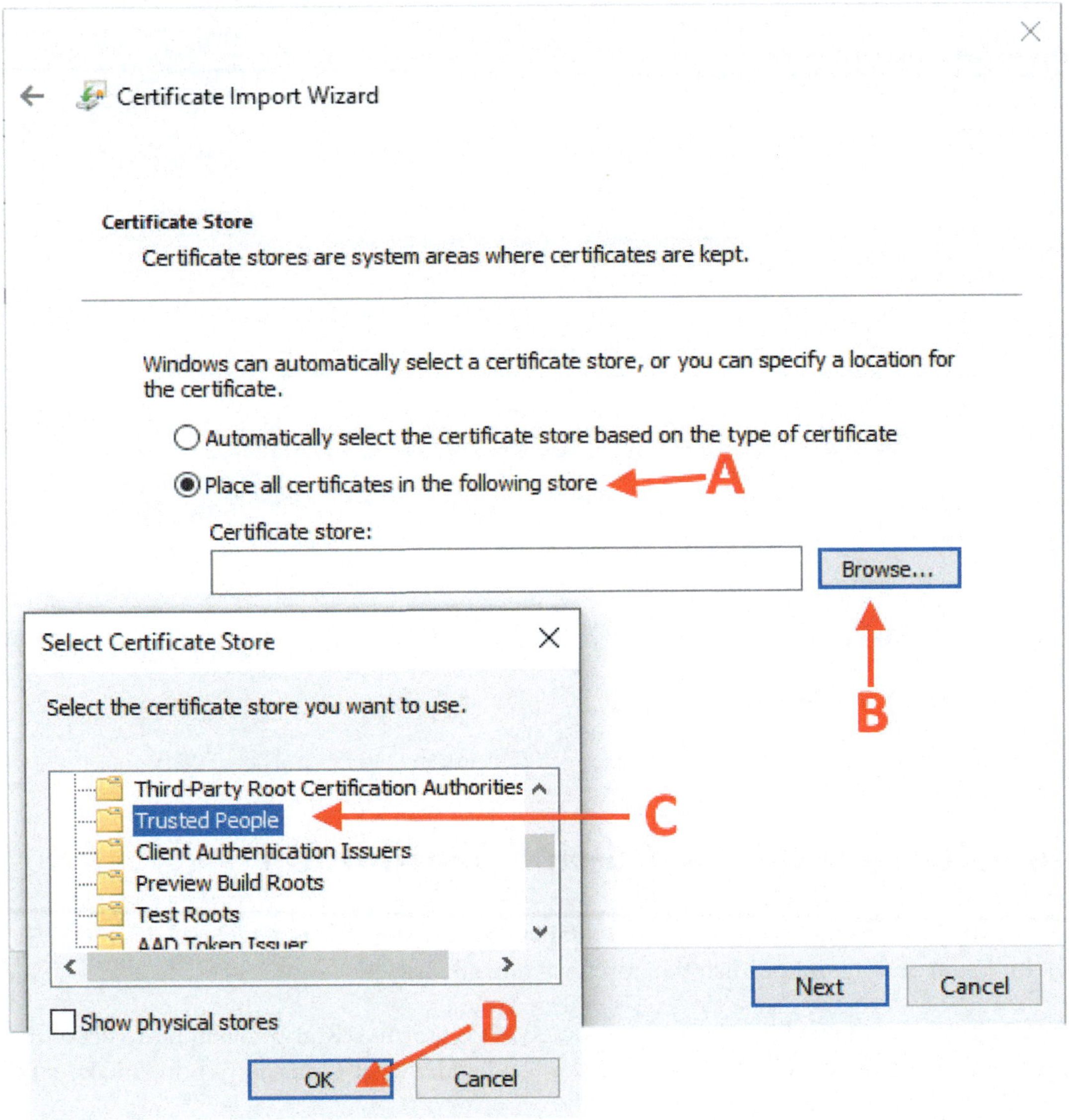

Hit Next and then Finish. You should see a message confirming that the import was successful. Click OK on each opened window.

If you now double-click the MSIX file, the Install button will be enabled:

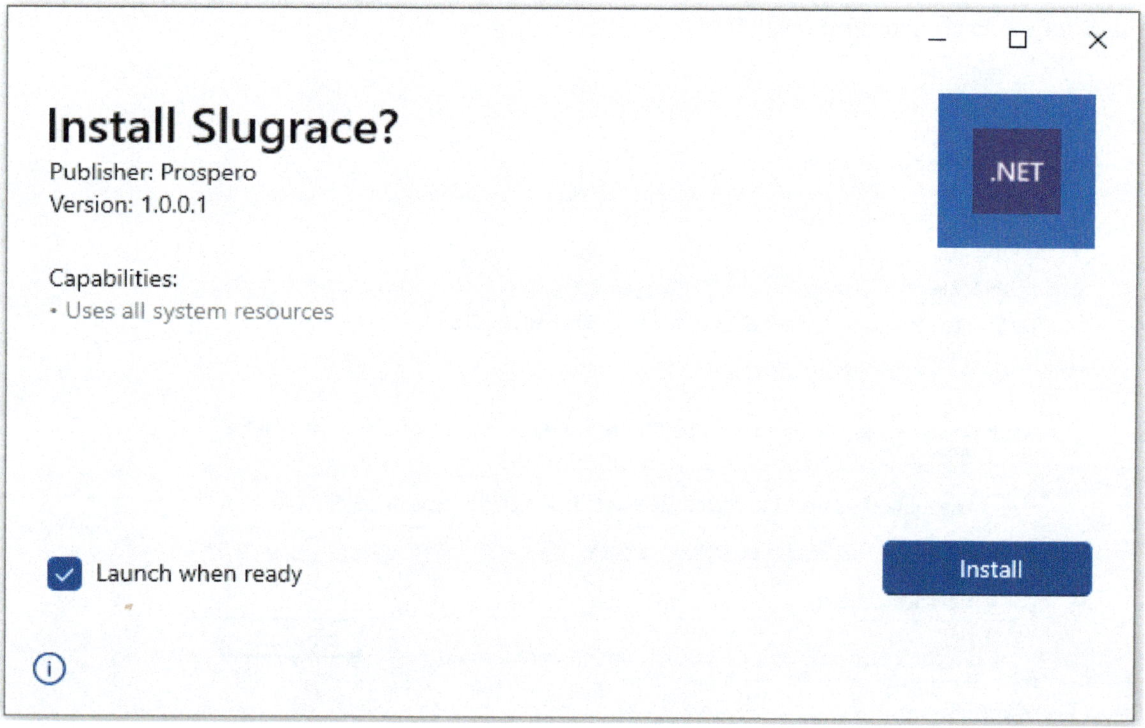

Hit it to install the app. When the app is installed, just play and enjoy.

Good. And now let's publish the app for Android.

Publishing for Android for Ad-Hoc Distribution

With ad-hoc distribution we can make the app available for download from a website or server. So, let's go back to Visual Studio and publish the app for Android.

For Android deployment we need the Android Package (APK) format. Right-click the project in the Solution Explorer and select Properties. Then, under Android, select Options (A) and make sure apk is selected in the Release drop-down (B):

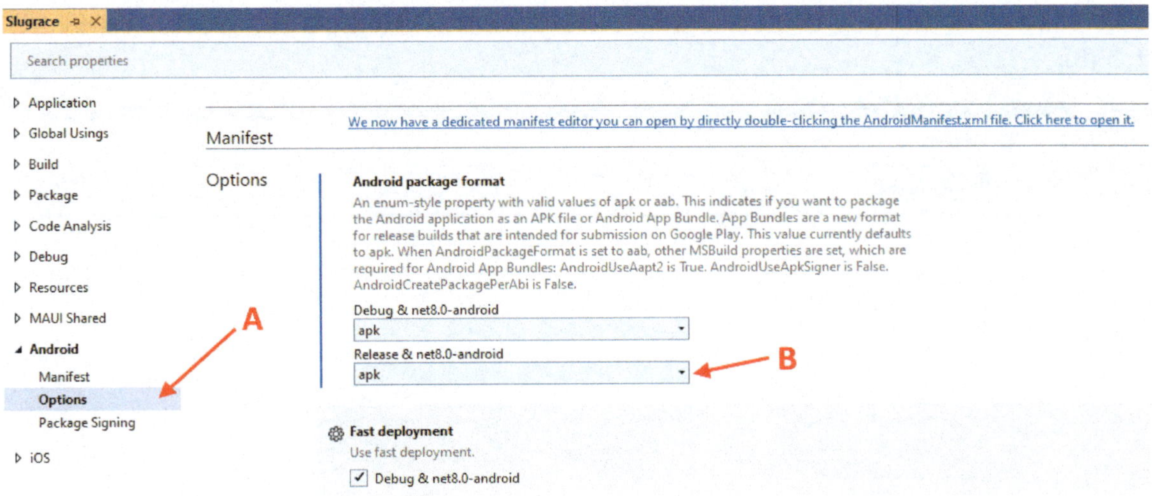

As the debug target select your Android emulator (A) and select the Release configuration (B):

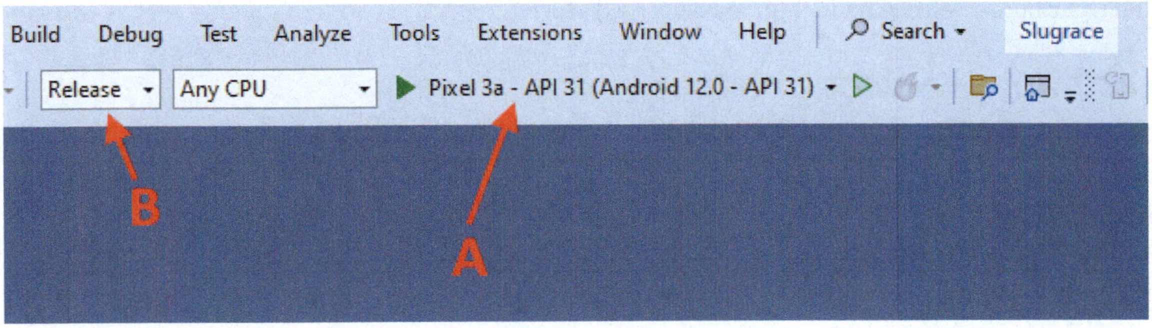

Right-click the project in Solution Explorer and select Publish... This will open the Archive Manager in a new tab. Visual Studio will start to archive the app bundle:

This may take a while. After that, make sure the archive is selected (A) and hit the Distribute… button (B):

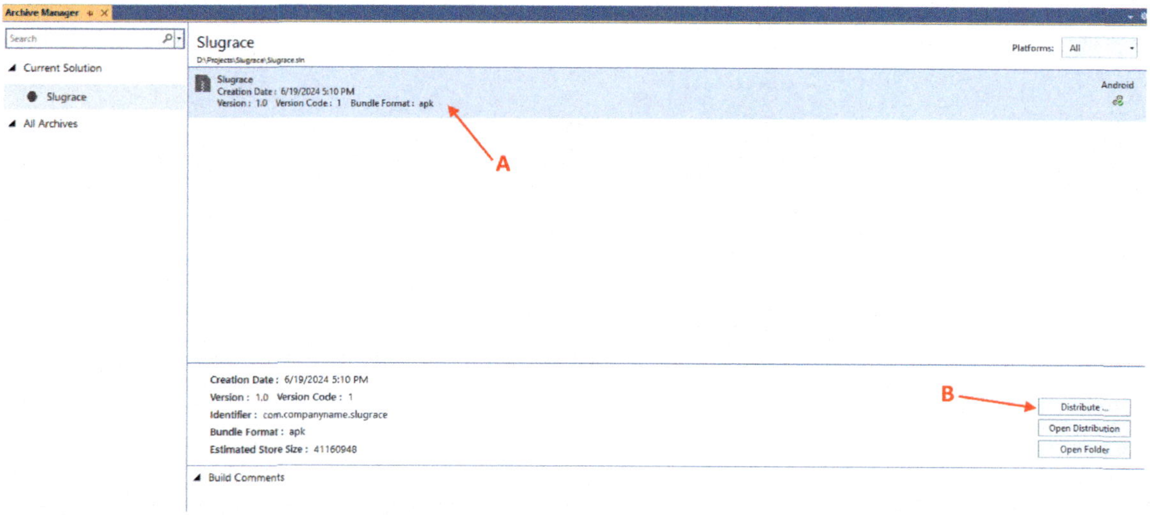

In the Distribute - Select Channel dialog select Ad Hoc:

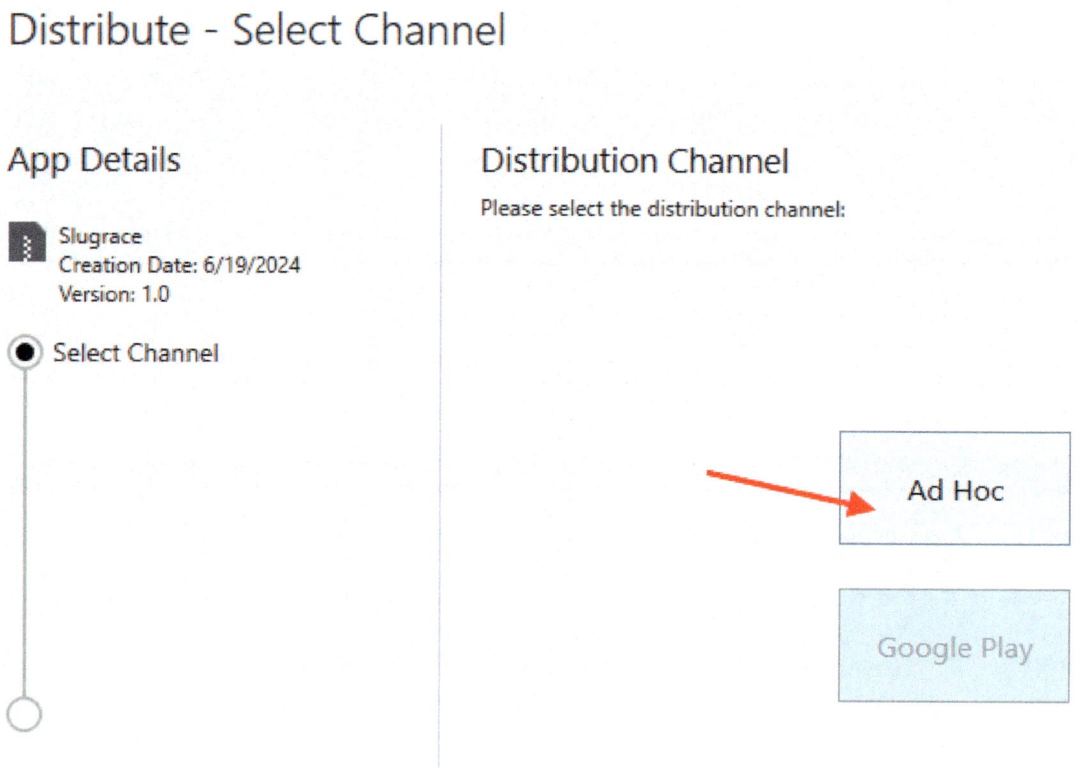

In the next dialog select the + button to create a new signing identity:

Next, the Create Android Keystore dialog opens. Enter an alias and a password. The alias should identify your key. You also have to provide at least some information below. It will be included in your certificate. Then hit the Create button.

Keep the password in a safe place. You're going to need it in a moment.

Select the signing identity you just created (A) and hit the Save As button (B):

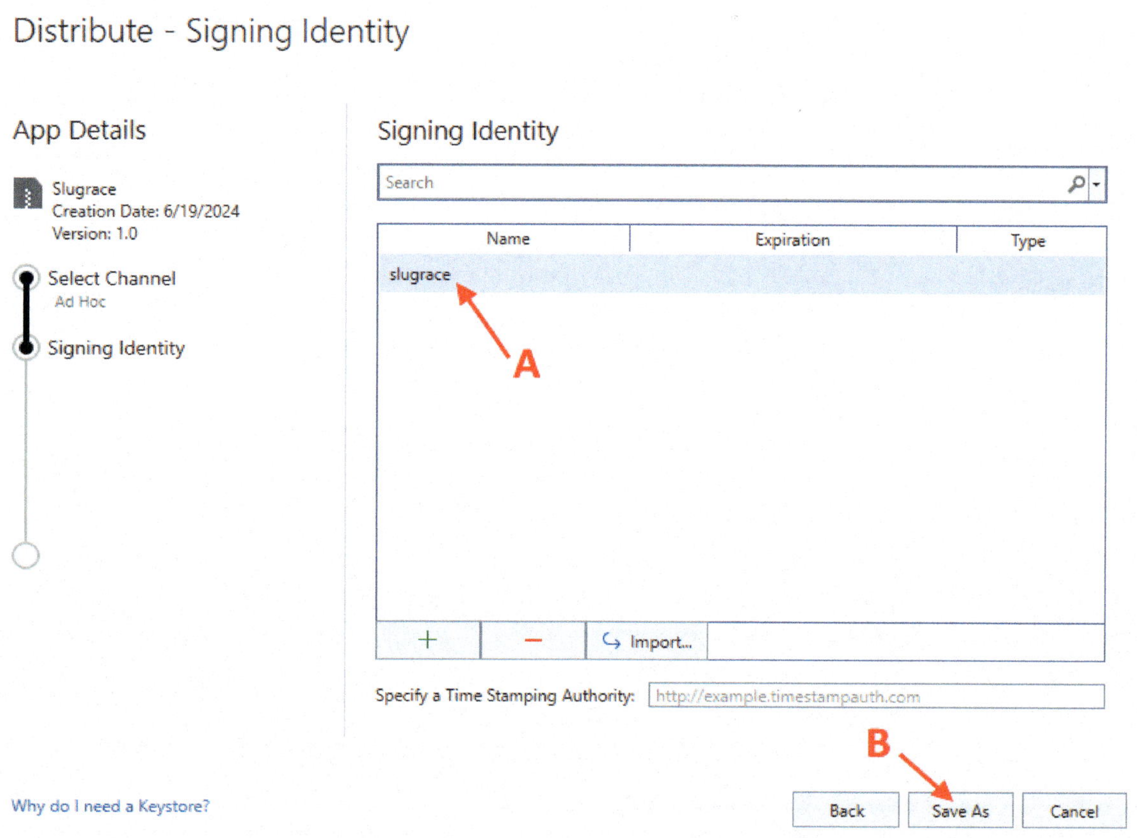

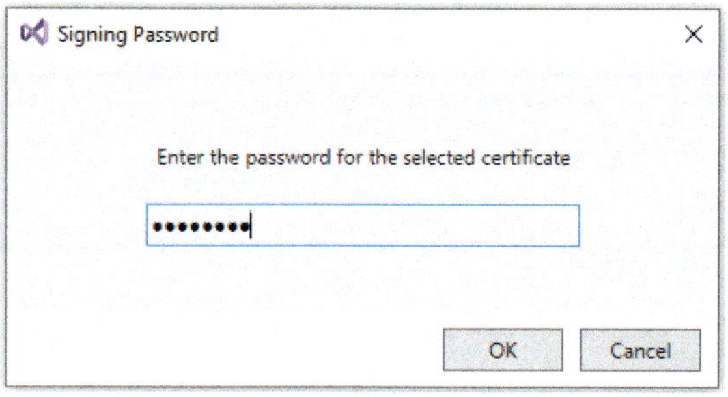

Select a location for your file and hit Save. When the Signing Password dialog shows up, enter the password you used before and hit the OK button:

Next, hit the Open Distribution button:

This will open the folder where the published app is. You can then distribute the app through a website or server.

You can also install it directly on your device. To do that, just copy the APK file to your device. In the file explorer select the file and in the menu or popup that shows up select Install (you may need to allow installing apps from external sources in the settings first). When the app is installed, tap Done or Open and enjoy the races.

Conclusion

This is it. We just created our first fully functional .NET MAUI app. I hope you enjoyed my book. Now we're ready to create other beautiful apps for all the available platforms. .NET MAUI is a relatively new framework and it's developing rapidly. You can build nearly anything with it - the sky is the limit, so just go wild and show off your skills. See you in another book or on my Prospero Coder blog.

Index

ABOUT THE AUTHOR

My name is Kamil Pakula. In 2011 I graduated from the Warsaw University of Technology where I had studied computer science. Since then I've worked on many projects using such programming languages as C++, C#, Java, JavaScript and Python. Recently I've been using mostly .NET technologies to create desktop, mobile and web applications, as well as games. I also work as a content writer for Code Maze and I run my own programming blog that you can find at prosperocoder.com. I'm also employed as a full-time .NET developer.

Printed in Great Britain
by Amazon

47055275R00258